HENRY NEWMAN

AN AMERICAN IN LONDON 1708–43

HENRY NEWMAN
An American in London
1708–43

by

LEONARD W. COWIE

Published for the Church Historical Society

LONDON
S·P·C·K
1956

First published in 1956 by
S·P·C·K
Northumberland Avenue, London, W.C.2
Printed in Great Britain by
Richard Clay and Company, Ltd., Bungay, Suffolk

CONTENTS

ILLUSTRATIONS

*Reproduced by kind permission of the Trustees of the British Museum
†Reproduced by kind permission of the Trustees of the National Portrait Gallery

PREFACE

ARTICLES on Henry Newman have appeared in the *Dictionary of American Biography* and J. L. Sibley's *Biographical Sketches of Graduates of Harvard University*, but until Dr W. K. Lowther Clarke included two essays on him in *Eighteenth Century Piety* in 1944, little notice had been taken of him in this country and no life written. This may be due partly to Newman's own modesty and humility, for he took an important part in many activities of his time. The grandson of a Puritan divine who emigrated to New England in the time of Archbishop Laud, he was a graduate and librarian of Harvard College and followed a commercial career as a young man. He then settled in London and was secretary of the S.P.C.K. from 1708 to 1743, during which time he was prominent in its widespread undertakings. These included the charity schools, the distribution of Christian literature, and the sending of Continental religious refugees to the new colony of Georgia. In addition, Newman was a colonial agent for New Hampshire and performed many services for individuals and institutions in the American colonies. This involved him in constant correspondence, most of which has survived, and I have tried to allow his well-written and vivid letters to speak for themselves as much as possible.

This work was originally a thesis approved by the University of London for the award of the degree of Ph.D. I am grateful to have been allowed to use material from archives in both this country and the United States and for the help I have universally received from librarians and others. I wish particularly to thank Dr Robert W. Greaves, Reader in History at Bedford College, London, for his constant help and advice, which have been invaluable during the whole period I have been working on this subject, and Dr Charles L. Sanford, of Harvard University, who, while himself writing the life of Jeremiah Dummer, Newman's contemporary as colonial agent for Massachusetts, generously made it possible for me to visit the United States in search of material. My wife has shared much of the work with me and also compiled the index.

I have modernized the punctuation and largely dispensed with the numerous capital letters when quoting from the correspondence of Newman and other contemporary writers. I have used the old (or English) calendar and the modern notation of years throughout.

L. W. C.

St Mark and St John's College, Chelsea,
12 July 1955

1

EARLY YEARS IN AMERICA AND ENGLAND

THOUGH he spent most of his life in London as secretary of a great society of the Church of England, Henry Newman came of an eminent Puritan family in New England. His grandfather, Samuel Newman, was among the American divines whose lives were recorded by Cotton Mather in his *Magnalia Christi Americana*; and in 1729 Henry Newman wrote an unfinished draft of a letter to Thomas Prince, the Boston theologian and bibliophile, who had asked him for information about his family. In this he described his own life as far as 1698 and added a little to supplement the account of his grandfather in the *Magnalia.*[1]

Samuel Newman, according to Cotton Mather, was born at or near Chadlington, a village in Oxfordshire, about 1600. Newman said, "My grandfather was born at Banbury in Oxfordshire", but this may mean that the family afterwards moved there. It may be that he had some connection with Banbury, for nearby was Broughton Castle, the seat of William Fiennes, eighth Baron and first Viscount Saye and Sele, one of the earliest and greatest of the Parliamentarian leaders, who was reputed to have made Banbury the most Puritan town in England, so that Samuel Newman, like Ben Jonson's Rabbi Zeal-of-the-Land Busy, may also have been "a Banbury man". The first definite date in Samuel Newman's life is that he went to Magdalen College, Oxford, in 1617 as a servitor, but transferred to St Edmund Hall, where he graduated in 1620. "Afterwards", continued Newman, "he went into Yorkshire and preached in the Vicarage of Halifax." The only record of this period of his life is that he was preacher at the Chapelry of Cross Stone in the parish of Halifax, about twelve miles west of the town, from 1622 to 1623, but he may have been longer in the parish.[2]

[1] *D.N.B.*; Cotton Mather, *Magnalia Christi Americana*, 1702, III, 113 f.; Rev. Mr Prince to HN, 4 March 1729, Colonial Soc. of Mass. Publications, XXVIII, 101–3; HN to Rev. Mr Prince, 16 July 1729, *New Eng. Letters.*

[2] Abraham Newell, "Cross Stone": *Halifax Antiquarian Soc., Papers, Reports, etc*, 1928, 204.

Then there came, as Newman said, "the persecutions of the Puritans under the Laudean faction". From 1628 to 1640 the two successive Archbishops of York, Samuel Harsnett and Richard Neile, were both friends of Laud and upholders of his policy. They made the same effort to introduce into the parish churches a uniformity of worship which was objectionable to the Puritans, whose practice and preaching they attacked by prohibition and deprivation. It is not surprising, therefore, to learn that Samuel Newman suffered under them. According to Cotton Mather, "The Episcopal molestations compelled him to no less than seven removes".

Nor is it surprising that he should finally have joined the "great Puritan migration" which brought some 20,000 men, women, and children to New England between 1630 and 1643. Boston was established in 1630 as the headquarters of Governor John Winthrop of the Massachusetts Bay Company, and Samuel Newman spent the rest of his life ministering in settlements around the town. He became minister of Dorchester about the end of 1636 and of Weymouth in 1638, finally in 1644 becoming first minister of Rehoboth, to which he gave its name. He would have had an important position in these settlements, for the early growth of the colony, though so rapid, was not haphazard, but by groups managed by the organized congregation under the leadership of the minister on lines derived from Continental Calvinism. Cotton Mather described him as an industrious student, a hospitable pastor, and an imaginative preacher, but, above all, as *Bibliander Nov. Anglicanus*, an outstanding Biblical scholar, who compiled the fullest concordance yet made in Europe, which he further enlarged in America—"Thou, Newman, hast excelled them all". He died at Rehoboth in 1663, his last words being, "And now, ye Angels of the Lord Jesus, come do your office".

Newman's grandfather died seven years before he was born. The influence of the Puritan pioneer upon his grandson must not, therefore, be exaggerated. At the same time, Newman grew up among the scenes and stories of his ministry. Later, he would also have met people in England who valued Samuel Newman's work, such as Ralph Thoresby, the Leeds merchant and historian, who noted in his *Diary* in 1714, "till eleven at the Committee of the Society for Promoting Christian Knowledge; dined privately with my good friend the Secretary, Mr Newman, had refreshing discourse concerning his pious grandfather, the author of that useful book, called the Cambridge Concordance".[1] Moreover, though he abandoned his grandfather's doctrine and country, Newman never entirely relinquished the Puritan outlook. The combination of earnestness, humility, and industry to be found in his character must owe much to the inheritance of his grandfather. One is reminded strongly of the grandson in what Cotton Mather said of Samuel Newman—"But of his family discipline there was no part more notable than this one; that once a year he kept a solemn day of humiliation with his family and once a year of thanksgiving; and on these days he would not only inquire of his household what they had met withal to be humbled, or to be thankful for, but also he would recruit the memoirs of his diary."

If it was as well written as his grandson's letters, Samuel Newman's diary must have presented a valuable picture of life in early New England, but unfortunately it was lost, and Mather had less to say about him than about many of his contemporaries. Similarly, when Newman came to England, his father's papers were lost in the coasting vessel that took his baggage from Portsmouth to London, so that he could give Thomas Prince few details about him. Samuel Newman

had three sons, Antipas, Samuel and Noah. *Antipas* was, I believe, born at Weymouth and lived to be minister of Wenham and had two sons, John and Samuel, the last of whom died in the West Indies, the eldest was sometime representative for the town of Wenham. *Samuel* lived and died a plain useful layman at Rehoboth, leaving two sons, Samuel and David.[2] *Noah* was born at Rehoboth, about the year 1646, where he was educated under his father and lived to succeed him, though not immediately, because he could not be above seventeen years old when his father died, supposing that he died as Dr Mather's *History* mentions in 1663. Noah, after his being settled as his father's successor, married Mrs Joanna Flint, a daughter of the Revd Henry Flint of Roxbury, about the year 1669, by whom he had three children, viz. Henry, born the 10th of November 1670, and Samuel and Mary, who died young. Noah died of a consumption about 1678,[3] leaving only his wife, who died of a consumption about a year afterward, and Henry to the care of a benign Providence.

Newman, then, was left at the age of 8 an orphan and with no brothers or sisters. He seems to have led the common life of a

[1] Ralph Thoresby, *Diary*, 2 vols., 1830, II, 256.

[2] "14 Dec. 1710. Mr Samuel Newman of Rehoboth dies; he sat in one Court as a Justice of Peace; was a very good man." "Diary of Samuel Sewall": *Sewall Papers, Mass. Hist. Soc. Collections*, Fifth Series, VI, 295.

[3] "16 April 1678. Mr Noah Newman, Pastor of Rehoboth Church, died." "Sewall's Commonplace Book", op. cit., VI, 12.

homeless child, passing under the care of his mother's relations. Among these were his grandmother and his aunt, Mary (Willett), wife of the Reverend Josiah Flint, who graduated at Harvard in 1664. She was the mother of Henry Flint ("Father Flint"), who was a tutor at Harvard from 1699 to 1754 and one of the great College characters of the century, while one of her daughters married John Quincy, a descendant of Edmund and Judith Quincy, who had sailed to Massachusetts with the Reverend John Cotton in 1633. Her sons, Edmund and Josiah, became merchants of Boston, and Newman later had many dealings with them in sending things to or from America. Newman remembered with gratitude these relations of his mother's family. In 1737 he was glad to hear news of them, "particularly of my good Aunt Flint and her daughter, my Cousin Quincy, of whose many civilities above forty years ago I have a grateful remembrance, as well as those I received above fifty years since in my Uncle Quincy"; and two years later he recalled "my old cousin John Quincy, whom I have reason to remember with gratitude for many good offices he did as a kind of guardian to me under Judge Sewall in my young days when I had no parents to advise with".[1] His father's relations, on the other hand, had no place in Newman's memories, nor did he keep in touch with them. In fact, when "a very weak man in understanding" came to him in London in 1739, stating he was a son of his cousin, John Newman, and whose purpose "he bluntly told me at our first meeting was to be my heir", Newman "could only consider him an impostor till Mr Winthrop, whose aunt was mother of the Newmans at Wenham, owned him and very kindly took care to send him back to New York".[2]

Newman was educated, as might be expected of a boy with no settled home, in several schools. He "was put to school at Roxbury, Dorchester, Dedham and, last of all, at Braintree under the guardianship of Mrs Flint, his grandmother, Mr Benjamin Tompson being his master at this last place". The free schools in New England provided a good education. In most of the northern and middle colonies they were at least as good as in England, particularly in Massachusetts and Connecticut, where from the beginning every township of fifty householders had to provide an elementary

[1] HN to John Winthrop, London, 26 Feb. 1737; to Edmund Quincy, Braintree, 27 July 1737, *New Eng. Letters*.

[2] HN to Messrs Edmund and Josiah Quincy, Boston, 14 Sept. 1739, *New Eng. Letters*.

school and those of one hundred a higher school. The Puritans of the seventeenth century, both in England and America, placed great emphasis upon the learning of the ancient languages as a means "to the intensive study of the Scriptures and *pietas literata*" [1]; and at his successive schools Newman would have been well-grounded in the "holy tongues" of Latin and Greek. Newman's only reference in his letters to his schooldays illustrates the careful supervision of the pupils' morals which was also part of Puritan educational ideas. "When I was at school", he wrote in 1724, "I learnt from some of my playfellows to say *Odzuckers, Oddsliffikins, the Dickens is in it*, and *the Duce take it*, not knowing the tendency of these phrases to oaths and curses, but those who had the care of my education, I thank them, soon convinced me of my error, and taught me to keep at the utmost distance from expressions so unbecoming a Christian and a gentleman." [2]

Newman's schooldays came to an end when he was 13, for "he was sent to Harvard College 1683 before he was qualified for it (during Mr Roger's Presidentship), Mrs Flint being very desirous to see him and other of her grandchildren pushed into the world before she left it". The entrance requirements at Harvard were not unduly high for a grammar-school boy—an ability to translate Cicero and to write and speak Latin, together with some knowledge of Greek grammar—but it was not easy to enter the College. Before the founding of Yale in 1701, Harvard was the only college in New England and usually took only a dozen boys a year, some of whom came from outside New England.[3] This suggests, therefore, that for Newman to have been accepted by the College in this way was due to special circumstances, perhaps because of his undoubted Puritan ancestry and likely prominence later in the life of the colony. Certainly among Newman's contemporaries at Harvard were a number who achieved distinction—Gurdon Saltonstall and Jonathan Law, Governors of Connecticut; Jonathan Belcher, Governor of Massachusetts and New Jersey; John Winthrop, F.R.S., a cousin of Newman; Paul Dudley, F.R.S., Chief Justice of Massachusetts; Benjamin Lynde, Peter Burr, and Edmund Quincy, all colonial justices, and the last another of Newman's cousins; Dudley Woodbridge, Judge of Admiralty in Barbados;

[1] Foster Watson, *The Old Grammar Schools*, Cambridge, 1916, v.

[2] HN to Rev. Mr Croxall, Hampton, 7 Jan. 1724, *Society's Letters*.

[3] S. E. Morison, *Three Centuries of Harvard*, Cambridge, Mass., 1936, 22; C. K. Shipton, "Secondary Education in the Puritan Colonies", *New England Quarterly*, VII, 646.

Benjamin Wadsworth, President of Harvard; Timothy Cutler, Rector of Yale and Christ Church, Boston; Benjamin Colman, herald of liberal Congregationalism; and William Vasey, first Rector of Trinity Church, New York.

Newman's youth was a time of transition in Massachusetts. The first generation of settlers, the contemporaries of Samuel Newman, had passed away. The motives of these pioneers who had left the Church of England and suffered persecution were mainly religious, "a great hope . . . of laying some good foundation . . . for the propagating and advancing of the gospel of the kingdom of Christ"[1]; but by now many who came to the colony were attracted by the economic advantages in the new land which the others had opened. Merchants and fishermen were laying the foundation of the colony's prosperity, and their influence was generally hostile to Congregational orthodoxy.[2] The keynote of the colony had been the creation and maintenance of a Bible commonwealth in which Church and State should be fused together. The franchise had been restricted to the narrow circle of Church membership, itself dependent upon the relation of a personal transformation by what was believed to be the grace of God. The fathers, however, had not always succeeded in passing their own experiences and convictions to their children and grandchildren, who were baptized but often could not become full members of a Church through inability to present evidence of "regeneration". Admission to this partial membership or "Halfway Covenant", as it was nicknamed by its critics, preceded the new charter of Massachusetts in 1691, which was to transfer the franchise to the mass of property-owners with ultimately fatal results for the old dominant theocracy.[3]

There were other signs that the reign of the divines was ending. The Church of England was establishing a foothold among "the Lord's godly and free people" in the sacrosanct territory around Massachusetts Bay, as typified by the growth of an Anglican congregation worshipping in the King's Chapel, Boston, before the end of the seventeenth century. Within Congregationalism itself, this was also a period of reaction from the intensive preaching of

[1] *Bradford's History of Plymouth Plantation 1606–1646*, ed. W. T. Davis, New York, 1908, Chap. 2.

[2] W. B. Weeden, *Economic and Social History of New England, 1620–1729*, 2 vols., Boston, 1890, I, 88–90; Perry Miller, *Orthodoxy in Massachusetts, 1630–1650*, Cambridge, Mass., 1933, xi, xii.

[3] Luther A. Weigle, *American Idealism*, New Haven, Conn., 1928, *passim.*

the founders of the colony. Instead of strict Calvinism with its doctrine of predestination, the second and third generation preferred to emphasize the power of the individual to exert his will and repent. With this disbelief in the sharper points of Calvinism began the liberalism of eastern Massachusetts, which was to be strengthened during the eighteenth century by the reaction from the excesses of the Great Awakening of George Whitefield and Jonathan Edwards and lead to the Unitarian separation at the end of the century.[1] None realized better that changes were taking place than Cotton Mather, who lamented: "The *old spirit* of New England hath been sensibly going out of the world, as the old *saints* in whom it was have gone; and instead thereof the *spirit of the world* with a lamentable neglect of *strict piety* has crept in upon the rising generation." [2]

Harvard College was inevitably affected by these changes, and when Newman went there it was on the eve of one of the most important events in its history since its foundation in 1636. In 1685, Increase Mather, Minister of Second Church, Boston, and father of Cotton Mather, accepted the post of President of Harvard. He did so on condition that he retained the ministry of his church and that it was only a temporary appointment until a permanent and resident President was found; but he remained President until 1701, although in charge of his church the whole time and away in England on a political mission from 1688 to 1692. This meant unusual opportunities for the two tutors and resident Fellows, William Brattle and John Leverett, who practically managed the affairs of the College from 1686 to 1692, when they both married and resigned their Fellowships. Both men came from the rising New England merchant class and shared a sociable disposition and cultured tastes. They were not outstanding scholars and left no published works, but they exercised a deep influence on their pupils and had a reputation as preachers. No suggestion was ever made that their doctrinal opinions were not of strict Calvinist orthodoxy, but manuscript notes taken of Brattle's sermons by John Hancock, one of his pupils, indicate as strong an interest in ethical questions as in Puritan theology. He insisted upon election, the divine decrees, and the majesty of God, but also emphasized God's delight in mercy and Christ's mission to save sinners, and

[1] Williston Walker, *A History of the Congregational Churches in the United States*, New York, 1894, 170–80, 267–79.
[2] Cotton Mather, *Magnalia Christi Americana*, II, 334.

exhorted his hearers to "follow peace with all men" and "let us excite within us compassions".[1] The effect of Brattle and Leverett, the historian of Harvard has said, was to induce their pupils to be "friendly toward the Church of England and inclined to overlook or explain away some of the rigours of Calvinist theology", so that many of them in their turn "dropped preaching on fine points of theology" in favour of "practical discourses on the divine attributes and human conduct".[2]

The prescribed course at Harvard was based upon the seven liberal arts and three philosophies, as studied in medieval universities, and comprising largely the reading of classical belles lettres and the study of the learned tongues. It placed special emphasis upon logic and rhetoric, Greek and Hebrew, ethics and metaphysics, but was weak in mathematics. Brattle and Leverett made few alterations in the formal curriculum, but introduced the students to reading and studies outside it. They were offered instruction in French, while Cotton Mather, who only gradually realized what was happening in Harvard, accused the students of reading "plays, novels, empty and vicious pieces of poetry, and even Ovid's Epistles, which have a vile tendency to corrupt good manners".[3] Above all, the students were introduced to recent Anglican divinity, particularly the works of John Tillotson, later Archbishop of Canterbury, who "reformed the style of preaching and transformed its content, advocating probity on grounds of common sense and piety on grounds of common prudence".[4] They were also introduced to Henry More's *Enchiridion Ethicum* and other writings by the Cambridge Platonists.[5] Brattle and Leverett, therefore, sought to make their pupils aware of the main intellectual movement of the time among English theologians, who felt the need to transcend controversy and to concentrate upon what they considered vital in the religious tradition. Their aim, in this later part of the century and in another Cambridge, was like that of Whichcote's preaching, as described by his eighteenth-century editor, " to preserve a spirit of sober piety and rational religion in the University and Town of Cambridge, in opposition to the fanatic enthusiasm and senseless canting then in vogue".[6] They appear to have won the regard of their students,

[1] Abiel Holmes, "History of Cambridge", *Mass. Hist. Soc. Collections*, VII.
[2] S. E. Morison, *Harvard in the Seventeenth Century*, 564.
[3] Josiah Quincy, *History of Harvard University*, 1840, I, 559
[4] Charles Smyth, *The Genius of the Church of England*, 1947, 35. [5] *D.A.B.*
[6] Quoted, Basil Willey, *The Seventeenth Century Background*, 1946, 134.

many of whom were themselves sympathetic towards the changes of opinion taking place in the colony. Their work, to quote again the historian of Harvard, saved the College "from becoming a sectarian institution, at a time when the tendency of most pious New Englanders was to tighten up and insist upon hundred-per-cent puritanism in the place of infiltrating ideas that heralded the Century of Enlightenment".[1]

The effect of these two men upon Newman was profound and permanent. It was through them, he said, that he later became an Anglican. He stated this in several letters to defend himself against criticisms of his correspondence with New England Dissenters.

> They were the only tutors [he avowed] at that time in the College that recommended to their pupils the reading of Episcopal authors as the best books to form our minds in religious matters and preserve us from those narrow principles that kept us at a distance from the Church of England, and this at a time when there was a President that thundered out anathemas upon all that went to the Church of England as apostates from the primitive faith. The first time I preferred to go to the Church of England I should have been publicly admonished for it or expelled if those gentlemen had not generously interposed and protected me.

Their influence in Harvard, he held, was immense for they

> have had an opportunity and improved it effectually for making more proselytes to the Church of England than any two men in all America, as I can easily demonstrate by their having been the instruments in rescuing the greatest part of the men of education in the country from those narrow principles which kept them at a distance from the Church of England. And I am not ashamed to own that I am one of their proselytes.[2]

Indeed, Newman retained much of their religious outlook for the rest of his life. He always admired not only Tillotson's writings, but also his gentle and accommodating nature. In a letter to Benjamin Colman, he told a story about

> Dr Increase Mather, when Dr Bates had introduced him to dine with Archbishop Tillotson. After their return from Lambeth, Dr Bates said, "Well, brother, how do you like our Archbishop?" "Why truly," replied Dr Mather, "I like him so well that if you always had such Archbishops, New England had never been." It was about this time that Archbishop Tillotson went in a coach and six to visit Dr Bates in his cottage at Hackney, whose curate the Archbishop had formerly been in Cromwell's time at St Dunstan's-in-the-West, but those prospects of

[1] S. E. Morison, *Three Centuries of Harvard*, 44–5.

[2] HN to Dr Smalridge, Dean of Christ Church, Oxford, 9 March 1714; to Mr Taylor, Secretary of S.P.G., 29 March 1714, *Society's Letters*.

reconciling the Dissenters to the Established Church vanished on the death of that truly great man and the late glorious Queen Mary, to which I have reason to believe Bishop Burnet and other prelates were hearty well-wishers.

Having been brought to the Church of England himself by the personal influence of his tutors, Newman seems to have placed great hopes in the good results that kindness by Churchmen towards Dissenters would produce. He emphasized his view to Colman by telling him another story about "a society of clergymen in the west, that met alternately in one another's houses friendly to confer about the state of their respective cures" at the time of Sacheverell's trial, who resolved to rebuke one of their number for being too friendly with Dissenters, "particularly that it was observed no Dissenting minister could ride through the town, but stopped at his gate and was welcome to a pipe of tobacco and a glass of cider, etc.". His reply was to ask them whether they had converted any Dissenters to the Church, and when they said they had not—" 'Why then,' says the supposed delinquent, 'I can glory and bless God for it in being instrumental to gain many', which he named, some of which were well known to them, and the gentleman says, 'You may do it if you have a mind to enlarge the Church by Christian methods.' Upon which their admonitions were turned into congratulations, and the good man acquitted of being thought a betrayer of his Church." [1] This may argue on Newman's part a too simple faith that differences of doctrine and discipline could be resolved by affable archbishops and hospitable clergy, but it may well reveal the impression made upon Newman at Harvard by the broad-minded religion and personal kindliness of his tutors.

Nor did Newman in later life, even in the busiest days of his secretarial work, lose his wide interest in reading which was another inheritance from his Harvard tutors. One week he spent "several evenings very agreeably" with Thomas à Kempis and wondered whether *The Imitation of Christ* was "one of those books which may be thought proper to be put into the hands of piously disposed persons". To a correspondent oppressed with melancholy, he advised the reading of Bishop Simon Patrick's *Advice to a Friend* and offered to lend him a copy. He hoped that "our Harvard gentlemen" read Sir Isaac Newton's philosophy and would also attempt the sermons of Dr Samuel Clarke, despite the hetero-

[1] HN to Rev. Dr Colman, Boston, 24 Sept. 1736, *New Eng. Letters*.

doxy of his Arian tenets, "for notwithstanding his peculiarities, he must be allowed to have been a great divine"; and in a codicil to his will he left to Governor Belcher's son "ten volumes of all of Dr Clarke's sermons in 8vo. as an acknowledgement of the pleasure he has given me in reading them". To Governor Belcher himself he wrote: "Having lately read Voltaire's *History of Charles XII of Sweden*, I thought, if it be not new to you, I could not present you with a more agreeable entertainment in the next winter evenings than the perusal of it." The Governor replied: "You have gratified me extremely in your handsome present . . . of which I have had a good character and shall read it these winter evenings." Another bequest in his will to a friend was "all the volumes of *Spectators* and *Tatlers*", and, indeed, he was a good example of the interest in contemporary literature which Leverett and Brattle instilled into their students.[1]

Moreover, Newman's years at Harvard changed his choice of a career. When he went to the College, "he was designed by his friends for the ministry". Such students began their professional study of theology only after they had taken their first degree, and it seems that Newman, after graduating B.A. in 1687, made at least the first steps towards this, for there is still a book in the College Library—William Twisse's folio *Vindiciae Gratiae Potestatis ac Providentiae Dei*—on the fly-leaf of which he inscribed, "This book I borrowed of my Aunt Flint, and all these. Alting's common places, Jeane's Scholastick Divinity, Another Folio of Doctor Twisse's Works, Voetius his Divinity, Another of Alting's Works in 4to. Borrowed the 15: 9th: 1687."[2] Before long, however, his changing religious sympathies and growing interests led him to abandon all intention of following in his father's and grandfather's footsteps. He took advantage of Leverett and Brattle's liberal policy to undertake different studies from those contained in his late uncle's theological books. "His want of several qualifications and his genius strongly inclining him to travel instead of studying theology, he learned the French language, read chiefly mathematical books and travels after he had taken his first degree at Cambridge and acquired the French language by spending a

[1] HN to Mr Archdeacon Deane, Rochester, 6 Nov. 1742, *Miscellaneous Letters*; to Mr Brudnell, 9 March 1714, *Society's Letters*; to Jonathan Belcher, Jnr, Boston, 20 May 1731; to Gov. Belcher, Boston, 15 Sept. 1733, *New Eng. Letters*; Gov. Belcher to HN, "Belcher Papers", *Mass. Hist. Soc. Collections*, Sixth Series, VII, 475; P.C.C. Wills Principal Probate Registry, 1743, Boycott, f. 205.

[2] S. E. Morison, *Harvard in the Seventeenth Century*, 272.

summer at the French town of Narrangansett [1] that he might be ready to ramble when opportunity offered."

In this way he spent the time pleasantly at Harvard while waiting the traditional three years before taking his M.A. The requirements for this at Harvard, as in England, were very slight. It was not even necessary for the candidate to reside in College as long as he returned to Cambridge in time to discuss a philosophical problem or give a "commonplace" (a model sermon), hand in a synopsis of Arts, and reply to a *quaestio*, prepared beforehand on a printed subject, at the Master's Commencement.[2] Newman took his M.A. in 1690, when he replied in support of the *quaestio* at the Commencement Exercises, "*An Morbi sint Contagiosi?*"—"Are diseases contagious?"—which could suggest that the range of reading allowed to post-graduate students was wide indeed.[3]

After taking his second degree, Newman stayed still longer at Harvard, being from 1690 to 1693 Librarian of the College. This was the library to which John Harvard had left his own library of some 400 volumes. It was predominantly, though not overwhelmingly, theological and philosophical, and used mostly by graduate students. Newman was always proud of having held this post, and equally proud of the library with which he had been entrusted. Writing to Benjamin Colman in 1740, he compared it favourably with the library in the churchyard of St Martin-in-the-Fields founded in 1684 by Archbishop Tenison, where "you cannot take a book down without being covered with dust, whereas when I lived at Harvard College I was ambitious of nothing more than to keep it so clean that strangers, particularly Sir Francis Wheeler and the officers of his Squadron, when they saw it confessed that they never saw any college library at Oxford or Cambridge in England come up to it, and when I afterwards came to England, I was surprised to find many college libraries inferior to ours in all respects." [4]

A memorandum at Harvard states that on 3 September 1691 Newman was paid £3 for his services as library keeper, but he must have had private means as well as this small salary. In fact, he seems to have inherited land from his father. In 1689 his name appeared among the non-resident proprietors of Rehoboth, and

[1] I.e., the Huguenot settlement at Narrangansett, R.I.
[2] S. E. Morison, *Three Centuries of Harvard*, 34–5.
[3] J. L. Sibley, *Harvard Graduates*, 1885, III, 369.
[4] HN to Rev. Dr Colman, Boston, 20 Nov. 1740, *New Eng. Letters*.

one of the last letters he wrote, several weeks before his death, inquired about "some lots amounting to 45 acres of land belonging to me in that and the township of Attleborough adjoining", which, it appears from his will, were being farmed by his cousins, Samuel and David Newman.[1] In keeping with his later character, his only known expenditure in this period was a charitable one. In 1691 he joined several friends in promising money to Ruth Green, of Cambridge, widow, to enable her son Joseph to attend Harvard; he gave twelve shillings. Joseph Green was later Minister of Salem Village, Massachusetts, and exercised a great reconciling influence during the frenzied witchcraft delusion there.[2]

While Librarian at Harvard, Newman was able to extend his interest in mathematics to astronomy. There was a flourishing school of astronomy at Harvard. A telescope had been presented to the College in 1672 by Governor John Winthrop, F.R.S. With this Thomas Brattle made observations on the comet of 1680 that won Newton's commendation in his *Principia*, and in the summer of 1694 Newman assisted him in observations with a quadrant on the solar eclipse, as mentioned by Brattle in the account he sent to the Royal Society. Moreover, from 1646 and probably earlier, the Cambridge printer had chosen a recent Harvard graduate to make the calculations and prepare the copy for an annual almanac. This was the most widely diffused form of literature and, indeed, the only periodical literature in New England. It was, therefore, important in the life of the country, for, as has been said, these "annual New England almanacs, compiled largely by tutors and resident B.A.s, informed the farming population on the discoveries of Galileo, Kepler and Gassendi". Newman compiled the almanacs for 1690 and 1691. The first, called *Harvard's Ephemeris*, contained a "Postscript Exhibiting somewhat Touching the Earth's Motion", which quoted "for experimental reason the exquisite observations of the industrious Monsieur Azout"; the second, *News from the Stars*, had an account "Of Telescopes", a summary of astronomical discoveries made up to that time.[3]

Newman always retained these scientific interests he had gained

[1] L. Bliss, *History of Rehoboth*, Boston, 1836, 57, 129; HN to Thos. Hutchinson, 29 April 1743, *New Eng. Letters*; P.C.C. Wills, Principal Probate Registry, 1743, Boycott, f. 205.

[2] S. E. Morison, "The Commonplace Book of Joseph Green (1675–1715)", *Colonial Soc. of Mass. Publications*, XXXIV, 238.

[3] S. E. Morison, *Three Centuries of Harvard*, 31; S. E. Morison, "The Harvard School of Astronomy in the Seventeenth Century", *New England Quarterly*, VII, 3; *Philosophical Transactions of the Royal Society*, XXIV (1704, 1705), 1630–1.

at Harvard. His correspondence contains descriptive passages which reveal him as a keen observer of natural phenomena, as this account of

a very fine Aurora Borealis [which] shewed itself here to above 100 thousand spectators, which I now hear has been seen above three score miles round London, and how far further a little time may show, but I think the observations already made place it far above the atmosphere, and must, therefore, puzzle all our philosophers to account for. If it was seen in France and Ireland, etc., it will be a demonstration that there are vast materials in the region of the air, which the great Creator vouchsafes to disclose to ignorant mortals as he did the magnet and the use of microscopes, etc., after they had been concealed for many ages from learned inquisitive philosophers.[1]

Often when he wrote to correspondents overseas, he sought to exchange information with them, as when writing to Samuel Palmer, a merchant in India.

Cometical astronomy has been mightily improved here of late years. You may perhaps be pleased to see a treatise lately published by Mr Whiston on that subject, and therefore I have herewith sent it. Pray what discoveries of this kind have the philosophers in your parts made? What footsteps of the Deluge have you remaining with you? Whether the earth lies *in strata super strata* in all pits and cliffs with you as it does here, and whether the more ponderous bodies are found in the lower parts of the earth? [2]

Soon Newman's studies took a yet more practical turn. The desired opportunity of travelling abroad came when he became a sort of lay chaplain in a New England merchant ship trading with Europe. By the time of the Restoration, Massachusetts had developed through Boston and neighbouring ports "an all-round trade by which it supplied the Plantations with foodstuffs, took their sugar and other produce in return, exchanged them with continental Europe for manufactured goods to be distributed throughout the colonies",[3] a trade it now continued despite the outbreak of hostilities with France in the War of the Grand Alliance. As Newman was by now considering a career in commerce, the offer was the more welcome, apart from the interest and excitement it brought him.

In 1692 he was invited by Mr Marston of Salem, the owner of a ship commanded by John Beal of Marblehead, to take a voyage to Bilboa in Spain in a merchant ship of which he was chief owner. This invitation

[1] HN to Rev. Mr Wheeler, Warpenham, 5 Oct. 1726, *Society's Letters*.
[2] HN to Sam. Palmer, Persia, 16 March 1714, *Society's Letters*.
[3] *Cambridge History of the British Empire*, I, 251.

was very acceptable, his duty being only to read prayers and on Sundays a sermon to the crew. At this time it was he applied himself to understand the art of navigation and whatever else might qualify him for business. He went three voyages to Bilboa in this ship, and though in every voyage the ship was engaged with French ships and lost men, she always cleared herself of them by the bravery of the Captain and his men and afterwards made an agreeable tour back to New England as once by way of Cadiz, another time by the Cape de Verde Islands, Barbados and Tortugas, and the last voyage 1694 he got leave at Bilboa the latter end of 1694 to embark in the *Falkland*, commanded by Captain Long, to England, whereupon his arrival at Falmouth, some distance from the town, he prostrated himself upon the ground to kiss it and with humble thanks to God for having preserved him through so many storms and engagements with French ships, in one of which he was wounded in the thigh by a small shot, and last to bring him to the land of his forefathers, which he had so long impatiently wished to see. Some of the boat's crew that were with him, thinking he had been in a fit, ran up to him to know what was the matter, which he soon explained to them by kissing every post and tree as they passed on to the town.

Newman evidently received his wound on his last voyage, for William Brattle wrote to another of his Harvard friends in the spring of 1695, "Have no news but that Mr Newman was wounded in his thigh in a fight Captain Beal had (in getting into Bilboa) with a French man-o-war." [1] He suffered no serious effects from this wound, though it troubled him at intervals for the rest of his life. In 1712 he wrote that "being come with the return of pain of an old strain I received at sea, I am advised to use rest or all other applications will be ineffectual", and in 1718 that he was "so lame that I am obliged to rest as much as I can to get rid of it".[2] Despite this legacy of his voyages, he always looked back on them with happiness. In writing to a merchant in India in 1729, he thanked his daughter for "the *History of St Jago*, which she sent to your servant maid, and which I read with pleasure, as it revived my remembrance of that island, when I happened to go ashore, in the same place where their ship watered, about 35 years ago".[3]

It was on this last voyage, too, that Newman made an interesting heraldic suggestion to Harvard, prompted perhaps by a desire to see the College able to compare favourably in all respects with the English colleges. It was that he should have the College arms carved in stone at Bilboa to adorn Old Harvard Hall. On 11

[1] Wm Brattle to Rowland Cotton, 9 March 1695, *Mass. Hist. Soc. Misc. MSS.*, Vol. V.

[2] HN to Mr Melmoth, 4 Feb. 1712; to Sir Humphrey Mackworth, 29 July 1718, *Society's Letters.*

[3] HN to Zachery Gee, Fort St George, 20 Feb. 1729, *Society's Letters.*

June 1694 the College minutes recorded, "Mr Newman's proposal about procuring the College arms at Bilboa is left to the President's consideration and determination". Increase Mather evidently approved of the idea, for on 20 July 1694 the minutes stated, "Cash pd. Mr Henry Newman £5 pr. order of the Corporation to procure the College arms to be cut in freestone or in marble"; but for some reason Newman acted like Jack in *Jack and the Beanstalk* with his mother's cow, and invested the sum at Barbados in a parcel of twenty-seven cane-joints for walking-sticks at 4*s*. 6*d*. each. It was not a good bargain, most of them, the College Treasurer noted in 1696, "being short, scabby and of no substance". Newman sold three himself, but the College had to dispose of the rest at half-price, barely recovering its £5 and obtaining no achievement of arms.[1]

This transaction hardly augured well for a commercial career, but Newman had friends among the merchants of Boston. When regular fishing voyages from English ports had been interrupted by the Civil War, merchants found bases for their operations in New England ports, and an active commerce had sprung up. Ships from Boston or Rhode Island carried meat and flour to St John's to sell to the Newfoundland fishermen and there to be freighted with fish and train oil for sale in the ports of southern Europe. This trade grew rapidly after the Restoration, despite a set-back caused by the ravaging of the little English settlements in Newfoundland by D'Iberville, the brilliant subordinate of the Comte de Frontenac, Governor of Canada.[2] This was the trade Newman was to enter.

On landing in England, he went to London, where

he found with a few letters of recommendation many friends, and in a few months soon after he was invited to a partnership with Mr Francis Taylor, who had lived some years as a merchant at Stockholm, to go with him to Newfoundland, in behalf of a company at London to negotiate as factors a stock of ten thousand pounds proposed to be circulated from London to New England and thence in provisions to Newfoundland, the produce of which to be remitted either directly to England or in fish, etc. to Spain and Portugal, but his project was soon laid aside by the news of the French having destroyed the principal settlements of the English, and therefore after about fifteen months stay in London, he returned with a cargo of about £500 sterling on

[1] S. E. Morison, *Harvard in the Seventeenth Century*, 493–4; J. L. Sibley, op. cit., III, 369; *Mass. Hist. Soc. Proceedings*, First Series, VI, 352–3; *Leverett MS. Diary*, 67 (Harvard Coll. Library).

[2] *Cambridge History of the British Empire*, I, 181–2.

commission to Boston, where he commenced merchant 1696, and by the time he had spent a year there, the same project of settling a factory at Newfoundland was revived at London upon the peace of Ryswick, and Mr Taylor following him to Boston, Articles of Partnership for seven years were there agreed on, and both proceeded in different sloops laden with provisions to St John's, Newfoundland, 1698.

The draft of Newman's letter of 1729 to Thomas Prince ended here, and he gave no further account of his life. Only occasional references can be discovered about the years immediately after 1698. Two entries about him occur in the Diary of Samuel Sewall, the strict Puritan New England judge—the first on 4 November 1697, King William III's birthday, when at Boston "about 8 Mr Brattle and Newman let fly their fireworks from Cotton Hill; Governor and Council went thither with a trumpet sounding"—as later in England, such public occasions strongly appealed to his patriotism and delight in pageantry; the second, on 4 January 1699, concerns Newman's attendance at the worship of the Huguenot congregation in Boston on the previous Christmas, to the indignation of Sewall, who repeatedly recorded his protest against the religious observance of the day as a grievous sin—"This day I spake with Mr Newman about his partaking with the French church on 25 December, on account of it being Christmas-day, as they abusively call it. He stoutly defended the Holy-days and church of England." Apparently, though he had not yet broken with the creed of his birth, Newman found the appeal of Anglicanism as strong as when at College.[1]

Presumably Newman was as much in Newfoundland as in Boston during these years. The occasional references to Newfoundland in his later letters did not praise the island. He held that it "claims the preference in respect of wildness in all places", and that "the inhabitants of Newfoundland are too much disposed to ridicule all things serious".[2] The colony at this time was very small, with a permanent population of less than a thousand, while a French colony was also established there and existed side by side with the English until the Treaty of Utrecht in 1714. Most of the fishermen returned to English ports, so that there was little political development on the island. Until it achieved a regular government in 1728, it was administered like a man-of-war, the captain

[1] "Diary of Samuel Sewall", *Mass. Hist. Soc. Collections*, Fifth Series, V, 462 and 491.

[2] HN to Elizabeth Sheldon, Stroud, Glos, 31 Aug. 1727, *Private Letters*; to Rev. Mr Henry Jones, Bonavista, Newfoundland, 25 Feb. 1729, *Society's Letters*.

of the convoy administering justice during the summer visits of the fishing fleets. The fishermen made ceaseless complaints of the lawlessness of the colonists, and in 1701 the convoy captain appointed "one Mr Henry Newman, a merchant" to be "Register" or magistrate at St John's, being "given such instructions as are necessary . . . that if any pirates should happen to be seized . . . there cannot be any error in the proceedings".[1]

This appointment in Newfoundland, which cannot have been very easy or congenial, is the last that is known of Newman as an American merchant. The next news of him is that in the summer of 1703 he visited Oxford with a fellow Harvard graduate, Nathaniel Saltonstall,[2] and he was to spend the rest of his life in England. Nothing can be learnt from Newman about his activities immediately after the expiration of his articles of partnership; but in 1710 Colonel Joseph Dudley, Governor of Massachusetts, spoke of him as "a person of great probity, who had lived some years in the Duke of Somerset's family", and when proposed as Secretary of the S.P.C.K. he was described as "late in the service of His Grace the Duke of Somerset".[3] This was Charles Seymour, sixth Duke of Somerset, "the proud duke", who obtained through marriage the estates and territorial influence of the Percys. Newman was presumably in his employment from about 1703 to 1708, when the Duke was a prime favourite of Queen Anne, being Master of the Horse and a commissioner for the union with Scotland.[4] He was prominent in Court life, and though Newman never mentioned it in his letters, he must himself have been there with his employer, judging by his acquaintance with Court ways and personages. "When you go the errand you propose", he told a correspondent, "you have only to take your opportunity any morning and ask for the Lord of the Bedchamber in waiting, to whom it will be necessary to present a copy of your book, that he may be the better able to speak to it when he presents you to the King. Sunday is not a proper time, because it is a publick day, attended with a great crowd, and Thursday is much like it, but if you attend any other day soon after 12 noon you will be in time." [5] This is the advice of a man intimate with the Court at some time in his life.

[1] *Calendar of State Papers, Colonial Series, America and W. Indies* (1701), 430.
[2] Newman's letter to his kinsman, Henry Flint, already a tutor at Harvard, describing his Oxford visit, is printed in *Colonial Soc. of Mass. Transactions*, XXVIII, 95–9.
[3] T. Hutchinson, *History of the Colony and Province of Massachusetts Bay* (ed. L. S. Mayo), 3 vols., Cambridge, Mass., 1936, II, 140; *S.P.C.K. Minutes*, 17 June 1708.
[4] *D.N.B.*
[5] HN to Mr Zachery Williams, London, 6 Dec. 1739, *Private Letters.*

Somerset, despite his trimming politics, had never wavered in support of the Protestant succession since he had taken up arms in 1688, and was to be present at the fateful Council when Queen Anne from her death-bed handed Shrewsbury the Treasurer's white staff. Newman was to remain steadfast to the Hanoverian cause all his life. He feared the schemes of the extreme Jacobites in the anxious concluding years of Anne's reign. "No man is wise enough to foresee which way things will turn yet," he wrote to Leverett in 1710, "but so restless are some men to get into the saddle that they seem to make light of the peace of the Kingdom so they may advance themselves. I don't care to say what I think on this head, but hope your prayers and those of other good men will prevail that God would direct the Queen and her Council wisely to govern this great people." [1] The High Church cause, although Anne's reign was its Indian summer, did not win his sympathy. Looking back some years later, he spoke of the "rout" made by Sacheverell and "the train of admirers that followed him as under a delirium for the time it lasted".[2] In the last months of the reign he thought, "As to political affairs we are very unsettled and can hardly ever be otherwise until the House of Hanover come hither to give us a prospect of a race of princes never to be extinct." [3] Nor did he change his mind after the Hanoverian accession. Opposition to the "most august family of Hanover", as he called it, was "downright madness". George I was "the best of princes" and his son equally to be praised.[4]

For the rest of his life also Newman was attracted by the Court and its spectacles. This was, perhaps, fostered by his service with Somerset, who was a chief mourner at the funerals of Charles II, Mary, William III, Anne, and George I, as well as bearing the orb at four coronations, and whose "handsome figure appeared to advantage in pageants of this character, for which he showed an extraordinary predilection".[5] At any rate, the arrival in England of George I, the execution of the Jacobite conspirators in 1723, the coronation of George II, the marriage of Princess Anne with William IV, Prince of Orange in 1733, and the quarrel between George II and Frederick, Prince of Wales—all interested Newman

[1] HN to President Leverett, Harvard, 26 June 1710, *Harvard College Papers*, I, f. 95.
[2] HN to Rev. Dr Colman, Boston, 24 Sept. 1736, *New Eng. Letters*.
[3] HN to Mr Hales, Hanover, 23 Feb. 1714, *Society's Letters*.
[4] HN to Mr Hales, The Hague, 27 Aug. 1714; to Rev. Mr Tatam, Sutton-on-the-Hill, Derby., 1 Aug. 1718, *Society's Letters*.
[5] *D.N.B.*

keenly, and he provided his New England correspondents with full accounts of them.[1]

Yet Newman never seems to have aspired to be a courtier or a politician. It was not a career that would have suited his character. As he told a discontented young lady at Stroud, who wished to be at Court: "I own I go thither sometimes because I love the Royal Family, but I bless myself that my lot is not to live among them, that I am a spectator at liberty and not a trainbearer or some other fine thing confined to a place abounding with vanity and insincerity." [2] His years with the Duke of Somerset were not to determine his life in England; they were to be followed by a post much better suited to his pious and charitable character.

[1] Several of these letters are printed in W. K. Lowther Clarke, *Eighteenth Century Piety*, 42–7.
[2] HN to Elizabeth Sheldon, Stroud, Glos, 31 Aug. 1727, *Private Letters*.

2

SECRETARY OF THE S.P.C.K.

THE mounting attack by High Church upon Low Church and Dissent have made the reigns of William III and Anne known as a time of political and ecclesiastical strife, but it was also one of religious revival and activity. According to the Tory pamphleteer, Charles Davenant, this had its origin in the Romish attack on the Church of England under James II. This writer recalled, in the early years of Anne's reign, how "the measures King James the Second took to change the religion of the country roused up fresh zeal in the minds of all sorts of men; they embraced more straitly what they were in fear to lose".[1] One effect of this moral and religious movement was to encourage the religious societies which had already been formed under the influence of some of the great preachers in London. They had attracted "groups of serious young men", who met to strengthen each other in religious life and practice by prayer and worship, charity and good works. By 1710 there were forty-two of these societies in London alone, and they were the forerunners of the Methodist "societies" later in the century. Another group of religious societies, which came into being after the Glorious Revolution, were the Societies for the Reformation of Manners, designed to check the licence of the age, mainly by securing the enforcement of the law against vice and intemperance among the poor.[2]

The Society for Promoting Christian Knowledge came into being on 8 March 1699, and in its origin had much in common with these other religious societies. It was founded on the initiative of that energetic divine, Dr Thomas Bray, who was joined by four of his friends, persons of "honour and quality"—Mr Justice Hooke, a lawyer; Colonel Colchester, a country gentleman; Sir Humphrey Mackworth, M.P., a capitalist and economist; and Lord Guilford, son of Lord North, the Lord Chancellor. Largely through Bray's vigorous leadership, the Society met frequently—sixty times in the first year—and increased its numbers by electing further members, both clerical and lay. Some bishops joined, but

[1] Charles Davenant, *Collected Works*, IV, 396.
[2] J. H. Overton, *Life in the English Church, 1660–1714*, 1885, 214.

none were active in its affairs, which continued to be managed by laymen, whose aims were expressed in the agreement all had to sign—"Whereas the growth of vice and immorality is greatly owing to gross ignorance of the Christian religion, we whose names are underwritten do agree to meet together, as often as we can conveniently, to consult (under the conduct of the Divine Providence and assistance) how we may be able by due and lawful methods to promote Christian knowledge." [1]

These aims distinguished it from the other religious societies. Bray intended it to work along the lines of the *Congregatio pro Propaganda Fide* of the Roman Church; his first scheme called it "a Protestant Congregation or Society".[2] Therefore, although it had much in common with the Societies for the Reformation of Manners, the S.P.C.K. always insisted that its work was on different lines—"This Society hath sometimes been mistaken for that of Reformation of Manners; and though the end of both is directed to the glory of God and the good of mankind, yet the measures taken by each are different: The Societies for Reformation applying themselves chiefly to the putting the laws in execution against profaneness and debauchery, whereas the endeavours of this Society are immediately directed to the Promoting Christian Knowledge, especially amongst the poorer sort of people." [3] That it successfully maintained this purpose is shown by the recognition given it in 1712 by the author of a guide to contemporary religious societies—"I cannot but take notice with great thankfulness to God of a very honourable and beneficial society, erected in 1699 in this City, by which the promoting of Christian Knowledge is vigorously endeavoured, which seems to fill up all that could be thought deficient in the methods that were before set on foot in order to the general amendment of the lives and manners of men. For whilst the Societies for Reformation pluck up the weeds and prepare the ground, this sows the good seed." [4]

The main purposes of the S.P.C.K., as Newman explained to Sir Hans Sloane in 1731, were "to encourage the erecting of charity schools and workhouses and to disperse good books among the

[1] T. B. Murray, *Jubilee Tract; being an Account of the Chief Proceedings of the Five Original Members of the S.P.C.K., in March 1698–9*, 1849, 5; W. O. B. Allen and E. McClure, *History of the S.P.C.K.*, 16.

[2] H. P. Thompson, *Thomas Bray*, 1954, 36.

[3] S.P.C.K., *The First General Letter to Correspondents*, 1700.

[4] J. Woodward, *Rise and Progress of the Religious Societies*, 4th ed., 1712, 67.

people who are not able to buy them", but this was not all, "as they are a Voluntary Society, they are not confined to any part of the world, but wherever the interest of religion and virtue can be served by their good offices, they have readily concurred in the use of such means as were in their power to advance them".[1] By calling it a "voluntary society", Newman was contrasting it with the Society for the Propagation of the Gospel, established three years later by royal charter. He had often to explain this difference, particularly to his American correspondents. "The Society for Propagating the Gospel in Foreign Parts", he told one, "were originally formed out of this Society, but by having a Charter are confined to the English Plantations in America and tied up to several rules, not one of which can be altered or violated, but on penalty of forfeiting their Charter, without a dispensation under the Great Seal." The result was, he told another, that "when the Mother Society came to consider of the limitations they were under by their Charter, they chose to keep up their voluntary capacity".[2] And during Newman's secretaryship, this freedom enabled it to engage in an increasing number of world-wide religious activities.

What brought Newman into the Society can only be conjectured. Perhaps it was through Dr Bray, who went to Maryland in 1699 as Commissary for Bishop Compton of London and was in America for over three years, when Newman might have met him; or perhaps it was through Dr Snape, Chaplain to the Duke of Somerset and an early member of the Society. Certainly Newman was later described in the Society's minutes as "well known to Dr Snape, His Grace's Chaplain, and to Dr Bray",[3] while the first mention of him was on 13 May 1703, when he was made "a Corresponding Member for Newfoundland". The next month, at his first meeting, he was given 250 copies of a pamphlet called *The Obligations Christians are under to Shun Vice and Immorality* and "100 Packets for the Commanders of Merchant Ships", to be "dispersed in the English Settlements in Newfoundland".[4] This, again, may have been through Bray's influence, for he had learned while in America that though England drew a rich trade from Newfoundland, "there never was, nor yet is, any preaching, prayer or sacraments,

[1] HN to Sir Hans Sloane, 1 Sept. 1731, *Sloane MSS.*, 4052, f. 4.
[2] HN to Rev. Mr Colman, Boston, 20 Oct. 1722; to Rev. Mr Barnard, Marblehead, Mass., 25 Sept. 1727, *New Eng. Letters*.
[3] *S.P.C.K. Minutes*, 17 June 1708.
[4] Ibid., 13 May and 3 June 1703.

or any ministerial or divine offices, performed on that island", and he had condemned "this indifference of ours in propagating the religion we profess to believe".[1]

Samuel Sewall, who had sent Newman books in Newfoundland, wrote to him: "Whatever diminutive thoughts you may have of yourself, I hope true religion will be the more successfully promoted for your being admitted a member of that Society. It would be well if you could set on foot the printing of the Spanish Bible in a fair octavo, ten thousand copies, and then you might attempt the bombing of Santa Domingo, the Havana, Porto Rico and Mexico itself. I would willingly give five pounds towards the charge of it, if it shall be agreed to be convenient to be done. Mr Leigh commends the Translation of a Cypriana Valera, which I am an owner of in folio."[2] When Newman became Secretary of the Society, he was to receive many such suggestions from people who wanted him to put their favourite ideas into practice.

Newman not only frequently attended meetings of the Society, but in August 1705 became Secretary of the body later known as Dr Bray's Associates, whose purpose was to establish parochial libraries for the clergy. Bray's original plan, when appointed Commissary for Maryland, was to establish them for the American clergy, since "none but the poorer sort of clergy could be persuaded to leave their friends and change their native country for one so remote; that such persons could not be able sufficiently to supply themselves with books; that without a competent provision of books, they could not answer the design of their ministry; that a library would be the best encouragement to studious and sober men to undertake the service"; but he soon decided to include the clergy of England and Wales, for, being unable to afford books himself, "he became thereby more sensible of the wants of his brethren" and realized "that we had poor cures and poor parsons enough in England, and that charity should begin at home".[3] Newman's experience as Librarian at Harvard would have been valuable here, and though a part-time post, it gave him a knowledge of men and methods useful when he took the more arduous post of Secretary of the S.P.C.K.

[1] H. P. Thompson, *Thomas Bray*, 58

[2] Sam. Sewall to HN, 4 April 1701 and 6 March 1704, *Mass. Hist. Soc. Collections*, Sixth Series, I, 256 and 297.

[3] *Rawlinson MSS.*, D.834, f. 44; *Publick Spirit, illustrated in the Life and Designs of the Reverend Thomas Bray, D.D.*, 1746, *passim.*

This, by an unusual appointment, had been held since 1702 by Humphrey Wanley, the Anglo-Saxon scholar and an Assistant in the Bodleian Library, Oxford, until, having spent most of the year 1699 collating Anglo-Saxon manuscripts in Cambridge and planning to continue his researches in the Cotton Library in London, the Bodleian objected to his absence from Oxford. Possibly through George Hickes, Non-juring Bishop of Thetford and antiquarian, he obtained the patronage of Robert Nelson, the Non-juror and author of *Festivals and Fasts of the Christian Year*. Nelson, an early member of the S.P.C.K. and often chairman at its meetings, secured for Wanley the post of Secretary of the Society at a salary of £40 a year, and promised to support him—"You are so well qualified to serve the Society whose prosperity I am most zealously concerned for, that, as that engaged me first in your interest, so it will always incline me to favour and promote it; and if I find upon any occasions some of our members less sensible of it, I shall endeavour to set your merits in a true light."

For Wanley his time as Secretary was not wasted. He collaborated in the valuable report on the Cottonian Manuscripts and produced his own greatest work, the final volume of Hickes' *Thesaurus*. For the Society he translated from the French in 1704 the *Grounds and Principles of the Christian Religion* by Jean Frédéric Ostervald (1663–1747), the Swiss Protestant divine who gave a powerful stimulus to the religious life of Calvinism on the Continent. Dr Bray and other members of the Society were keenly interested in the Reformed Churches abroad, and this treatise, like others by Ostervald, sought to give religious life a more practical character, so that it seemed very suitable for the Society to publish in England.

This, however, did not justify Wanley's appointment to all the members of the Society, and Nelson soon had to protect him from the criticisms of John Chamberlayne, first Secretary of the Society from 1699 to 1702 and now Secretary of Queen Anne's Bounty. "I cannot sufficiently wonder why Mr Chamberlayne should trouble the Society with his complaints", wrote Nelson to Wanley. "I must confess I have that opinion of your conduct as to believe it will always be seasoned with piety and prudence"; and again, "I am sorry Mr Chamberlayne continues to give you so much uneasiness; he is resolved to make your patience as your other good qualities." Wanley's patience with his predecessor was not tried long, for in 1708 he obtained the highly congenial position of

Library Keeper to Robert Harley, who was building up his great collection of manuscripts.[1]

Wanley did not tender his resignation to the Society until 3 June 1708, but as early as the previous March the Reverend Henry Shute, Treasurer of the Society, sounded Newman on the possibility of his succeeding him.[2] Newman seems still to have been in the Duke of Somerset's service and gave no definite reply. "There is nothing could have been more agreeable to my inclinations", he said, "thus to serve the Committee of the Society in what you proposed, were I free from any other engagement which happens at present to engross so much of my time that I must not pretend in any tolerable manner to be capable of executing both. And I must own if I had been free, though the business itself had been most agreeable, yet I should have found some difficulty to accept a salary from the Society out of what is collected for pious uses." He suggested instead that the Society's business should be shared between four or six gentlemen, each serving for two or three months, with a messenger and a charity-school boy as the only paid servants. Perhaps in suggesting this he was mindful of criticisms that Wanley had not justified his salary. At any rate, he calculated, "Some such expedient as this would in seven years' time save near £500, which, with their usual management, would erect a great many charity schools or purchase not a few books." He did, however, agree that, "if, as I am promised, the summer affords me much leisure, I shall be proud to devote it all to the service of the Society". He was as good as his word, for when he was proposed for the post by one of Dr Bray's friends on 17 June 1708, he accepted a week later and attended his first meeting of the Society in that capacity on 1 July "with abundance of thanks for the honour they did him".[3] He was to hold it until his death, almost exactly thirty-five years later, on 15 June 1743.

Newman was suited for the post. He knew the ways of both business and the Court, understood Latin and French, and had some private means, while the years were to reveal how congenial he found the work and how conscientious he was in undertaking it. It may well be, however, that political considerations also were concerned in the appointments of both Wanley and Newman.

[1] D. C. Douglas, *English Scholars, 1660–1730*, 2nd ed., 1951, 98–118; C. F. Secretan, *Life of Robert Nelson*, 1860, 104–12.

[2] *S.P.C.K. Minutes*, 3 June 1708; HN to Rev. Mr Shute, 25 March 1708, *Society's Letters*.

[3] *S.P.C.K. Minutes*, 17 and 24 June, 1 July 1708.

Dr Bray sought support for the Society from men of all parties in Church and State, and it included among its earliest members men of such differing views as Thomas Tenison, Gilbert Burnet, White Kennett, Simon Patrick, Thomas Wilson, Robert Nelson, and Samuel Wesley.[1] But it was impossible for the Society to remain aloof from the political struggle of Anne's reign. Nelson was a Non-juror until 1710, and there were others among the Society's members. For one so devoted to the cause of the S.P.C.K. as Nelson, it was strange to have urged the appointment of Wanley as Secretary, but if it were at the instigation of Dr Hickes, it might well represent a natural attempt by the Non-jurors to win the Society for their cause when it was not yet irretrievably lost. The Society was certainly divided in its loyalties—"Good Dr Bray said how happy and religious the nation would become when the House of Hanover came and was very indignant when Mr Mason said that matters would not be mended when that family came thither."[2] The appointment as Secretary, therefore, of one as thoroughly devoted to the Hanoverian cause as Newman would strengthen the position, on the eve of the crisis in Church and State, of Bray and his friends, who did not wish to see the Society involved in the struggle for the succession.

Another matter upon which Newman and Bray were agreed—as, indeed, were most Englishmen at the time—was their fear of Popish machinations against the Church and government. Dr Bray was writing his *Martyrology or Papal Usurpation* (published in 1712), but thought it best "to conceal his name, because he shall depict in this history some hellish practices among the Papists, for which if he were known, he might be in danger to be treated as Sir Edmundbury Godfrey".[3] Newman shared these fears, which for Englishmen were inspired by memories of Romanist power at Whitehall under Charles II and James II and fear of French aggression under Louis XIV, and for him were doubtless increased by his upbringing in New England, where "the proximity of French Jesuit missionaries and their intrigues with the Indians, and resentment at the political interference of the Pope, helped to keep the colonists intensely hostile to Roman Catholicism".[4] The Spanish War of Succession made him apprehensive. "Popish priests come daily over to us from Dunkirk to pave the way for

[1] J. H. Overton, op. cit., 217.
[2] W. Whiston, *Memoirs, Written by Himself*, 1753, 134.
[3] HN to Mr Bewick, Barrow, Leics., 23 Aug. 1711, *Society's Letters*.
[4] *Cambridge History of the British Empire*, I, 403.

some design which they seem to be big of, and there are already many instances of perversion to their bloody religion, which show that they are not idle", he wrote in 1712; and again the next year, "As to publick affairs, everything seems to have a melancholy aspect . . . only those vermin French priests swarm in many places as a presage of some catastrophe at hand." [1]

In 1718 Newman revealed to Archbishop Wake "a piece of secret history" of this time: "A number of gentlemen, both of clergy and laity, of honour as well as fortune in Great Britain and Ireland, did dare in the last three years of Queen Anne's reign to watch the advances of Popery and to meet weekly to communicate to one another such intelligence as came to their knowledge and to consider of the best means to countermine the devices of the enemies of the Protestant Succession." [2] Newman was their Secretary, and they "used to meet at Whitehall", probably in his rooms.[3] Their minutes from November 1712 to July 1715, written in Newman's hand, are in the possession of the S.P.C.K., and largely record reports by members of Mass Houses opened in different parts of the country or of such Popish activity as that Lord Petre "keeps 200 horses in his stable", whereupon they resolved to make "further enquiries about Lord Petre's equipage". They also "dispersed books" and collected material "for a Bill to prevent the growth of Popery" and were "resolved to be martyrs in the cause, if it pleased God to call them to it", though Newman sought to make this less likely by indicating the members' names in his minutes only by letters. He never revealed the names of these gentlemen, but very likely they included Bray and other members of the S.P.C.K.

Newman's business was to gather news about Papist activity all over the country. Thus, he asked a correspondent at Dover for "advice as occasion offers concerning such Popish priests or emissaries as come into England through your town", including "the names as well as the numbers of such persons as they arrive from France or elsewhere. Be pleased also to signify whether any register has been kept of such persons by any person and by whom it is kept, or if not, what numbers have lately come to England under your observation." [4] His inquiries ranged far—to Car-

[1] HN to Mr Hales, The Hague, 25 Nov. 1712, *Society's Letters*; to President Leverett, Harvard, 22 Jan. 1713, *Harvard College Papers*, I, f. 98.
[2] HN to Abp Wake, 11 June 1718, *Wake MSS.*, Arch. W. Epist. 15.
[3] HN to Chas. Talbot, Lincoln's Inn, 31 Dec. 1718, *Private Letters*.
[4] HN to Mr Henry Austen, Dover, 12 May 1713, *Society's Letters*.

marthenshire, "I shall be glad to know the names of the Popish priests that are so busy in your parts and any particular practices used by them to pervert people, and the names and places of abode of those people, because the Papists here would have it believed that there is no such thing as practices to pervert people in the country"; to Principal Carstaires of Edinburgh University, "Whether Popish priests are lately increased among you? 'Tis said the convents abroad belonging to the three Kingdoms are almost entirely deserted by the best Britons"; and even to Colonel Kane of the British troops in Minorca, "Pray what number of Popish inhabitants remain with you and have they any priest allowed to them?"[1] He also distributed "small books proper to be put into the hands of such as are in danger of being infected by the corruptions of the Church of Rome and its emissaries", as a gift from this "society of private gentlemen to whom I happen to be related". Among those to whom he sent them was the Governor of Fort William, since he was sure the Papists were "very intent to propagate superstition and ignorance in the Highlands as the best means to preserve an interest for their purpose among the inhabitants".[2]

Some correspondents were able to tell him of Popish subterfuges or intimidation. In Lincolnshire "a Popish priest in the parts of Lindsey was taken some months ago baptizing a child (and I think the child of a Protestant). The Minister of the parish had notice of what was doing, took a constable and some neighbours and seized him in the very midst of the solemnity and carried him before a Justice of the Peace, but by some shuffling betwixt the Justice and a Roman Catholick gentleman, who appeared for the prisoner, the further examination (for it was then late at night) was put off till next morning, and the priest was spirited away and so escaped punishment."[3] Or again, Anne Millington, a London girl of 15, whose Protestant father had died, was kept by her mother, "a Papist by education", because the girl had a legacy of £15 a year. "A Popish priest has been often to visit the daughter to instruct her, but the girl will not hearken to him. Her mother has frequently compelled her to go to Mass with her, but the girl takes all occasions to give her the slip and go to the Church of England, for which she is beaten when she comes home under the pretence that she goes thither, not for the sake of religion, but to

[1] HN to Mr Vaughan, Carmarthen, 10 Oct. 1713; to Principal Carstaires, Edinburgh, 11 April 1713; to Col. Kane, Port Mahon, 27 June 1713, *Society's Letters*.
[2] HN to Sir Wm Gordon, Fort William, 29 June 1713, *Society's Letters*.
[3] John Disney, Lincoln, to HN, 18 Feb. 1713, *Stowe MSS.*, 748, f. 99.

fall into ill company. By this means the girl leads a dog's life and would go into any service to be out of reach of her mother." Newman wondered whether the Lord Keeper could set her at liberty and "require an account of her fortune to be lodged in Chancery or with Protestant guardians".[1]

Newman feared the Popish danger all his life. He warned a Swiss correspondent of "the tyranny of Rome, whose machinations will never be at rest to embroil all Protestant countries and this Kingdom in particular, till the Prophecies of St John's Revelation, Chap. XVIII, are fulfilled".[2] In the 1730s, as war with Spain approached, his apprehensions increased. "It is scarce credible the insolence of the Papists among us of late", he told the Archbishop of Dublin in 1735, "so that I am informed several private Mass Houses have dared once more to open themselves in this City that has suffered so much by them. God forbid that there should be less zeal in the Protestants of Great Britain and Ireland to defend their knowledge and profession of the true religion than there is in the Romanists to introduce Egyptian darkness." [3] He regretted, therefore, that this company of gentlemen "met regularly till the happy accession of King George to the throne, from which time their fears being at an end, they ceased their solicitations, with that indolence which is usual among Protestants when a present danger that threatens them is over".[4]

It was well for Newman, however, that their solicitations and his letter-writing for them did come to an end, for his work as Secretary of the S.P.C.K. was increasing. In November 1713 a committee of inquiry, appointed by the Society to examine its books and papers and report on its administration, found that in the five years and four months Newman had been Secretary he had written 6340 letters, made abstracts of all letters received, made fair copies of the minutes and important documents, indexed letter and minute books, kept the accounts, supervised Dr Bray's Parochial Libraries, and compiled records of charity schools throughout the Kingdom.[5] As a result of this report his salary was raised. Wanley had received £40 a year when Secretary and been given a gratuity of 20 guineas on resigning.[6] When Newman was

[1] HN to Mr Miller, 21 Jan. 1713, *Society's Letters*.
[2] HN to Rev. Mons. Pelier, Lausanne, 14 Nov. 1723, *Miscellaneous Letters*.
[3] HN to Ld Primate of Ireland, Dublin, 2 Jan. 1735, *Private Letters*.
[4] HN to Abp Wake, 11 June 1718, *Wake MSS.*, Arch. W. Epist. 15.
[5] *S.P.C.K. Minutes*, 12 Nov. 1713.
[6] Ibid., 3 June 1708.

appointed the Society decided his salary was "not to exceed sixty pounds per annum", and added "they may have it in their power further to reward his diligence and industry".[1] He was now given a gratuity of £50 and a salary of £80 a year, which was further raised in 1717 to £100 in consideration of his work "in transacting the affairs relating to the Protestant Mission in the East Indies".[2]

The next year, when he moved to the Middle Temple, though the Society paid £40 a year for the rent of his chambers and £10 in "parish dues", besides being responsible for repairs, it only took £10 a year from his salary. He considered this so generous that he not only engaged a clerk to help him at his own expense, but also paid for any occasional extra help. In 1718, however, the writing of a long postscript to the annual printed Circular Letter sent to members compelled him to "pay 2*d.* a dozen and sometimes more" for such help. That year the total cost "for extraordinary assistance in writing in the services of the Society" was £5 0*s.* 6*d.*; and as he paid his clerk "8*s.* a week (besides what he has for victuals, for which I reckon nothing)", he felt he could no longer "bear the expence of it". As the Society's correspondence was still increasing, it met his bill and agreed to pay 4*s.* a week towards his clerk, divided as to "one half between the Society and the Malabar Mission", which caused most of the extra work.[3] Early in 1721 his salary was raised by another £10 on account of "the great increase of business incumbent on the Secretary by reason of the Society having engaged to promote the design of printing the New Testament and Psalter in Arabick"; and when he had pleurisy the next year the Society voted him a gratuity of 10 guineas towards convalescing at Hampstead, besides another gratuity at the end of the year "for his extraordinary trouble in the affair of the Mission".[4]

This was more than Newman expected, and for the next five years, so that he "might not be thought to prey upon their goodness", he again paid his clerk's salary, but in 1727 he found he could no longer do this. He had to find £10 a year for rent, £20 16*s.* with board for his clerk, and £20 12*s.* with board for his housekeeper, which meant that one half of his salary went in rent and wages. He asked that he might again "charge the Society with 4*s.* for the assistance of my clerk"; but the Society did more

[1] *S.P.C.K. Minutes*, 17 June 1708.
[2] Ibid., 3 Dec. 1713 and 16 May 1717.
[3] HN to Rev. Mr Mayo, 18 Dec. 1718, *Private Letters*.
[4] *S.P.C.K. Minutes*, 19 Jan. 1721 and 11 Dec. 1722.

than that. It increased his salary to "£100 per annum clear of all deductions" and allowed him "£5 per annum for incidental expenses of fire, candles, etc.", "£24 per annum for the maintenance of a clerk", besides "£50 as a gratuity for his past services, £30 on account of the Arabick impression and £20 on account of the Malabar Mission", even though Newman had asked that there might be no "motion for a gratuity, while the allowance of the Society is so generous as it is".[1] Finally, in 1735 his salary was raised to "£140 per annum . . . for himself and clerk", and he was given "£50 as a gratuity for his extraordinary trouble and charge . . . in relation to the distressed Protestant emigrants from Saltzburgh".[2]

In explaining his financial position to the Society in 1727, Newman said: "It gives me not a little uneasiness that I can't serve them upon the same terms as their Treasurers do." The Treasurers of the Society at that time, following the death of Henry Shute in 1722, were Richard Mayo, Chaplain of St Thomas's Hospital, and John Deane, Archdeacon of Rochester. These two clergymen acted in an honorary capacity, but it would have been quite impossible for the Secretary to have done so. Only a full-time official could have performed his duties. The Treasurers had only to receive subscriptions for the several funds of the Society and make authorized payments; they did not even attend all the meetings of the Society. Newman's correspondence alone could hardly have been done on a part-time basis. This, "my indispensable duties at my scrutoire", as he once termed it, was always one of his main duties, and it increased as his own and the Society's activities widened. " 'Tis past eleven o'clock", he observed in a letter, and he must have often had to sit up writing late at night.[3] More important letters he wrote directly himself, but his usual practice was to write rough drafts, which were copied out by his clerk for his signature. Fifty-two volumes of these drafts are still in the archives of the S.P.C.K. Together with letters in England and America, they provide nearly all the information about Newman.

The chief occupation of Newman's clerk was to produce these fair copies of his letters, but he had other duties. He lodged with his employer and acted as valet or personal servant to him. Some

[1] HN to Rev. Mr Mayo, 30 Jan. 1727, *Private Letters*; *S.P.C.K. Minutes*, 11 June 1728.

[2] Ibid., 16 Dec. 1735.

[3] HN to Sir Thos. Lowther, Paris, 18 Feb. 1720, *Society's Letters*; to Marquis Du Quesne, 19 Nov. 1723, *Letters to Jamaica*.

of Newman's successive clerks are known only by their handwriting, but others were good or bad enough to be mentioned in his correspondence. An early one was "honest Mr Banks", who came to him at Whitehall in 1711. He was the "son of an eminent merchant at Hamburg, who fell into decay"; but his health was bad. In 1711 Newman sought medical advice for him because he was "afflicted with a great weakness in his eyes", and two years later he asked Robert Nelson's help to get him a new job since "a kind of cramp in his right hand has disabled him from writing so well as is necessary in my business". He told Nelson: "He is capable of being a butler or gentleman to dress a person of quality. . . . He is married, but that has not given him any hindrance since he lived with me. . . . He will be content to conform himself to the orders of the family where he shall happen to live notwithstanding this circumstance." Eighteen months later Banks was still without fresh employment, for Newman wrote to Chamberlayne in the hope that he might use his official connections to the man's advantage. He told Chamberlayne that he was "naturally a tight clean fellow" and spoke "High Dutch" (German), which might recommend him to the King or some of his Court "in such a station as Page of the Back Stairs, Door Keeper, Waiter or Groom of Chambers". By 1719, however, Banks was dead, leaving a widow "in a very destitute condition with two little children", and Newman asked a member of the Society, "If you please to recommend her to Mr Auditor Harley for chamber keeper at his office in Lincoln's Inn, which I understand is vacant, it will go a good way towards her support and will be a great act of charity." [1]

Banks was succeeded by Thomas Adams, of whom Newman complained that if left alone "he either does nothing for want of sense to do it or does all wrong, as he has no long time since than this day. The poor man has worked hard to write me two sheets of paper very fair considering the season, and yet 'tis but waste paper to me, because he has transferred a whole paragraph in both sheets so as to make them complete nonsense." Newman kept him, however, for nearly seven years, because "he behaved himself with great sobriety and integrity", until he also broke down in health with "a swelling in his neck", for which he "attended a consultation of physicians and surgeons at St Thomas' Hospital", where these "gentlemen were of opinion that the fittest means to remove

[1] HN to Dr Stare, 9 June 1711; to Mr Nelson, 4 April 1713; to Mr Chamberlayne, 2 Oct. 1714, *Society's Letters*; to Mr Hoare, 31 July 1719, *Private Letters*.

it were internal medicines and that the country air would help the operation of them". The Society gave him two guineas from its Charity Box "in consequence of his faithful service and diligence in the service of the Society" and agreed to recommend him for the mastership of the charity school at Tiverton in Devon.[1]

After Adams, Newman seems to have had several clerks in quick succession. John Meyrick was an early one. "He was", Newman said, "the quickest and correctest as well as the fairest writer that I ever knew. I had not parted with him if I could have afforded the wages he desired; from me he went to Mr Chamberlayne, and since his death he has kept a school at Farnborough in Kent, the laboriousness and uncertain profits of which has induced him to endeavour to return to his old practice of clerkship." That was in 1727, when Newman was writing to help him find a job.[2] Then there was Robert Lynn, who remained with Newman several years until dismissed in 1730 because "he has disappointed me in business often by his intemperance". After dismissal, he forged Newman's name to a letter of recommendation and obtained money from some half a dozen members of the Society.[3] There was also Mr Delagarde, presumably a "poor proselyte", who was dismissed in 1734, Newman finding "he was of little more service than as a spectator in the office . . . fickleness and constant application to dramatick amusements disposed him to neglect my business". But he was followed by Mr Norman, the best of Newman's clerks, who remained with him until he died within a year of Newman's own death.[4]

The letter-writing, which occupied so much of the time of Newman and his clerks, shows the width of the Society's interests and business. These often made necessary letters to Ministers of State, particularly Sir Robert Walpole (though he rarely replied), and dignitaries of the Church, of whom Edmund Gibson, Bishop of London, and William Wake, Archbishop of Canterbury, appear most often, both being revealed as sympathetic towards the Society whenever asked for their advice or opinion, while Thomas Wilson, Bishop of Sodor and Man, actively assisted it in its publishing and missionary ventures.

[1] HN to Mr Chamberlayne, 11 Jan. 1716; to Mr Hoare, 27 Dec. 1721, *Society's Letters*; *S.P.C.K. Minutes*, 21 April 1720.

[2] HN to Vigerus Edwards, 21 Sept. 1727, *Society's Letters*.

[3] HN to Sir Wm. Perkins, Chertsey, 18 Aug. 1730; to Rev. Dr Heylin, 28 Nov. 1730, *Society's Letters*.

[4] HN to Archdeacon Deane, Rochester, 20 July 1734, *Society's Letters*.

The interest in the Protestant Churches of the Continent taken by Dr Bray and in his friends—and, indeed, by many in the Church of England at this time—was reflected in the correspondence the Society had opened up with foreigners distinguished for their active piety. These included Ostervald of Neuchâtel, Jablonski of Berlin, and, above all, Francke of Halle.[1] Augustus Hermann Francke was Professor of Oriental Languages and later of Divinity at the University of Halle, the centre of the Pietist movement in the Lutheran Church. In 1698 he founded the Hallischen Waisenhause, an orphanage for deserted children who were maintained, educated, and set to work. Its fame spread beyond Germany and influenced the English charity school movement, for Robert Nelson had his interest in this orphanage at Halle aroused by a Non-juror friend, Francis Lee, and it was doubtless through him that two Germans attended a very early meeting of the S.P.C.K. and—through John Chamberlayne as interpreter—told the members about Francke's work.[2] Francke was soon made a Corresponding Member, and Newman's correspondence with him was increased by the East India Mission, which owed its inspiration and many of its missionaries to him, and when he died in 1727 and was succeeded by his son, G. A. Francke, the settling of the Salzburg refugees in Georgia brought Newman into correspondence with him also.

Most of Newman's correspondence, however, was with clerical and lay members of the Society. These were of two sorts: Residing Members (later called Subscribing Members), who subscribed between two and ten guineas a year, and Corresponding Members, living not only in all parts of the British Isles but on the Continent and in America and India as well, who gave what they chose to the Society. "A Subscribing Member is one that subscribes to pay quarterly or annually a certain sum towards promoting the designs of the Society", Newman once explained. "A Corresponding Member is excused making such subscriptions because he, living for the most part in the country, is supposed to be at an expense in promoting the designs of the Society by encouraging Charity Schools and distributing good books among the poor, in which he bears one part of the expense and the Society the other, but in many instances our Corresponding Members have become Subscribing Members voluntarily out of zeal to advance their

[1] J. S. M. Anderson, *History of the Colonial Church*, 3 vols., 1856, II, 409.
[2] H. P. Thompson, *Thomas Bray*, 42.

designs."[1] While Newman was Secretary the Subscribing Members remained about a hundred in number, but the Corresponding Members increased until in 1733 there were, Newman said, "between four and five hundred members at home and abroad with whom I am obliged to keep up a correspondence".[2]

The Corresponding Members, clerical or lay, were intended to be, through Newman, the link between the Society and its activities. Such a member had to be invited to join by the Society, which generally desired to have only one in each town or neighbourhood, and he was encouraged to form a local Society to promote the Society's aims in his district. In a letter to an unknown newly-appointed member at Bristol in 1712, Newman told him this was the way the Society thought he might best further "the discouragement of vice and advancement of piety". He should "prevail with such of the clergy and laity of your neighbourhood as you find best disposed and able to join you in this charitable work", being assured that "when you have set up such a society, though at first it consists of not more than three or four such persons . . . you will find your work much easier than you imagined". On its side, "the Society will present you with a small packet of such books and papers [as] they at present disperse for the promoting Christian knowledge and practice", with the promise that "if you should be mindful at any time to give some of them amongst your poor neighbours, the Society will assist you in obtaining such as you desire at the lowest rates".[3] Another correspondent was congratulated on behalf of the Society by Newman on forming such a religious society among his neighbours, who were "associating as brethren to solace one another in the pleasures of religious conversation", and told "it would be a great pleasure to them to see more such fraternities formed in other parts of the Kingdom".[4]

Despite, however, the Society's extensive activities and large correspondence, it had a London dominance. The distinction between the two sorts of members assisted this, for only Subscribing Members could vote at the Society's meetings, though any Corresponding Member in Town might attend. In practice only a few active Subscribing Members living in London attended with any regularity the general and committee meetings at which all decisions concerning the Society were made. When Newman be-

[1] HN to Rev. Mr Bowyer, Martock, Som, 15 April 1735, *Society's Letters*.
[2] HN to Rev. Mr Sam. Mather, Boston, 15 Sept. 1733, *New Eng. Letters*.
[3] HN to ?, Bristol, 5 Feb. 1712, *Bristol Public Archives Repository*.
[4] HN to Rev. Mr Hughes, Clyst Hidon, Devon, 11 Feb. 1718, *Society's Letters*.

came Secretary the average attendance was from six to eight, but later rose to between twelve and fifteen. Newman himself attended every meeting, taking notes for the minutes and sometimes drawing rough sketches of the members on pieces of blotting-paper which still remain between the pages of his notebooks. At first the most regular members were Dr Bray, John Chamberlayne, Robert Nelson, and Henry Shute. After their deaths the only ones to rival them were Sir John Philipps and Lord Perceval; but in the 1730s, when the Society was concerned with the new colony of Georgia, General Oglethorpe, John Wesley, and George Whitefield attended quite frequently. Before Newman's death, a new generation was represented by Sir Erasmus Philipps, the late Sir John's son. The strong lay element in the Society's councils was a reflection of the "steady laicisation of religion" of the times, when the laity, individually and collectively, took an increasingly active part in religious organization and philanthropic work.[1] It was probably another reason for the Society's London dominance, making it uncertain how much it might rely on clerical support or work through the ordinary diocesan and parochial system. As it recorded in 1710, "The Society have always been very tender of doing anything that might look like dictating to the revd clergy and especially to those that are dignified with an episcopal character." [2] Later, as the Society acquired a more important position in the Church, it did something to remedy this defect. Chamberlayne, Wanley, and Newman—the first three Secretaries of the Society—were laymen, but their successors have all been clergymen.

It is difficult to determine what part Newman took in the Society's decisions. He avoided prominence for himself. Within a month of his appointment as Secretary, he asked his correspondents "hereafter to omit the style of Secretary to the Society in your superscriptions to me, because the less they are known (except to their Correspondents, and those they are well-assured wish well to their designs) the more 'tis in their power to do good in an envious age".[3] Similarly, when Samuel Mather of Boston wished in 1736 to dedicate a book to him, he replied: "As to the compliment you propose to make me in some work you are about to publish, I must intreat you to consider my unworthiness and

[1] G. M. Trevelyan, *English Social History,* 1944, 362.
[2] *S.P.C.K. Minutes,* 20 Nov. 1710.
[3] HN to Rev. Mr Pye, Mon., 10 Aug. 1708, *Letters to Correspondents.*

obscurity, and that the last is my consolation next to God's mercy in Christ under all my defects, which you will so far deprive me of as you publish anything inconsistent with my meanness and obscurity, an error I have too much reason to fear from my friend and therefore beg you will turn the edge of your compliments to some persons more worthy of them."[1] Again, though it is clear that Newman joined in the discussion at the Society's meetings, he never referred in the minutes to any view expressed by himself.

His relations with members of the Society seem to have been pleasant; but he twice fell foul of the energetic John Chamberlayne, who had been a thorn in the flesh of his predecessor. The first time was when Chamberlayne asked to be lent the Society's minute book and was annoyed when Newman was "so squeamish all of a sudden as to refuse sending it out without the consent of the Society". He thought it was "perhaps without precedent in any company in England, where a man in any of them might sit down and transcribe all their minutes at any time if he pleased to take that trouble, but this is not the first instance you have given one of an unconquerable *opiniabreté* which some time or other will do you much harm". Consequently, he told him, "I desire you to look upon me no longer as a member of that body, and then you will be justified without consulting anyone to refuse me what I shall be an entire stranger to."[2] But he did not resign and some years later had a difference of opinion with Newman at a committee meeting, for which Newman apologized the next day: "The presumption of yesterday was meant with all the respect and love as Lord William Powlett's servant lately shewed to his master when he presumed to take him by the beard when he fell from his horse."[3]

That the Society was satisfied with Newman's services was shown by their treatment of his salary and his long continuance in office. After his appointment as Secretary, his earlier travel and various employments were exchanged for a life in London centred in the Society's work. When he became Secretary, he had lodgings in Whitehall—"my chamber up the Chapel Stairs in Whitehall", he described it, while a correspondent addressed him as, "Mr Newman at his lodgings over Whitehall Gate".[4] The Chapel Royal,

[1] HN to Rev. Mr Sam. Mather, Boston, 3 April 1736, *New Eng. Letters*.

[2] Mr Chamberlayne to HN, 7 Nov. 1712, *Rawlinson MSS.*, C.933, f. 77.

[3] *S.P.C.K. Minutes*, 21 Aug. 1722; HN to Mr Chamberlayne, 22 Aug. 1722, *Society's Letters*.

[4] HN to the Trustees of the Blackguard School, 4 June 1713, *Society's Letters*; Mr Richard Goodwin to HN, 2 May 1711, *Rawlinson MSS.*, D.834, f. 6.

BARTLETT'S BUILDINGS, HOLBORN
From a water-colour by T. Hosmer Shepherd, 1838

Whitehall, had disappeared with most of the Palace in the fire of 1698. The chapel stairs were in the east of the Palace, between the river and the Banqueting Hall, the only fragment built of Inigo Jones' contemplated Palace and the only part surviving to-day. The view enjoyed by Newman from these lodgings was described by Celia Fiennes about 1703 as "all along the prospect of the Thames on one side and a large park on the other, walled in, which is full of very fine walks and rows of trees, ponds and curious birds, deer and some fine cows".[1] This was St James's Park, the "public walk" of the century for those who wished to be seen and those who wished to see, for fine folk, ministers, courtiers, and ladies as well as those who went to jostle and stare; and when the Assembly of Massachusetts was more than usually troublesome, Newman could only hope, "God Almighty give the sages of New England wisdom to prevent the impending storm, and if those persons who have raised it, could be selected and sent over thither to walk in St James' Park for one month in Parliament time or any other time, I am persuaded they would recover their senses and be ever after able to serve their country." [2] No less impressive was the Thames on the other side of Whitehall. Though coaches and carts in the London streets were increasing, the river was still the most crowded highway, and "above Bridge" was a constant traffic of barges and lighters as well as the wherries and tilt-boats of the watermen, whom Newman heard forecasting in 1713 that Sacheverell would be Bishop of Rochester.[3]

When the Society considered the appointment of Wanley's successor as Secretary, it stated, "We judge it convenient that he do live near the Treasurer", Henry Shute, who was Lecturer of Whitechapel and had a house in Bartlett's Buildings, Holborn.[4] Newman continued to live in Whitehall, but this was not convenient for the Society's meetings, every Thursday afternoon, at four o'clock in winter and five in summer, in Shute's house. Committee meetings were either in the chambers in Lincoln's Inn of William Melmoth, the pious lawyer and Treasurer of the S.P.G., or in the Nandos Coffee House in Fleet Street, near the Inner Temple and much patronized by lawyers. Newman must often, therefore, have had to travel up to the City and back, particularly as he asked his correspondents to direct their letters to

[1] *The Journeys of Celia Fiennes*, ed. C. Morris, 1947, 292.
[2] HN to Benjamin Colman, 10 Sept. 1723, *Mass. Hist. Soc.*, *Colman Papers*.
[3] HN to the Trustees of the Blackguard School, 4 June 1713, *Society's Letters*.
[4] *S.P.C.K. Minutes*, 17 June 1708.

"the Revd Mr Shute's in Bartlett's Buildings near Holborn", this being "for the convenience of keeping those on a public account from those on a private".[1]

He was, however, able to store the Society's books near him by renting from the Lord Almoner "the second floor and part of the garrett in his apartments at Whitehall". This was originally for the books for the parochial libraries of Dr Bray's Associates, and in 1709 he had 5521 such books in quires besides those of the S.P.C.K.[2] Early in 1714 George Smalridge, Dean of Christ Church, Oxford, became Bishop of Bristol and Lord Almoner. Newman tried to continue the arrangement, writing to Smalridge even before he became Lord Almoner: "If the Dean of Christ Church succeeds in that trust, as I hope he will, and has not occasion for these rooms otherwise, I only beg he would allow me to be the first of all the beggars to put in for them, and then I question not but he will admit my pretensions to be at least equal to those that have interest enough to be in other places." But Smalridge required the rooms, and a month later Newman wrote: "Mr Sharpe has removed most of the goods this day from the Lord Almoner's Lodgings in order to give your Lordship possession of them." [3]

The Society suffered similarly a few weeks later when the Bishop of London—John Robinson, newly translated from Bristol—"granted Mr Treasurer Shute leave to live in London House, Aldersgate Street", this being the Bishop's town residence bought after the Restoration to replace the old London House in St Paul's Churchyard. Shute announced, "He shall quit the house in Bartlett's Buildings and desires to know whether the Society will meet in Aldersgate Street or will accommodate themselves elsewhere".[4] Fortunately, a member, Mr Mellows, offered "chambers he has in the Middle Temple to be vested in the Society". After inspecting them, the Society accepted and offered Newman "these lodgings whilst he was in the service of the Society", to which he replied that "he had compared the advantages and disadvantages of his lodgings at Whitehall with the Society's chambers, and that though there were several reasons which induced him to prefer his present situation, yet if the Society were pleased to consider it

[1] *Circular Letter to Correspondents*, July 1708; HN to Rev. Mr Edwards, Embleton, Northumb, 6 March 1712, *Society's Letters.*

[2] *An Account of Books Received, Rawlinson MSS.*, D.834, f. 56.

[3] HN to Dr Smalridge, Oxford, 2 March 1714; to Bp of Bristol, 5 April 1714, *Society's Letters.*

[4] *S.P.C.K. Minutes*, 29 April 1714.

would be for their interest that he should remove to the Temple, he should always submit his judgement to theirs whilst he has the honour of serving them". Whereupon, "the chambers were ordered to be repaired and the Secretary to move into them with the Society's books and papers, the Society to pay the duties and repairs, and £10 per annum to be deducted from the Secretary's salary on that account".[1]

So Newman moved eastwards towards the City in the summer of 1714. He described his chambers variously as "in Garden Court No. 1, four pairs of stairs high on the north-east part of the staircase", or "No. 4 the head of the stairs going up by the First Fruits Office near the Water Gate in the Middle Temple", or "in Barebone's Buildings, the lower end of Middle Temple Lane, near the Water Gate".[2] From this it is clear they were in the substantial and ornamental brick building with four chambers to a floor completed on the order of the Middle Temple by Dr Barebone, son of Praise-God Barebone of the Commonwealth and, according to Roger North, the originator after the Great Fire of large-scale speculative building in London.[3] Whatever their disadvantages compared with Newman's lodgings in Whitehall, they were nearer the Society's meeting-places, and the courts and lanes of the Temple were an oasis from the turmoil of the thoroughfares of traffic between Charing Cross and St Paul's and as pleasant and uniquely English as a cathedral close or an Oxford or Cambridge college. Newman once spoke, in typical eighteenth-century appreciation, of the similar "polite wilderness and gardens" of the Charterhouse, and in old age recalled his Middle Temple chambers: "I lived in them fourteen years with great pleasure whilst my legs were younger to go up them".[4] Among his neighbours in the Middle Temple was a fellow New Englander, Jeremiah Dummer, colonial agent for Massachusetts when Newman was agent for New Hampshire.

As before he was near the river, and here also of the two references in his letters to his life in the Middle Temple, one concerns the watermen. The volleys of abuse between boatmen and

[1] *S.P.C.K. Minutes*, 27 May, 3 and 10 June 1714.

[2] HN to Mr Brunker, Under-Treasurer of Middle Temple, 21 Oct. 1732, *Society's Letters*; to Mr Sam. Mather, Boston, 21 May 1718, *Private Letters*; to Rev. Mr Hildrop, Marlborough, Wilts, 27 March 1772, *Society's Letters*.

[3] *Autobiography of Roger North* (ed. A. Jessopp), 1887, 53–7; M. D. George, *London Life in the Eighteenth Century*, 78; J. B. Williamson, *History of the Temple*, 1924, 641.

[4] HN to Rev. Dr King, Master of Charterhouse, 19 May 1721, *Society's Letters*; to Rev. Mr Gibb, Bristol, 26 Dec. 1741, *Miscellaneous Letters*.

bargees were a traditional accompaniment to traffic on the Thames, and he told of "a gentleman in the Temple who lived near the crowd of watermen that ply there, who used often to get into a storm of cursing and swearing with one another, at which time he used to throw out of his window two or three books against swearing enclosed in a paper with these words: 'Give this to the man that swears.' Though it did not cure them of swearing, it laid the storm for that time and set them scrambling for the books—which it is hoped some read to good effect." [1] The other reference illustrates again Newman's love of royalty and pageantry. He described how on Candlemas Day 1736, "the ancient custom of revels was so far revived that the Inner Temple presented my Lord Chancellor and the judges of their houses with a feast and a ball in their hall at the same time to compliment Sir R. Walpole who, it seems, is a member of that house, and several of the judges belonging to the Society. At this entertainment they had the King's musick, and the Prince and Princess did them the honour to pass an hour with them." [2]

The Society intended the Secretary only to live in the Middle Temple chambers. Shute allowed it a store-room for books and papers in London House, and for some years Newman headed his letters there. The Society met "upon courtesy in the same chambers in Lincoln's Inn where the Commissioners for the Fifty Churches met", where Thoresby at the end of a meeting "looked at the curious and noble models of many churches proposed to be built"—fifty-two within the Bills of Mortality according to the Act of Queen Anne, but only sixteen were completed before the scheme stopped under the Hanoverians.[3] This arrangement lasted until 1716, when the Commissioners moved to Westminster, and Newman was ordered to seek a large ground chamber somewhere near the Temple. He thought he had found it in the chambers "at the lower end of Essex Street, now occupied by the Hon. Peregrine Bertie", whom he asked for "the use of his great room (without trespassing on his bedchamber)", adding by way of reference that "the Archbishop of Canterbury, the Bishop of London, and other worthy Prelates and Members of Parliament are members of the Society".[4] The Hon. Peregrine was not per-

[1] HN to Rev. Mr Sam. Disney, Wakefield, 17 Feb. 1741, *Miscellaneous Letters*.
[2] HN to Ld Perceval, 3 Feb. 1726, *Egmont MSS.*, H.M.C., 7th Report, 248.
[3] Ralph Thoresby, *Diary*, II, 244.
[4] *S.P.C.K. Minutes*, 10 May 1716; HN to Mr Whitingham, 14 July 1716, *Society's Letters*.

suaded by such good company, so Newman applied to Sir Isaac Newton to be allowed "to meet at the house of the Royal Society in Crane Street for two or three hours one day in the week". Newton referred this to the Council of the Royal Society, which desired "some two gentlemen of this Society might attend to inform them of the nature of this Society"; a week later one of the two reported that "though they had not rejected the Society's request, yet upon what he could discern of the inclination of the members of the Royal Society, he could not think it advisable to persist in desiring of it, for fear of a negative".[1]

Finally, the Society obtained the use of St Paul's Chapter House, but this was "found inconvenient for the Society". Many members lived in the new London growing up on both sides of the Tyburn Road with the building of Cavendish Square, Hanover Square, Grosvenor Square, New Bond Street, and other fashionable streets and squares of the west; they did not want to travel often across to the narrow, dark, damp lanes of the City. It was decided, therefore, while continuing the Society's meetings at the Chapter House, to have committee meetings in St Dunstan's Coffee House by the Church of St Dunstan-in-the-West just beyond Temple Bar. The membership of both meetings was much the same, and at first both met weekly, but in 1722 "the weekly meetings of the Society were changed into monthly ones, the first Thursday of every month, at St Paul's Chapter House, and the . . . intermediate committees every Tuesday at St Dunstan's Coffee House", thus further reducing the members' journeys into the City. The Society's books and papers remained at London House until April 1719, when "the inhabitants of London House being warned to leave it", the Society "ordered that the chambers in the Middle Temple be fitted up to receive the Society's books and papers". Though this had advantages for Newman, it must have made his chambers less comfortable, as the growing activities of the Society added to the books and papers stored there, and soon more space was needed, which was secured by fitting up shelves in a hired room in St Dunstan's Coffee House.[2]

This dispersal of the Society's meeting and storage places added to Newman's labours, but not to the efficiency of the Society. He described to a member its disadvantages. The Society, he said, "have two rooms adjoining to St Dunstan's Coffee House, near the

[1] *S.P.C.K. Minutes*, 15 and 22 Nov. 1716; *Royal Society, Journal Book*, 15 Nov. 1716.
[2] W. O. B. Allen and E. McClure, op. cit., 130; *S.P.C.K. Minutes*, 23 April 1719.

centre of the residence of their members, one for a place to meet in weekly, and the other for a store-room, but both these are become so strait as to be scarce able to receive their company or their books. . . . The Dean and Chapter of St Paul's are so kind to permit us to have our general monthly meetings at St Paul's Chapter House, but that is only in a common room for two or three hours in a month where we have not a book or paper to consult but what is carried by a messenger to every meeting." [1] The situation became worse in 1727, when Henry Godolphin was succeeded as Dean by Francis Hare, who proceeded to foreshadow Lord Hervey's condemnation of him as "haughty, hot-headed, injudicious and unpopular" when Walpole wished him to succeed Archbishop Wake.[2] "The new Dean of St Paul's," Newman wrote, "having thought fit to decline favouring the Society with the liberty of meeting in the room at the Chapter House above stairs, as they used to do, they are permitted to meet in the Court Room below stairs, but as that is very inconvenient now and will be more so in the winter, so that the Society have been obliged to think of providing themselves with a better accommodation." The S.P.G. and the Society for the Sons of the Clergy, who had also used the same room in the Chapter House, were in the same position. The former society, Newman reported, "has taken a house in Warwick Court for their committees, their secretary and their library", and the latter "has taken a house in Salisbury Court for their register and his papers".[3]

As was obviously best, the S.P.C.K. followed their example and returned to Bartlett's Buildings to a house suitable for all its meetings and possessions. Late in 1727 Newman told the landlord of his Middle Temple chambers that the Society "have this day agreed to treat with Mr Melmoth about a house in Bartlett's Buildings, belonging to a relation of his, four doors from that where Mr Shute lived. . . . The rent is £44 per annum besides parish taxes. For my own part I am content with the apartments which by your goodwill I enjoy, being better accommodated in many respects for disposing of the Society's books and papers than I can expect to be in the house proposed, excepting that the Society will have a room for their meetings more convenient than they have at present." [4] Newman moved into his new dwelling the

[1] HN to Rev. Mr Robinson, Leeds, 4 Nov. 1725, *Society's Letters.*
[2] Lord Hervey, *Memoirs*, II, 101–10.
[3] HN to Mr Mellers, Wrexham, Denbigh, 7 Aug. 1727, *Society's Letters.*
[4] HN to Mr Mellers, 14 Nov. 1727, *Society's Letters.*

next spring with typical quietness, for when Dr Colman wrote from Boston to Thomas Hollis, a Harvard graduate living in London, enclosing a letter for him to give to Newman, he could only write back that he had "had my servant shove it under the door of his chamber in the Temple, where he will find it when he goes thither, for he don't lodge there, nor does he let any of his neighbours know where he does lodge".[1] Newman still kept some connection with the Middle Temple. Its Register records that he was admitted a member on 10 July 1728,[2] and the Society continued to possess the chambers, for which Newman, not without difficulty, found a tenant: "My chambers were vacant six months before I could get a tenant for them, and then I was glad to take up with £19 per annum, after laying out about £10 in repairs for painting, etc., to tempt a tenant up three pairs of stairs, which the young men don't love, though in reality they are in that respect better for a student by that height till he comes to practise the law."[3]

Bartlett's Buildings, described by Hatton in 1708 as "a pleasant square court, near against Hatton Street", were off Holborn Hill, almost due north of the Middle Temple by a steep climb up Fetter Lane and opposite the gardens of the Bishop of Ely's Palace, where the Society kept its library until the Bishop needed the room.[4] No further away from the West End, it enabled the Society at last to have Secretary, store-room, and meeting-place all under the same roof. From now all the Society's business was conducted here, except once, in 1735, when the committee "adjourned to Sir John Philipps' house, in regard his cold would not permit him to come abroad with safety".[5] This was more convenient for Newman, but his surroundings were not as pleasant as in his two former lodgings. The house had a garden with a summer-house, in which Newman wished to hang an engraving of Harvard College, but these older parts of eighteenth-century London were not agreeable, and in 1720 the nearby churchyard of St Andrew's, Holborn, was "so offensive" that it was shut up by order of the King and Council for a time.[6] The house needed immediate repairs, and Newman gave

[1] *S.P.C.K. Minutes*, 4 April 1728; Thos. Hollis to Benjamin Colman, *Hollis MSS. 1718–1774*, f. 67, *Harvard College Library*.

[2] *Register of the Middle Temple*, "July 10 1728. Henry Newman, of the City of London, gent."

[3] HN to Mrs Gibb, Bristol, 26 Dec. 1728, *Society's Letters*.

[4] E. Hatton, *A New View of London*, 2 vols., 1708, I, 4; *S.P.C.K. Minutes*, 23 Nov. 1731.

[5] Ibid., 15 March 1735.

[6] HN to Gov. Belcher, 19 Feb. 1731, *New Eng. Letters*; M. D. George, op. cit., 353.

"a *Whole Duty of Man* for a poor labourer that assisted".[1] When further repairs were needed in 1734, Newman wished to improve the building "by pulling down the back part and carrying the staircase into the garden, so as to have the first floor flush in one great room fit to receive the library on one side, rebuild the alcove in the garden with brick, which is now wood not worth painting over any more and bestow iron railings by the front door"; but the committee only authorized a minimum of repairs, "securing the tiling and chimneys of the house and alcove", with the result that more repairs were necessary about three years later, which delayed Newman's correspondence because "several workmen were repairing my house and my papers so blocked up that I could not come at them to put anything in its place".[2]

It was easier for Newman to identify himself closely with the Society because he was a bachelor and never seems to have contemplated marriage. His work, he assured a young lady correspondent, absorbed his whole life, compensating him for lack of both wife and wealth: "For my own part, as Providence has denied me the happiness of a wife, I endeavour to love my masters and my business as other men do their wives. The charity children throughout the Kingdom and my canary birds with my cat and her kitten at home supply the place of children as they engross so much of my time to take care of them, and while it pleases God to give me health and the use of my limbs, I walking afoot, envy no man that rides in his chariot and wants that privilege to compensate for the gout or some other infirmity which I thank God I am a stranger to." [3]

Nor, though a bachelor, was Newman lonely in London. He was, to quote the *Dictionary of American Biography*, "deeply sympathetic with that movement of reform which, slowly gathering momentum in the later seventeenth century, branched out into a wide variety of humanitarian endeavour during the years of his London life"; and he had as friends the most prominent men in these endeavours. Among the members of the S.P.C.K. were Sir Hans Sloane, the physician, John Perceval, first Earl of Egmont, Sir John Philipps, pioneer of Welsh education, and many other of the clergy and laity. Ralph Thoresby was a member, attending

[1] *S.P.C.K. Minutes*, 16 July 1728.

[2] HN to Archdeacon Deane, Rochester, 20 July 1734, *Society's Letters*; *S.P.C.K. Minutes*, 18 March 1735; HN to Rev. Mr Gigg, Bristol, 22 Oct. 1737, *Miscellaneous Letters*.

[3] HN to Elizabeth Sheldon, Stroud, Glos, 31 Aug. 1727, *Private Letters*.

the meetings when in London and often calling on "my old friend, Mr Newman, the Secretary".[1] An early friend was the Reverend A. W. Böhme, Lutheran Chaplain to Prince George of Denmark, who joined the Society in the year Newman became Secretary, and whose death in 1722 was a great grief: "In him I have lost one of my dearest and intimate companions, and every place where I used to enjoy him seems desolate as if one half of me was gone to the grave." [2] Fresh activities later brought him new friends, like General Oglethorpe, founder of Georgia, and Thomas Coram, originator of the Foundling Hospital. New England merchants in London relied upon him for help and advice, and his service with the Duke of Somerset made him known in political circles. He knew Joseph Addison, Under Secretary of State from 1706 to 1709, and even better, Richard Steele, whose struggle on behalf of the Whigs at the end of Anne's reign he admired: "I do not know that any man living hath a greater sense of the service you have done the nation." [3] He particularly enjoyed the company of young men, and when the sons of his correspondents came to work or study in London, he befriended and helped them. He told an Irish correspondent that nearly every day he dined or supped with his son, when they discussed religion or philosophy together, while the son of Governor Belcher of Massachusetts, who read law at the Temple, remained his friend for the rest of his life.[4]

His want of home life was hardly supplied by the amusements or entertainments of the time. It was not to be expected that he should go to the theatre, which still exhibited a licentiousness inherited from the Restoration dramatists.[5] Thinking of the brothels around the theatres in East London and other social evils which seemed inevitably connected with them, he held that "the degeneracy and licentiousness of this great city" was largely due to "our theatres, where everything that is sacred is made a jest of, and the youth will resort to them though they rob their parents or masters to support the expense of attending those assemblies".[6]

[1] Ralph Thoresby, *Diary*, 19 March 1723, II, 358.

[2] HN to Rev. Mr Cotton Mather, Boston, 31 Aug. 1722, *New Eng. Letters*.

[3] HN to Sir James Lowther, M.P., Whitehaven, 8 Oct. and 3 Nov. 1713, H.M.C., 13th Report, App. VII, 247; HN? to Richard Steele (Feb.? 1714), *Rawlinson MSS.* (in a volume of papers collected by Newman and letters addressed to him); HN to Sir Richard Steele, Carmarthen, 16 Aug. 1726, *Society's Letters*.

[4] HN to Mr Nicholson, Sligo, 23 Nov. 1717, *Society's Letters*.

[5] M. D. George, op. cit., 227–8.

[6] HN to Rev. Mr Marshall, Naunton, Glos, 10 March 1733, *Society's Letters*.

Social reformers regarded the London pleasure-gardens differently, since, in offering simple amusements and cool evenings out-of-doors, they raised public morals during the century. Newman does not seem to have gone to any, but he knew enough to answer a lady correspondent's questions about the Marylebone Gardens in 1740.[1] His attitude towards the popular lotteries was not so clear. He wrote the spendthrift Marquis Du Quesne a sermon on "lotteries and bubbles of all kinds", insisting that "the encouragement of them discourages industry and all lawful enterprises for acquiring wealth";[2] but he bought lottery tickets for himself and his friends, lay and clerical. The difficulty was that some members of the Society approved them—"Good Mr Gibson has dedicated a ticket in the present lottery to pious uses, $\frac{1}{5}$ to the Corporation Society,[3] another $\frac{1}{5}$ to that for Promoting Christian Knowledge, $\frac{1}{5}$ to the Malabar Mission, $\frac{1}{5}$ to Glancha Hospital,[4] and the remaining $\frac{1}{5}$ to the Vicar of Kirkdale in Yorkshire. The number is 54 in 361, for the success of which he desires the prayers of all good men"[5]—but others did not. "Your Lordship has been rightly informed", he assured the Bishop of Dromore in Ireland, "that there is no such thing as a project on foot for assisting the Saltzburghers or the Georgian undertaking by a lottery, and I believe the well-wishers to both those charities would decline accepting of such a medium as in the opinion of many sober men carries the appearance of a kind of gaming which the lower part of the world are already too fond of." Newman was ignorant that General Oglethorpe had already asked Lord Perceval to speak to Sir Robert Walpole about "lottery tickets for the advantage of the Carolina colony", and this was probably the only time that Walpole's inertia assisted rather than disturbed Newman's peace of mind.[6]

Rather than by organized pleasures, Newman's want of home life was supplied by the coffee-houses and taverns which filled a large share of Londoners' social activities. They abounded in the City, particularly along the Strand and Fleet Street, many set apart by custom for men of particular professions or interests. The

[1] HN to Mrs Forman, 6 June 1740, *Private Letters*. Printed in W. K. Lowther Clarke, *Eighteenth Century Piety*, 46.
[2] HN to Marquis Du Quesne, 14 Aug. and 19 Dec. 1723, *Letters to Jamaica*.
[3] I.e., the S.P.G.
[4] That of Professor Francke at Halle.
[5] HN to Rev. Mr Gibb, Bristol, 26 Feb. 1734, *Society's Letters*.
[6] HN to Bp of Dromore, 5 Nov. 1734, *Private Letters*; *Egmont Diary*, 19 March 1731, *Egmont MSS.*, Add. MSS. 47061, f. 7.

easy-going conviviality of the age was leading to the development of clubs in the coffee-houses, and Newman referred to two of these to which he belonged: "Sir Hans Sloane's Club", which met for an "evening conference at Mayor's Coffee House in King Street", and doubtless consisted largely of members of the Royal Society of which Sir Hans was Secretary; and "the Crown Tavern in my neighbourhood", which may have been the Crown and Anchor Tavern in the Strand, where in 1710 the Academy of Antient Music had been instituted by some gentlemen and masters for vocal and instrumental concerts and the establishment of a musical library. At any rate, in 1723 Newman went there to a concert of "about 40 performers in musick" by which the festival of the patron saint of music, "St Cecilia was commemorated with great magnificence".[1]

Moreover, though less general as the century went on, it was an old-established practice for coffee-houses and taverns to be used as places of call and business by lawyers, physicians, and merchants. The S.P.C.K. did this, both for business meetings and for the annual anniversary meeting, the most important event of its year, which was held from 1704 mainly for the benefit of the Subscribing Members in Town, of whom only a small proportion regularly attended the weekly meetings. It was usually towards the end of January, though in 1715, when it coincided with "the day for electing Members of Parliament for the County of Middlesex, so many gentlemen of the Society were obliged to give their attendance at the election as made it necessary for the chairman and stewards to order notice to be given for suspending the Anniversary Meeting of the Society".[2] It took place first at Sion College, then at "the Guest Rooms adjoining to St Dunstan's Church", until "several members having found great inconvenience by attending the Anniversary Meeting in so cold a room as St Dunstan's Guest House, the Society have agreed to have that Meeting at the Leg Tavern in Fleet Street". This tavern had to be abandoned in 1723, "it being now kept by a Papist", but the practice remained of holding it in one of the larger taverns which had great rooms used for formal dinners, concerts, or meetings—"the Sun Tavern in Fleet Street" in 1724; "the Rose Tavern in Cursitor's Alley" in

[1] HN to Marquis Du Quesne, 19 Nov. 1723, *Letters to Jamaica*; to Rev. Mr Wheeler, Warpenham, Northants, 21 Nov. 1723, *Society's Letters*; to Ld Perceval, 24 Nov. 1723, *Egmont MSS.*, Add. MSS. 47030, f. 77.

[2] *S.P.C.K. Minutes*, 27 Jan. 1715.

1727; "the Blue Post Tavern in Portugal Street" in 1740; and "the Crown in the Strand" in 1743.[1]

The usual attendance was about forty, "mostly clergymen, but never a bishop or dean", said Lord Perceval in 1737. The charge was 2*s*. 6*d*. each, and a collection, averaging £10, was made for some charitable object. The arrangements were made by six members of the Society as stewards, and a chairman was appointed to preside. The company met at one o'clock, "dinner being served up, after a blessing asked". The meal began with the reading of "Matthew XXV or part of it" (the Parables of the Virgins, the Talents, and the Sheep and the Goats) during the earlier years, but later this was changed to 1 Corinthians 13. It was usually read by "the Messenger belonging to the Society", but once the Society, judging "the Messenger's voice not proper for reading a chapter intelligibly to the Society while they are at dinner, ordered that one of the charity boys at St Dunstan's School be procured to read a chapter", for which he was given 5*s*. "At the end of the dinner, before thanks given (the servants, etc. being withdrawn), the Secretary read an abstract of their proceedings for the preceding year." Usually the dinner was "plain and wholesome", but in 1723 "the King's health was drunk in Tockay wine", imported "by a learned Transylvanian, Mr Baba" to be sold to buy a printing press for the Hungarian Protestants[2]; and the Society took the opportunity both to embellish its meal and to take its part promoting the common desire of the time that the Church of England should set itself at the head of the Protestant interest in Europe. Several members of the Society expressed their enjoyment of this annual dinner—to Robert Nelson it was a "sociable and friendly meeting", and to Ralph Thoresby it seemed "like the primitive Agapé or Love Feasts, before corrupted".[3] To Newman one of its attractions must have been that it was one of the few things he did not have to arrange himself.

Such was the background to his work as Secretary of the S.P.C.K. After his appointment, he not only never left England again, but seems not to have gone far out of London. His work

[1] W. O. B. Allen and E. McClure, op. cit., 126; HN to Rev. Mr Watts, 27 Dec. 1710; to Mr Dundas, 3 April 1711; to Capt. Morris, 22 Nov. 1712; to Ld Perceval, 1 Jan. 1721, *Society's Letters*; to Ld Perceval, 17 June 1723, *Egmont MSS.*, Add. MSS. 47029, f. 293; 7 Feb. 1724, 47030, f. 114.

[2] H.M.C., *Egmont Diary*, I, 224, and II, 364; *S.P.C.K. Minutes*, 12 and 14 Jan. 1719; Dr James de la Faye to HN, 5 Dec. (NS) 1722, *Egmont MSS.*, Add. MSS. 47035, f. 20.

[3] C. F. Secretan, *Life of Robert Nelson*, 106; Ralph Thoresby, *Diary*, 20 May 1714, II, 214.

kept him there, and holidays were almost unknown then, as also was travel. Despite the work of the Societies for the Reformation of Manners, even the streets of London could be unpleasant and dangerous, and not long after he became Secretary, he had to record that there was not a quorum for one of the Society's meetings because the members were at the funeral in St Clement Danes' of one of their number who was "murthered by three soldiers of the guard while he was assisting a constable that was assaulted for having carried a lewd woman to the watch house".[1] As for long-distance travel, Newman had perhaps heard how, when the future Emperor Charles VI came to England to visit the Duke of Somerset in 1703, his coach capsized a dozen times before he reached Petworth, owing to the bad state of the roads. Newman's travels were confined to a convalescence on the heights of Hampstead and visits, mainly on business, to such outlying villages as Hackney, Newington, Chelsea, Walham Green, or Kensington, where wealthier members of the Society had retreats. Not that these short journeys were without their troubles, for once he came to grief in the kennel or gutter in the middle of London streets along which the filth flowed: "I this day got on horseback to wait on you at Ealing, but in Long Acre had the misfortune to be thrown off into the kennel and made so dirty that I was obliged without any other harm (thank God for it) to return home and strip myself from head to foot." [2]

He made a much more pleasant journey into the country in 1726:

I lately spent a day at Putney on purpose to have an hour's consolation with Mr Law, the author of the *Practical Treatises*, etc., and had the satisfaction of two or three hours in Mr Gibbon's delightful garden, where he lives. Among other things, I asked him how he came to fall into that happy way of thinking he seemed to be master of and whether he could prescribe any rule for other people to obtain that happiness by? He told me he had long addicted himself to the study of the heathen moralists, who had a way of thinking uncommon to the rest of mankind; that he could not help considering Plato, Socrates, Seneca, Epictetus, etc. as lesser lights sent into the world by God to prevent the Gentiles among whom they lived from being abandoned to all immoralities till the great light by Jesus Christ should come into the world; that though their notions of futurity were very dark, yet their thoughts upon the excellence of virtue and detestableness of moral evil were so sublime, that he could not help thinking sometimes that they were

[1] *S.P.C.K. Minutes*, 24 March 1709; H. P. Thompson, *Thomas Bray*, 96.
[2] HN to Dr Mangey, Ealing, 4 June 1726, *Society's Letters*.

divinely inspired; that if he had any felicity in his way of thinking, perhaps he had derived it in some measure from his great esteem of the ancient moralists and their inimitable way of expressing themselves.[1]

[1] HN to Erasmus Philipps, M.P., Picton Castle, Pem, 30 July 1726, *Society's Letters*. Cf. William Law, *A Serious Call to a Devout and Holy Life*, Chap. XVIII: "Human wisdom or right use of our reason, which young people should be called to by their education, is nothing else but the best experience, and finest reasonings, of men that have devoted themselves to the study of wisdom, and the improvement of human nature. . . . The youths that attended upon Pythagoras, Socrates, Plato, and Epictetus, were thus educated. Their every-day lessons and instructions were so many lectures upon the nature of man, his true end, and the right use of his faculties; upon the immortality of the soul, its relation to God, the beauty of virtue, and its agreeableness to the Divine Nature; upon the dignity of reason, the necessity of temperance, fortitude, and generosity, and the shame and folly of indulging our passions."

Law was at this time employed by Mr Gibbon, a wealthy merchant, as tutor to his son, who was to be the father of the historian. Edward Gibbon, *Autobiography*—"My father's study . . . contained some valuable editions of the classics and the fathers, the choice, as it should seem, of Mr Law."

3

BOOKS AND TRACTS

NEWMAN continued as Secretary to Dr Bray's trustees for provision of parochial libraries after becoming Secretary of the S.P.C.K. This sometimes led to a natural confusion between the two bodies, and Newman had to set it right. "The design of the parochial libraries is not carried on by the Society at Bartlett's Buildings, but by another body of men, most of whom are indeed of the Society, but are in this thing independently. I happened to serve them as their Secretary before I had the honour of serving the Society."[1] While he was its Secretary the work of the trustees was given statutory recognition by Parliament through "An Act for the Better Provision of Parochial Libraries in that part of Great Britain called England" in 1709,[2] and rules were drawn up to govern the provision of the libraries. Since Dr Bray intended that libraries should be for "poor cures and poor parsons", they could be established "only in livings not exceeding £30 per annum" and were to be for reference only, so as to ensure they were not dissipated or used for other purposes. As Newman explained to the Bishop of Bangor, who informed him that the money given for the establishment of a parochial library at Bangor was conditional upon it being a lending library, "The founders had rather return the money than recede from the rule of not allowing any books to be lent. These libraries consist of a collection adapted to the use of a country clergyman that is destitute of books or ability to buy them, and if the collection be not kept entire they will not be useful to him, and if lending were allowed they would be in danger of being embezzled, and the incumbent would have a good excuse to his diocesan if upon a visitation they should be half wanting."[3] Another rule, which reflected Dr Bray's recognition of the importance of religious instruction, was that every incumbent having a library had "to make a catechetical discourse

[1] HN to Rev. Mr Grave, Lewes, Sussex, 2 July 1713; to Mr Harrison, Cambridge, 20 Sept. 1711, *Society's Letters.*

[2] *Publick Spirit, illustrated in the Life and Designs of the Reverend Thomas Bray, D.D.*, 1746, 69.

[3] HN to Bp of Bangor, 15 Feb. 1711, *Society's Letters.*

every Lord's Day or to catechize the children or expound the catechism when he does not do the former".[1]

Each parish receiving a library had to pay a premium of £5, in return for which the trustees supplied some seventy religious books, "contained in a wainscot box or press" of four shelves and "worth above twenty guineas". These included bulky tomes such as Eusebius' *Ecclesiastical History* (£1 1*s.* 6*d.*) and Tillotson's *Works* in three folio volumes (£2 8*s.*), smaller books such as Nelson's *Address to Persons of Quality* (3*s.* 6*d.*) and *Festivals and Fasts of the Christian Year* (5*s.*), Archbishop Wake's *Sermons* (4*s.* 6*d.*) and Bishop Pearson's *On the Creed* (10*s.* 6*d.*), and tracts such as Bishop Burnet's *Pastoral Care* (2*s.* 6*d.*) and Dr Bray's *Catechetical Instructions* (1*s.* 6*d.*). It was a sound selection of writings upon which contemporary Anglican thought and practice were based and presupposed some learning and diligence in the clergy for whom they were intended. As Newman said: "The Society have nowhere in their proposals for erecting libraries so much as supposed ignorance in the reverend body, the very end of their design being as much as in them lies to prevent such an imputation"; and again: "If the libraries they erect don't consist of all the books requisite to make a man a compleat scholar, yet they may be sufficient to furnish a man with the knowledge necessary to undertaking a parochial charge, and it must be owned that the narrowness of their funds has obliged them to content themselves with an essay which they hope may occasion an accession that may hereafter make amends for all deficiencies in the beginning." [2]

The trustees were never able, however, to supply more than a handful of parochial libraries. On the establishment of Queen Anne's Bounty in 1704 it was estimated that out of nearly 10,000 benefices in England and Wales, no fewer than 2122 were under £30 a year and 1200 under £20.[3] By 1711 only forty-five parishes had received libraries; in 1716 it was fifty-four; and in 1723 sixty "besides the two sent to the plantations, at Virginia and Montserrat".[4] Newman had to confess that the scheme did not attract subscriptions, particularly in competition with the growing activities of the S.P.C.K.—"The demand of several other charitable designs has occasioned this, which entirely depends on casual and

[1] HN to Rev. Mr Washington, Cambridge, 20 Feb. 1729, *Society's Letters*.
[2] HN to Rev. Mr Collins, Swansea, 21 April 1712, *Rawlinson MSS.*, D.834, f. 16; to Rev. Mr Tatam, Sutton, Derby., 1 Aug. 1716, *Society's Letters*.
[3] N. Sykes, *Church and State in England in the Eighteenth Century*, 212.
[4] "List of Parochial Libraries", *Rawlinson MSS.*, D.834, ff. 9 and 34.

Mandata DEI. *Exod.* xx. à *ver.* 2. usque ad *ver.* 18.

وصايا الله

انا الله ربّك الّذي اخرجتك من ارض مصر من
بيت العبوديّة • لا يكون لك معبودًا اخرًا من دوني •
لا تصنع لك منحوتًا ولا شبهًا لما في السّمآء من العلوّ
وما في الارض سفلًا • وما في المآء تحت الارض • لا
تسجد لها ولا تعبدها لانّي الله ربّك القادر الغيور • مطالب بذنوب الابآء
مع البنين والثّوالث والرّوابع لشانئيّ • وصانع الاحسان لالوف
من محبّيّ وحافظيّ وصاياي ✲ لا تحلف باسم الله ربّك باطلًا • لان الله
لا يبرّئ من يحلف باسمه باطلًا ✲ اذكر يوم السّبت وقدّسه • ستّة
ايّام تخدم وتصنع جميع صنائعك • واليوم السّابع سبت تسبت فيه لله
ربّك • لا تصنع شيًا من الصنائع انت وابنك وابنتك وعبدك وامتك •
وبهائمك وضيفك الذي في محلّك • لانّ الله خلق في ستّة ايّام •

السّموات

THE TEN COMMANDMENTS IN ARABIC

"A specimen of the new cast letter, to be used in the printing of the Psalter and New Testament . . . to be distributed *gratis* among the poor Christians in *Arabia*, *Syria*, *Palestine*, &c." (See pp. 67–71)

not annual benefactions, to proceed more slowly, and this is the reason that the gentlemen concerned in that charity meet but seldom, what has been done hitherto being for the most part out of their own pockets." [1] Dr Bray had realized the problem of raising the standard of clerical scholarship, but it was increased stipends and cheap printing in the nineteenth century which was to do most towards solving it.

The literary activities of the S.P.C.K. were both more ambitious and successful. One of the original aims of the Society was the wider task of distributing Christian literature throughout the country. "In Great Britain", Newman told Sir Hans Sloane, "their chief cares have been to encourage the erecting charity schools and workhouses and to disperse good books among the people who are not able to buy them." [2] The Society acted as a distributor of books rather than publisher in the modern sense, its usual method being to select books and tracts already of proven worth as Christian literature, which it then either had specially reprinted or bought in large quantities, chiefly at this time from its bookseller, Joseph Downing of Bartholomew Close. Since it was the only body doing this, its business was valuable; on the death of Mr Downing in 1734 there were, Newman said, "six candidates of booksellers or printers" seeking to succeed him.[3]

The Society, indeed, could make its wishes felt. In 1742, for instance, Newman complained to a firm of stationers that the paper and printing of their latest edition of *The Whole Duty of Man* were so bad that the Society "will be obliged to leave it out of the catalogue of books they disperse among the poor if it be not rectified" and, since the Society acted as "annual customers for a considerable number", asked for a reduction in price "in consideration of their being disposed of to charitable uses". The stationers sent a specimen of a new edition of a book and offered a reduced price, both of which the Society accepted on condition it could "exchange . . . the copies of the old imperfect edition remaining undisposed of", Newman adding, "I am ordered to recommend it to you to give directions for printing the devotions at the end of the new edition in as good, if not larger, letter than the body of the book for the sake of such as use them at the Communion Table." [4]

[1] HN to Col. Kane, Port Mahon, 3 Sept. 1720, *Society's Letters*.
[2] HN to Sir Hans Sloane, 1 Sept. 1731, *Sloane MSS.*, 4052, f. 4.
[3] HN to Rev. Mr Marshall, Naunton, Glos, 6 Sept. 1734, *Society's Letters*.
[4] HN to Messrs Mount and Co., Stationers, Tower Hill, 3 and 10 Dec. 1742, *Miscellaneous Letters*.

For the distribution of most of its books, the Society relied on its members, who here also acted as the link between the Society and the country, and the buying of these books for them formed its largest expenditure. "The chief article of their expense is in books, printed by their orders or bought at a cheaper hand, to disperse among their Residing and Corresponding Members . . .", wrote Newman. "Besides this there are several other articles which, being of a publick nature, they are necessitated to be at, as the carriage of these books into all parts of the Kingdom, salaries and gratuities to their servants or those that have deserved encouragement from them." [1] At first, members who wished to disperse books were treated liberally. From its foundation to the end of 1703, "the Society had chiefly printed the books at their own expense and dispersed them gratis" to each member as he required them, but from then members were encouraged to contribute towards the cost of their orders, so that, to quote the minutes in 1705, "packets are now frequently paid for". This, however, did not meet the mounting expenses caused by the steady increase in the Society's members and publications, and in June 1719 it was decided "to send the bound books at the prime cost, the Society paying the binding, and the books in quires at half-price, and a catalogue with the prices to be printed and dispersed". Members still received annually all the Society's new books until by 1732 these "common packets" had become "so bulky that the last year exceeded the value of the casual benefactions, and it was agreed for the future none be sent to new members, but only an abstract of a *Letter from a Residing to a Corresponding Member*, with a printed catalogue of books dispersed".[2]

Members, therefore, could have "Bibles, New Testaments, Common Prayer Books and all other bound books mentioned in the catalogue" at the cost of the quires and "the little practical Tracts . . . which are only stitched" at half the actual cost. Newman had to emphasize that only members could have books at these prices from the Society, "their fund for this purpose appropriated being but £200 per annum, it would soon be exhausted to the prejudice of their members, if the like privilege were allowed to others who were not of the Society". Nor did the Society intend "to sell Bibles, etc. to the poor at the prices mentioned in their Circular Letters, a thing which they can't propose to do, because

[1] HN to Mr Dundas, 3 April 1711, *Society's Letters*.

[2] W. O. B. Allen and E. McClure, op. cit., 169–87; *S.P.C.K. Minutes*, 2 June 1719 and 2 March 1732.

if their fund were fifty times larger than it is, it might not be sufficient to answer all demands in such a manner, and they would inevitably draw on themselves a clamour from the booksellers in all parts of the Kingdom as if the Society were undermining their business". In sending the catalogues, he continued, "Their intentions were to facilitate the giving away Bibles, etc. absolutely to the poor and to desire their Correspondents as much as they could to avoid all appearance of the sale of the books mentioned in the Circular Letters, and that where a fund can't be raised to supply the wants of the poor gratis, that they only be allowed the advantage of having them on the terms mentioned in the Letter, and that the rich be allowed only to have them on the said terms to give away among the poor." Obviously this arrangement was open to abuse, but, Newman concluded, "The Society must rely upon the prudence and integrity of their Correspondents not to embarrass a well-intentioned method for assisting the poor." [1]

Presumably the members were trustworthy, for they were allowed literature in this way for the rest of Newman's period of office. His job was to arrange the dispatch of parcels of books, which by itself was no light task. "We have", he wrote in 1735, "about 500 members to whom packets are sent as they occasionally desire them, but about half that number are most active in desiring books for charitable uses." [2] Moreover, some orders were large. In 1720 Ralph Thoresby noted that he wrote to Newman "with an ample commission for above 850 books, to advance the good of souls, most to be distributed to the poor in these parts"; while quite a usual packet dispatched by him on 24 October 1720 comprised "10 *Bibles*, 6 *New Manuals of Devotion*, 25 *Christian Monitors*, 12 *Worthington on Resignation*, 50 *Christian's Way to Heaven*, 50 *Necessary Duty of Family Prayers*, 50 *Persuasives to the Serious Observance of the Lord's Day*, 50 *Kind Cautions to Prophane Swearers*, 50 *Dissuasives from the Sin of Drunkenness*, 50 *Rebukes to Uncleanness*".[3] In contrast with such orders were occasional requirements for a few copies of some book, such as the Leicestershire vicar who wanted eight copies of "Books entitled *Divine Recreations*", and Newman remarked: "I doubt they will be no more agreeable to the taste of your parishioners than the last were." [4]

[1] HN to Rev. Mr Rayner, Tiverton, Devon, 24 Feb. 1726; to Rev. Mr Allen, Kettering, 8 Dec. 1719, *Society's Letters*.
[2] HN to Rev. Dr Hales, Teddington, 28 Jan. 1735, *Society's Letters*.
[3] Ralph Thoresby, *Diary*, 31 Dec. 1720, II, 307; *Rawlinson MSS.*, 844, f. 30.
[4] HN to Rev. Mr Fenwick, Hallaton, Leics, 30 Aug. 1737, *Miscellaneous Letters*.

Some recipients put the books to enterprising uses. A Wiltshire vicar "built a room joining to the chancel" of his church and "contrived in it a bookpress to be locked up and opened every Sunday to contain at least two of a sort of the books sent him by the Society" in hopes of stopping "the youngest sort of people of lingering many precious hours in the churchyard upon the Lord's Day before and after Divine Service".[1] In the porch of the little church of Ducklington, near Witney in Oxfordshire, may still be seen, chained to a shelf, the books placed by a vicar in 1708 with the inscription, "Preay do not abuse the books". And though intended for the poor, the books sometimes gained wealthy supporters for the Society, notably in 1729, when Newman wrote: "The Countess of Huntingdon, meeting with some of the Society's books this summer in the country, has desired to be entered on their list of contributors for ten guineas per annum from midsummer last and since that she has engaged my Lady Harpur in her neighbourhood to be entered on the same list for five guineas per annum."[2] This was Selina, Countess of Huntingdon, later closely associated with George Whitefield in the Methodist revival.

Though most of the Society's books were for general distribution, a few were for particular classes. In 1709 correspondents received three copies of an *Essay upon the Execution of the Laws, etc.*, being asked in the Society's usual cautious way to "present one of them to the Chairman of the next Quarter Sessions in your neighbourhood and the other two to such Justices as you shall think proper. Only this you are desired, not to deliver them when you are upon the bench, but in the most private and discreet manner as becomes the nature of the thing." Four years later the annual packet contained "*Prayers for Prisoners under Sentence of Death*, as a tract of which you may have occasion to make very good use of whilst your lot happens to be to live in a place where the county gaol is kept", and the *Oath of a Constable*, to be given, "according to your discretion, to such as are sworn to discharge the oath of a constable".[3] These special tracts show how the members of the S.P.C.K., while continuing attempts of the Societies for the Reformation of Manners to secure the enforcement of the law, were also beginning to concern themselves with the spiritual needs of those who came under the law. Mr Justice Hooke himself

[1] Rev. Mr Geo. Millard, Box, Wilts, to HN, 17 April 1714, *Abs. Correspondence.*
[2] HN to Mr John Meller, Wrexham, 31 July 1729, *Society's Letters.*
[3] *Circular Letters to Correspondents*, Aug. 1709 and Oct. 1715.

took a hundred copies of *Prayers for Prisoners under Sentence of Death.*[1]

Most of the Society's literature was distributed through its correspondents, but Newman sent some directly to persons with particular needs, at home and abroad. An inquirer about charity schools was sent Robert Nelson's *Address to Persons of Quality*, Newman saying, "There being no index to the book, I have put in a memorandum pointing at some of the good things therein mentioned." The Secretary of the London Hospital, founded in 1740 at Whitechapel for seamen, labourers, and others, received 100 copies of the *Christian Monitor* and a hundred of the *Bishop of London's Advice to Persons Recovered from Sickness*. A merchant captain was given a packet of books for "the English that reside on Madagascar, destitute of all spiritual instruction but what they can receive from good books", and Newman, perhaps drawing from his own practice in Newfoundland, hoped he would "enjoin those to whom he gives these books to read part of them every Lord's Day at the least".[2]

Much literature was sent to the army and navy, usually the *Soldier's Monitor* or *Seaman's Monitor*. The largest consignments of both were royal gifts. In 1722 George I ordered 10,000 *Soldier's Monitors* for the army and the next year the same number of *Seaman's Monitors* for the navy.[3] Apart from these exceptional consignments, the Society often gave packets to sympathetic officers and chaplains for their ships or regiments. Captain Studley of the *Norwich* at Portsmouth received a packet containing fifteen items, including, besides the *Seaman's Monitor*, copies of *An Address to the Officers and Seamen in Her Majesty's Navy*, *A Kind Caution to Swearers*, and *A Dissuasion from the Sin of Drunkenness*; while a gift "to the officers and soldiery encamped near Colchester" during the Spanish War consisted of fifty *Soldier's Monitors* and 150 each of Dr Woodward's tracts on *Prophane Language*, *The Sin of Uncleanness* and *Drunkenness*. Nor were men serving abroad forgotten. Upon the recommendation of George Whitefield, then in Georgia, books were sent to Dr Cunningham, Chaplain of the Gibraltar garrison, and also to George Barry, a sergeant there, "for the religious and

[1] H. P. Thompson, *Thomas Bray*, 41.

[2] HN to Rev. Dr Pelling, 25 July 1715, *Society's Letters*; to Mr Richard Neal, London Hospital, 23 April 1743, *Miscellaneous Letters*; to Capt. Rogers, 25 April 1716, *Society's Letters*.

[3] HN to Gov. Shute, 14 July 1722, *New Eng. Letters*; to ?, 15 Sept. 1723, *Rawlinson MSS.*, B.376, f. 29.

well-disposed soldiers in the garrison at Gibraltar". The troops in Minorca received special consideration, most of the books sent to Colonel Kane, Lieutenant-Governor of Port Mahon, being designed "to preserve them in the Protestant religion and to furnish them with arguments against Popery". The titles included *A Short Refutation of the Principal Errors of the Church of Rome*, *A Dialogue between a Protestant Minister and a Romish Priest*, and *An Account of the French Protestants' Sufferings on board the Galleys*, and Newman told Colonel Kane that he had had them "bound that they may endure being carried in the soldiers' pockets, to be read at leisure hours to one another, not only to fortify them against Popery, but enable them to become as it were missionaries among the common inhabitants, and to let the Papists see that our common people have better arguments to defend the Protestant religion with, than they have against it or in defence of Popery".[1]

The Society also considered "printing and publishing the Holy Scriptures, etc. in the Spanish and Italian languages with a view to introduce the knowledge of them among His Majesty's subjects at Minorca, whence it may please God to lead other parts in the Mediterranean to a knowledge of those Fountains, which antichristian tyranny has for many ages concealed"; but nothing came of it.[2] The Society did not engage in Protestant propaganda on the Continent. It sent literature to a few foreign correspondents, and some members sent packets to acquaintances abroad, but Newman was doubtful about such activities. He doubted their effectiveness and feared political complications. He and, indeed, most members could not share the enthusiasm with which French Huguenot refugees tried to persuade the Society to engage in propaganda in their native country. A Monsieur Guarriges in 1724 "applied to the Society to take some copies of his translation into French of *The Laws against Heretics* to disperse in foreign parts". Newman wrote to Archbishop Wake, being "ordered humbly to ask your Grace's opinion of the performance and how far it may be usefully dispersed abroad". Wake's reply is not recorded, but the Society does not seem to have taken any of the tracts.[3] Another Frenchman, Colonel Valogne, sent through the

[1] HN to Capt. Studley, *Norwich*, Portsmouth, 8 May 1714, *Society's Letters*; to Capt. Bolton, Soho, 25 Aug. 1741; to Rev. Dr Cunningham, Gibraltar, 29 April 1738; to Rev. Mr Whitefield, Georgia, 20 May 1738; to Sergeant Barry, Gibraltar, 20 Jan. 1739, *Miscellaneous Letters*; to Col. Kane, Port Mahon, 28 Aug. 1717 and 26 Oct. 1718, *Society's Letters*.

[2] HN to Rev. Mr Leith, Bedford, 26 Oct. 1717, *Society's Letters*.

[3] HN to Abp of Canterbury, 16 April 1724, *Society's Letters*.

King's Packet "among his friends in France what he calls bombs and hand grenades against the Church of Rome". The Society had supplied him with such printed ammunition, and towards the end of 1726 he asked for more. Townshend then was pursuing a policy of alliance with France against the threatening combination of Spain and the Empire. Newman asked Lord Perceval whether he thought it "advisable" to give him tracts which might give "umbrage and offence" to the French Court "at a time when we are soliciting their friendship". Perceval replied that he saw no reason why sending them "to be dispersed discreetly abroad will give more umbrage or offence to the French Court at this time than at any other if discovered, for there is room enough for re-crimination". So the Colonel had his tracts, and presumably distributed them discreetly enough to avoid any international incident.[1]

Lord Perceval, indeed, favoured extending the Society's activities to the Continent, and on his travels abroad had suggested that "some books of our religion could be sent to . . . open the eyes of Roman Catholicks".[2] He was not the only member to urge the Society to additional literary undertakings. Some of the most prominent had ideas of their own which they expected it to adopt. John Strype, to whose lives of Tudor Churchmen Newman subscribed, wished the Society to do more "dispersing books against Popery"; Newman tactfully referred it to the committee and it got no further.[3] Sir Hans Sloane thought the Society might publish and distribute the New Testament in Ethiopic, but Newman was gently dissuasive, reminding him that "there being little or no canal for trade from England to Abyssinia, the access to instruct the natives of it will not be easy".[4] He could always urge finance as the reason for declining new suggestions. "The Society are already engaged in so many charitable designs at home and abroad", he told a correspondent, "as call for all the aids they can afford and even more if it were in their power." [5]

In fact, the Society was wary of fresh literary ventures, whether overseas or not, if they might involve official disapproval. Its relations with the Bishops were not easy. Here they particularly give the impression of standing apart from its activities, ready to

[1] HN to Ld Perceval, 14 Nov., 1 and 14 Dec. 1726; Ld Perceval to HN, 3 Dec. 1726, *Egmont MSS.*, Add. MSS. 47031, ff. 417, 430, 432, 436.
[2] Ld Perceval to HN, 5 July 1723, *Egmont MSS.*, Add. MSS. 47030, f. 17.
[3] HN to Rev. Mr Strype, Low Leyton, Essex, 9 Sept. 1712, Add. MSS. 5853, f. 545.
[4] HN to Sir Hans Sloane, 23 Aug. 1736, *Sloane MSS.*, 4054, f. 294.
[5] HN to Rev. Dr Mawer, Richmond, Yorks, 11 April 1738, *Miscellaneous Letters.*

approve some publications, but equally ready to condemn others. The Society tried to avoid dispersing books likely to arouse episcopal objections. When a member wanted "Bishop Bull's intended letter to his clergy" printed, Newman had to tell him the committee thought "it will not be advisable for them to concern themselves in an affair of that nature", not only because "in all likelihood every Bishop in the Kingdom would have Bishop Bull's *Life* and see his letter in it", but also "it could not be expected that any Bishop would recommend to their clergy a thing of this nature, but in their own words, and that it would not consist with that caution which the Society have always used not to do anything which might look like assuming to direct their superiors for them to have a hand in publishing what might be construed by some as a reproof to those Bishops who should omit giving that advice Bishop Bull did".[1]

Several episodes showed the need for caution. In 1709 Archbishop Tenison "expressed some resentment that a little book entitled *A Further Instruction to those that have learned the Church Catechism* had been recommended by the Society" without authority. Newman was ordered to search the minutes and fortunately was able to announce at the next meeting that "200 of them were sent to the Society by an unknown benefactor, but the Society never recommended it". Mr Chamberlayne was asked to wait on the Archbishop to explain this.[2] A clearer example of the need for walking warily came in 1725. At the desire of several members, the Society considered publishing a collection of metrical psalms by Sir Richard Blackmore. Newman, while agreeing about "the slowness of our country musick and the inconvenience that attends reading line by line", had to say that the Society "seemed to think it would be too assuming in them to publish such a collection and recommend it to the Kingdom, when the Bishops themselves doubt of their power to recommend such a performance to their respective dioceses, though there are precedents to justify the minister of a parish doing it to ease his parishioners and as an instruction to the clerk". In 1725, however, Newman told Sir Richard Blackmore that the Society would publish his collection because Bishop Gibson's *Directions to the Clergy of his Diocese* recommended "a course of singing psalms for half a year" and his *Directions to the Masters and Mistresses of the Charity Schools* condemned "introducing

[1] HN to Mr Vaughan, Carmarthen, 10 Oct. 1713, *Society's Letters.*
[2] *S.P.C.K. Minutes*, 2 and 16 June 1709.

into the Church compositions merely humane, how fine and elegant soever they may be thought, as a liberty not strictly warrantable in itself nor wholly free from ill consequences". But the assumption was not correct, and Newman apologized to Gibson, explaining that the Society had decided on publication thinking "it was made agreeable to your Lordship's new scheme for regulating Psalmody, but when they are informed that what they intended as a compliment will give disgust to your Lordship, I am sure they will make no difficulty to desist from it".[1]

The Society had previously, in 1718, had an experience in dispersing a collection of psalms which was most unfortunate because it unwittingly touched upon the Trinitarian controversy of the early years of the century. "Some of the Society's correspondents having desired to see a collection of psalms in metre proper for common occasions, they agreed to recommend to them a set of select psalms and hymns", namely, *A Collection of Psalms used in the Parish Church and Chapels of St James, Westminster*, made by Archbishop Wake when Rector of the parish. This must have seemed safe enough, and the Society ordered 750 copies of the 1709 edition from the proprietor for the annual packet. At once a correspondent in Doncaster complained about "alterations made in the doxologies and other parts" of the psalms. The Society investigated and, Newman told Strype, "to their great surprise, after they had bought and dispersed several hundreds of them amongst their members, they find a copy has been imposed upon them by the said proprietor, with several omissions and alterations, and more particularly in the doxologies, insinuating an opinion dissonant to the doctrine of the Established Church concerning the Ever-Blessed Trinity . . . [and] likewise leaves out the Lord's Prayer and Ordination Hymn, disagreeing the copy they approved". This had been done, "without the knowledge of the Archbishop, as appeared by the surprise and concern which His Grace expressed in the first hearing thereof", by the present Rector of St James's, Dr Samuel Clarke. Newman might admire his sermons, but in 1712 Clarke had published his fiercely-attacked *Scripture Doctrine of the Trinity*, in which he maintained that the Father alone is Supreme God, that the Son is a Divine Being only in so far as divinity is communicable by this Supreme God, and that the

[1] HN to Rev. Mr Wheeler, Warpenham, 1 Dec. 1724 and 11 March 1725; to Sir Richd Blackmore, Boxsted, Essex, 3 April 1725; to Bp of London, 13 Aug. 1725, *Society's Letters*.

Holy Spirit is inferior both to the Father and the Son, not in order only, but in dominion and authority. The Society did not want to be identified with such views. It "declared their disapprobation of the copy as it has been dispersed by them" and ordered Newman to write "to all the Corresponding Members to whom copies have been sent, asking for its return".[1]

Nor did the Society wish to provoke Dissenters. Though a Church society, it remained firm to Dr Bray's ideal of promoting a common Protestant Christianity and shunned controversy. "The Society", Newman explained, "have purposely declined (as foreign to promote Christian knowledge) to concern themselves with the controversy between the Established Church and Dissenters, except in the instance . . . of defending infant baptism, the common result of disputes among Protestants being rather a lessening of charity than conviction of truth." [2] An author was told by Newman that it could not "approve of the dispersing in their packets of the *Duty of Publick Worship Proved*" as suitable for instructing children, as it might "lead them into controversies which might beget in them an uncharitable opinion of other Protestant Churches", and a correspondent that it declined a book (discreetly unnamed) even though by a bishop who "is a member and annual contributor to the designs of the Society", because it would draw the Society into "a controversy which they have always industriously avoided as foreign to their designs of promoting Christian knowledge on principles allowed by all Christians except Papists. And though many things have been well wrote against the Sectaries, the Society . . . declined dispersing of them and rather pray to God to heal our divisions and to open the eyes of those who are misled to acknowledge the truth as exhibited in the Holy Scriptures." [3]

Quite apart from such principles, the Society could only afford to disperse books likely to be needed. Many submitted manuscripts, and Newman sometimes gave these would-be authors advice. To one he said: "I remember to have read it somewhere that if an author will suffer his composition to lie by him a year or more and then peruse it, it will come forth with more advantage, and he will not repent the delay of his publication." To another, a

[1] *S.P.C.K. Minutes*, 23 and 30 Oct. 1718; HN to Rev. Mr Strype, Low Leyton, Essex, 29 Nov. 1718, Add. MSS. 5853, f. 575.

[2] HN to Rev. Mr Paley, Leeds, 27 May 1727, *Society's Letters*.

[3] HN to Rev. Mr Fox, Potterne, Wilts, 14 May 1720, *Society's Letters*; to Thos. Carew, Culbone, Som, 8 Nov. 1735, *Miscellaneous Letters*.

clergyman who sent him some "Essays in Poetry", he advised: "As you propose, God willing, to devote yourself to theological studies, you would find your account in it to be deaf and blind to Belinda's charms, the contemplation of which will never yield an established tranquillity to the mind, but instead of it may perhaps give a bias which may cost many a struggle to conquer." He was most scathing to the Chaplain of the Duke of Portland, Governor of Jamaica, who sent a sermon which "was twice as long as the sermons usually are here", and he asked him: "Pray how can you afford in respect to your health and your hearers to make such long sermons in such a hot country? If you commonly practise it, it must be a great prejudice to your health, if not disgusting to your auditors." [1]

Since the Society usually only distributed books already printed and published, Newman tried to persuade writers to submit only printed works, sometimes even declining to forward a manuscript to the Society. To a Berkshire clergyman who sent him a manuscript, he explained: "I was tempted to lay it before the Society . . . but they have so often declared their aversion to perusing manuscripts, that I had not courage to do it. For their rules require that a manuscript shall be perused by four different members at four different times, and when each have found out objections, they have either differed with one another about them or been unwilling to expostulate with the author to make the alterations desired, so that a printed book, which may be in several hands at the same time, has a better chance to be accepted than a manuscript." And he concluded: "I hope notwithstanding it may see the light and shall gladly recommend it to the Society when printed to make it as publick and useful as you intended it." [2] Manuscripts that did reach the Society were often rejected without this elaborate consideration, as was a "manuscript recommending the charity of contributing to Briefs", because "the reputation of Briefs is now so low that an advocate for them is not only heard very coldly, but is in some danger being thought a friend to the abuses of them", and a "copy book" claiming "to contain all the principles of the Christian religion" on the grounds of being "too expensive to be attempted".[3] It is difficult to see why Newman

[1] HN to Mr Whitelocke Bulstrode, 7 Dec. 1720; to Rev. Mr Barrett, 3 April 1711, *Society's Letters*; Rev. Mr Galpine, Jamaica, 30 Sept. 1723, *Letters to Jamaica.*

[2] HN to Rev. Mr Peery, Faringdon, Berks, 24 Jan. 1738, *Miscellaneous Letters.*

[3] HN to Rev. Mr Burghope, Burton Agnes, Yorks, 2 Feb. 1720; to Mr Nelson, 16 Dec. 1710, *Society's Letters.*

forwarded the latter, except that it was submitted by so prominent a member as Robert Nelson, a friend of its author.

So seriously did the Society take its literary activities that even when an author offered to present copies of his work for free distribution, its standard was as high. The book had to be both acceptable doctrinally and likely to be effective. A Yorkshire clergyman offered 150 copies of his *Admonition against Drunkenness*. The Society accepted, but for future editions Newman told him: "If the texts referred to had been printed at large, whether it might not have been more instructive to those into whose hands it may come, who perhaps are not provided with a Bible to turn to them or have not leisure to do that office for themselves, is submitted. Reproof is one of the most difficult lessons to be managed successfully, especially for inveterate crimes where the offender seems hardened against all admonition, as in the case of drunkenness, where the constitution is so often vitiated into a habit that pleads a kind of necessity to support it." [1]

Yet, with all its caution, the Society was not narrow in its literary activities. Its desire to strengthen relations between the Church of England and Continental Protestants made it ready to introduce foreign religious literature into the country. In 1714, ten years after Wanley had translated J. F. Ostervald's *Grounds and Principles of the Christian Religion*, it received a copy of the new liturgy composed by him for the Reformed church in his native city of Neuchâtel of which he was pastor. It contained a catechism and "arguments and exhortations used before and after reading the Holy Scripture in the Churches". Newman told him that the Society was pleased to "observe so good a disposition in the Reformed Churches abroad to restore the use of liturgies to their ancient dignity"; and the Society had it translated by John Chamberlayne and published "for their Corresponding Members for the instruction of the Charity Schools and the poorer sort of people".[2] It was a good example of the way in which most English Churchmen of the time felt able largely to identify themselves in doctrinal matters with Protestants abroad, but wished to lead them to liturgical worship.

Again, in 1731, Professor Callenberg of Halle in a letter to Mr Ziegenhagen, one of the King's German Chaplains, told him of

[1] HN to Rev. Mr Disney, Wakefield, 17 Feb. 1741, *Miscellaneous Letters*.

[2] HN to the Dean and Pastors of the Churches of the Sovereignty of Neuchâtel and Vallangin, 16 June 1714; to Mr Hoare, 9 Jan. 1716; to Rev. Mr Osterwald, Neuchâtel, 16 May 1716; to Rev. Mr Holyday, Saxby, Lincs, 26 Nov. 1734, *Society's Letters*.

"a remarkable disposition among the Jews in Germany to read Christian books, occasioned by a book printed at Halle in the German Hebrew dialect entitled *Light in the Evening* wrote by a learned Christian in the Oriental style proving that the Messias is come". Newman saw the letter and told the Society about it. Upon the Society expressing interest in the book, which was by John Moeller, Callenberg offered "any number gratis that the Society shall desire for the use of Jews in England". The Society took a year before telling him, "If you please to transmit 100 copies in quires, they will make the best use they can of them." Newman did not think the book would be of much use. He thought "the worldly-mindedness of our Jews in general gives little hope of these books being so well received here as by the religious Jews in Germany", while in any event "our Jews being mostly Portuguese Jews, it is doubted whether they will understand the German dialect".[1] Newman evidently only knew the Spanish and Portuguese Jews of the Sephardim, mostly rich and respected, though the first synagogue of the Ashkenazim, which used the German ritual, had been established in Duke's Place, Aldgate, in 1722 by Jewish refugees from central Europe, who came in increasing numbers in the eighteenth century.

One of the Society's most ambitious schemes while Newman was Secretary, the printing of "the Psalter and New Testament in Arabick", indicated the interest also taken in England in the Eastern Church. Early in the century several Orthodox clergy had been received by Archbishop Tenison, while there was a proposal that, to help "the true primitive religion so early and so long flourishing in the Greek Church" in its struggle against "the pressure of the Mohametans and the Romish imposture", some twenty Greek youths might "be brought over to England and instructed in the fundamentals of religion and learning, whereby at their return they might be capable to defend the faith".[2] When, therefore, Mr Böhme laid before the Society in 1720 a letter from Solomon Negri, a native of Damascus living in England, with "a proposal for printing the New Testament in Arabick for the use of the Christians in the Eastern countries where the Arabick is used, but for want of printing, books of any sort, and especially of the Holy Scriptures, cannot be obtained but at such prices as very few can reach to", it was interested and asked Archbishop Wake's advice

[1] HN to Rev. Mr Fox, Reading, 20 April 1731; to Prof. Callenberg, Halle, 6 April 1732, *Society's Letters*.
[2] E. F. Carpenter, *Thomas Tenison*, 1948, 358.

about the project. Wake replied that he "was of opinion that the Society should cheerfully go on with the same in the method proposed". The Society decided to print the Psalter as well as the New Testament.[1]

Newman had to make the arrangements. First a separate fund had to be raised by subscriptions. Then it had to be decided whether the printing should be done in England or Holland. Newman learnt from correspondents in Holland that it could be "done cheaper and better" there, but when Wake's advice was again asked, he considered "that it would be more advisable for the Society to print the Arabick New Testament in England, notwithstanding the difference of the expense, because the benefactors will be better disposed to encourage a thing under their eye". This advice was followed, which meant "a new font of types" had to be cast by a printer, Mr Palmer of Great Swan Alley near Charterhouse. Before this, however, Newman had to secure "a specimen of a fine Arabick letter, worthy of their imitation", and with typical thoroughness in 1721 and 1722 he inquired about Arabic manuscripts in the Bodleian Library, Oxford, received "beautiful Arabick copies of the Psalter and New Testament" from Rowland Sherman, "a learned English merchant at Aleppo", and borrowed from Humphrey Wanley "a very fine manuscript Alcoran in a small Arabick letter" out of the Earl of Oxford's library. When work began, Solomon Negri benefited from having suggested the scheme by being made "supervisor and corrector of the press". He was lodged with Mr Palmer and paid £6 a quarter, £9 10*s*. being advanced to pay his present and previous lodgings, "besides what shall be thought necessary for apparel, linen and other necessaries", all of this coming from the fund. The printing of the Psalter began first, and by the end of 1724 over 6000 copies were printed and 2000 sent at once to Rowland Sherman to distribute.[2]

The Arabic New Testament had now to be printed. Since the type was cast, this could have begun at once but for the supreme

[1] *S.P.C.K. Minutes*, 24 March and 28 June 1720.

[2] HN to Sir Hans Sloane, 1 Sept. 1731, *Sloane MSS*. 4052, f. 4; to Mr Hastings, Utrecht, 1 Nov. 1720; to Sir Robt de Neville, Leyden, 26 April 1720; to Rev. Dr King, Charterhouse, 19 May 1721; to Rev Mr Gagnier, Oxford, 22 April 1721; to Dr Stratford, Oxford, 18 July 1721, *Society's Letters*; to Rowland Sherman, Aleppo, 9 June 1724, *Rawlinson MSS*. C.743, f. 58; to Mr Wanley, Dover St, 4 and 27 June 1722, *Harleian MSS*. 3780, ff. 250 and 252; to Mr Philpot, M.P., 22 Aug. 1719, *Private Letters*; to Rev. Dr Wilkins, Lambeth, 25 Nov. 1720; to Rev. Mr Shute, 23 Dec. 1720; to Richd Wilson, Leeds, 17 Nov. 1724; to Rowland Sherman, Aleppo, 23 Dec. 1724, *Society's Letters*.

problem of finance. Newman had worked hard for subscriptions for the Psalter and received money from many sources. Archbishop Wake gave 20 guineas, the Duchess of Bedford £50 and "the Presbyterian congregation at Nottingham" £21 5*s*. 7*d*., while £100 came from "the principal promoter of it", John Tylor, Bishop of Llandaff, and formerly an East India Company's chaplain. The South Sea Bubble in 1720 made subscriptions difficult, but Newman raised in time the sum of over £600 needed to get the Psalter through the press. It seemed unlikely, however, that private subscriptions alone would provide for the bulkier New Testament, and even before the Psalter appeared Newman sought another source of money.[1]

Early in 1721 he secured an introduction to Lord Stanhope, one of the Secretaries of State, told him of the project and asked him "to be pleased to commend it to the King for His Majesty's encouragement". Stanhope was sympathetic, but a short time later died after making his vehement speech on the South Sea question. Newman had, therefore, to begin again with Stanhope's successor, Lord Townshend, who after two or three months informed him that the King had promised £500. The promise was, however, easier to obtain than the money. Townshend had yet to secure the warrant for the royal bounty, and Newman could not hasten him. In the autumn of 1721 he told John Robethon, the King's Huguenot secretary, that he had waited on Townshend "at the back stairs humbly to put him in mind of his speaking to His Majesty, and I was in great hopes that it might then have done to put an end to the frequent solicitations with which I have troubled His Lordship, but after waiting there some time His Lordship was pleased to tell me that he had again forgot me, but would certainly remember it this morning". But Newman had to wait upon Townshend for nearly four years. Not until the summer of 1726 was the King's warrant signed, and even then Newman's labours were not ended. Still no money came to the Society, and he found that Sir Robert Walpole had to sign a "subsequent warrant . . . which is to be directed to my Lord Halifax". For a month he "attended every week at the Treasury . . . excepting when Sir Robert Walpole was in Norfolk" in an attempt "to put him in mind of signing the subsequent warrant, which was every Treasury

[1] HN to Hon. Mr Robethon, 9 Jan. 1721; to Dr Stratford, Oxford, 13 July 1721; to Mr Chamberlayne, 21 Oct. 1721; to Rev. Mr Hardy, Nottingham, 14 May 1722, *Society's Letters*.

Day laid before him", only to be told eventually "it would be necessary to get some friend that had an interest in Sir Robert" to induce him to do it. He asked Sir John Philipps to act for him, and after a further two months finally received the £500 from the Exchequer.[1] He had, however, one more disappointment. He hoped to follow up the receipt of the royal bounty by a deputation to Frederick Prince of Wales to interest him in the project; but the domestic differences of the royal family frustrated this intention. The Archbishop of Canterbury declined to join as he "had no hand in recommending the affair to the King, which might give umbrage to some people as want of respect to His Majesty if he should do it in the present case", and the Bishop of London said he "never goes to the Prince's Court except on days of compliment when he can't avoid it without manifest disrespect", upon which the Bishop of Durham, who had earlier promised to approach the Prince "by himself or the Lord of the Bedchamber in Waiting", now withdrew "because he is of another Province".[2]

Nevertheless, the royal bounty enabled the Society to go ahead with the Arabic New Testament, 10,000 copies being printed. The Society distributed them and the Psalters through its correspondents at Aleppo, Rowland Sherman, the merchant, and Nevil Coxe, the British consul, and made every effort to ensure their success. The Archbishop of Aleppo's approval was obtained, but at the same time, to defeat possible Popish opposition, the publication was done anonymously, "that the Popish clergy, if they pleased, might arrogate the glory of having done it at Rome, so they will but let the copies be dispersed quietly through Palestine, etc". Unfortunately for some reason—Newman put it down to "the ferment of late years among the Ecclesiasticks of the Greek Church in those parts"—the distribution did not go well, and the Society found itself with several hundred Psalters and New Testaments on its hands. Some were sent to the Danish missionaries in India, some to the Minister of the German Church at St Petersburg to be distributed "among the oriental readers", some to the "Rev. Mr Rodde at Narva in Livonia" to go to "some Persian prisoners in the Russian garrisons", and some to General Oglethorpe for

[1] HN to Abp of Canterbury, 12 Jan. 1721; to Ld Townshend, 24 Feb. 1721; to Hon. Mr Robethon, 31 Oct. 1721; to Ld Townshend, 20 Nov. 1724; to Erasmus Philipps, M.P., 30 July 1726; to Sir John Philipps, Picton Castle, 2 Aug. 1726, *Society's Letters*; to Sir Robt Walpole, 7 July 1725, *Rawlinson MSS.*, C.379, f. 60; to Ld Perceval, 11 April 1726, *Egmont MSS.* 47031, f. 389.

[2] HN to Abp of Canterbury, 15 Oct. 1726; to Ld Perceval, Charlton, 28 Dec. 1726, *Society's Letters*.

"the Mohametan Africans in Carolina". So the stock was exhausted, but the Society did not regard this venture as a success and was discouraged from attempting other foreign publications during Newman's lifetime.[1]

The Society was more successful in publishing Welsh books. As the charity school movement spread to Wales, an increasing demand for books in the native language resulted. Even before Newman was Secretary, requests reached the Society for Welsh Bibles and Prayer Books and "good books" translated into Welsh, and Newman organized the purchase and distribution of such as he could find. When these were exhausted the Society published new editions, particularly 10,000 copies of a new impression of the 1630 edition of the Welsh Bible in 1717 and another impression in 1728. Newman was not concerned in this as in the Arabic printing, since its chief promoters were Moses Williams, Vicar of Llanwenog, prominent in the Welsh charity school movement, and Sir John Philipps, who gave many of the Bibles away himself to cottagers.[2]

When Sir John Philipps died in 1737, the leader of Welsh education was already his friend and son-in-law Griffith Jones, Rector of Llanddowror, who wrote in 1731 to the Society asking for "40 or 50 small Welsh Bibles" for a charity school in his parish. From this beginning came his scheme for the circulating charity schools of Wales. Realizing that the existing charity schools were too few for the scattered population of Wales, he asked the clergy to allow a teacher to come for three months at a time to hold a school in the parish, so that each teacher would instruct the children in four villages every year. By this means Griffith Jones hoped to give every child in Wales a chance of learning to read the Book essential for Salvation. By 1738 he had established 37 such schools, and the number increased yearly. Each school meant a further request to the S.P.C.K. for Welsh literature, particularly Bibles; and in 1737 alone the Society sent the circulating schools 740 Bibles, many Psalters and Catechisms and 13,000 other Welsh books. Newman tried to satisfy the demand in these last years of his life, but Welsh Bibles became so scarce that they cost the Society 15*s*. each to buy in London. Newman saw that

[1] HN to Sir Hans Sloane, 1 Sept. 1731, *Sloane MSS.* 4052, f. 4; to Mr Thos. Jones, Bristol, 2 Jan. 1724, *Society's Letters*; to Sir Gerard Conyers, London, 9 July 1736; to Rev. Mr Ludovick Trefurt, St Petersburg, 31 May 1737; to Gen. Oglethorpe, 13 April 1738, *Miscellaneous Letters*; *S.P.C.K. Minutes*, 6 Feb. 1728.

[2] HN to Rev. Mr Moses Williams, 21 May 1714, *Letters to Correspondents*; M. G. Jones, *Charity School Movement*, 294–6.

the Society must undertake a fresh impression, but, once again, expense was the obstacle. It was not so colourful a venture as the Arabic New Testament to appeal to the public. Moreover, the Society came up against the ambitious and litigiously-minded King's Printer, John Baskett, who was seeking a monopoly of the royal privilege of printing the Bible. The Society had successfully resisted him in "printing the Scriptures in Arabick without his being employed", but having admitted his right in its previous impressions of the Welsh Bible, Newman considered it would have to do so now. This meant it would have to be done by the King's Printer in London, since the cost of transport made Oxford or Cambridge too expensive. Nevertheless, the Society decided in the spring of 1743 to undertake a new "impression and distribution of Bibles in the Welsh language". Newman began raising funds, estimating that "£40 or £50 a year" would be needed, but he died on the very threshold of the venture. The new edition appeared in 1746 and was followed by others promoted by the Society, which played their part in the Welsh religious and national revival of the eighteenth century.[1]

The literary activities of the S.P.C.K. during Newman's time as Secretary show how important, in this alone, the Society had become in the religious life of the country. As has been said, "This important function [of publishing educative literature] had now been controlled almost to monopoly by the Society for Promoting Christian Knowledge, which thus became the chief and more permanent influence in stemming the tide of irreligion and immorality." [2] Never before had any organ of the Church of England attempted this, and it was not easy for the S.P.C.K. It had to contend with episcopal suspicion and even opposition; it made mistakes, particularly in printing the Arabic Psalter and New Testament; but its energies were persistent and usually well-directed. It sought to serve, not only the Church of England, but the wider cause of Christianity wherever it seemed possible. Above all, it refused to be engaged in controversy with Dissenters or be diverted in any other way from its main purpose, the furtherance of Christian education and the promotion of a higher standard of morality and charity.

[1] HN to Rev. Mr Griffith Jones, 17 Jan. 1741; to Bp of St Asaph, 6 April 1743; to Rev. Dr Wilson, 17 May 1743, *Miscellaneous Letters*; *S.P.C.K. Minutes*, 19 April 1743; *Welsh Piety: or a Collection of the several Accounts of the Welsh Circulating Charity Schools from their first Rise in the year 1737 to Michaelmas 1752*; M. G. Jones, op. cit., 297–302.

[2] Norman Sykes, *Edmund Gibson*, 197–8.

4

THE CHARITY SCHOOL MOVEMENT

THE founders of the S.P.C.K. stated that their aims were "immediately directed to the promoting Christian knowledge, especially amongst the poorer sort of people", and this was to be done, not only by dispersing religious literature, but still more by encouraging charity schools. At its first meeting of 8 March 1699 the Society "Resolved that we consider to-morrow discussing how to further and promote the good designs of erecting Catecheticall Schools in each parish in and around London".[1] Although some such schools, designed to provide the children of the poor with religious instruction and elementary education, had already been founded, the establishment of the S.P.C.K. marked the real beginning of the charity school movement, which became a popular public benefaction in the first half of the eighteenth century. It had made remarkable progress when Newman became Secretary, as shown by the figures the Society regularly published. In 1704, 54 schools had been established in and about London, which educated 2131 children; three years later, the number of schools in London itself was 55 and in the country 216, with an average of nearly 50 children in each London school and just over 17 in each country school; by 1714 there were more than 1000 schools in the country which had bound apprentice over 2000 children.[2]

The first members of the Society placed great hopes in the schools. Their letters show them acutely anxious about the prevalent immorality and wickedness, particularly of the town population, "that inundation of profaneness and immorality, which we find of late upon us, puts all serious persons here into no small consternation at the prospects of those judgements, which according to the ordinary course of Divine Providence overtake an apostasized people", as Dr Bray said in a letter to the Governor of Jamaica, adopted by the Society in 1701.[3] The charity schools

[1] S.P.C.K., *First General Letter to Correspondents*, 1700; *S.P.C.K. Minutes*, 8 March 1699.
[2] *Account of the Charity Schools*, 1704–14.
[3] *S.P.C.K. Minutes*, 6 Jan. 1701. "The historian of moral and religious progress is under the necessity of depicting the period as one of decay of religion, licentiousness of morals, public corruption, profaneness of language—a day of rebuke and blasphemy" —Mark Pattison in *Essays and Reviews* (8th ed. 1861), 254.

were to meet this situation. "The chief design of our charity schools", a charity preacher said, "[is] to reform the lives of a class of mankind, which, to the utmost degree, needed reformation";[1] and their moral purpose was uppermost in the minds of their founders. Their influence might extend beyond the present generation, as "godly nurseries, which give us a fair specimen of the reformation of manners in this age, and I hope in God, will compleat and perfect it in the next at least".[2] Newman shared this hope. When the Rector of Broseley in Shropshire told him about the irreligion of the colliers in his parish, Newman made several suggestions. The owners of the coal-mines might assist the Justices of the Peace and the parish officers to "put in practice some regulations which may with God's blessing cure those disorders or at least restrain them". Local members of the Society might also "persuade the proprieters of the mines to consent to the colliers being paid their wages on Saturday noon, in order to their going then to market for what they are now forced to trespass on the Sunday to do". But, above all, he should establish a charity school for "the amendment of the next generation, so far as that they may not be without instruction for want of ability to read; and these when so taught may be able to read to the present adult people who are not so happy as to be able to read themselves, but yet may be well disposed to hear others read to them, at all proper intervals of time in the business Providence has allotted to them, especially on Sundays."[3]

Much of Newman's time, particularly during his first years as Secretary, was taken by the charity schools, but not in direct control or management. The Society did not itself establish or conduct schools. The movement was characteristic of the period in relying on local initiative. Usually, the first annual *Account of the Schools* stated, the initiative was taken by the incumbent or prominent parishioners, who advertised "the necessity and usefulness of the design" to raise funds for its establishment. They "commonly met with so good success" that they soon did this, and thereafter both funds and administration of the school were vested in trustees, usually members of local families.[4] The Society had no power over them, and Newman's office towards them was much

[1] William Dawes, *The Excellence of the Charity of the Charity Schools*, 1713, 16.

[2] Andrew Snape, *Sermon on Charity Schools*, 1711, 25.

[3] HN to Rev. Mr Richard Hartshorn, Broxley, Salop, 18 June 1737; to Mr Francis Freeman, Bristol, 18 March 1738, *Miscellaneous Letters*.

[4] *Account of the Charity Schools*, 1714.

the same as Bagehot described that of a modern monarch towards his ministers—to be consulted, to encourage, and to warn.

As schools could only be started by local effort, Newman's duty was to urge correspondents, if suited, to do this. The ideal qualifications, he once said, for this were "a large acquaintance, reputation, leisure, estate";[1] but he approached any who might be able to do it in some way or another. When Dr Waddington became a Fellow of Eton, in congratulating him, he said the Society "had long desired to see a Charity School set up at Eton where there are abundance of poor children that want such an advantage" and hoped he would "recommend such an undertaking to the Revd Provost and Fellows of Eton".[2] The Society desired trustees should be "composed both of clergy and laity, which will creat a good understanding between the ministers and their neighbouring gentry";[3] and Newman wrote severely to the Vicar of Great Gidding, who complained his parishioners would not support his charity school: "I cannot imagine how the people refusing so small an expence as 50 shillings towards fitting up a school room for the charity children must necessarily put you upon destroying yourself. If you have by a pragmatical domineering conduct (pardon the expressions, for I can't help considering your case in such a light from your own letters) laboured to extort the benevolence of your neighbours in such a matter wherein they were entirely free to do or not to do according as they were inclined, consider whether you have not industriously brought upon yourself the contradictions you groan under." [4] He assured the founders of schools of both immediate and future rewards. "The Rewarder of cups of cold water given to His disciples won't forget your labours love on this score," he told one, "and you have thereby entitled yourself to the respect from the Society which you wish for and when you have stood proposed so long as their rules prescribe, I can't doubt but I shall have their commands to signify to you their choice of you for a Corresponding Member." [5]

Newman's advice to founders of schools rested on some personal experience. As early as 1689 the King in Council had ordered "that those idle and vagabond boys, commonly called the Blackguard, be kept from harbouring themselves or coming into St

[1] HN to Capt. Campbell, 27 April 1713, *Society's Letters*.
[2] HN to Rev. Dr Waddington, Eton, 29 Aug. 1721, *Society's Letters*.
[3] S.P.C.K. *Third Circular Letter to the Clergy Correspondents*, 1700.
[4] HN to Rev. Mr Robt Watts, Great Gidding, Peterborough, 31 July 1712, *Society's Letters*.
[5] HN to Mr Poole, Oswestry, Salop, 15 May 1714, *Society's Letters*.

James' Park, Whitehall or any other places near Their Majesties".[1] This was a darker side of London life, the homeless, deserted children and young vagrants, living in the streets by begging, robbing, and other public disorder and growing up to form gangs of thieves as described by Defoe in *Colonel Jack*. Late in Anne's reign Newman envisaged a "Blackguard School" for them, especially "such as are altogether friendless and who by being born in Flanders or Spain are strictly of no parish in Great Britain, such whose parents have been knocked in the head in the service of Her Majesty". He formed trustees, who met in his chambers, but needed "20 or 30 good subscribers" before he could "set it going". He approached the Duke of Ormond and the "Board of General Officers" and also John Sharp, Archbishop of York. On the dismissal of Smalridge from the Lord Almonership for refusing to sign the declaration against James Edward, the Old Pretender, Sharp had succeeded to the office, and he was also spiritual adviser to the Queen, so Newman asked his permission to call the school the "Lord Almoner's School" because "your name would recommend it more than the gift of 100 guineas from another person"; but Sharp died soon afterwards, and the venture "proved abortive by reason of the unhappy divisions that then prevailed".[2] Five years later he tried again, relying upon ladies to raise subscriptions—"they ask in so powerful a manner that they'll get 100 guineas in the time that men would get 20"—though he hoped the only expense would be a schoolmaster, since he believed he had "found out a way to maintain a school for them about Court, without a subscription or charge to anybody" by having "a place for a schoolroom in Scotland Yard or the mews now unemployed".[3] But this attempt also came to nothing, perhaps because there were by then five charity schools for boys in the district.[4]

About this time Newman was also interested in "a charity school lately erected at Whitchurch in Middlesex in which honest Cholmondley has laboured with such success that though he had but here and there but half a crown by some of his friends to bring it about, there are now 24 poor girls taught . . . and clothed".

[1] *Privy Council Register* (P.R.O.), P.C. 2—73, 159.

[2] HN to Mrs Ketteridge, 12 June 1713; to Trustees of Blackguard School, 4 June 1713; to Capt. Gardner, 20 Aug. 1713; to Mr David Kennedy, Secretary to Duke of Ormond, 24 June 1713; to Abp of York, 8 May 1713, *Society's Letters*.

[3] HN to Mr Robt Hales, The Cockpit, Whitehall, 4 March 1718, *Society's Letters*.

[4] M. G. Jones, *The Charity School Movement in the Eighteenth Century*, 1938, 372–3.

In 1714, hearing that the Dean of Lincoln would be in the district over Whitsun, he asked Chamberlayne to persuade him to preach a charity sermon for the school and perhaps himself "hold a plate at the church door". When Lord Carnarvon became the school's patron, Cholmondley founded a new school at Hampton to which Newman promised, despite the Rector of Whitchurch's protests, "about £10 from his friends in London . . . transferred from Whitchurch School". Here also Newman sought a sermon by a prominent preacher, which would "not only be agreeable to the gentry thereabout, but draw down 30 or 40 people from London to throw in their mites"; and the trustees should arrange that "30 or more proper objects of such a charity will be looked out to be presented at the time in the best rags they have"; but in that summer of 1718 all excused themselves—the Archbishop of Canterbury, "being persuaded to go out as far as Camberwell a month since to preach a charity sermon, His Grace got such a cold that he has not had two days' health since and is now under a course of physick"; the Bishop of London, "on account of a bleeding which in this hot season might be in danger of returning upon His Lordship if he did not refrain from preaching". The Bishops of Gloucester and Lincoln also declined, though each was assured "his own time shall be conformed to and a coach provided, if His Lordship pleases, that will carry him out in the morning and return him in the evening of the Sunday he shall choose". Eventually the sermon was postponed, Newman fearing "the presence of the Court will be fatal to the charitable design at Hampton by drawing away the company that it is wished might be at the church". He had already sent the Vicar of Richmond "sheet accounts" of the school to gain "the encouragement that would be given by the royal family in a place so near the Court".[1]

Since the Society had no funds for schools and made no attempt to set up a central fund, Newman's experience of the ways of raising money for a school—subscriptions, patronage, sermons, and the like—was useful in advising trustees. When he heard of successful schemes he noted them for their benefit, from the Somerset parson who "applied the offerings at the Sacrament and the perquisite of a Burial Cloath", to the Subscribing Member

[1] HN to Mr Chamberlayne, 23 April 1713, 26 April 1714, 9 and 12 July 1718, *Society's Letters*, and 23 June 1718, *Private Letters*; to Mr Nicholson, Hampton, 20 June 1718; to Rev. Mr Boroughs, Hampton, 12 July 1718, *Society's Letters*; to Rev. Mr Gunn, Whitchurch, 24 June 1718; to Rev. Mr Harris, Richmond, 6 June 1718, *Private Letters*.

who "being at Tunbridge, used his good offices for having a charity sermon preached there by Dr Lupton and prevailed with my Lord Perceval and Lord Castlemain to hold the basins . . . which had so good success that about £80 was collected at the church doors and upon the walks".[1] Besides this, the most the Society did was to transmit earmarked gifts for particular schools and sometimes help hard hit schools by, as Newman told a correspondent in 1711,

> allowing persons appointed for that purpose to give from 40*s*. to £5 towards setting up a school in parishes where poor children were very numerous and by such a subscription from an unknown hand, the parishioners have been allured to subscribe from £30 to £50 per annum and sometimes more. At other times, upon the declining of a school within the cities of London and Westminster, to animate the neighbourhood to support their subscriptions, the Society have been at the expense of fitting up the school with tables, benches, Bibles, Prayer Books, catechisms and everything necessary to accommodate the children, but these articles do not occur so often as they did some years ago, because the example of the neighbouring parishes is now grown a sufficient incitement to this kind of charity, and where poverty is their excuse, they are assisted by collecting in the wealthy parishes of the City, as most of those within the walls, having no poor children of their own, adopt some school in the suburbs to bestow their charity upon.[2]

If a school was failing, the Society tried to save it. Hearing that Brentford Charity School was "in a very declining condition and would in all likelihood drop if a speedy care were not taken to prevent it", because "Mr Justice Clitheroe has been a generous benefactor . . . but that upon some disgust at the management of it, he had withdrawn his charity", Newman asked several influential gentlemen to persuade him to renew it.[3]

The charity sermon was the popular way of raising money. Newman helped trustees to arrange these and urged "parishes in London that have no poor children" to have one for "such parishes in the suburbs as have most need of it to support charity schools".[4] In 1708 sixty charity schools in London and twenty-one churches had charity sermons, monthly, quarterly, or annually; [5] and from 1704 one was held annually for all schools in London and Westminster, "when all the boys and girls maintained at the schools in

[1] HN to Rev. Mr Bowyer, Martock, Som, 9 Nov. 1734; to Mr Jennings, Bristol, 28 Aug. 1722, *Society's Letters*.

[2] HN to Mr Dundas, 3 April 1711, *Society's Letters*.

[3] HN to Mr Gee, 2 March 1715; to Mr Jennings, 21 March and 4 May 1715; to Mr Parnell, 3 June 1715, *Society's Letters*.

[4] HN to Mr Capel Berrow, Totteridge, Herts, 16 Aug. 1709, *Letters to Correspondents*.

[5] E. Hatton, *A New View of London*, II, 580.

their habits walked two and two with their masters and mistresses, some from Westminster and some through London, with many parish ministers going before them".[1] It was held at St Sepulchre's Church each year on Thursday in Whitsun Week and organized by a Society of Patrons of the Anniversary of Charity Schools established by Robert Nelson and others, though the S.P.C.K. paid the cost—"The charge of erecting seats for the children in London, etc. at their Anniversary Meeting, etc. is defrayed by the Society because no parish or private persons can be chargeable with it, neither are the Society known to be at the expense, but it is done in the name of a member and nobody disapproves of a decency that costs them nothing." [2] Newman, therefore, had little to do with the arrangements, but in 1722 he had to insist that the Society must have "no material objections to the preachers named by the Trustees"; [3] and as the schools increased, he twice tried, in 1712 and 1715, to have it held in St Paul's Cathedral, but both times Wren held "the accommodations for the children and spectators" would damage the interior, so it was not transferred there until 1782.[4] After each occasion, he had to obtain, not without difficulty, a copy of the anniversary sermon from the preacher for printing in the S.P.C.K.'s annual account of its proceedings. The worst offender was Dr John Thomas, favourite Chaplain of George II through having learnt German when previously Chaplain to the English Factory at Hamburg. He preached the anniversary sermon in 1740 before going to Hanover with the King, who told him: "The next time I come to Hanover, you shall come over with me, and then if a prebend or deanery should happen to fall, you will have a good chance of succeeding to it." There, as Newman sardonically told a friend, "the pleasures and amusements of a Court are too many to allow any leisure for copying work", and not until Dr Thomas duly became Dean of Peterborough the next year did he supply his sermon and permit publication of the Society's proceedings.[5]

Newman sought support every year for the anniversary meeting.

[1] J. Strype (ed.), *Stow's Survey of London*, V, 43.

[2] HN to Mr Dundas, 3 April 1711, *Society's Letters*.

[3] HN to Abp of Canterbury, 7 April 1722, *Society's Letters*; *S.P.C.K. Minutes*, 5 April 1722.

[4] *S.P.C.K. Minutes*, 3 April 1722; HN to Mr Hales, 23 May 1712; to Dean of St Paul's, 8 Dec. 1715, *Society's Letters*; to Dean and Chapter of St Paul's, *Miscellaneous Letters*.

[5] HN to Sir Erasmus Philipps, Rome, 8 May 1740; to Rev. Dr Thomas, Hanover, 30 May 1740; to Dean Copping, 31 July 1740; to Francis Freeman, 20 Feb. 1741, *Miscellaneous Letters*.

Steele wrote in 1712 two essays in *The Spectator* on St Bride's Charity School. Soon afterwards it ceased publication for eighteen months. When it reappeared, Newman told him: "When you are at leisure to bestow a letter on the charity schools, you will very much oblige the well wishers to them. I am sure you would have been pleased to have been at St Sepulchre's yesterday where you would have seen above four thousand children in their best clothes at their devotions while a prelate read prayers and another prelate preached."[1] Steele was too immersed in politics to write on the anniversary meeting or anything else, but Newman continued to solicit influential or wealthy friends. In 1724 he told Lord Perceval: "The Bishop of Man preaches to-morrow at the Anniversary Meeting of the Charity Schools at St Sepulchre's, where about five thousand children are to be assembled, one of the most affecting sights of the kind that I believe is to be seen in the Christian world. To see and hear with what readiness all the children join in the several parts of divine service, wherein they seem to be as exact and uniform as the King's Guards are at their exercise."[2] He similarly invited the Countess of Hertford in 1731 to attend, adding, "I am sure Lord Beauchamp and Lady Betty will thank your Ladyship for the pleasure of accompanying you to such a sight as the nation and perhaps all Europe cannot parallel."[3]

As the charity school movement grew, endowments were left by men and women who had been subscribers in their lifetime, but these often went astray. A form of bequest drawn up by the Society "so as to prevent any scruple about paying it" was not always used. Urgent letters came from trustees unable to secure legacies left to their schools and complaining that benefactions were "swallowed up without attaining the end proposed". Newman wanted "a Bill to be brought into Parliament for the recovery of small gifts and legacies to pious and charitable uses at less expense than in the common way of suing under a commission for charitable uses under the Great Seal". While he was Secretary several such Bills were introduced into Parliament, but none became law. In default of this, Newman had another suggestion. As early as 1711 he wrote: "The concealed or misapplied legacies have induced me to believe that many more might be detected if the Archbishop of Canter-

[1] *The Spectator*, No. 294, 6 Feb., and No. 380, 16 May 1712; HN to Mr Steele, 21 May 1714, *Society's Letters*.

[2] HN to Ld Perceval, Pall Mall, 27 May 1724, *Society's Letters*.

[3] HN to Lady Hertford, 28 April 1731, *Society's Letters*.

bury would authorize some person to inspect the register of wills in Doctor's Commons. If only one will in 50 would yield any advantage, it would abundantly answer the pains of our inquisition. They are mostly gifts in reversion that are subject to this fate."[1] This was not done either, but Newman got the Society to allow him to pay half a guinea as a "premium to the examining clerks at the Prerogative Office for intelligence of legacies to the said Society". Soon the Society for Reformation of Manners asked him to do the same for it, and he recovered several legacies for both societies.[2]

The S.P.C.K. also published books and pamphlets suitable for the trustees of schools—model regulations for teachers, rules for pupils, instructions for parents, and forms of prayer—which were sent them on request. Thus the beautiful and philanthropic Lady Betty Hastings received in 1737 from Newman "books proper for Selby School", including "rules for governing charity schools" and "copies of the prayers used in them".[3] The Society's books emphasized the all-important influence of the teachers in the schools, and Newman often reminded trustees of the need for care in their appointments. He had his own standards:

The success of either boys or girls schools depends very much on the choice of a good master or mistress, who are the Pole Stars of those little seminaries. And among all the qualifications required in the choice of those persons, much knowledge does not seem to be so necessary as to be good Christians of a meek and humble behaviour. These latter qualities have made some of our masters and mistresses, who were very unpromising in other respects, outshine in the discipline of their schools those who valued themselves much upon their parts and skill in writing and arithmetick, not but that it is most desirable to have all good qualities to meet in the persons devoted to this service. But that being a thing rarely to be found, the discretion and prudence of a person with a tolerable degree of knowledge seem to be preferable to the skill of reading and writing well without much discretion.[4]

For this reason, Newman was anxious that when the Society acted as a sort of appointments bureau, whether on behalf of trustees or teachers, it should take care and not just draw up a register of applicants without inquiry. "Mr Bickerton, a clergyman, was this day with us to recommend William Harrison of

[1] M. G. Jones, op. cit., 54.
[2] HN to Mr Welham, Prerogative Office, 23 Feb. and 21 April 1714, *Society's Letters*; to Mr Jos. Acres, Newbury, Berks, 21 Sept. 1736; to Mr Meyrick, Prerogative Office, 23 Jan. 1738; to Archdeacon Deane, 15 Oct. 1741, *Miscellaneous Letters*.
[3] HN to Lady Eliz. Hastings, Ledstone, Ferrybridge, Yorks, 12 March 1737, *Miscellaneous Letters*.
[4] HN to Sir Geo. Wheeler, Durham, 1 March 1715, *Society's Letters*.

Droitwich for your school", he told a Gloucestershire trustee. "We told him the Society would not recommend any person who they had not personal knowledge of and good testimonials as to his past life, but that if he thought it would be worth while to come to Town to be discussed with about his qualifications, the Society might be able in a little time to have it in their power to recommend him if he answered the character given him." [1] He received reports about teachers from agents appointed by the Society to inspect charity schools and was ready to recommend the pupils of outstanding teachers to be teachers themselves. One such master was Henry Dixon, whom Newman persuaded to go in 1711 to the Bluecoat School at Bath, founded by Robert Nelson and Edward Jennings, and who was so successful that Newman said of him: "He hath done so much good in a short time as many men would be glad to be able to say they have done in the whole of their lives." [2] Another master, "Mr Sims of Cripplegate", had so many pupils teaching in London schools that Newman affectionately called him "one of the Fathers of the Charity Schoolmasters in London".[3]

The London schools had no difficulty in finding teachers and rarely asked Newman's help. He told a Devonshire schoolmaster, anxious to come to London, that it was no more than "once in three or four years, so many candidates appear to fill up every vacancy".[4] The London salaries largely explained this. "The salary here", he told a country correspondent, "is £30 per annum [for a master] and for a mistress £20 or £25 per annum, with coals and sometimes house rent free." [5] This compared favourably with grammar-school salaries. At two prominent free schools each with a staff of three—Birmingham Grammar School and Manchester Grammar School—the annual salaries at this time were respectively £68 15*s*., £34 6*s*. 8*d*., £20 and £60, £28, £12; while the average stipend of curates was between £30 and £40 a year.[6] Country trustees, however, could not pay such salaries. Newman offered the Devonshire schoolmaster a school in Ealing at "£20

[1] HN to Rev. Mr Gregory, Wotton-under-Edge, Glos, 11 Feb. 1721, *Society's Letters*.

[2] HN to Robt Nelson, 2 and 16 June 1711; to Mr Leakon, Bath, 22 May 1712, *Society's Letters*.

[3] HN to Mr Hughes, Kilmesdon, Som, 18 July 1718, *Society's Letters*.

[4] HN to Mr Karfoot, Tiverton, Devon, 26 Dec. 1741, *Miscellaneous Letters*.

[5] HN to Mr Chancellor Lloyd, 26 May 1713, *Society's Letters*.

[6] G. Griffith, *Free Schools of Birmingham*, 1861, 7–8; W. R. Whatton, *History of Manchester School*, 1834, 105; N. Sykes, *Church and State in the Eighteenth Century*, 206, 212.

a year for teaching all the poor children of the town", which together with a house and one cauldron of coal a year from the trustees was "all the encouragement they could afford". This, being "a fine healthy situation, about seven or eight miles from London, and two or three from the Thames", might attract a country master, but not a London one. Country trustees wanted teachers with "experience in London methods", trained by Sims or other good men, but Newman could rarely oblige them. "It were to be wished you might have had a master that had been practised for some time in a school here," he told one of them, "but those that are eminent meet with so good encouragement from their patrons that there is no aiming at it without taking some time to treat with the trustees of such a school and bidding above the usual allowance to masters." [1] It was the same all the time he was Secretary. "Masters don't care to go into the country, but upon consideration of having so much as they have here", he explained in 1713; and again in 1739, "A man in London capable of such a charge and worthy of recommendation for sobriety and other qualities will have some dependencies here, which he either can't or won't quit without wages equal to what is generally given in London and more in proportion if he carries a wife and family with him." [2]

As a result country trustees sometimes sought a way of acquainting their own teachers with "London methods". Very early in its existence the Society was asked "to consider of some methods of training up masters for charity schools in the country who are very much wanted there".[3] In grammar schools a man gained experience as an usher, but when Lady Betty Hastings wanted a young master in one of her charity schools to serve this way in a London school to fit him for a larger school, Newman had to reply: "Our charity schools here never keep ushers because they can't afford it, but the masters make some of the elder boys assist them in teaching the lesser in large schools, which answers the end of ushers, for which they have no consideration other than being preferred to service the first opportunity by the favour of the trustees. This being the case, I am sorry it is not in my power to serve the young man recommended by your Ladyship. If he continues in the school where he is, he will still be improving himself till

[1] HN to Mr Haynes, Bristol, 16 March 1714, *Society's Letters*.
[2] HN to Mr Chancellor Lloyd, 26 May 1713, *Society's Letters*; to Rev. Dr Wilson, Tunbridge Wells, 4 Sept. 1739, *Miscellaneous Letters*.
[3] *S.P.C.K. Minutes*, 7 and 14 Oct. 1703.

Providence shall open a door for his preferment."[1] Newman helped some trustees by arranging with suitable London schoolmasters to give a short training to their candidates or existing teachers. He advised one country patron, unable to find a master for his school, to "choose a discreet man out of his town or neighbourhood on such terms as he can agree upon and send him to London to be instructed, where . . . one of the masters has promised me in fourteen days to qualify him for such a trust provided he writes and understands keeping common accounts"; and another, dissatisfied with his schoolmaster, to send him "if he can be spared in your Easter holidays, to St Giles' School to learn of Mr Marriott".[2]

The connection of Newman and the S.P.C.K. with the schools was not, however, confined to such day-to-day matters as finance or teachers. The movement was unfortunately caught up in party politics, and the Society could not stand aside. If the appointment of Newman as Secretary marked the failure of the Tories to control the Society, it did not stop their attack on the charity schools. It was the time when sympathizers on the governing bodies of the great endowed schools brought them into the political arena by appointing headmasters with High Church and Tory views in such important schools as Eton, Westminster, Winchester, and St Paul's.[3] The charity schools suffered similarly. The Society's conception of religious education in these schools was expressed by an early charity preacher: "I don't mean that I would have them taught the niceties of speculation or controversy, which are so much brought into religion, for that would not do them service; but to acquaint them as much as possible with the Christian life."[4] Often the teaching in parish schools was such that Dissenters sent their children to them and subscribed to them, sometimes more liberally than Churchpeople.[5] As a result of the Tory offensive, it was alleged that disaffected persons "endeavoured to get the management of the charity schools into their hands and to make them instrumental in nourishing and spreading an aversion to the Protestant succession", and "preachers distinguished for their discretion, temper and moderation in the early days of the move-

[1] HN to Lady Eliz. Hastings, Ledstone, Yorks, 15 June 1734, *Society's Letters*.

[2] HN to Mr Chancellor Lloyd, 26 May 1713; to Mr Pacey, Boston, Lincs, 31 March 1726, *Society's Letters*.

[3] H. C. Maxwell Lyte, *Eton College*, 288–9; J. Sargeaunt, *Annals of Westminster School*, 109; A. K. Leach, *History of Winchester College*, 370–1; J. F. Kirby, *Annals of Winchester College*, 386; M. F. G. McDonnell, *History of St Paul's School*, 297.

[4] R. Willis, *Charity Sermon*, 1704, 6.

[5] M. G. Jones, op. cit., 111.

ment were replaced by men who very indiscreetly fell a-railing at the Dissenters and did very unreasonably publish how much the charity would tend to put an end to their schism".[1] Often, it was asserted, "under the disguise of charity schools, children are brought up in disaffection to the government, malice against Protestant Dissenters, and the way prepared for singing dirges and requiems for the dead".[2] When the Dissenters, as Isaac Watts later explained, "found by sufficient experience, that the children were brought up in too many of these schools in principles of disaffection to the present government, in a bigoted zeal for the word church, and with a violent enmity, and malicious spirit of persecution, against all whom they were taught to call presbyterians, though from many of their hands they received their bread and clothing. It was time then, for the dissenters to withdraw that charity which was so abused."[3]

The local independence of the schools made it difficult for the S.P.C.K. to deal with this situation. Though Newman tried "to persuade those violent opposers of Whiggish charity to reason",[4] both Secretary and Society realized that political events would finally decide the fate of the schools. Their policy was to count upon the Hanoverian accession and secure future official goodwill. One of Dr Bray's friends, Robert Hales, was at the Court of Hanover, and Newman sent him long letters about the Society and the schools, while in 1713 he wrote to the Electress Sophia about "the care that is taken to preserve the Protestant Religion in these Kingdoms by providing a means of instruction for the poor who at present make too considerable part of the nation to be neglected", and the success of "the method of charity schools", which though only

> about fifteen or sixteen years standing, it has pleased God so wonderfully to prosper the design that above a thousand schools have been erected in that time at which above twenty thousand poor children are now instructed and about ten thousand more have been put out apprentices. This has laid such a foundation for securing the Protestant Religion and of consequence the succession of your illustrious family to the throne of these Kingdoms as will, I hope, for ever frustrate all attempts to introduce Popery or overthrow the settlement on which the future happiness of this nation so much depends.

[1] *Wake MSS.*, Arch. W. Epist. 15, Universities, Charities and Religious Societies, 1715–18. Memorial Representing the Origin and Design of the Charity Schools, the First Method of Supporting them, etc.

[2] Ambrose Barnes, *Life*, Surtees Soc., 8.

[3] Isaac Watts, *An Essay on Charity Schools*, 1728.

[4] HN to Mr Chancellor Lloyd, 26 May 1713, *Society's Letters*.

Having received a favourable reply from her, the Society sent her early the next year "a Collection of the Charity Sermons preached at the Anniversary Meetings of the Charity Schools . . . bound up in blue Turkey leather."[1]

Later in the year, when events had taken the turn hoped for, a display of charity children was arranged for George I's entry into the City. This had been done in the previous year on the Thanksgiving Day for the Peace of Utrecht, "when 3,925 charity children, boys and girls, new clothed, with masters and mistresses" were seated on an eight-tiered gallery in the Strand "in full view of both Houses of Parliament in their procession to St Paul's upon that occasion". The Society gave "sixpence for each child" towards the expenses of the display, and the Society's messenger distributed the *Account of the Charity Schools* "on the Thanksgiving Day to every coach and chariot as they went to St Paul's Cathedral".[2] After George I's entry into the City, Robert Nelson, the High Churchman and former Jacobite, reported to the Society how "about 4,000 children of the charity schools appeared on a machine containing six ranges of seats, 600 feet long from east to west, on the north side of St Paul's Cathedral, erected at the charge of the trustees of the several charity schools, and that as the King passed by and during most of the procession, the children sang the first six verses of the 21st Psalm, according to Sir John Denham's version". Newman, in his account to Mr Hales, said: "The charity children made a goodly appearance in St Paul's Churchyard, which the King and Prince were extreamly pleased with, so that His Highness said he never saw anything so fine, and that he only wished he had his own children with him to see them at the same time."[3]

These two public displays did not serve to absolve the Society and the schools from suspicion. Their past reputation was strengthened by the anxieties of the rising of 1715. *The Flying Post* in the spring of 1715 attacked the Society, whose protest brought only partial retraction. "The Society", Newman told the Bishop of Bangor, "thought it more for the interest of the design that no further public notice should be taken, but that strict rules should

[1] HN to Princess Sophia, 3 Aug. 1713; to Mr Hales, Hanover, 23 Feb. 1714, *Society's Letters*; *S.P.C.K. Minutes*, 28 Jan. 1714.

[2] Ibid., 16 April and 7 July 1713; HN to Mr King, Exeter, 27 June 1713, *Society's Letters*.

[3] Ibid., 23 Sept. 1714; HN to Mr Hales, Hanover, 24 Sept. 1714, *Society's Letters*.

be made to prevent the appearance of misbehaviour in the children for the future." But this really concerned the trustees, not the Society. The Jacobites had nicknamed it "the Presbyterian Club", so little did it favour them, and "it cannot be expected that they should answer for the indiscretions of some charity schoolmasters, whom they have had no hand in appointing any nor power to displace, but . . . the Society have never been wanting when notice has been given to them of such delinquents to procure an humble application to some of my Lords the Bishops or other persons vested with authority to admonish them for it".[1]

Schoolmasters being seldom without detractors, complaints enough reached the Society. Newman compiled a secret "list for the satisfaction of such of our Society as should desire to see it", in which he marked those reported to be "infected by the madness that prevailed the latter end of the late reign and those of a contrary disposition"; [2] but when complaints were investigated, few were substantiated. The Master of St Anne's Charity School, accused of being a Non-juror, replied "he ever was and is now ready to take the oaths whenever they shall be tendered to him".[3] When this was done, a few refused, like Mrs Mary Harbin, Mistress of St Martin-in-the-Fields Charity School for girls, who was dismissed by the trustees in 1716 for refusing to take the oaths and pray for George I.[4] Later that year it was alleged to the Society "that the Master of the Charity School in Addle Lane had drunk the Pretender's health under several fictitious names and at other times had used the most scandalous speech against the King and his Government". The Society found the accusation "forged, false, scandalous, and malicious" and voted "that the schoolmasters in general were very well affected to King George and his Government".[5]

This did not satisfy everyone. The Whigs knew the slight power the Society had over the schools and suspected that many trustees had High Church sympathies, to them synonymous with Jacobitism, and sheltered disloyal teachers. The government decided to reform the schools at the same time as the select or close vestries of the metropolis, long regarded as Tory strongholds. The Close

[1] *The Flying Post*, 26 and 30 April 1715; HN to Bp of Bangor, 19 May 1715, *Society's Letters*.
[2] HN to Mr Chamberlayne, 22 Dec. 1714, *Society's Letters*.
[3] *S.P.C.K. Minutes*, 14 June 1716.
[4] John McMaster, *St Martin-in-the-Fields*, 268–9.
[5] *S.P.C.K. Minutes*, 5 July 1716; *S.P.C.K. Circular Letter*, 1716.

Vestries Bill of 1716, besides proposing to transform the vestries, intended to give the power of appointing teachers and selecting pupils in the parish charity schools to an elected body. Attempts by Newman to persuade members to vote against it could not prevent it passing the Commons; but it was heavily defeated in the Lords after a speech against it by Archbishop Wake, who would not support Whig policy to the extent of endangering the Church. Having saved the schools, he tried to persuade them to reform themselves. He urged the trustees of the London charity schools to dismiss "all such masters and mistresses as instil any factious or seditious principles into their children". The trustees met and "proceeded to censure some masters after they had acquitted all the masters in general at the beginning of their meeting". Wake also asked the S.P.C.K. to confine its membership to those well-affected to the King and Government and its assistance to schools where the teachers' loyalty was beyond doubt.[1]

The Society could not ignore the situation, even if the schools had escaped official ill will. Suspicion might still harm them, especially financially. As Newman put it: "Occasion may be thereby given to those who may be too ready to lay hold of such handles to withdraw their charity from these schools." [2] The Society accepted both of Wake's requests and also decided "to promote that loyal spirit among those concerned in the charity schools".[3] It drew up "Orders to be read and Given to the Parents on the Admittance of the Children into Charity Schools. To be set up in their Houses", and "Orders to be Observed by the Masters and Mistresses in the Government of the Charity Schools". The former ordered parents not to allow their children to take part in Jacobite demonstrations, "much less to show any the least disaffection to our most gracious Sovereign King George and the Royal Family"; the latter that teachers should see their pupils' "minds be not tinctured with any new and singular notions, either in religion or government; and that they be restrained diligently from speculations of all kind and confined to such doctrines and principles as more immediately concern faith and a good life". The schools received 18,500 copies of these papers. Newman also

[1] M. G. Jones, op. cit., 115–17; Abp of Canterbury to Trustees of London Charity Schools, 6 June 1716; to HN, 21 Aug. 1716, *Abs. of Correspondence*; *S.P.C.K. Minutes*, 10 May 1716.

[2] HN to Mr Jennings, Great Gramden, Herts, 12 June 1715, *Society's Letters*.

[3] *S.P.C.K. Minutes*, 30 Aug. and 6 Sept. 1716; HN to Abp of Canterbury, 8 Sept. 1716, *Wake MSS.*, Arch. W. Epist. 15.

sent a copy of each to Archbishop Wake and enclosed a list of London schools where masters had proved their loyalty by whipping boys for such crimes on 29 May as "being at a bonfire", "wearing bows in their caps" or "crying, 'High Church and Ormond for ever!' "[1]

For a time the Society's leaflets and the schoolmasters' rods allayed public opinion, but in 1718 some Low Churchmen presented a Memorial to Archbishop Wake asking that control of the schools should be transferred to a body corporate, appointed by the Crown and under the presidency of the Archbishop.[2] Wake was again opposed to any intrusion upon the rights of the Church and merely suggested to the Society that all teachers should not only take the oaths to the government, but also "sign a solemn declaration acknowledging His Majesty King George to be the only lawful and rightful King of these Realms". Newman promised to lay his letter before the Society at its next meeting, "being well assured that they will most readily conform themselves to everything in their power to render the charity school masters and mistresses throughout the Kingdom as eminent for their loyalty to King George as some of them have been remarkable for their folly and disaffection"; and at its meeting the Society resolved "to recommend what your Grace proposes" to the trustees "in your Grace's name, lest the name of the Society might give an umbrage that might hinder the effect of your Grace's advice".[3]

Unfortunately the Jacobite Plot of 1722 fostered fresh rumours about the schools. In the summer of 1723 "Cato" in an article in the *British Journal* questioned the loyalty of this "newfangled charity" where children were "bred up traitors before they know what treason signifies" and teachers "staunch Jacobites or furious High Churchmen". An unsigned letter in the *London Journal* defended the schools from "Cato's" attacks, and a letter of thanks from Newman to Wake for his approbation of it indicates that he was its author. In it, Newman defended the general character of the schools, since "Care is taken to appoint such Masters and Mistresses to these schools as are eminent for their Humility and Modesty, rather than abounding in Knowledge more than is necessary to teach the Children to be good Christians and good

[1] HN to Abp of Canterbury, 2 Oct. 1716, *Wake MSS.*, Arch. W. Epist. 15.

[2] *Wake MSS.*, Arch. W. Epist. 15. Memorial Representing the Origin and Design of the Charity Schools, etc.

[3] Abp of Canterbury to HN, 2 June 1718; HN to Abp of Canterbury, 2 and 13 June, *Wake MSS.*, Arch. W. Epist. 15; *S.P.C.K. Minutes*, 12 June 1718.

Servants". He challenged "Cato" to make good his accusations of disloyalty: "If the Publisher of this Invective would discover any Instance of a Master or Mistress disaffected to the Government, or teaching the Children under their care to be so, he would deserve the Thanks of the Publick for such Service." And he concluded by asking him to show himself capable of something better than mere criticism: "He is earnestly desired, instead of decrying by hard Names and unchristian Raillery what he does not offer to mend, to propose any Scheme by which the Charity Schools may be conducted with any more Profit to the Publick than now they are."[1]

"Cato's" attacks, however, attracted the notice of Edmund Gibson, Bishop of London, who was anxious to clear his diocese of suspicion of Jacobitism. He was himself an irreproachable Whig and ecclesiastical adviser to Walpole, but he wished to be absolved of any accusation of condoning disaffection to the government. Accordingly the Society was "informed that the Bishop of London was very much affected with the insinuations therein made to reproach the design of charity schools". Newman was instructed to wait on him "to receive his Lordship's wishes therein". He reported "that his Lordship said that he did not expect such a compliment from the Society and that at present he only desired to be furnished with a list of the masters and mistresses of the charity schools in his diocese or in the Bills of Mortality". After nearly three weeks, Newman sent him a revision of the list he had made in the previous scare. He apologized for the delay: "The privacy I am obliged to use in collecting names and characters has taken up more time than I expected, occasioned by the many alterations since seven years", but assured him that teachers formerly suspected of Jacobitism "are very much altered in their behaviour to what they were, occasioned partly by the great ferment in 1716 when some were turned out and partly by the check which the subscribers who are well affected to the government have upon them". Gibson did nothing for over a year. Then he summoned "all the Masters and Mistresses within the Bills of Mortality which were in his diocese, to the Chapter House of St Paul's", and delivered a charge to them in which he warned them they must inculcate the spirit of loyalty in their schools and that he would "make enquiry from time to time into the conduct and

[1] *British Journal*, 19 June 1723; *London Journal*, 20 July 1723; HN to Abp of Canterbury, 21 Aug. 1723, *Society's Letters*.

behaviour of the several masters and mistresses, so that if he should find any who neglected or avoided the giving such easy proofs of their loyalty . . . he must conclude them to be persons disaffected and very unfit to be entrusted with the education of children in a Protestant country". The Society thanked him for these directions and obtained leave to print them and send a copy to all their members and all the schools in the country.[1]

After this the agitation died down. The Society did not want the powers of the trustees changed, but encouraged them to persist in its first conception of general moral and religious education and to regain the friendship of the Dissenters. In 1717, upon learning that the Master of Monmouth Charity School was a Dissenter, "the Society made no attempt to get the choice of the master reversed, but rather chose means to reclaim the person on whom the choice fell by presenting him with a packet of books proper for his instruction as a Christian and a charity schoolmaster, and they hope their endeavours will have some good effect".[2] Newman congratulated schools which put this policy into effect, such as Tiverton Charity School, where the trustees were able to "excite some of the Dissenters, not only to be subscribers to the school, but also to entrust their children under your instruction".[3]

Doubts about the schools' politics made the Society the more anxious that their moral purpose should be above reproach. In 1712, when the political struggle was mounting, John Honeycott, Master of Clerkenwell Charity School, increased its worries. Like modern educationalists, he believed in school drama and with his pupils "publicly acted the play called *Timon of Athens* and by tickets signed by himself had invited several people to it", but he met the fate of pioneers. The Society agreed "that the acting of the said play by the master and children of the Charity School at Clerkenwell is a great reproach to the design of charity schools and to bear testimony against it as scandalous and of pernicious consequence to the charity schools in general". Henry Compton, Bishop of London, wrote to Newman, "to signify his resentment of the great offence thereby given" and "intimated his intention to reform that abuse". Newman's reply showed him as scandalized

[1] *S.P.C.K. Minutes*, 18 and 25 June, 2 July 1723, 17 Nov. and 3 Dec. 1724; HN to Bp of London, 20 July 1723, *Society's Letters*; *The Daily Courant*, 16 Nov. 1724; N. Sykes, *Edmund Gibson*, 202–6.

[2] HN to Rowland Cotton, Etwal, Derby, 2 July 1717, *Society's Letters*.

[3] HN to Mr Wilson, Tiverton, Devon, 6 Aug. 1730, *Society's Letters*.

by the play-acting as anyone: "The Master, being a headstrong, conceited man, had acquired such an influence over the Trustees of the School . . . that they, instead of hindering him, seemed rather to countenance him", so that "all that wish well to the design of charity schools would be glad to see some signal token of your Lordship's displeasure upon the Master, if not upon the parish", for their purpose was to "train up children to be ornaments of the Church" and not "to be comedians or, in other words, to officiate in the devil's chapel". The next Sunday Sir William Dawes, then Bishop of Chester and later Archbishop of York, was to preach a charity sermon at the Church of St Magnus the Martyr for the school, but insisted that the collection went to another school. The Society in alarm asked Mr Jennings and Mr Nelson "to wait on the Bishop of London to request him to withdraw Mr Honeycott's license", whereupon the trustees of the school asked for a meeting with the Society's representatives, which "severely reprimanded Mr Honeycott, who made his humble submission accordingly". Newman told the trustees he had acquainted the Bishop "with what has been done in the affair" and hoped "the course you have taken with Mr Honeycott may prevent him being guilty of the like misbehaviour in the future".[1] That this incident was taken so seriously at a time of political excitement shows the harsh side of eighteenth-century philanthropy, dominated by fear of crime, starvation, and vagrancy. The anxiety of the promoters of the schools to preserve children from the moral dangers of the London streets and the iniquities of the Blackguard stimulated a dread of the theatre which took serious alarm even at Mr Honeycott's school play.

Despite the Society's care, criticism of charity school education mounted. In the same year as "Cato's" attack in *The British Journal* a more serious blow was struck by Bernard Mandeville, whose poem *The Fable of the Bees, or Private Vices Public Benefits*, a widely controverted insistence on the essential vileness of human nature, appeared in a second edition bound up with an essay by him *On Charity and Charity Schools*. Mandeville was also an opponent of the High Church party, but his essay urged the social and economic rather than the political threat of the schools. Newman earnestly defended the schools against the "aspersions cast on them

[1] *S.P.C.K. Minutes*, 7 and 14 Feb. 1712; HN to Bp of London, 7 and 14 Feb. 1712, *Society's Letters*; to Trustees of Clerkenwell Charity School, 9 April 1712, *Letters to Correspondents*; C. F. Secretan, op. cit., 129–31.

by the author of the *Fable of the Bees*", who was "an author without any modesty" to write "so vile a book". Some of Mandeville's sweeping charges, indeed, were unfair. He accused trustees of improperly apprenticing children when they left school, because they "don't deliberate so much what is best but what tradesman they can get that will take the boys with such a sum", so that children "are bound, at least most commonly, either to sots and neglectful masters, or else such as are very needy and don't care what becomes of their apprentices, after they have received the money".[1]

Newman denied this accusation: "It is a general rule through London and Westminster among the trustees for those schools to bind out a poor charity child to a kennel raker and give money with him rather than let him go a footman to a man of quality for nothing, except that man of quality or gentleman that takes him will give security to bind him out to some trade or handicraft after three or four years' service as an errand boy, and even this they decline doing except they are well satisfied in the character of the master as well as the security given."[2] Certainly tradespeople asked Newman to vouch for them in applying to trustees for apprentices. For Mrs Cooper, a "clear starcher", desiring "a charity girl for an apprentice", he wrote she had "washed my linen for four or five years past to great satisfaction, and during that time I have always heard a good character of her, and her mother assures me that she constantly goes to church every Lord's Day and will set any servant she has a good example in that as well as other respects" and would "teach her to understand and do the business by which she gets a good livelihood"; and he told the Treasurer of the Greycoat School, Westminster, of an applicant who wanted a boy "to learn him his trade of a tailor", that he and his wife were "persons religiously disposed and such as will be very careful of any child committed to their care".[3] Instances such as these show that many trustees, unlike the parish officers who apprenticed pauper children, took care to bind their children to employers of good character and into trades that would enable them to earn their livelihood later on.

Another of Mandeville's criticisms was that the schools deprived the country of the labour of the poor, especially in agriculture.

[1] B. Mandeville, *Essay on Charity and Charity Schools*, *passim*.
[2] HN to Rev. Dr Bundy, 29 March 1733, *Society's Letters*.
[3] HN to Mr Thos. Greene, Westminster, 1 Oct. 1720; to Mr Wisdom, Westminster, 22 Sept. 1721, *Society's Letters*.

"The more a shepherd and a ploughman know of the world, the less fitted he'll be to go through the fatigue and hardship of it with cheerfulness and equanimity", he wrote. "To divert children from useful labour until they are 14 or 15 years old is a wrong way to qualify them for it when they are grown up." [1] This was no new complaint. In 1712 correspondents asked the Society to consider the inconvenience caused "by putting of the children of charity schools apprentices to mechanick trades rather than to husbandry in the country where they are most wanted", which resolved to recommend trustees to "put out the children to services rather than to apprentices". Newman, reporting the discussion at the meeting to a correspondent, said: "Some members were of opinion that next to inculcating Christianity itself, a greater service could not be done to the nation and to the design of charity schools in general than to propagate a true judgement of the importance of agriculture in the nation." [2] Since "the main industry of the country during the first six decades of the eighteenth century was still agriculture", with land ownership bringing both political power and economic rewards, while prevailing mercantilist theories stressed ample food production at home to maintain a favourable balance of trade, the schools were criticized for imperilling agriculture by encouraging poor children to seek other employment.[3] This criticism was strongest in London, which, despite high death rates, grew through constant immigration from the country. As Arthur Young later noted, "young men and women in the country villages fix their eyes on London as the last stage of their hope".[4] Not all who came were able to fulfil their hopes or avoid joining the paupers and vagrants of the poorer quarters of the City, so that opinion in the metropolis was sensitive to any drift from agriculture and ready to accuse the charity schools of responsibility for it.

Newman claimed he could refute such suggestions: "I can assure from several letters I have by me from the north and west parts of England that it is an unjust calumny upon the charity schools in those countries where agriculture is the business of the country that the children of those schools forsake their country, and I believe it may be safely affirmed that of the thousands of vagabonds

[1] B. Mandeville, op. cit., *passim*.
[2] *S.P.C.K. Minutes*, 20 March and 31 July 1712; HN to Rev. Mr Francis Fox, Potterne, Wilts, 2 Aug. 1712, *Society's Letters*.
[3] Basil Williams, *The Whig Supremacy, 1714–1760*, 101–5.
[4] Arthur Young, *Farmer's Letters*, 1771 ed., 353.

in London streets come out of the country, there is not one of them that ever belonged to a charity school, of which my curiosity has led me sometimes to make the enquiry." [1] Some London trustees tried to place their children in agriculture, including those of St Sepulchre's Charity School, Holborn, well known to Newman. They wanted to "encourage husbandmen and gardeners to employ their children", and put advertisements in the newspapers, but the treasurer of the school told him, "only one boy has been put out to a gardener upon the recommendation of that advertisement, the rest being generally put out to watermen, tailors, shoemakers and such other trades". This was because, Newman thought, "The children of this town seldom incline to a country life, nor do their constitutions often favour going into a laborious employ, except to the gardeners near the town, where country boys are generally more acceptable, being more robust; but our town boys excell the country youth in all fine handicraft for the weaving and toy trades, etc." In the last year of his life he still thought the same, telling Thomas Secker, then Bishop of Oxford and later Archbishop of Canterbury, "The children of the charity schools bred in the country [are] more robust for their business when they are bound . . . [but] children bred up in London are generally better qualified for handicrafts of which there is a great call in the lower branches." [2]

While anxious to prove that the schools did not endanger the country's economic order, Newman had less sympathy with criticisms that they threatened the social order by depriving the wealthy of servants. When the ever-vocal John Chamberlayne mentioned this, his reply was emphatic:

It is not to be wondered at, that a footman or postillion's place should be filled with more difficulty when thirty thousand of the dregs of the nation, it might be said four times that number, since the first institution of charity schools, are drawn into a life of better views, for these creatures were hitherto the disease of the nation, as they are still in France and in all countries where oppression and poverty reigns. And those that will have four footmen and a postillion to attend them whenever they go abroad, I hope may be enabled by the growing wealth of the nation to send to France and Germany for them, when they can no longer find in England that will devote themselves to so insipid a life. Every waterman's boy stands fairer to serve his country more usefully than any duke's footman that is capable of nothing else. The rise of wages is a consequence of wealth and that the children do

[1] HN to Rev. Dr Bundy, 29 March 1733, *Society's Letters*.
[2] HN to Rev. Mr Fox, Reading, 27 Jan. 1736; to Rev. Dr Thomas, Soho, 29 April 1737; to Bp of Oxford, 20 and 22 April 1743, *Miscellaneous Letters*.

find better business than being footmen, which is a comfortable omen to the Kingdom.

Newman did, however, allow some criticism of the schools and in this same letter to Chamberlayne significantly remarked that their curriculum should now be changed. The first design of rescuing poor children from ignorance of their duty to God and man had "been wonderfully helped"; over 30,000 children were now taught reading and the catechism, but "twenty four years of experience had shown that a working school is in all respects preferable to one without labour and more in keeping with the present trend of public opinion".[1]

Public opinion always impressed this on the Society by requests that the children might be "inured to labour", and in 1712 it urged teachers to "instruct the children under their care particularly in the duties of servants".[2] Education of poor children should be primarily occupational, a preliminary to apprenticeship and dependent upon social status, to make them self-supporting and used to labour as soon as possible. Newman held that this must precede even religious instruction. He told a correspondent: "The thoughts of your friends concerning the teaching of our charity children the Book of Psalms is certainly very just . . . but the children being generally designed for servants, by the time they are thoroughly instructed in the Christian religion and taught to read and write, they are put out to service and have no leisure afterwards but in the ordinary kinds of devotion, wherein it is well if they can preserve what they have learned." [3] This ideal led many trustees to introduce means of inuring children to labour and contributing to their support, most commonly by spinning for the cloth industry, which Defoe had approvingly noticed was performed in the woollen districts by children of 4 or 5 years old in their parents' cottages.[4]

Newman, like the Society as a whole, strongly favoured this and was ready to advise trustees about adopting it. When Gilbert White of Selborne, grandfather of the later more famous incumbent of the same name, wished to establish a working school, Newman told him:

The methods when a working school is erected are to get sober men or women, that understand spinning, weaving, sewing, knitting, mend-

[1] HN to Mr Chamberlayne, 15 Dec. 1722, *Letters to Correspondents.*
[2] *S.P.C.K. Minutes*, 31 July 1712.
[3] HN to Mr Hales, 27 Aug. 1713, *Society's Letters.*
[4] D. Defoe, *A Tour through Great Britain, passim.*

ing or making clothes or shoes, to teach the children certain hours of the day in these faculties; by which means much of the expense of clothing and mending the clothes of the children [is saved]. And when they have made any proficiency, so that they don't spoil their work, the overseers or their friends send in wool or flax and have it wrought up at such reasonable rates, that they scarce ever want work when once they have acquired a reputation of doing it well. As their stock increases they get conveniences for brewing and baking, etc., within themselves, whereby they save another considerable article of expense . . . The labour of such a school, after it has once gained an establishment, shall very nearly entirely support itself, though oftener the produce of the labour is much less than the expense.[1]

Newman realized, unlike many members of the S.P.C.K., that schools were not likely to pay their way. The children's unskilled labour, the teachers' incompetent supervision, the trustees' imperfect business capacity usually made this impossible; but he still considered it valuable training for the children and urged trustees to adopt it when convenient. When the school at Hackney was revived in 1735, he suggested the trustees considered "adding to the instruction of the children in reading and writing, some cheap and easy labour very consistent with their other learning", as "the children, though they cannot maintain themselves, are taught to do a great deal towards clothing themselves and by that means are inured so much to labour as to be qualified to make better servants wherever the Providence of God shall place them".[2]

Newman also made a list of successful working schools to which he referred inquirers for further advice. Some were in London—"the boys and girls schools at Lambeth and some in and near Spitalfields . . . the first by spinning of stocking and mop yarn, the last by winding raw silk, etc."; "St Clement Danes trustees are rich, and having 140 children under their care, have resolved to make a trial of some employ for their children"; "St Martin's-in-the-Fields employ their children by a rotation of one-third at a time, so that every boy works two days in the week"; "St George's-in-the-Fields, Southwark, where the master, being bred a wool-comber, has by his industry discovered some improvements that may perhaps be thought worthy of imitation." [3] But he most esteemed as a model working school that at Artleborough in

[1] HN to Rev. Mr Gilbert White, Selborne, Hants, 1 May 1710, *Letters to Correspondents*.

[2] HN to Mr Stephen Ram, Hackney, 4 July 1735, *Private Letters*.

[3] HN to Rev. Dr Thomas, Soho, 29 April 1737; to Mr Gyles, Holborn, 8 Dec. 1735, *Miscellaneous Letters*.

Northamptonshire, through its first mistress, Mrs Harris, whose "industry and success has drawn upon her the trouble of advising others how to pursue her method". She astutely traded the produce of her pupils' spinning and knitting to dealers in Northampton and Wellingborough for a good price, while the children kept part of their earnings as encouragement. "It is worth while for any gentleman minded to set up a working school", Newman told Chamberlayne, "to go thither to see how eagerly the children press to go to school by five o'clock in the summer mornings and grudge every hour they spend out of it; they make reading and writing their diversion, and the gain they make by their labour makes them impatient to return to it again, and all this conducted by one old woman, who could scarce write her name when she first opened her school." [1]

To help his correspondents better, Newman sometimes passed their questions on to other schools, and these letters show what problems troubled them. To trustees at Liverpool, "being informed that the children of your charity school or schools are employed in some useful work without prejudice to their learning to read, write and cast accounts", he asked about, "the nature of the work they are employed in? How many hours in the day they are employed? Where you get the materials, that is whether they are bought as a stock for the house or furnished by tradesmen to be wrought up? What may be the annual profits of their labour and to whom that is given? Whether to the parents or to the common stock for clothing the children and other expenses of the house?" [2] When the Honourable Society for Promoting English Protestant Schools in Ireland was founded, he was made a Corresponding Member and took advantage of this to ask about "any new attempts for employing the poor children in Ireland", particularly in "agriculture where land can be obtained for that service".[3] He also tried to learn from abroad, obtaining from the Directors of the Charitable Society at Lausanne particulars of the poor children's "cotton manufacture", though he did not think it could be copied in England because "the material of it is a foreign product", and asking Lord Perceval, when in France in 1722, whether the charitable establishments there showed "how the poor may more easily be provided for" by being taught to work,

[1] HN to Mr Tugg, Artleborough, 18 Feb. 1719, *Society's Letters*; to Mr Chamberlayne 15 Dec. 1722, *Letters to Correspondents*.
[2] HN to Mr Blundell, Liverpool, 18 Nov. 1735, *Miscellaneous Letters*.
[3] HN to Mr Hansard, Dublin, 6 May 1737, *Miscellaneous Letters*.

but Perceval was in too much of a "perpetual hurry" to inquire for him.[1]

In such letters Newman explained he was thinking of the "common charity school where the children go home every day to their parents and are employed part of their school time in some manufacture or branch of husbandry, besides learning to read, write, etc."; but in his lifetime some schools were changed. Trustees often had difficulty in enforcing regular attendance upon their pupils or controlling their behaviour after school-hours. They might make rules requiring the children to go to school and church and punish offenders with the ever-ready birch-rod, but they could not coerce parents or nurses, with whom many charity children were boarded out by parish overseers, if they made the children work or beg in the streets. Thus, the trustees of St Anne's Charity School, Soho, ordered in 1700 that truants were to "be whipt" especially severely before the vicar when he "pleased to call at the school", but no amount of corporal punishment and public disgrace inflicted upon the boys deterred the real offenders, and when one was summoned, after her charge had been frequently flogged, to be admonished for keeping "her nurse child from school and sending him to work in the brick-fields with his coat on, she replied that she did not owe the trustees so much service and neither could nor would come".[2] At Bath it was even worse, for when the charity school mistress similarly chastised girls for absence from school, some "barbarian mothers" abused her before the children "in a clamorous manner" so that "the discipline of her school was seriously hindered".[3] Many people, therefore, wanted schools where children were wholly under discipline as boarders without intermission or interference. William Seward, for instance, told Newman that he hoped in Georgia "the two great objections in charity schools will be effectually remedied in Mr Whitefield's orphan house, the children being employed in labour suitable to their years and kept from the evil examples of their parents at home. I wish all the charity schools were put on the same foot." [4]

Few such schools were possible, however, mainly for reasons of expense. Something was done at Bath to enable the mistress to correct at least some of her pupils without maternal interference,

[1] HN to Rev. Mons. Polier, President Ecclesiastique, Lausanne, 23 Sept. 1736, *Miscellaneous Letters*; to Ld Perceval, 7 Aug. 1725; Ld Perceval to HN, 22 Sept. 1725, *Egmont MSS.*, Add. MSS. 47031, ff. 11 and 24.

[2] J. H. Cardwell, *Soho: The Story of a Charity School, 1699–1899*, 1899, 15–16.

[3] *Abs. of Correspondence*, 17 Aug. 1715.

[4] *Colonial Records of Georgia*, XXII (2), 300–1.

for the S.P.C.K. was told that they were maintained in "a house where they may be lodged and dieted, and the girls taught to wash and scour and do other house labour [as] may be highly serviceable to inure the children to labour and keep them humble".[1] And, indeed, girls' schools were almost the only ones profitably transformed into boarding schools, usually as a solution to the perpetual problem of finding trained and respectful domestic servants. To this end many a charity school became a boarding establishment for girls from 7 or 9 to 14 or 16 years, who, besides receiving religious and moral instruction, were taught straw-plaiting or lace-making and trained for domestic service with emphasis on the necessary virtues of humility, submissiveness, and industry. They were taught to read and write when young and then did the cookery and cleaning, laundrywork and needlework until put into service in neighbouring houses. They had cropped hair and wore large round cloaks with tight-fitting hoods; they rose early, worked long hours and ate plain food; they were whipped for unpunctuality, incivility, or untidiness, a punishment from which they might not later be immune as maidservants.[2]

This development scarcely appears in Newman's letters, partly because it mainly occurred after about 1725, when the Society's zeal was gradually transferred from charity schools to overseas missions and book-publishing, and its influence over the trustees declined. As the century progressed, the welfare of many schools was left to individual clergymen and village squires—and their wives. The lady of the manor or vicar's wife usually created and managed such girls' boarding schools where learning was combined with domestic labour, and few were linked with the Society, which had an entirely male membership. Even Lady Betty Hastings, founder of many charity schools, was only a subscriber and not a member of the Society. In any event, the Society continued to uphold the ideal of catechetical schools. Newman always thought it important that poor girls should be educated because as mothers they could later bring up a family religiously. The energetic ladies who thought of them rather as potential servants and often themselves governed a school, drawing up rules, instructing teachers, and birching girls, were not likely to turn for advice to the bachelor Secretary of the Society.

Newman did assist, however, towards the end of his life in the

[1] *S.P.C.K. Minutes*, 2 July 1713.

[2] M. G. Jones, op. cit., 94–5; C. Cappe, *Account of Two Charity Schools for the Education of Girls in York*, 1800, *passim.*

establishment of a boarding institution for children whom the charity schools had largely neglected—the poverty-stricken children of the streets, like the Blackguard who had aroused Newman's efforts earlier. The foundation of an institution for these children had long been suggested. Robert Nelson, in his *Address to Persons of Quality and Estate*, deplored: "We have neither school or hospital for the distressed children called the Blackguard. Many also of the parish children are vagrants and exposed to a multitude of temptations by not being kept together in one house, which could be done at much less charge to the parish as well as much greater advantage to the poor children." [1] Addison in *The Guardian* had proposed that existing charities should be extended to provide for foundlings, which would diminish the abandoning of children and child-murders and emulate the great hospitals of Paris, Madrid, Lisbon, Rome, and other Continental cities, a proposal which Defoe later supported in a novel in which the heroine lamented "had this been the custom of our country, I had not been left a poor desolate girl without friends, without clothes, without help or helper, as was my fate".[2]

That the S.P.C.K. did not extend its assistance to these children whose plight troubled some of its members showed its declining zeal for charity schools and their loss of popularity among its supporters. Luckily their cause was taken up by a man of energy and determination, Thomas Coram, a sea-captain, who having spent ten years in Massachusetts and married a Boston woman, on his return to England settled at Rotherhithe, then a homely and well-gardened river suburb. Going to and from the City, he passed early in the morning and late at night abandoned and unwanted infants, "sometimes alive, sometimes dead and sometimes dying", left in the streets as victims of poverty or prostitution or orphanhood. Though a common sight in large towns, it so shocked him that he determined to procure an institution for their care. For seventeen years he urged their cause, going round London offices, seeking signatures for a petition in favour of the plan. Eventually he persuaded twenty-one aristocratic ladies to sign a manifesto, agreeing to support such a hospital if the King gave a charter. "Names like these", said Pugh, "could not fail of succeeding", and the duchesses broke through the obstruction and apathy against which Coram had struggled. In 1739 he received a charter

[1] C. F. Secretan, op. cit., 149–50.
[2] *The Guardian*, No. 105, 1 July 1713; Daniel Defoe, *Moll Flanders*, 1721, 1.

of incorporation for "the Hospital for the Maintenance and Education of Exposed and Deserted Young Children", and had enough subscriptions to begin.[1]

Newman was an old friend of Coram. Their association, doubtless originating in common connections with New England and active philanthropy, was strengthened in 1732 when Coram became a trustee for Georgia. Although the S.P.C.K. had no connection with Coram's charity, Newman became, as soon as it was incorporated, "one of the Governors and Guardians, in company with about 400 others, including all the Privy Council", and attended their meetings regularly until his death. At Coram's request, he wrote to Sir Erasmus Philipps, then travelling in Italy, to ask him, since Addison had mentioned the institution for foundlings at Rome, to "inform yourself of the economy of it and of any other foundation for such purpose that you may happen to meet with in your travels", and again to discover "how the children are marked that are received into such hospitals abroad, if in the foot, what part of it and with what materials, so that the Corporation here may follow or improve on the practice abroad as they shall think fit".[2] The Foundling Hospital began with 19 boys and 11 girls on 25 March 1741 in a house in Hatton Garden, not far from Bartlett's Buildings, and Newman rejoiced at each sign of its growth, as when Coram told him he could "take in 30 or 40 more children" in 1742. By then the building of the permanent Hospital in Lamb's Conduit Fields had begun, and though Newman died before its completion, he had been able to assist in some alleviation of the lot of the most wretched of the poor children of London, whose sufferings had aroused his own concern in his earlier life.[3]

Newman's career as Secretary of the S.P.C.K. largely covered the first and most important period of the charity school movement, which was still novel and popular when he became Secretary. Schools were founded all over the country to provide poor children with Christian knowledge and elementary education, and the Society regarded the encouragement of these efforts as one of its most important duties. Newman, while supporting individual schools, fulfilled the task which the strangely loose relationship between the Society and local trustees placed upon him. When the schools underwent criticism and unpopularity, through

[1] *D.N.B.*; John Pugh, *Remarkable Occurrences in the Life of Jonas Hanway, Esq.*, 1787, 159.

[2] HN to Sir Erasmus Philipps, Rome, 24 Aug. 1732 and Venice, 31 Oct. 1740, *Miscellaneous Letters.*

[3] HN to Jonathan Belcher, Jnr, Dublin, 31 Dec. and 9 Nov. 1742, *Miscellaneous Letters.*

political entanglement and distrust of their social and economic utility, he undertook their defence and advised on the introduction of schemes of work. By the time of his death, the schools were less popular, and "it was clear that they had failed to fulfil the promise of fifty years earlier, while the need for popular education had become much more pressing".[1] The failure of the working schools, except the girls' schools, through lack of money and experience, caused zeal for the movement to decline, and after about 1725 the Society's competing activities led to diminished interest in it.

Newman's continued compassion, however, for the most desperate of London children led him to support Coram's charity, and he never himself lost faith in the charity school movement. Despite its weaknesses, he believed it would "promote the publick good, by putting the helpless poor in a condition to be useful to the publick instead of being a burthen as they are at present".[2] Many aspects of the movement, which he favoured, would be condemned to-day, but neither he nor the movement could have been other than part of the times. In an age of well-marked social distinctions, he and his friends naturally agreed with prevailing views that charity children, whether it were possible to "inure them to labour" or not, should be prepared for servile work, but they did also show an active compassion and sense of responsibility for these children whose spiritual and physical needs were so great and so neglected. The Regulations of the Foundling Hospital in 1739 carefully stated that the children would only be educated for the meanest services, but Newman, who more than a quarter of a century before had pitied these children as "altogether friendless", must have known that their very lives would probably be saved by the charity.[3] "The charity school movement", it has been said, "was, in the first place, a religious movement, and in the second place, a social movement. It was only through the bearing of education on religion and society that it was also an educational movement." [4] This may be so, but it is also true that, under the influence of Newman and other like-minded men, it was also a movement which, despite its failings and disappointments, was to rescue generations of poor children from complete ignorance and destitution.

[1] J. W. Adamson, *A Short History of Education*, Cambridge, 1919, 137.
[2] HN to Mr Blundell, Liverpool, 18 Nov. 1735, *Miscellaneous Letters*.
[3] HN to Mrs Ketteridge, 12 June 1713, *Society's Letters*.
[4] R. H. Tawney, *Economic History Review*, IX, 202 (Review of M. G. Jones, *The Charity School Movement*).

5

THE EAST INDIA MISSION

"YOU will reasonably expect I should give you some account how the Society came to be concerned in the East Indies", Newman wrote to a correspondent in 1713. "You will please to know that an account of the success of the Danish missionaries at Tranquebar having been published here, it was so well accepted that several offered to contribute to their assistance if anybody would undertake to receive and convey money to them. The Society for the Propagation of the Gospel, considering that their charter confined them to Her Majesty's Plantations in the West Indies, declined concerning themselves in it, and our Society, though their chief province be in Great Britain, yet being under no restraints but by the laws of the land and common discretion, they gladly embraced the opportunity of receiving and remitting succour to those missionaries."[1]

It was strange that the S.P.C.K. should become associated with the beginning of Protestant missions in India. The founders of the Society had not intended that it should engage in overseas missions; the S.P.G. was founded three years later, in 1702, as a separate society for this, and it began work in the British possessions in America, though not in India, already another sphere of British overseas influence. At the beginning of the century the English East India Company had three principal settlements—on the west coast, Bombay, part of the dowry of Charles II's Queen, Catherine of Braganza, and other subordinate posts on that side of India; on the east coast, Madras or Fort St George, founded in 1639, and its dependent factories on the Coromandel Coast and in the Bay of Bengal; and in Bengal, Calcutta, or Fort William, founded in 1690. Newman's years of Secretary of the S.P.C.K. coincided almost exactly with the period in the history of British expansion in India, which began with the death of the last Great Mogul in 1707 and the formation of the United East India Company in 1708 and ended with the arrival of Dupleix in India in 1741 and of Clive in 1743. It was a time of steady and quiet

[1] HN to Rev. Mr Ayerst, Utrecht, 27 Jan. 1713, *Society's Letters.*

prosperity for the British in India. Though their territory was negligible in area, comprising only a few square miles, and their numbers small, Madras having only 300 Englishmen, of whom two-thirds were soldiers, their prospects seemed bright. Portuguese and Dutch power in India was declining. Anglo-French rivalry was on the way, but postponed by the pacific ministries of Walpole and Fleury. The Company's first concern was still the increase of trade. Its mercantile representatives were content to devote themselves to commerce and avoid Indian politics or wars, but the factory period of the Company was really at an end and the time at hand when it would seek territory as well.[1]

It might have been thought that the S.P.G., as the missionary society of the Church of England, would have been very ready to engage in activities in India. The Roman Catholic version of Christianity had been brought to India in the sixteenth century, first by the Portuguese, who in 1536 established the Bishopric of Goa, while in 1542 St Francis Xavier and two other Jesuits landed in India. Though accurate figures are unobtainable, the Roman Catholic missions in India made considerable headway, and by 1700 there were perhaps about a million Roman Catholics in India, of whom about half a million were in the Portuguese possessions on the west coast and about 450,000 in Madura and other missions around Madras. In the eighteenth century the decay of Portuguese power, its replacement by first the Dutch and then the English, and dissensions among the Roman Catholic missions themselves caused a decline in numbers and morale among the Roman Catholics in India from which they took over a century to recover.[2]

The situation in India, therefore, was not unfavourable for intervention by the S.P.G., but it shunned this mission field because religious responsibility was supposed to rest with the East India Company; and from the very early days of the Company some of the London merchants who joined it were eager for the conversion of the peoples of India. The Company tolerated Roman Catholicism and non-Christian religion in its territories, but wished the children of Englishmen to be reared as Protestant Christians. It appointed chaplains to its chief settlements, eighteen between 1667 and 1700, and in 1680 the first English church in India was built when Governor Streynsham Masters founded St Mary's Church, Madras. The new charter of the Company in

[1] V. A. Smith, *Oxford History of India*, 2nd ed., Oxford, 1923, *passim*.
[2] K. S. Latourette, *A History of the Expansion of Christianity*, 5 vols., 1939, III, 249–73.

1698 and of the United Company in 1708 required that "there should be provided in every garrison or superior factory one minister and one decent and convenient place for divine service only"; these chaplains were expected to learn Portuguese (the *lingua franca* of these posts) and the language of the natives, "the better to instruct the Gentoos that shall be servants or slaves of the Company and of their agents in the Protestant religion". In 1694 the Company had the English Liturgy translated into Portuguese at Oxford and printed and dispatched several hundred books to its factories; daily prayers were held in its establishments; schoolmasters were sought for the European and Eurasian children in the settlements. There was as yet no sign of the hostility to missions which characterized the policy of the Company in the latter part of the eighteenth century, and Newman always found the Directors favourable enough to religious efforts.[1]

Unfortunately the Company's servants in India were not usually of the same mind as the Directors. Most were not only too much occupied in the pursuit of wealth to concern themselves with missions, but feared that Christianity, by uniting natives of different faiths, might render untenable their foothold in India. As the Danish missionaries told Newman in 1714, "this is the general temper of our Europeans when they come to the East Indies, they are so much bent upon treasures of India, that the treasures of the world to come, declared in the Gospel of Christ, are laid aside, whilst those that endeavour to put them in mind of such never-failing riches are for their pains persecuted and hissed at".[2]

In this atmosphere, it is not surprising that most chaplains did not exceed their duties as laid down in the charter. "The English chaplains", Newman told a correspondent, "generally confine their care to the English congregations in the garrisons where they are, excepting a few Indian slaves who happen to become domestics among the English." [3] Some who tried to work among the natives had little encouragement. "'Tis a common observation here in India that the first thing the Portuguese undertake in any factory is to build a church, the Dutch a fort and the English a punch house", wrote Richard Cobbe, Chaplain of Bombay Castle, in 1716 to his father in a bitter letter shown to Newman. "There

[1] H. W. Tucker, *The English Church in Other Lands*, 1886, 13; F. Penny, *The Church in Madras*, 3 vols., 1904, I, 122.

[2] Rev. Messrs Ziegenbalg and Gründler, Tranquebar, to HN, 12 Oct. 1714, *Abs. of Correspondence*.

[3] HN to Rev. Mr Walton, Carlisle, 11 Dec. 1718, *Society's Letters*.

was a church once designed to be built and sufficient contributions were raised for it, but the money has long since been perverted and the walls remain a standing monument of reproach to the nation even to a proverb, viz. 'when the English church is finished'." [1]

Though the S.P.G. was not able to remedy this, its foundation led to the sending of the first Protestant missionaries to India, the Lutherans mentioned by Newman. The Danish East India Company, founded in 1616, four years later established its chief trading post at Tranquebar, on the east coast and in a centre of European rivalry, between a French factory at Korikal and an English one at Fort St David, while further north were the most important French and English stations on that coast, Pondicherry and Madras. There were Lutheran chaplains at the Danish fort, but they seem only to have ministered to the Danes and Germans of the factory. King Frederick IV of Denmark, however, knew of the S.P.G. through the friendship of its members with the chaplains of his uncle, Prince George of Denmark, Consort of Queen Anne, and the King hoped that what the Anglican Church was doing in America might be emulated by the Lutheran Church in India. He was assisted and encouraged by one of his chaplains, a German, Franz Julius Lütkens. No men able and willing to go as missionaries to India were to be had in Denmark, but Lütkens knew Professor Francke of Halle, who found two pastors in his seminary, Bartholomew Ziegenbalg and Henry Plutschau, willing to be missionaries, and Frederick IV promised to pay them 200 rix-dollars (£30–£40) a year. Arriving at Tranquebar in July 1706, they built a church, learnt Portuguese and Tamil, and began their labours despite shortage of supplies, ridicule, and opposition from their fellow-countrymen, and even imprisonment by the Danish Governor. They won converts both from Hindus and from nominal Roman Catholics of mixed Portuguese and Indian blood who were numerous in Tranquebar as in other European trading-posts. In 1709 they were joined by John Gründler from Denmark, while Mr Böhme, Newman's friend among Prince George's Lutheran chaplains, translated into English a collection of letters from the missionaries and dedicated the book to the S.P.G., inviting help for the mission. The S.P.G. being prevented by its charter, the S.P.C.K. agreed to support it instead.[2]

[1] HN to Rev. Mr Geo. Lewis, Dublin, 1 May 1716, *Letters to Correspondents*.

[2] H. P. Thompson, *Into All Lands: The History of the S.P.G.*, 1951, 174–5; W. O. B. Allen and E. McClure, *Two Hundred Years: The History of the S.P.C.K., 1698–1898*, 1898, 258–62; Eyre Chatterton, *History of the Church of England in India*, 1924, 101–3.

The Society collected subscriptions for the mission from English sympathizers and arranged for them to be "annually remitted in money or goods" to India. The first consignment was sent by Newman late in 1710. It included £100 in Spanish pieces-of-eight, but, more important, "a printing press, 500 weight of Roman types with utensils belonging thereto, 100 reams of paper and also a printer".[1] The printer was Jonas Finck, who brought the equipment from Halle. The Society heard that the missionaries spent much money on copying books for distributing and thought this was the most practical help it could send. The East India Company granted free freight and passage, but the voyage was costly and difficult. Off Rio de Janeiro the gunner and six seamen deserted the ship in a pinnace and took with them the chests containing the money for the missionaries. Then the ship was captured by a French privateer, being eventually ransomed for £3500, of which the Society had to pay £150 for its goods, but on the resumed voyage Jonas Finck threw himself overboard in a fever off the Cape of Good Hope. Fortunately, when the press reached Tranquebar in 1712 a soldier of the Company understood it enough to assist the missionaries until Francke sent another printer, a schoolmaster and a youth to help the printer together with "a font of Malabarick types".[2] The missionaries made good use of the press. By its aid Ziegenbalg published in 1714 the first translation ever made into Tamil of the Gospels and the Acts of the Apostles; and within six years some 20,000 copies of Lutheran catechisms, hymn books, and religious treatises in Portuguese and the native vernacular had been produced.[3]

The dispatch of the annual cargo for the missionaries in India was always Newman's duty. "The ships bound to Fort St George generally depart hence about Christmas", and it made him busy at the end of each year. Letters had to be written and purchases made. All goods for the missionaries had to be ready a fortnight before the ship sailed, and each "left open in order to be viewed by a committee of the East India Company and afterwards sealed up with their seals". Then he had to arrange for them to be entered

[1] HN to Ct of Directors of East India Co., 8 Dec. 1710, *Letters to Correspondents*.

[2] HN to Rev. Mr Lewis and Mr Wm Jennings, Fort St George, 21 April 1712; to Mr Melmoth, Lincoln's Inn, 26 May 1712, *Society's Letters*; to Rev. Mr Lewis and Mr Wm Jennings, Fort St George, 31 Dec. 1712, *Letters to Correspondents*; to Mr Hales, Clerk of the Council, 20 June 1718, *Private Letters*; Messrs Ziegenbalg and Gründler to HN, 23 Oct. 1712, *Letters from India*; *S.P.C.K. Minutes*, 29 Feb. and 4 March 1712, 6 Jan. 1713.

[3] *The Daily Courant*, 19 Dec. 1719.

at the Customs House, taken to the wharf, and freighted on a hoy to go to the ship at Gravesend. No wonder he was glad when it was done. He apologized for not replying to a correspondent in 1718 because of "a constant hurry that has taken up my thoughts for 5 or 6 weeks past in buying and shipping a small cargo consisting of many particulars for our missionaries in the East Indies which, God be thanked, were despatched for this year the day before yesterday, so that I shall now have a little rest".[1] It was the same in 1742, when he could not meet a correspondent visiting town, having "been for a month past continually engaged in buying or packing up goods and writing letters to the Society's correspondents in East India, which now, thank God, is in a manner over for this year".[2] In 1734, when it seemed Britain might be drawn into the War of the Polish Succession, he was more than ever rushed owing to "the sudden departure of the ships to avoid a press that is soon expected for supplying the King's ships with men".[3]

The East India Company each year allowed goods to "go freight free in one of their ships to Fort St George" and gave free passages to outgoing and returning missionaries, which, Newman gratefully recorded, was "a vast saving of expence to the Society and the missions".[4] The Company's agents in India were not as friendly to the mission as the Directors. In 1712 they sent back reports from Fort St George that it was "an imposition upon the credulous", a charge which Newman rebutted at the Court of the Company so well that the Directors told the Governor and Council of Fort St George "the designs of the Society here are truly great and noble, and we would be willing to encourage the putting them in practise".[5] Yet the Directors sometimes suspected subjects of a rival nation in India, and when Ziegenbalg and his wife were to return to India in 1715, they would not at first grant free passages; only when asked "again for Mr Ziegenbalg as a German and not as a Dane" did they agree.[6] The formation, with the Emperor's support, of the Ostend Company, which trenched on British

[1] HN to Abp of Canterbury, 14 April 1718; to Capt. Morris, Carlisle, 11 Jan. 1718, *Society's Letters*.

[2] HN to Sir John Gordon, Brentwood, 30 Jan. 1742, *Miscellaneous Letters*.

[3] HN to Messrs Schultze and Geister, 31 Jan. 1734, *Society's Letters*.

[4] HN to Rev. Mr Woodrow, Glasgow, 4 Jan. 1733, *Society's Letters*.

[5] HN to Thos. Wooley, Secretary to East India Co., 10 Oct. 1712; to Governor and Council of Fort St George, 2 Feb. 1713, *Letters to Correspondents*; Dispatch of Directors of East India Co. to Governor and Council of Fort St George, 2 Feb. 1713, *East India Co. Papers*.

[6] HN to Rev. Mr Boehm, 27 Oct. 1715, *Society's Letters*.

preserves in India, caused further difficulties. Newman had to write to the missionaries in 1720: "The Honourable East India Company, having received advice that the Danes at Tranquebar have given shelter and liberty of trade to an Ostend trading ship, they seem to resent it so much as to threaten to withdraw their assistance to the mission and take it very ill that whilst they cherish you in spirituals, you should destroy their temporals."[1] But the suppression of the Ostend Company in 1725 and the collapse of the Danish East India Company in 1728 made matters easier, and Newman wrote regularly to the Company with the "thanks of the Society for the ready concessions", "the generous concession to all their requests".

Each annual shipment from the Society to the missionaries consisted of both money and goods, including gifts, sometimes from abroad, such as "a Malabarick cross" from Denmark or "366 three-quarter ounce pieces-of-eight" collected at Halle, sometimes from individuals at home, like the Mr Smith who gave "four large parcels of Grotius' *De Veritate Religionis Christianae* in Arabick", and Newman had to get "help in collecting of them in order to their being bound".[2] When subscriptions were sufficient, the Society sent considerable presents. The printing press was followed by a Portuguese version of the New Testament, specially reprinted at Amsterdam. Here Newman had not only to make sure from John Evans, Bishop of Bangor (who had once had to resign a chaplaincy with the East India Company for engaging in private trade), that "books printed in the Portuguese as spoke in Europe are generally understood in India" and arrange for the sheets to be bound in vellum, but also seek subscriptions. Cambridge University gave £40 and in return a copy of the edition was sent to each college and hall; Oxford, despite suggestions from Newman to Fellows he knew, gave nothing, so only one copy was sent to the Bodleian.[3] The Society also sent paper for the press until 1716, when the missionaries built their own paper-mill.[4] Another former Indian chaplain, William Stevenson, suggested that "to the books which the Society now sends to the missionaries, there might be some few added concerning the theory and practice of Physick,

[1] HN to Messrs Ziegenbalg and Gründler, 15 March 1720, *Society's Letters*.

[2] HN to Rev. Mr Wm Carstares, Edinburgh, 12 Dec. 1710; to Rev. Mr Lewis, Fort St George, 4 Jan. 1711, *Letters to Correspondents*.

[3] HN to Bp of Bangor, 12 Feb. 1711; to Mr Harrison, Cambridge, 20 Sept. 1711; to Mr Salmon, Oxford, 17 Oct. 1711; to Francis Boynton and Geo. Davis, Beverley, Yorks, 19 Feb. 1712, *Society's Letters*.

[4] HN to Mr Chamberlayne, 4 Oct. 1716, *Society's Letters*.

for I know nothing that will more endear them to the natives and facilitate their conversion than a complete skill in curing diseases and a charitable, generous practice of it".[1] The missionaries themselves made suggestions. They "informed [the Society] that the Romish missionaries in India, by their skill in the Mathematicks, do very much insinuate themselves into the good opinion of the natives", and asked for apparatus to enable them to do the same. They were sent "mathematickal instruments for teaching navigation, surveying and other parts of the mathematicks", such as globes, telescope, barometer, thermometer, a double microscope, and "a month pendulum clock". Included with these was "a chest of English beer containing fourteen dozen", which the missionaries found so acceptable that all later shipments included "a chest of beer and Cheshire cheese covered with lead as usual"; and their German carpenter, Christopher Adler, "a very ingenious man, made a font of lesser types at Tranquebar out of the leaden covers of the Cheshire cheeses which in several years had been sent by the Society as presents to them".[2] The Society wished the missionaries to ask for goods: "For the future be as particular as you please in expressing your wants, for the East India Company won't let us send you a considerable sum of money without some goods. They themselves being under some rule by Act of Parliament to export a tenth part of their bullion in the manufactures of Great Britain expect at least that proportion to be observed by those that freight in their ships." [3]

The missionaries, made Corresponding Members of the Society, were also asked to give periodical accounts of their work. By 1712 they reported that they were teaching seventy children in five schools and had made "117 baptized converts in the *Tamil* or *Malabarick* Church and 83 in the *Portuguese* Church, to which be pleased to add fifteen *Malabarick* and five *Portuguese* Catechumens".[4] These distinctions indicated the two languages in which their work had to be done in order that they might evangelize both native Hindus and those of mixed blood who spoke Portuguese.[5]

Such accounts of the missionaries' achievements were sent by

[1] Rev. Mr Stevenson, Morningthorpe, Norfolk, to HN, 8 Dec. 1719, *Letters from India*.

[2] Rev. Mr Gründler to HN, 16 Jan. 1716, *Letters from India*; HN to Mr Ziegenbalg, 1 Feb. 1717, *Society's Letters*; to Missionaries at Tranquebar, 8 Feb. 1737, *Miscellaneous Letters*.

[3] HN to Missionaries at Tranquebar, 23 Jan. 1736, *Miscellaneous Letters*.

[4] W. O. B. Allen and E. McClure, op. cit., 262.

[5] K. S. Latourette, op. cit., III, 278.

Newman to subscribers and prospective subscribers. In the earliest days of the mission, among those who received one of these reports was Samuel Wesley, the incumbent of Epworth in Lincolnshire. It was read by his wife, Susanna, upon whom the work of Zeigenbalg and Plütschau made a deep impression. "For several days", she said, "I could think or speak of little else." She resolved to give a weekly missionary lesson to her children, and her son John said in later life that he had never forgotten what he learnt there.[1]

Newman was also glad to receive from the missionaries curiosities and specimens of their own work, which he also used to stimulate interest in the mission. Ralph Thoresby recorded in 1712, "Mr Newman presented me with a leaf of the palm-tree, with part of the Gospel impressed on it in the Malabaric character and language, with a reviving account of the success of the Protestant Missionaries in propagating the Christian religion amongst the poor heathens in the East Indies", while in 1714, "he showed me . . . a curious manuscript of the Danish Missionaries concerning the heathen Malabar deities, with their horrid pictures"; and in 1723, "he gave me a specimen of the paper invented and made by the Protestant Missionaries at Tranquebar; he showed me also Tate and Brady's Psalms, printed there in English".[2] Cambridge University Library received a copy of Ziegenbalg's Tamil version of the New Testament, while Chamberlayne presented "a Catechize according to the Reformed Religion printed at Tranquebar in the East Indies" to the Royal Society, which was placed in its library.[3]

The Society also saw something of the missionaries themselves. In 1712 Plutschau came back from India and was received by a special assembly of the Society at which a Latin speech was delivered "to thank him for the service he has done to the Christian religion in India and to assure him that the Society will do all that is in its power to procure encouragement to the Protestant mission in India from the British nation". He did not go back to India, but accepted work at home. Two years later Ziegenbalg visited England, leaving the mission in Gründler's charge; he, too, was received by the Society, which ordered Newman "to show him the remarkables of London on such proper occasions as may present,

[1] E. A. Payne, *The Growth of the World Church* (1955), 31.
[2] Ralph Thoresby, *Diary*, II, 100, 256, 372.
[3] HN to Rev. Mr Sherlock, Cambridge, 1 Nov. 1715, *Society's Letters*; *Journal Book of the Royal Society*, 30 July 1713, X, 510.

while he stays in London", and when he left to be with him "at the customs house and give him all the assistance he can".[1]

After staying at Halle to supervise "printing the Malabarian grammar", Ziegenbalg returned to Tranquebar early in 1716 and laid the foundation of a new church for the increasing converts. This was consecrated in 1717, in which year he baptized thirty converts, and fifty the next year. But in February 1719 he died aged only 36, and Gründler died the next year, the last months of both men being saddened by differences between themselves and the Mission College in Copenhagen which supported them. After Ziegenbalg's death a letter reached India written to him and Gründler by Archbishop Wake, who said: "Let others gain titles and honours, for which they have neither gone through trouble nor danger, but lived perhaps in idleness or in the common round of their profession amongst Christians, but you will gain both a lasting fame in time and a great reward in eternity, for you have laboured in the vineyard, which you yourselves planted in faith, you have made known the name of Christ amid innumerable dangers and difficulties, you have assembled a congregation where His name was before unknown, and you have faithfully remained by it to support it." [2]

The devotion of the Danish missionaries emphasized the absence of British missionaries in India. Many members of the Society felt this; Newman himself did not think it enough merely to support the Danish mission, but doubted whether they could raise money to maintain their own missionaries. "Depending only on voluntary contributions," he told Mr Lewis, Chaplain of Fort St George in 1711, "they are not at present in a capacity to send and maintain any missionaries of our own nation, and therefore they would gladly encourage those that are already there and have given proofs of the zeal and ability to undertake the providing of missionaries." The next year, however, he told him the Society hoped to establish schools in India, first at Fort St George and then at other British settlements: "It seems to be on all hands agreed that the Indian children are as capable of instruction and large attainments in learning as any of the Europeans. If this be so, it may be hoped that a few persons sent from hence well qualified for all useful instructions may soon form a nursery for catechists and

[1] *S.P.C.K. Minutes*, 13 Nov. 1712, 22 and 29 Dec. 1715, 3 Jan. 1716; HN to Mr Dolins, 7 Nov. 1715, *Society's Letters*.

[2] W. O. B. Allen and E. McClure, op. cit., 263–4.

schoolmasters." Accordingly, the East India Company was informed and asked to give free passages and protection to "the Protestant missionaries and schoolmasters against the power and artifices of the Papists, Mohamedans and heathens".[1]

The Society had yet to find men to go to India. Newman wrote to those likely to know any, including Bishop Wilson of Sodor and Man, telling him the Society had "been long endeavouring to find out fit persons for so great a work, but have not yet met with any who are both sufficiently qualified and also willing and at liberty to undertake it. They would gladly have men of a sober and religious conversation, endowed with a meek and humble spirit, men pretty well mortified and dead to the world and worldly advantages, of some experience in the care of souls and zealous for the glory of God and the salvation of men. If with these divine qualities, they have learning and an aptitude to learn languages, it will be a great advantage." To another correspondent he laid more emphasis on the human qualities of the sort of man they wanted. He should be "of a pious disposition, capable of teaching all the *credenda* and *agenda* of the Christian religion" and also "have so much knowledge of the Latin tongue as to be apt of learning and capable of teaching other languages grammatically, as there shall be occasion", as well as "have some knowledge in the mathematicks or at least a disposition to learn them", being finally "an Englishman, a single person, of a good aspect and healthy constitution". And, Newman concluded: "It may not be an easy thing perhaps to find a person, in whom all those qualifications may meet, disposed to go into so remote a country." [2]

So it proved, but at that time it seemed the Society had a suitable man. In October 1712 Sir John Philipps informed Newman: "There is a very worthy clergyman in Carmarthenshire whose name is Jones that has lately discovered an inclination to go to Tranquebar." This was none other than Griffith Jones. Newman was instructed by the Society to make him an offer of "going as a schoolmaster to the East Indies", where he would "settle at Fort St George"; but Jones was undecided, because of "the extreamly miserable blindness of his own country". For a year Newman urged him to decide: "Please to remember the longer you delay

[1] HN to Rev. Mr Lewis, Fort St George, 19 Dec. 1711 and 31 Dec. 1712; to Ct of Directors of East India Co., 3 Dec. 1712, *Letters to Correspondents*; C. F. Pascoe, *Two Hundred Years of the S.P.G.*, 1901, 472.

[2] HN to Bp of Sodor and Man, 17 Oct. 1713; to Mr Macbeth, 18 Sept. 1712, *Letters to Correspondents*.

your answer, the worse for yourself if you do go and for the Society if you do not go"; "Dear sir, you know my thoughts fully in this affair, so that I need say no more but to pray as I do that the same spirit which directed St Paul in his course, the sixteenth of the Acts, may direct you"; "'Tis your own heart, upon a humble prayer to the Disposer of all things, that must determine you in this case. Friends may advise, but all their arguments will signify nothing, if you have no heart to the undertaking, nor courage to encounter all manner of difficulties that can oppose you in so glorious a cause. Such a cause as I can't help thinking is worthy of the greatest prelate in Christendom to engage in at the expense of resigning all his honours and revenues here." But Griffith Jones finally replied that "he thinks himself obliged to decline it upon the prospect he has of doing more service to religion in his native country than he can propose to do abroad".[1]

If he had gone, the history of British missions in India might have been very different; but the Society was left with no prospect of finding anyone. "The greatest difficulty they have to struggle with", Newman told Professor Francke, "is to find missionaries endowed with apostolic qualifications whose friends will not oppose their going." [2] Yet the Society continued to be urged to establish schools. From India the Governor and Council of Fort St George asked for a school "for the education of poor Protestant children, such as are born of mixt parents and for want of due care have been very frequently seduced by the Roman Catholick missionaries", under a teacher capable of "instructing children in reading, writing and accompts and, above all, in the Christian religion", while Ziegenbalg, writing of the British settlements in India, "wished that the places situate among the heathen might prove an inducement to their nation to plant Christian knowledge in such parts as are subject to them".[3] At home the chief advocate of schools was James Wendley, formerly Chaplain at Fort St George, whom the S.P.C.K. invited on his return in 1709 to join its committee. The Society decided, therefore, to establish schools without a missionary to supervise them. "I am sorry to say I can't

[1] Sir John Philipps to HN, 30 Oct. and 20 Nov. 1712; Griffith Jones to HN, 9 Oct. and 22 Nov. 1713, *Abs. of Correspondence*; HN to Griffith Jones, 22 Aug. and 12 Oct. 1713; to Bp of Bristol, 4 Aug. 1713, *Society's Letters*.

[2] HN to Dr Francke, Halle, 14 July 1713, *Letters to Correspondents*.

[3] Governor and Council of Fort St George to HN, 26 Jan. 1716 and 17 Sept. 1717, *Letters from India*; Rev. Mr Ziegenbalg to Rev. Mr Boehm, 31 May 1715, *Abs. of Correspondence*.

inform your Lordship of any missionary sent from hence," Newman told Bishop Wilson, "the gentlemen of our universities being bred too delicately to undertake so hardy a service, but the Society have given directions for creating a charity school at Fort St George and another at Fort St David to be furnished with schoolmasters from the natives educated at Tranquebar under the Danish missionaries." [1]

This was only possible through the labours of William Stevenson, Chaplain at Fort St George from 1712 to 1718 and the most clear-headed and practical of the Company's chaplains during this period. He founded a school at Fort St George and then one at Cuddalore; Richard Cobbe, who had already got work on the church at Bombay restarted, founded a school there as well.[2] But the attempt met with only brief success. The year after Stevenson returned to England, Gründler reported to Archbishop Wake that the schools "did not answer our expectation, chiefly [because] there was no particular missionary to look after them. For during the stay of the Rev. Mr Stevenson in these parts, who took especially care about the schools, they flourished and did well, but for want of a good inspector after his return to Europe, they came to nothing, except that of Cuddalore, which is still in being." [3] Wake seems for a time to have considered "dispensing with some beneficed clergyman's absence from his cure or obtaining some preferment without cure to be bestowed on such persons as should be found qualified to undertake such a service", while Newman wondered whether "some fellowships at Oxford or Cambridge might not be devoted to this service"; but these suggestions were too revolutionary to be taken really seriously.[4]

In any event, the Society now thought it was not likely to find anyone willing to go to India. "We are too much addicted to the world to take any pains to win the heathen to Christianity," Newman admitted to one of Francke's colleagues at Halle, "and God knows when we shall do better. Some small attempts are making towards it, but we want a primitive spirit to do anything to purpose. The most we pretend to do at present is to assist the Danes in the worthy enterprise"; and to Ziegenbalg's widow he said:

[1] HN to Bp of Sodor and Man, 12 Nov. 1714, *Society's Letters.*

[2] Rev. Mr Stevenson to HN, 15 Sept. 1715 and 7 Oct. 1716; Rev. Mr Cobbe to HN, 11 Oct. 1715, *Letters from India*; HN to Wm Jennings, Fort St George, 22 Jan. 1717, *Society's Letters.*

[3] Rev. Mr Gründler to Abp of Canterbury, 12 Dec. 1719, *Letters from India.*

[4] HN to Abp of Canterbury, 14 April 1718; to Mr Dawson, 28 June 1716, *Society's Letters.*

"Such is the degeneracy of Europe through the prevalence of luxury and sensuality that if it pleases God to continue His blessing on the labours of the missionaries, posterity will in all likelihood see in the compass of a few years congregations of better Christians from among the heathen in India that can now be found in Christendom. There are several presages of this, which afford but uncomfortable prospect to us in Europe, but must be very agreeable to those who live in India and more to those who are the instruments of Providence in bringing about so glorious a change." [1]

Another reason for the Society's discouragement at this time was the failure of an attempt to establish a mission in Africa. In October 1721 two Africans were introduced to the Society. They had been brought to England by a shipmaster and claimed to be "Princes of Delagoa near over against Madagascar on the south-east coast of Africa", who were empowered to treat for "the concluding of a contract between the African and East India Companies about settling a factory at Delagoa, the country belonging to the King, their brother". Such was contemporary ignorance about Africa that they were believed, and for a year the East India Company and the Africa Company disputed as to which had the right to trade with Delagoa. The East India Company finally withdrew its claim that Delagoa was within its monopoly, and the Africa Company gave them a "princely education". They were "well cloathed and rigged" and "tied to swords". A tutor was engaged to educate them and Dr Bray to instruct them in the Christian religion. Dr Bray also introduced them to the S.P.C.K. with the idea that missionaries should return with them to Delagoa. This occasioned a debate, in which the whole question of overseas missions was raised again, and Dr Waddington said, "The Society is not instituted to promote Christian knowledge otherwhere than in England", but it was decided to approach the Africa Company, which had now signed a contract with the Africans, and "to give an engagement for subsisting two discreet persons proposed to be sent over to Delagoa with the two Africans in the same manner as the Malabar Mission is encouraged". This mission was offered to two seamen, lately returned from Barbary captivity, but they preferred not to go to Africa again. Eventually only one catechist, Marmaduke Penwell, "a sober mechanick",

[1] HN to Prof. Relandus, Halle, 13 Oct. 1713; to Madam Ziegenbalg, 28 Feb. 1719, *Society's Letters*.

who was "qualified as a charity schoolmaster", was found. The Society decided to send him with the Africans "and if the attempt succeed hereafter to endeavour to prevail with one or more revd divines to go over". He was to be paid £30 a year, but also had £20 to enable him to share the "fresh provisions and brandy" of the captain's table on ship. They sailed from Gravesend, but the ship struck a rock and put into Exmouth for repairs. The Africans quarrelled violently and continually until one of them "in a phrenzy" one night "went out about eleven o'clock and was found next morning hanging by his garters on an apple-tree". Penwell and the surviving African resumed their voyage, only to be unable to land at Delagoa because the Dutch, who had "settled a factory there with great expense and the loss of three hundred men's lives", would not allow them to leave the ship, which had to proceed to the Cape of Good Hope. The captain of the ship had always maintained that Prince John (the surviving African) "was a villain to impose so much upon the African Company in telling them that he was a prince", and he was "set ashore in a very barbarous country". The ship returned to the Guinea Coast, shipped slaves from there to the West Indies and sailed back to England. The epilogue to this tragi-comedy was written nearly twenty years later by Newman when he sent Penwell's Journal to Bishop Gibson to read: "Penwell was a plain, illiterate man, as his Journal will show, but honest and well-recommended to the Society; and his behaviour in this voyage recommended him to the service of the African Company in which he died." [1]

This African episode was no encouragement to the S.P.C.K. to persist in establishing an Indian mission of its own; and William Stevenson, on his return to England, also dissuaded it. He was convinced that it would be a mistake to mingle together in the mission field workers of different beliefs in Christian doctrine and government.[2] The Society decided, therefore, to content itself for the time being with increasing its support for the Danish mission. Three new recruits from Halle arrived there to soften the blow caused by the deaths of Ziegenbalg and Gründler. During their stay in London, before sailing to India, they impressed New-

[1] H. P. Thompson, *Thomas Bray*, 93–4; *S.P.C.K. Minutes*, 5 and 26 Oct. 1721, 23 Jan., 1 and 13 Feb. 1722; HN to Ld Perceval, 26 Jan., 2 and 27 Feb., 11 May, 1 Dec. 1722; Mr Penwell to Ld Perceval, 2 and 30 Dec. 1722, *Egmont MSS.*, Add. MSS. 47029, ff. 194, 202, 215, 241, 279, 307, 308; HN to Rev. Mr King, Topsham, Kent, 29 March and 19 Oct. 1723, *Society's Letters*; HN to Bp of London, 8 Jan. 1740, *Miscellaneous Letters*.

[2] Rev. Mr Stevenson to HN, 25 Aug. 1716, *Letters from India*.

man strongly. In a letter to Bishop Wilson, he compared them with "the produce of Oxford or Cambridge", who were "not inclined to go so far from their country and friends and to deny themselves of that comfortable way of living they have been used to here, to take up what the Indies affords". The Society was, "therefore, glad to assist those excellent men that are there and pleased to see Professor Francke sending more after them, though he seems to have no more visible fund than we have". "The three gentlemen", whom he had met in England, "are in a manner sent abroad without purse or script and yet they want nothing, but are everywhere met with by favours conducted by the same kind Providence which has so wonderfully supported the College at Glaucha." Moreover, the missionaries at Tranquebar "are content with plain living and seem to have all things in common amongst them, one chest sufficing for their stores and one room to lodge in, and an Arabick or Syriack book is of more value to them than a suit of clothes above what they at present want". And Newman concluded: "I am afraid we shall never find these qualities in the education of Great Britain, but I don't despair of them in the Isle of Man if there were a fund to train up missionaries under your Lordship's example and direction." [1] Newman did, however, find a little consolation in the fact that in this matter Denmark showed up only a little better than England, for the missionaries were predominantly Pietist clergy from Halle and only a very few from the Mission College in Copenhagen.

Though not "possessed of a fund sufficient to maintain above half an [English] missionary with due decency", the Society now decided to pay one of the Danish missionaries the same salary as he had been receiving from Denmark. The missionary supported by the Society was Benjamin Schultze, one of the three new recruits. An accomplished linguist, he finished the Tamil translation of the Bible begun by Ziegenbalg; but he was a preacher as well as a scholar, holding that "*viva voce* preaching, the testimony of a living man, has a great advantage over the private reading of books". In 1726 three more Lutheran missionaries arrived at Tranquebar. Schultze took advantage of this to tour Cuddalore, Fort St George, Publicat, and other British settlements, as a result of which he expressed a wish to start a mission at Fort St George.[2]

[1] HN to Bp of Sodor and Man, 27 Jan. 1719, *Society's Letters*.

[2] HN to Mr Christian Ludowick, Leipzig, 18 April 1720, *Private Letters*; W. O. B. Allen and E. McClure, op. cit., 264–5.

The Society had long wished that this might be done, but was careful first to obtain permission from the East India Company. Newman asked "that the like attempts for propagating Christianity might be made in the British territories in India", and the Company ordered: "At the desire of the Society for Promoting Christian Knowledge, That if any Danish missionaries shall visit or reside at places under the Company's Jurisdiction, our Governors and Officers may give them their protection. We heartily consent thereunto upon supposition that they behave themselves respectfully and suitable to the Rules of the place." [1] So the Society agreed to Schultze's plan, which made it more than ever necessary for Newman to retain the good offices of the Company and its agents. To the Court of Directors he sent copies of "a sermon and account lately published wherein a short mention is made of the Protestant mission in the appendix and how much it owes to the generosity of the Court"; to Governor Richard Benyon of Fort St George, on his appointment in 1736, he offered his congratulations and recommended the missionaries to his "favour and protection", later informing him the Society "thought themselves obliged to make you the compliment of being a Corresponding Member, in hopes you may be pleased . . . to countenance the Mission which Providence has directed them to attempt founding at Madras".[2] He even sought the acquaintance of the captain of the Company's ship which had taken missionaries to India and told him he wished "to present you with a dish of what you would like best and a bottle of wine . . . at what tavern you please".[3] Whether due to Newman or not, the extension of the mission into its territory caused no friction with the Company, and the Governor and Council of Fort St George reported to the Directors in 1730: "The Danish missionaries in this place behave themselves quietly and modestly." [4]

Schultze followed the policy of the mission at Tranquebar by opening a school at Blacktown in Madras. This received the support of the Society, but not of Stevenson. He, jealous perhaps that they should succeed where he had failed, maintained that in the

[1] HN to Mr Mole, Secretary of East India Co., 2 Dec. 1726, *Society's Letters*; *General Letter from the Hon. Directors of the East India Co. to the Governors and Officers within the Company's Jurisdiction*, 1727, para. 93.

[2] HN to Hon. Richd Benyon, 27 Jan. 1736 and 28 Jan. 1738, *Society's Letters*.

[3] HN to Capt. Micklefield, Commander of the *Colchester*, Jerusalem Coffee House, 22 Oct. 1740, *Society's Letters*.

[4] Governor and Council of Fort St George to Ct of Directors of East India Co., 18 Jan. 1730, *Letters from India*.

missionaries' schools "the boys, that are fit only to be menial servants, weavers or chintz-painters, had to understand their quarto catechism as well as the missionaries and be openly rebuked, brow-beaten and perhaps whipped for not mastering a theological folio". Newman kept his confidence in the missionaries, considering that "the real interests of the Company may hereafter be advantaged by it by entertaining those instructed by the missionaries either as soldiers, sailors or domestick servants in their respective factories, preferably to other natives, both for their fidelity and abilities in service". At any rate, the school started by Schultze rapidly increased. "He moreover received visits from so many adults that he had not time to speak with each separately, but was obliged to fix an hour daily for making known the word of God to all who wished to listen." By 1729 he was asking the Society for one or more assistants.[1]

The Society took this opportunity to try again to send an English missionary or even a Scottish one, for at a meeting of the Society Dr Bray was asked "to write to North Britain to enquire for a missionary for Fort St George", but he desired to be excused as he did not think it much use "from the experience he had had of persons from North Britain and Ireland", so Newman was asked to approach Bishop Wilson again. He wrote, however, both to a Scottish correspondent and to Bishop Wilson. "Our Society", he told them, "want a pious, learned young man to send as an assistant missionary in Fort St George in the East Indies." He again enumerated the qualifications demanded. "Besides a good knowledge in the Latin, Greek and Hebrew languages, it is wished that he might have a genius for learning any language because he must learn those that are spoke by above 100 thousand people of different nations." It was also to be wished that he had "some knowledge in natural philosophy, particularly in medicine and that he understood at least the rudiments of arithmetick, geometry, astronomy and musick and other parts of the mathematicks". The Society would furnish such a man with necessaries costing £100 and pay him a salary of £40 a year "with which they are informed a temperate man may live very comfortably".[2]

No candidate came from Scotland, but Newman could tell Schultze that Bishop Wilson "has just recommended the Rev. Mr

[1] HN to Rev. Mr Stevenson, Hereford, 28 Jan. 1727; to Mr Turner, Fort St George, 7 Feb. 1734, *Society's Letters*.

[2] *S.P.C.K. Minutes*, 9 Sept. 1729; HN to Bp of Sodor and Man, 11 Sept. 1729; to Mr Woodrow, Glasgow, 23 Sept. 1729, *Society's Letters*.

James Christian to be sent to your assistance, and he is now on the road to London". When he arrived, the Society arranged for him to preach in Lincoln's Inn Chapel on Acts 24. 18: "To open their eyes, and to turn them from darkness to light, and from the power of Satan to God, that they may receive forgiveness of sins, and inheritance among them which are sanctified by faith that is in me." Presumably he passed this test, for he was offered the post at Fort St George at £50 a year, but he expected to be paid as a Company's chaplain, who received £100 a year, and "upon a presumption that they did not expect from him to spend his life in their service and that he might be allowed, not only a competent support, but wherewith to enable him to return to Europe after spending some years in their service". The Society, however, was not prepared "to be at the expense of sending a missionary to Fort St George that would not be content to go thither out of zeal for the work of the mission and to deny himself any secular views that might subject the Society to the expense of sending another missionary whenever any temptation of preferment or other considerations might alter his mind". In other words, the Society wanted a man who would go as the Lutheran missionaries, "resolved to abide in the service of the mission without any limitation other than God Almighty's pleasure of sparing him life and health".[1]

Mr Christian's terms were the less acceptable to the Society because it had meanwhile heard from Halle that another candidate from the seminary wished to go to India, and though "there are some reasons why it is to be wished that a Briton might be sent preferable to a foreigner", the Society had almost decided to send the German before Bishop Wilson replied. He was, after all, from "Halle, where Mr Schultze was educated" and, therefore, likely to "be content to serve the mission in subordination to Mr Schultze, with whom it is absolutely necessary the assistant should live in perfect harmony, but who also should carry no scruples with him that might occasion any interruption to such a harmony in a design that will require their joint endeavours, *totis viribus*, to promote".[2] So not until 1789 was the first English missionary to be sent by the Society to India. Newman wrote a careful letter to Bishop Wilson, thanking him for sending Mr Christian, who entirely satisfied the Society, but had not been sent to India as Pro-

[1] *S.P.C.K. Minutes*, 1 and 13 Jan. 1730; HN to Rev. Mr Schultze, Fort St George, 18 Nov. 1729, *Society's Letters*; F. Penny, op. cit., I, 124.

[2] HN to Rev. Mr Woodrow, Glasgow, 11 Nov. 1729, *Society's Letters*.

fessor Francke had proffered a candidate. The Society had "defrayed all the extraordinary expenses of his journey to London" and secured him "the place of one of the Readers at the Church of St Martin's-in-the-Fields, which will be a decent support for him till he can be otherwise provided, if he be not sent hereafter as a missionary by the Society".[1]

In the event, Schultze was joined by two assistants from Halle, Sartorius and Geisler. Having never been employed by the Danish mission, they were the first sent out directly by the Society. The Society raised Schultze's salary to £60 a year and paid his assistants £45 each, besides providing for a catechist, a schoolmaster, one servant, the rent of a house, and support of the children in the school. It also sent them much the same supplies as the missionaries in Tranquebar: "books, paper, binding tools, knives, medicines"; "toys for the children, looking glasses, studs, sleeve buttons, ivory combs, blue glass necklaces"; "weather glasses and mathematical instruments"; "a Cheshire cheese, three chests containing three gross of beer and half a chest of wine".[2] In 1732 the Society faced more expenditure, for Schultze wished to build two new schools and "a new church and to enclose their burying ground, the hall of the mission house, which has served hitherto as a chapel, being much too strait for the congregation allowing a decent distance between the men and women who are Christians in a hot country and the heathen and Romanists who attend there out of curiosity".[3] The Society could not afford this until 1735 and then only on condition "that nothing be at but durableness and usefulness in these buildings, avoiding all unnecessary expense in vanity or show", laying down that for the church "a building of 40 feet square may at present be sufficient and so contrived that whenever the increase of the congregation shall require it, it may be enlarged by taking down one side and lengthened" and that the "missionaries lodge in the mission house and the two schools of boys and one of girls be kept along with the schoolmaster and schoolmistress in another house or houses fit for that purpose".[4]

[1] HN to Rev. Mr Woodrow, Glasgow, 11 Nov. 1729; to Bp of Sodor and Man, 7 March 1730, *Society's Letters*.

[2] HN to Bp of London, 18 Nov. 1732; to Mr Mole, Secretary of East India Co., 14 Jan. 1735; to Hon. Geo. Morton Pitt, Governor of Fort St George, 4 Feb. 1735, *Society's Letters*.

[3] Rev. Mr Schultze to HN, 25 Jan. and 24 Aug. 1732, 29 Jan. 1734; Rev. Mr Sartorius to HN, 24 Jan. 1733, *Letters from India*.

[4] HN to Messrs Schultze, Sartorius, and Geister, Fort St George, 4 Feb. 1735, *Society's Letters*.

Much of the success of the mission was due to Schultze, whose energy and linguistic gifts were as great as ever. Having found he must learn Telugu (or Gentoo), he soon mastered it, and by 1732 had translated the whole Bible and other books into it and written a Telugu grammar. In 1739 he began to study a third Indian language, Hindustani, then called Moorish because used by the Mohammedans. Before he left India in 1743 he had translated the New Testament and part of the Old Testament into it, besides writing a Hindustani grammar and a refutation of the Koran.[1] But he was not the ideal man to be in charge of the mission. Like many men of ability, he could not work easily with others. As early as 1726, William Stevenson thought from the way Schultze wrote that he was likely to "assume too great a superiority over his brethren".[2] Even when he went to Fort St George, his relations with the missionaries at Tranquebar were not easy. Newman wrote to him in 1730: "It is the earnest desire of the Society and what I am commended in the strongest terms to recommend to you to correspond with your brethren at Tranquebar in the most perfect harmony, and if there have been any misunderstandings between you and them to the prejudice of that Christian unanimity which should ever reign among you, the Society desire they may be cancelled by an act of oblivion on both sides, and that they may never hear of any tendency to disunion which may furnish occasion to the common enemy of mankind to frustrate your and their labours."[3] When joined by his younger assistants, Geister and Sartorius, he tried to rule them in a way they would not accept, and their disagreements brought about a crisis, not only in the mission, but also in the Society itself.

During 1733 and 1734 all three men seem to have written to Newman telling him of their grievances. Newman kept these letters to himself and tried to compose their differences. He did, however, show some of the letters to Isaac Hollis, who gave the Society "540 ounces of foreign silver", which paid for the new church and two school houses at Madras. This came to the ears of the members of the East India Committee, who naturally felt they should be given information about the mission before a New England subscriber, however wealthy. They summoned an extraordinary committee meeting, which resolved: "It is this day

[1] W. O. B. Allen and E. McClure, op. cit., 264–5.
[2] Rev. Mr Stevenson, Colwall, to HN, 27 Dec. 1726, *Letters from India.*
[3] HN to Rev. Mr Schultze, Fort St George, 24 Jan. 1730, *Society's Letters.*

ordered to be recommended to the Society, That the Secretary of the Society do not open any letter directed to him as their Secretary, but at some meeting of the Society or their Committee, nor communicate such letters to anyone but by their consent first obtained, nor act in anything relating to this Society but by their direction." But Newman was unrepentant. He told Mr Ziegenhagen, one of the King's German chaplains, and other members of the committee, that he had no intention of concealing the letters, but withheld them from the committee, lest communicating them might injure the interests of the mission. The missionaries' grievances, he considered, could not "be redressed by the Society any more than they could dethrone the Great Mogul", while Mr Hollis had to be told about the mission or he would withdraw his support. Newman defended himself equally vigorously on general grounds: "A discretionary power in common cases must be left somewhere, and he is not worthy to be the Society's Secretary who is left without the discretion or honour that may qualify him for such a trust." Such a power, he insisted, applied particularly to his correspondence. There must be a distinction between the Society's letters and his own private ones. Some of these required an immediate answer, while many people would not write to him unless their letters were treated as private. "Every member that knows me", he concluded, "I believe will vouch for my desiring to be trusted with no more power to promote their designs than is absolutely necessary for their service." Several meetings of the Society followed, at which Newman presumably put his views no less strongly, for finally an extraordinary general meeting amended the committee's motion into one less limiting on his actions: "That no foreign letter directed to the Secretary of the Society be opened by him, but in the presence of the Society, a Committee or of one Subscribing Member at the least." [1]

The differences between the missionaries were bound sooner or later, in fact, to come before the Society, since Newman's efforts to compose them were as unsuccessful as he had suggested those of the Society might be. At first the Society tried conciliation. The missionaries were told that their supporters "cannot but lament the unhappy animosities that of late have been among them and hope they will each of them do what in them lies to restore that Christian love, good agreement and harmony that is absolutely

[1] *S.P.C.K. Minutes*, 4, 7, 11 and 21 Jan. 1735; HN to Rev. Mr Ziegenhagen, St James' Palace, 4 Jan. 1735; to Mr Vernon, 6 Jan. 1735, *Private Letters*.

necessary to carry on the design of the mission in propagating the gospel in the heathen". When this failed, it decided "the only expedient left" was "to separate the contending parties", and in 1736 it asked Schultze to leave Madras and open a new mission at Cuddalore, the cost "to be defrayed out of the common fund" of the Society: "You have, good sir, we believe, as few failings as any missionary in India and as warm a zeal to promote the glory of God. Do what you can to sacrifice your chiefest failing to this zeal and to mortify the least degree of pride that can tempt you to a superiority or rule over your fellow labourers, although your merit may make you worthy of it and would probably commend it from them, if you did not assume it." Schultze, however, was not unnaturally disinclined to leave his well-established mission in Madras and begin again the task of founding a mission in a new place, so instead, in 1737, Sartorius and Geister went to Cuddalore. A year later Newman reported "things are much mended since the separation of the missionaries at Fort St George". Sartorius and Geister were "preparing to begin a school at Cuddalore as soon as the rainy season was over" and meanwhile were applying themselves "to learn the Malabarick language". Even more beneficial had been the effect of the separation for Schultze, who now had "two schools, Malabarian and Portuguese, for instructing sixty children, under the care of catechists and masters, natives of and educated in the country", and while in 1736, before the separation, twelve converts were baptized at Madras, this year the number was 132. At the same time the missionaries at Tranquebar reported they had "increased their congregation last year by an addition of 484 souls, of which 459 were heathen natives, mostly adult", and estimated their total number of living converts to be 2736.[1]

Such good news from the mission fields did not relieve Newman of worries at home connected with it. A number of problems became urgent during his last years. One was the validity of the Lutheran orders of the Missionaries. This was raised as early as 1713, Chamberlayne once again being the inquirer. His action, Newman told him, "occasioned a long debate", in which most members "seemed to wish the matter had never come in question before them, for it was no secret to them that the missionaries are

[1] W. O. B. Allen and E. McClure, op. cit., 264; *S.P.C.K. Minutes*, 20 Jan. 1736; HN to Messrs Schultze, Sartorius, and Geister, Fort St George, 4 Feb. 1735, *Society's Letters*; to Gov. Benyon, Fort St George, 28 Jan. 1738; to Archdeacon Deane, Rochester, 29 Aug. 1738, *Miscellaneous Letters*.

Lutherans or at least pass for such, in which it cannot be supposed they are countenanced and encouraged by the Society". Such reticence was not new, for, Newman explained, members seeking subscriptions

> thought it their prudence and charity to avoid as much as they could putting it into the heads of the benefactors that the missionaries were Lutherans or ministers not episcopally ordained, because mankind are too apt to catch at objections to save their purses, and they considered that if it should please God to make these men instruments of propagating Christianity under some disqualifications, it would not misbecome good men, not only to rejoice at it, but to encourage such instruments in hopes that their defects might by the good Providence of God be hereafter supplied. They considered that, though they assuredly wished to see the Gospel in its purity propagated without any bias to the sects or opinions that unhappily divide Christians, yet that it is rather to be connived at that the heathen should be Lutheran Christians rather than no Christians.

Finally, he reminded Chamberlayne that, as the Society could only get Lutheran missionaries in India, no one could really question their position: "You know with what application they have sought for English missionaries as one means to obviate the objection and how ineffectual all their labour hitherto has proved."[1]

With this Chamberlayne and others who doubted the validity of non-episcopal orders had to be satisfied, particularly as it continued to be impossible to engage English missionaries. As the need for subscribers increased with each expansion of missionary activity, Newman doubtless hoped the question would remain dormant, but it was revived in 1733, when the missionaries at Tranquebar ordained to the ministry a native named Aaron. This at once led members to ask whether Lutheran rules allowed of a "power vested in the missionaries at Tranquebar to confer orders on such persons", their argument being that as the Society seemed to recognize Lutheran orders, it should make sure that all it assisted were properly ordained in that Church. Mr Ziegenhagen was deputed to write to Professor G. A. Francke to ask his opinion of the missionaries' action, and when he replied assuring them of "the regularity of what the missionaries at Tranquebar have done and may further do as necessity may require on the like occasion", a General Meeting of the Society "unanimously expressed their entire satisfaction at the account" and declined to

[1] HN to Mr Chamberlayne, 19 Dec. 1713, *Society's Letters*.

raise the larger issue by "a comparison of the validity of episcopal with foreign ordinations, which could yield no service to the mission, but might do abundance of mischief". As Newman pointed out to Mr Wynch, Chaplain at Fort St George, one of those who had questioned Pastor Aaron's ordination, it was hardly able to do otherwise. "The sending over candidates for orders to Europe would be attended with insuperable difficulties", while "the Archbishop of Canterbury's opinion [was] in favour of ordinations in India". And to this correspondent, Newman concluded with his own views on the subject: "If the Primitive Christians had been as scrupulous on this head as some well-meaning persons nowadays are, how much would it have obstructed the progress of Christianity, and some perhaps would have blamed the forwardness of the eunuch in being baptized by Philip before he was better informed of his commission, but though some lay more stress on the external than the internal call to divine offices, it is certainly right to retain a regard for both with all the decency which prudence, the custom of different countries and the circumstances of different places will admit." [1]

Most members of the Society seemed to accept this view, and discussion on the question died down again. The Danish mission at Tranquebar continued to increase. It claimed 3700 Christians in 1740, and the next year another native pastor, Diogo, was ordained with the entire acceptance of the Society. But the question of orders was to be raised once more in Newman's lifetime. Sartorius died in 1738. The Society was able early in 1740 to send out from Halle Mr Kiernander (later the pioneer of missionary work in Bengal) to replace him as assistant to Geister at Cuddalore, and also arranged for two men from Copenhagen, Fabricus and Zeghlin, to reinforce the Tranquebar mission. When the Society sent out Sartorius and Geister to India, it had taken care to satisfy itself that they had regular Lutheran orders; Sartorius was ordained by one of the King's German chaplains, Mr Ruperti, in London in 1731; Geister in Wernigerode, also in 1731. Reasons of haste, however, prevented this with the three missionaries in 1740. Newman impressed upon the missionaries in India that he thought this a serious omission, "particularly of Mr Kiernander designed for a missionary from the Society", and made sure that

[1] *S.P.C.K. Minutes*, 19 April 1735; HN to Prof. Francke, Halle, 6 June 1735; to Rev. Mr Wynch, Fort St George, 4 Feb. 1736, *Miscellaneous Letters*; W. O. B. Allen and E. McClure, op. cit., 265.

the ordination took place at Tranquebar "to settle the matter on such a foot as to prevent all offence while it is practicable".[1]

By adopting this policy of insisting that there must be no doubt of the validity of the missionaries' orders from the Lutheran view, the S.P.C.K. seems to have satisfied its members then and throughout the century. The Society's relations with the mission in India reveal something more than the feeling of solidarity with Continental Protestantism which it displayed at this time. They reveal also the particular regard for the Lutheran Church which was felt by the Church of England and how the Lutheran connections of the English Royal Family contributed towards strengthening the contacts with Lutheranism, for Danish and German royal chaplains were members of the Society and introduced it to the needs of the Tranquebar mission. Though Newman's correspondence shows that some of the Society's members were worried by its support for Lutheran missions, it shows as well that the Lutheran Church seems to have occupied a special position in the eyes of many Anglicans. The historian of Anglican missionary relations concludes that though "the S.P.C.K. is not known to have ever made any formal statement on the validity of Lutheran ordination", yet nevertheless, "The most natural interpretation seems to be that by using these Lutherans the society did recognize the validity of their Lutheran orders. It is difficult to contest this interpretation, since it turns out to be the conception of that time, as far as it is possible to find any references to it."[2]

Another problem which the mission brought Newman in these last years was finance. From the time the first decision was made to help the Danish mission, the Society suffered more or less continuous anxiety over money to fulfil its obligations. As early as 1711, Chamberlayne told Lord Dartmouth, then Secretary of State, that it was very necessary the Bishops of London and Winchester should have directions to order their clergy to prepare sermons for Good Friday, when the Society might have "the proposed collection", seriously needed if it were to "go on with the Indian mission as they promised the Queen" or, indeed, if it were to do "anything else".[3] The upkeep of the Society's own

[1] Eyre Chatterton, *History of the Church of England in India*, 1924, 102; HN to Gov. Benyon, Fort St George, 20 March 1740; to Archdeacon Deane, Rochester, 8 March 1740, *Miscellaneous Letters*.

[2] Hans Cnattingius, *Bishops and Societies, A Study of Anglican Colonial and Missionary Expansion, 1689–1850*, 1952, 41–3.

[3] Mr Chamberlayne to Ld Dartmouth, 11 March 1711, P.R.O., State Papers, Domestic, Anne, 1711, 19/20.

missions at Madras and Cuddalore, as well as continued assistance to the Danish mission at Tranquebar, added to the money needed. The Society now had "three able missionaries wholly dependent upon casual benefactions . . . which for some years have proved very insufficient".[1] So Newman wrote in 1741, when finance was becoming even more difficult. In that year Schultze indicated that, through ill health, he wanted to return to Europe and asked for another missionary to replace him, but war with Spain since 1739 forced Newman to say it was unlikely the Society could face the cost of a "proposal for sending a new missionary to Fort St George"; it found it difficult to continue even the missionaries' salaries—"silver is so scarce and dear by reason of the war with Spain".[2]

To raise more money, the Society planned in 1742 to send "a circular letter to all their members as was done in the case of the Saltzburghers to very good effect".[3] To make it as effective as possible Newman wrote to the Archbishop of Armagh to ask permission to send it to the Society's members in Ireland, though privately he feared "the general decay of trade, the expense of the war and the prospect of the increase of publick taxes with other distresses will prevent the flow of benefactions which the circular letter in favour of the Saltzburghers produced [in] 1732, 1733 and 1734".[4] He was proved right. Early in 1743 he had to report that the fund for the East India mission "was at present not sufficient". It was decided to call an extraordinary general meeting of the Society to debate the whole question, "Whether it be proper for the Society to continue the East India Mission?" Newman did not conceal his own view that it should be continued. He wrote to a member the day before the meeting: "What will be thought of us in Germany and Denmark if we can go the length we have in founding a mission to propagate Christianity, purchasing and building houses, sending over at different times, not one by way of experiment, but several missionaries, and then abruptly discontinue the undertaking which they were animated by our zeal to pursue, not only in Tranquebar, but in the English settlements, by several large benefactions out of the fund at Halle." He ad-

[1] HN to Rev. Messrs Wynch and Howard, Chaplains at Fort St George, 28 Jan. 1741, *Miscellaneous Letters*.

[2] HN to Danish Missionaries at Tranquebar, 11 Jan. 1742, *Miscellaneous Letters*.

[3] HN to Bp of Chester, 31 July 1741, *Miscellaneous Letters*.

[4] HN to Ld Primate of Ireland, Dublin, 28 Nov. 1741; to Archdeacon Deane, Rochester, 8 Oct. 1741, *Miscellaneous Letters*.

mitted, "The present fund for supporting it is low, but Heaven can soon ordain the supplies necessary by some unknown benefactor", who might "grant more than we want if we have courage to depend on Providence and persevere in such measure as we are able to pursue till those supplies come. But if the door be once shut against accepting any supplies, the Society will not have it in their power even to be auxiliaries at Tranquebar, and the Romanists both at home and abroad will triumph at the defeating those measures which had been for many years a great eyesore for them. I hope God will direct the issue of the debate on this occasion to His glory." He was not disappointed. The next day the meeting "agreed *nemine contradicente* that the East India Mission be continued".[1]

So Newman had the satisfaction, in the last months of his life, of knowing that the Society would continue to support the East India mission, which by the end of the eighteenth century was estimated to have between 18,000 and 20,000 Christians attached to it, whose descendants "constituted the most stable elements in the Lutheran communities in the nineteenth and twentieth centuries".[2] Throughout the difficulties and criticisms which the undertaking had encountered, Newman's belief, as he told Cotton Mather, was that the Society should "not desist from giving the mission all the assistance they can and leave the success to the Lord of the Vineyard".[3] Like the first missionaries who laboured and died in Tranquebar and Fort St George, he trusted that great things would come of small beginnings. Indeed, his own hopes were no less than those expressed by Ziegenbalg in a letter to a member of the Society, which he copied in full in the Abstract of Correspondence: "After all, we look upon all these endeavours only as so many preparatory steps towards the ensuing great harvest of the heathen world. We do nothing as yet but break the ice, that those who are to come after us may find a way beat out for them and propagate the Gospel of Christ with the greater ease and expedition. And although we feel ourselves surrounded with many infirmities on our side, yet we confide in the Lord, that He will regard the sincerity of our intention and confer still greater blessing upon our endeavours than we have seen hitherto."[4]

[1] HN to Mr Philipps, Westminster, 14 Feb. 1743, *Miscellaneous Letters*; *S.P.C.K. Minutes*, 1 and 15 Feb. 1743.
[2] K. S. Latourette, op. cit., III, 281.
[3] HN to Rev. Mr Cotton Mather, Boston, 31 Aug. 1722, *New Eng. Letters*.
[4] Rev. Mr Ziegenbalg to Mr Henry Hoare, 11 Dec. 1713, *Abs. of Correspondence*.

6

THE VAUDOIS YOUTH AND PROTESTANT PROSELYTES

ONE of England's most dramatic interventions in foreign affairs during the Commonwealth was brought about by the massacre in 1655 by the Duchess of Savoy's troops of the Waldenses or Vaudois, whose Protestantism was older than the Reformation. Milton called on God to avenge the sufferings of the "slaughtered saints" whose bones lay scattered on the Alpine mountains. Oliver Cromwell headed a collection for the sufferers with a gift of £2000, and used Mazarin's desire for English friendship to make France persuade Savoy to end the massacres and reinstate the Vaudois in their valleys.[1] This brought satisfaction even to Englishmen who were not Puritans, and after the Restoration it still seemed natural to English Churchmen to regard the Persecuted Remnants on the Continent as their spiritual brethren. Jacobite danger and war with France in the eighteenth century strengthened this outlook, and in Anne's reign the Whig Government entrusted the Bishop of London with a royal pension of £60 a year towards the support of "two young men from the Valleys of Piedmont at the University of Cambridge in order to qualify them for the service of the Protestant Churches in those parts".[2]

What had begun as a political move by a government fighting for its life continued for similar reasons after the accession of the House of Hanover, but the application of the grant depended upon sympathetic individuals. These included French Huguenot refugees, who were able, through connections with the Continent, to arrange for Vaudois candidates to come to England. A Marquis de Rochgude went even further. He brought over a young man of his choice, Gaspard Manuel, had him admitted as a sizar at Clare Hall, Cambridge, in 1715, and was prepared to maintain him there, whether he obtained the royal pension or not; but the Marquis died of apoplexy in 1717 at Wesel in the Duchy of Cleves. He left £30 for "the Vaudois youth", but this was claimed by his

[1] C. H. Firth, *Oliver Cromwell*, 378–9.
[2] HN to Bp of London, 23 June 1722, *Society's Letters*.

tutor, Dr Loughton, who was still asking the next year for more than £25 to pay his debts. Clearly Manuel was in urgent need of help, the more so because he had "hitherto had only bare subsistence and little or nothing to lay out in books, much less towards taking his degree of Bachelor of Arts", and it had been planned that he should remain at Cambridge for a time after graduating "in order to recover his French". Nor could he expect to receive any royal bounty for at least another year.[1]

Dr Loughton wrote to Newman, presumably as one likely to take an interest in the case, telling him of Manuel's situation and asking whether he could secure support for the young man. Newman gained the interest of a notable Huguenot in England, the Marquis de Ruvigny, who had left France after the Revocation of the Edict of Nantes and served with distinction in the British army, being created Earl of Galway. He was prepared to contribute to Manuel's support at Cambridge until a pension was vacant for him, if Newman thought it worth while for him to continue his studies—"Whatever your opinion will be of what should be done with him, I shall follow." Finally, he agreed to pay the sum already owing to Dr Loughton and give a further £7 5*s*. each half-year, if Newman undertook to make it up each time by subscriptions to £12 10*s*., which Dr Loughton considered would be needed to maintain Manuel at Cambridge.[2]

Newman was thus made intermediary between Manuel and his chief benefactor, which was not easy. Before a year had passed, Dr Loughton complained that Manuel had not progressed in his studies. Newman induced Lord Galway to write him "reproving letters", but still he seemed "intractable to advice", and Newman asked his tutor for his "opinion of his genius, whether he be capable of arriving at that learning which is necessary for a Minister of the Gospel, for if he be not and must hereafter for his bread fall into a military or mechanick way of living, the sooner he goes to it the better". At this point, Manuel wrote to Newman, making it clear that he did not agree with his tutor's "method of instruction", but Newman warned him of his "power as a person of established reputation", whom he must satisfy to graduate, and added: "If such a compliance be grievous to you to bear, how can you expect

[1] HN to Earl of Galway, 12 Aug. 1718; to Bp of London, 24 Feb. and 18 May 1719, *Private Letters*.

[2] Rev. Dr Loughton to HN, 28 Jan. and 11 Feb. 1718; Ld Galway to HN, 29 Aug. 1719, *Rawlinson MSS*., C.933, f. 118, C.743, f. 48; HN to Rev. Dr Loughton, 9 July 1718, *Private Letters*.

to be able hereafter to conflict with trials of a more ardent nature when you return to your own country?" Newman made excuses for Manuel, who, he observed to Lord Galway, "if he does not mind his studies, must spend his time in sleeping, for though your Lordship's allowance be generous and large enough for a youth that minds his studies, it would not serve for one that rakes it at taverns". Moreover, he had heard that his tutor was "a worthy person, yet being overborne with pupils, he is obliged to study the most compendious ways of instruction, which it seems has not agreed with Manuel's prompt genius", and that "others have made the same complaint as Manuel". Dr Loughton, however, had not finished and told Newman: "He has behaved himself so ill amongst us for this year or two last past that our society, I believe, will not let him take his degree quite so soon as others of his standing do and can never give him any testimonial of his good behaviour." Newman asked him to explain these words, which might "include almost anything but murther and high treason", but the tutor's reply, he complained, was "full of resentment" and "leaves me as much in the dark as I was before". He took the bold step of writing to Dr Colebatch, Senior Fellow of Trinity College, whom he knew, asking him to intervene with the Master of Clare to allow Manuel to take his degree. It was a successful move. Manuel took his B.A. early in 1720, and a royal pension fell vacant for him at the same time.[1]

But neither Newman's efforts, nor Lord Galway's generosity, nor the King's pension were to secure their intended purpose. Manuel, no sooner than graduated, found that, having been born at Zurich in Switzerland, he was unable to "serve as a minister in Piedmont, not being a native of the Duke of Savoy's dominions". The previous holder of his pension indicated he "does not want to return to Piedmont, as he likes England better", while another was "no more a native of the Duke of Savoy's dominions than Mr Manuel". John Robinson, Bishop of London, complained that since he had been in office, of all who "have had the benefit of the King's pension, not one has gone to serve the Vaudois Churches". It was difficult to find candidates, and when they were found and qualified, there was either no vacancy for them in Piedmont or they went to Geneva, where there was no likelihood of persecution,

[1] HN to Dr Loughton, 25 April, 24 July, 4 Aug., 24 and 29 Dec. 1719; to Ld Galway, 12 May and 18 Aug. 1719, 30 Jan., 9 and 30 April 1720; to Mr Manuel, 4 Aug. 1719 and 3 Nov. 1720; to Rev. Dr Colebatch, 21 Jan. 1720, *Private Letters*.

while the Vaudois Churches preferred to send their candidates to nearer Protestant seminaries. Newman was now convinced that it was not possible to fulfil "the original intent of the settlement" and tried in vain to make the best of a bad job by urging, first Bishop Robinson and then his successor Bishop Gibson, to get the grant transferred to maintain one of two schoolmasters in Minorca "for preventing His Majesty's Protestant subjects in that island going over to the Church of Rome" and in the hope that "many of the natives would send their children to be instructed, who, of course, would embrace our religion, and their allegiance to the British Crown [could] be better depended on".[1] As for Gaspard Manuel, "the Vaudois youth", who gave Newman so much trouble, there is no further record of him, unless he be the "John Manuel" ordained deacon by the Bishop of London in 1722 and priest by the Bishop of Lincoln in 1732.[2] Though he disliked being a sizar at Cambridge, he might well have preferred a curacy in the Church of England to anything Piedmont could offer.

Newman's experiences with the Vaudois bounty, however, were as nothing compared with those in the administration of another fund concerned mainly with religious refugees in England, so important in the life of the country at this time. When the Edict of Nantes was revoked by Louis XIV in October 1685, there were some 400,000 Huguenots in France. Of these about a half escaped the jails and galleys, and it has been estimated that a quarter of the survivors, that is to say about 50,000, fled to England. It has been further estimated that no less than 80,000 refugees altogether arrived in England between 1670 and 1690, and more came during the next decade, at a time when the native population of England was between five and a half and seven millions.[3] The sufferings of the refugees moved religious people in England, and Newman mentioned a dinner in 1713 at the Leg Tavern in Fleet Street, which he and twenty other Englishmen gave for ten French confessors lately set at liberty from the galleys, whose "modesty and behaviour was so moving".[4]

Three years later he declined an invitation from Chamberlayne to be secretary of another society as well as the S.P.C.K. "Who-

[1] HN to Bp of London, 23 June 1722 and 31 Aug. 1723, *Society's Letters*.
[2] *Graduati Cantabrigiensis*, 310; J. and J. A. Venn, *Alumni Cantabrigiensis*, pt. i, III, 137.
[3] H. D. Traill (ed.), *Social England*, 1903, 450; J. H. Whiteley, *Wesley's England*, 1938, 59.
[4] HN to Hon. James Lowther, M.P., Whitehaven, 26 Dec. 1713, *H.M.C.*, *13th Report*, App. VII, 247.

ever undertakes it", he told him, "ought to speak and write Latin like an angel, but I can do neither. He ought to understand French Italian, Spanish and High Dutch, if not to speak them, but how little do I know of these languages." [1] His letter does not name the society, but it may well have been the Commissioners for Relieving Poor Proselytes, which came into being early the next year, when —in Newman's words—"a considerable number of worthy persons, English and French, having in the year 1717 received a commission from the Archbishop of Canterbury, my Lord Chamberlain and other lords by His Majesty's appointment, for relieving such proselytes from the Church of Rome as should be found real objects of charity".[2] If this be the society, then Newman changed his mind, for he was its secretary for the whole period of its existence. Chamberlayne was its treasurer, and as he was an eminent linguist, upon whom the S.P.C.K. relied when translation had to be done, no doubt he made good Newman's deficiencies in the work of this other organization.

This commission, the "Proselyte Society" as it was commonly called, was in origin a development from another commission set up for the relief of French refugees. In November 1695, William III in his speech to Parliament urged that provision should be made for these refugees, and £15,000 a year was voted out of the civil list for their relief. This money, together with voluntary contributions, was paid to the Lord Chamberlain, and to secure a just allocation of the funds, a commission of some fifteen persons, under the presidency of Archbishop Tenison, was appointed by royal licence in March 1699.[3]

Chamberlayne himself gave an account of the connection between this earlier commission and the "Proselyte Society" in his continuation of *Magnae Britanniae Notitia or the Present State of Great Britain*, which had been begun by his father, Edward Chamberlayne:

After the revocation of the perpetual Edict of Nantz established by Henry IV and so solemnly renewed by the Son and Grandson of that great King, whereby the free Exercise of the Protestant Religion became part of the Rights of all Frenchmen professing the same; and after the most dreadful Persecution that ever happened . . . it pleas'd God to move the heart of the great Assertor of the Religious and Civil Rights of Mankind, King William, of immortal Memory to consent that the sum

[1] HN to Mr Chamberlayne, 11 Jan. 1716, *Society's Letters*.
[2] HN to Lord Hertford, Marlborough, 14 Nov. 1723, *Private Letters*.
[3] E. F. Carpenter, *Thomas Tenison*, 326–7.

of £15,000 *per Annum* should be charged upon the Royal Revenues and appropriated by Act of Parliament, towards the Relief and Support of the vast number of French Protestants of all Degrees and Conditions, Ages and Sexes, that have been flying hither for Refuge from the year 1684, that fatal Epocha, to this Day. And for the rendring more effectual the aforesaid charitable Benevolence of our King and Nation, the said King was pleased to appoint some of the great Officers of the Kingdom, Privy Councillors and others, to superintend the distribution of the said sum of £15,000, and by their advice . . . that Sum has been managed with such Œconomy and Prudence that not only all the distressed Protestants or *Refugees*, as they are commonly called, have been assisted from year to year, but even many *Converts* from *Popery* of the same nation . . .

This has greatly increased the Objects of Church Charities, and the French Protestants have been satisfy'd to share with them part of that which was wholly appropriated to the said *Refugees*, his Majesty [1] has been graciously pleased to allow, that the Paymaster of the Pensions for the time being, shall issue the sum of £400 per annum in such manner and according to such directions as the Lord Archbishop of Canterbury shall give *for and towards the Relief of poor Converts from the Church of Rome*: by Virtue of which Powers the Archbishop of Canterbury, the Bishop of London, the Lord Chief Justice of the King's Bench and the Lord Chief Justice of the Common Pleas have agreed to appoint several eminent Persons to be Commissioners for the relief of poor Proselytes, and not only to receive and distribute the above mentioned £400, but also all such sums of money as shall be raised.[2]

The list of commissioners appointed in this way to relieve the poor proselytes, together with the minute books both of committee and general meetings, are in the possession of the S.P.C.K., where they were probably deposited by Newman. The original commissioners were twenty-six in number, of whom eleven seem to be foreigners, and included the Bishops of Carlisle and Norwich, the Marquis du Quesne and Monsieur Bouet, the King of Prussia's Resident, besides such prominent members of the S.P.C.K. as Lord Perceval, Sir John Philipps, and Dr Bray. The commissioners themselves added fifty-nine other names, including Newman and others who were also members of the S.P.C.K. They thus formed a semi-official body, but were unpaid, even Newman as secretary receiving no salary nor clerical assistance.

Despite this, they were always in financial difficulty. They had the royal bounty of £400 a year, but it was hoped that this would be supplemented by considerable private benefactions. At its first meeting, the committee resolved "that in order to encourage

[1] I.e., George I.

[2] John Chamberlayne, *Magnae Britanniae Notitia*, 25th ed., 1718, 293–4.

contributions, all members of the Society should contribute a certain sum yearly towards the support of the poor proselytes and that for the future none be admitted members of the Society without subscribing a certain annual sum to be paid quarterly during their stay in the Society".[1] But many members did not set a good example; subscriptions came in slowly; and Newman was several times instructed "to prepare a letter to be sent to such subscribers as have not yet paid their subscriptions". It was even more difficult to obtain donations from outsiders. In 1720, the year of the gambling mania, the committee appointed Newman and several other commissioners to make "an application to some of the South Sea Directors for obtaining a subscription in that stock towards the relief of poor proselytes". They failed, but Lord Perceval offered to lend them £100 "towards entituling them to a subscription in the South Sea for the benefit of the proselytes". Newman thanked him, but said: "It would not be for the honour of the Society to engage in such a way of raising money for them".[2] He was probably right to decline loans, even from enthusiastic commissioners, and that investment would not have been profitable; but subscriptions did not bring in much money. Income rarely exceeded £500 any year, and Newman remarked "as for the additional charities to the Royal Bounty, they are so inconsiderable that I question whether they will more than bear the charges necessary for supporting the name of the thing".[3]

Shortage of subscriptions was not matched by any shortage of proselytes seeking relief. Applications were continual and had to be investigated as circumstances allowed. At an early meeting, the committee divided candidates for pensions into four heads:

1. Those proselytes who after a strict enquiry have been found deserving the assistance and encouragement of the Commissioners, and of whose life and conversation the Committee have been reasonably satisfied.
2. Those whose characters hath appeared doubtful and suspicious to the Commissioners.
3. Those who, though of a good life and conversation, yet are not in the case allowed by the Standing Orders, as being able to maintain themselves without the help of the Commissioners or having allowances, pensions, etc.
4. Those who have appeared to the Committee to be unworthy to partake of this benefice.[4]

[1] *Committee Minutes*, 2 May 1717.
[2] Ibid., 24 July 1720; HN to Ld Perceval, 8 Sept. 1720, *Society's Letters*.
[3] HN to Mr Blunden, Hampstead, 11 Nov. 1723, *Private Letters*.
[4] *Committee Minutes*, 18 June 1717.

The commissioners then, as Chamberlayne described, granted a weekly allowance to each applicant while inquiries were made about his character and circumstance.[1] A few were placed in the last class and rejected without hesitation. They were proselytes whose conversion did not seem genuine, like "Mr Alvarado, of Saragossa in Spain, now in orders, the Committee is informed he has returned to Spain and while there professed himself a Papist, and since his return to Great Britain, he has been sometimes a Quaker and sometimes a Protestant, but always of an ill reputation". Others, such as "John Le Brun, of Mons in Flanders, a jewel cutter, his certificate seems suspicious", were deferred for further investigation and placed in the second class. Others were rejected under the third head, either because they were thought capable of supporting themselves, like "John Baptiste Bellanger, of Paris, a tailor, the Committee is informed that if he will work, he can earn his livelihood very well", or because they already received relief, like "Mr Poulet, of Languedoc in France, was formerly a soldier in Spain and is now a pensioner at Chelsea". The majority, however, came in the first class and were given half-yearly pensions ranging from 40*s.* to £8. A few of these needed only temporary help to put them on their feet, like "Lewis Nicolas de Chesau, a native of Champagne, formerly a Capuchin, having a prospect of being usher in a school, but wanting wherewith to put himself in a decent habit, etc.". A few also wanted their earnings supplemented, like "John Baptiste Treval, formerly Attorney in the Parliament of Paris and practises as a notary, having a wife and two children and but a small practice". But most in this class were, in Chamberlayne's words, "ministers, women, old persons, sick and infirm", entirely without resources. There was, for instance, "Vincent Pinna, a Sicilian, formerly a Capuchin, now in years, by the decay of his sight is disabled from following the business of making chains for watches, which he had undertaken", and "Mrs Mary Simon, formerly of Brussels, being in great want", and "Mr Claude Champion de la Motte, of Lorraine, formerly rector of a good family, being in a very destitute condition".[2]

Before long, the commissioners found their money fully expended on maintaining such people and were faced with the prospect of paying them pensions indefinitely. To avoid this, they tried, as Chamberlayne said, "to put them out to some good trade, by

[1] John Chamberlayne, op. cit., 295.
[2] *Committee Minutes*, 18 and 21 June 1717.

which they may support both themselves and families, or to send them abroad to some of His Majesty's Plantations, allowing them a sum of money for that purpose once for all". Being informed "that in all likelihood the Society may place such proselytes as are not able to work at any trade in the Isle of Man on very easy terms, upon making application to the Bishop of that island", Newman was instructed to write to Bishop Wilson, asking if this were so and also for a subscription. His reply to both requests was discouraging: "that since that place is a sort of asylum for people in distress, things are become as dear there as in England; and by the plenty of wine and brandy and the multitude of strangers, a man may be as soon corrupted there as in any one country; that he would very gladly be a member of the Society but cannot by reason he has been forced to advance to the poor clergy there part of his small income for their support, till they can obtain the arrears due to them from the Crown." [1] More promising might have been Sir Humphrey Mackworth's offer to find employment for them in Neath, but upon investigation, Newman had to explain that the commissioners would be glad to send a great number to so cheap a part of the country, but of their more than fifty dependants, nearly all were too old, had children, or were in occupations in London, so that they could only find one, Gio Antonio Fontana, a young Florentine, formerly a servant in the Venetian Embassy. He knew no English, but if there was a job suitable for him in Neath, the commissioners would gladly help to establish him in it.[2] The fate of Fontana is unknown, but the scheme came to nothing, since it proved easier to find jobs for those who could work in London, and the same applied to another idea of Newman's, that the Marquis Du Quesne might find some of them useful in Jamaica, where he was a military commander.[3]

The failure of large-scale settlement schemes left the commissioners only with the alternative of seeking places for individuals, a job which fell largely to Newman. Some refugees were deserters from the French forces, for whom it was comparatively easy to find occupations of some sort. Simon Roussell, who had served for twenty-six years in the British Army, finishing as a Sergeant of Dragoons in Spain until disbanded, entered "the good Duke of Chandos' service as a labourer at Cannons"; Francis Deprés, who

[1] *General Meeting Minutes*, 6 Aug. 1718 and 4 Feb. 1719.
[2] HN to Sir Humphrey Mackworth, Hampstead, 11 May 1720, *Private Letters*.
[3] HN to Marquis Du Quesne, 19 Oct. 1722, *Letters to Jamaica*.

had been taken prisoner late in the War of the Spanish Succession while a second lieutenant in the *Superbe* and chose "rather to spend his life in a free Protestant country, though it would be in a lower station", became a seaman in the *Royal Ann* galley.[1] But others seemed quite unemployable. Mary Simon, one of the original pensioners of the commissioners in 1717 and "always of a good repute among the proselytes", was still receiving £10 a year ten years later. She complained to Newman that "the allowance is what she cannot live upon and that she has been obliged to pawn her cloaks for rent and other necessaries", but actually, Newman told Bishop Gibson, "she is able to do nothing for a livelihood and is every year more crazy and necessitous . . . [and] was taken out of the Marshalsea some time ago and another time was rescued out of the hands of a bailiff".[2] Such cases were bound to make supporters of the Proselyte Society wonder whether it justified itself.

An even greater problem was that the commissioners constantly had reports that those adjudged worthy of charity as converts from Romanism were not what they pretended to be. In the first year of the scheme, they were told that "three pretended proselytes" receiving pensions were "secretly Papists and boasted privately of their having imposed upon the heretics and had a dispensation for doing so till Christmas next", and similar accusations followed.[3] It was difficult to discover whether such charges were true, but some seemed proved, as those against "Peter Ladier and his wife, peasants of Brigbere in the diocese of Countance in Normandy", of whom Newman reported in 1723: "Upon a thorough examination, we have found they never were Roman Catholicks, not having so much of the religion of that people as a *Pater Noster* or *Ave Maria*. We thence concluded that they are not only disqualified for receiving any money from the Society, but also notorious and criminal impostures, fit objects of punishment and of the Society's indignation and resentment." [4] An added difficulty was that some of the most suspicious cases had been referred to the commissioners by the Huguenot churches in London, who resented aspersions on their judgement. A prominent Huguenot resigned from the Society in 1723 and sent a printed letter "to all French Churches in and

[1] HN to Mr Arnold, War Office, 24 June 1718; to Mr Philpot, M.P., 5 June 1719; to Commander Swanton, Navy Office, 19 June 1719; to Brigadier Richards, Tower of London, 21 July 1719; to Capt. Willis, *Royal Ann* Galley, 31 Aug. 1719, *Private Letters*.

[2] HN to Bp of London, 28 April 1727, *Society's Letters*.

[3] *Committee Minutes*, 13 Nov. 1717.

[4] HN to Abp of Canterbury, 26 Oct. 1723, *Wake MSS.*, Arch. W. Epist. 27, f. 14.

about London", violently attacking the commissioners for examining afresh proselytes sent them by the French churches and for having "ordered an Italian proselyte to be arrested for the charity he had received after he was detected of being a cheat and going to mass in Westminster".[1]

The proselyte who caused the greatest disenchantment in the Society was not a foreign refugee, but a native-born Englishman. He was John Barrett, who claimed to have been born in Lancashire "of parents that were rigid Papists" and educated by the Jesuits in Rome. In 1721 he approached the commissioners as one who had "sincerely abjured the Church of Rome" and wished to be ordained in the Church of England. The committee "very much approved" a written "account of the motives of his conversion" and allowed him 4*s*. a week. "Soon after he had conformed to the Church of England", he claimed he "was stabbed in two places in his body as he was going home one night in the Strand", news sympathetically received by Newman as "a fresh argument of the valuableness of the man the Commissioners have taken into their protection". His estimation of Barrett increased when the latter wrote a book which he thought "a noble proof of his genius, great reading and prudent spending of his time, which if published will reflect honour upon the Proselyte Society". Parts of it, however, troubled him. Some expressions needed qualifying to remove an impression he "had wrote in favour of the tenets propagated by free-thinkers", while passages attacking "the mystery of priestcraft" seemed strange from one "desirous to assume the order", but no doubt he wished to distinguish "between the studied knavery and the honest simplicity of those that wear the sacred character". In a second work, *A Rational Compendious Way of Convincing Atheists of a Superior Being and of the Necessity of Religion*, he avoided such pitfalls, and Lord Perceval agreed with Newman that the manuscript was "strong and convincing".[2]

In 1724 Barrett was ordained by Bishop Gibson and became a "preaching curate" to the venerable Dr Bray at St Botolph's, Aldgate. Newman, having heard him, thought he acted "like a young beginner in his function" and advised him to read Eachard's

[1] HN to Ld Perceval, 16 July 1723; Ld Perceval to HN, 24 July 1723, *Egmont MSS.*, Add. MSS. 47030, ff. 18–20 and 22–24.

[2] HN to Ld Perceval, 31 Jan., 23 Feb. and 26 April 1723; Ld Perceval to HN, 9 March 1723, *Egmont MSS.*, Add. MSS. 47029, ff. 234–8, 301, 319; HN to Abp of Canterbury, 11 April 1721, *Wake MSS.*, Arch. W. Epist. 27, f. 105; to Bp of London, 26 March 1722, *Society's Letters*.

Contempt of the Clergy and Bishop Burnet's *Pastoral Care* "to avoid those failings young preachers are most inclined to". Barrett wanted a living, but the most Gibson would offer him was one in Maryland. He could only accept, but the ship on which he embarked was disabled in a storm off the Isle of Wight and he "came up to Town again on foot". The Proselyte Society decided this time to send him to Jamaica, Lord Perceval requesting the Duke of Portland, Governor of the island, to "favour him with a good living if there be one vacant in that island". But when the time came for the ship to sail, Barrett had disappeared; then news came that he had died at Stockport in Cheshire. At first Newman thought "the poor man is murthered by his own relations for having embraced the Protestant Religion". Investigation proved that he had died a natural death, but also revealed a sad story for Newman to tell Dr Bray about his former curate. His parents, both still living at Stockport, had always been "honest Protestants"; he had been educated at the grammar school at Stockport; he had travelled to Rome as tutor to a Protestant baronet, but had never been a Papist. Lord Perceval had allowed him "lodgings at his house in Pall Mall to save charges", but now the servants there said "he did not lie there scarce a week and some times not once in ten days". A woman came forward claiming to be Elizabeth Barrett, his wife, but Newman "suspected her to be his mistress"; and, finally, the captain of the ship on which Barrett had embarked for Maryland complained of his drunken behaviour and bad language. Newman stigmatized him as a "wicked fraud" and "one of the greatest impostors we have had to do with yet among the proselytes", but urged that his case "must remain a secret to the Proselyte Society", lest Huguenot critics might "triumph to know that the man which the English Committee always boasted of, was a cheat superior to any of 99 vagabonds that were gone back to France as innocent as they came".[1]

Such silence might be maintained, but this and similar cases discouraged the commissioners themselves, particularly Lord Perceval, one of the earliest and keenest of their number. Upon joining he told Berkeley: "The good we do and the mischief we hinder is so great that I heartily wish our fund were larger"; but

[1] HN to Ld Perceval, 16 July 1723, 24 May 1724, *Egmont MSS.*, Add. MSS. 47030, ff. 18, 137; 23 Jan. and 4 July 1724, *Society's Letters*; to Bp of London, 20 Dec. 1723; to Mr Aldersey, Spurstow, Cheshire, 16 June 1724; to Rev. Mr Dale, Stockport, 9 July 1724; to Rev. Dr Bray, Sheldon, War, 14 July 1724, *Society's Letters*; to Duke of Portland, Jamaica, 16 March 1724, *Egmont MSS.*, Add. MSS. 47030, f. 119.

three or four years' experience disillusioned him. In 1722 he presented a memorandum to his fellow-commissioners about their work. "We are", he alleged, "totally abandoned by the bishops and dignitaries of the Church", none of whom had attended their meetings for a long time and some had even withdrawn their subscriptions. The lower clergy gave little more support, so that most of the work fell upon two or three lay commissioners. Pensioners were dissatisfied because the fund was not large enough to give them adequate grants. Many proselytes, especially priests, "were no more than spies upon us", while the morals of others suggested that they "drew vile and scandalous persons from the Romish Communion who are a disgrace to any religion".[1] Faced with this, the committee decided to rid themselves of such undesirable pensioners by appointing two examiners, at a salary of £30 each a year, "to examine the case of the proselytes who do receive or shall apply for assistance from the Commissioners"; they were to "examine them upon the true motives of their conversion from the Church of Rome and what knowledge they have of the Protestant Religion" and inquire from "persons at home and by good correspondents abroad" into their characters so that they could furnish the commissioners with full information about each candidate for the award or renewal of a pension.[2]

Both Perceval and Newman, however, thought the committee's scheme inadequate. Newman now held that the royal bounty and the care of proselytes should revert to the original commission set up by William III, and Perceval agreed. He told Newman: "I heartily wish the French committee had the management of this affair and that at least we laymen were rid of it, since the clergy think so ill of us. I think the Archbishop should be acquainted with it." Newman took the hint. He wrote to Archbishop Wake and reported to Perceval that he "seems to have the same sentiments", for he had replied: "I am out of all hope in doing good in the business of the proselytes. You may try a little longer, but you will be forced to drop it in the end." [3] Emboldened by this, Newman submitted in October 1723 "Reasons humbly offered to the Commissioners for Relieving Poor Proselytes to Yield up their

[1] Ld Perceval to Rev. Mr Berkeley, Naples, 13 March 1718, *Egmont MSS.*, Add. MSS. 47034, f. 39; Lord Perceval's "Memorandum to Proselyte Soc.", *Rawlinson MSS.*, C.743, f. 51.

[2] *Committee Minutes*, 22 Feb. 1722.

[3] HN to Ld Perceval, 16 July and 26 Oct. 1723; Ld Perceval to HN, 24 July 1723, *Egmont MSS.*, Add. MSS. 47030, ff. 18–20, 22–4, 57.

Commission", stressing that, of those relieved, "the greatest part of them are such as are a disgrace to any commission, not for their poverty, but that they are generally so ignorant as to be scarce able to give any account of the religion they renounce and less of the Protestant Religion which they intend to embrace", while there were "above 50 that are detected of having been spies here or are now actually returned to Popery".[1]

The next month Chamberlayne died, leaving the Proselyte Society without its Treasurer. Newman wrote to the most active commissioners, urging them "to take this opportunity to resign the commission". This, he explained, "will not destroy the King's Bounty, but only return it to its old channel where it will perhaps be more usefully employed than it is now". The ill success of their efforts seemed to him evident. They had relieved about 250 persons as proselytes, of whom "above 100 have returned to the Church of Rome", including 41 who "were disposed of in good business for their subsistence", while about another sixty "are withdrawn from the Kingdom, as if their business here had been only to be spies or vagabonds seeking their fortune".[2] Lord Perceval supported him with another memorandum to the commissioners, this time in favour of relinquishing the commission.[3]

Their colleagues decided, however, as Newman told Perceval and Wake, "to go on with the commission after some alterations to the present rules, wherein I wish they may not be disappointed, as others have been before them", though the difficulties seemed "as insuperable as ever".[4] On hearing this, Wake sent Newman suggestions for the commissioners to consider. It would be "advisable to reduce the proselytes relieved to a certain number, suppose 30 or 40 or so many as could be found worthy of relief upon a strict enquiry, regard being had to the fund". Moreover, "monks are generally so ignorant and stupid that, except some of the order of Benedictines, they are looked upon abroad as the scum of the Church of Rome and can hardly be supposed to come over to us so much upon principle as upon some misdemeanour in their own convent, a desire for rambling from confinement or the

[1] HN's "Memorandum to Proselyte Soc.", Oct. 1723, *Society's Letters*.

[2] HN to Ld Perceval, 4 and 5 Nov. 1723, *Egmont MSS.*, Add. MSS. 47030, ff. 63, 65; to Mr Thos Blunden, Hampstead, 4 Nov. 1723; to Ld Hertford, Marlborough, 14 Nov. 1723, *Private Letters*.

[3] Ld Perceval's "Memorandum to Prosleyte Soc.", 2 Nov. 1723, *Egmont MSS.*, Add. MSS. 47030, ff. 85–8.

[4] HN to Ld Perceval, 14 Dec. 1723, *Egmont MSS.*, Add. MSS. 47030, f. 90; to Abp of Canterbury, 14 Dec. 1723, *Private Letters*.

view of marrying, and therefore such ought to be the last men admitted to partake of the charity, and that if any proselyte should marry after his embracing the Protestant religion that he be discharged from any further relief of the commission". And, finally, it would be well to "reduce the business of the commission so as to be done by 3 or 4 meetings in the year, which would greatly ease the commissioners, who are engaged for the most part in many other charitable designs".[1]

Newman forwarded the Archbishop's letter to the commissioners, who set up a committee "to examine the qualifications of all proselytes now upon the list" in order to reduce the number to fifty, five of whom were to have £20 a year, ten £15, fifteen £10, and twenty £5, making the annual total of the charity £500.[2] But the committee was most concerned with the continual problem of the reliability of applicants. It drew up a *Method of Proceeding in the Examination or Questions to be asked Proponents and Proselytes by the Examiners*, a printed list of forty-four questions with blank spaces opposite to be filled in by the examiners when interviewing applicants. The questions included: "How or in what ship they came over into England?"; "What account they can give of the Popish principles, worship and practice?"; "How they came to be acquainted with or sensible of the errors of Popery?"; "Whether they came here to be useful to the nation as members of it or whether they came only to be a charge to it?"; and (for a clerical convert), "Whether he did not leave his convent or cure out of wrath and a spirit of disobedience, having had some personal or particular quarrel with his bishop or superior, which does not relate to his religion, or whether he has not been expelled or driven from his place of abode for immorality or holding tenets of faith or doctrine which are contrary to the Christian religion in general?"[3]

Newman had already expressed fully to Lord Perceval his opinion of the futility of the scheme:

Such a commission in the nature of it is impracticable and cannot subsist without being liable to infinite mistakes, unless the managers of it could derive a power of looking into men's hearts to judge of their sincerity.

In answer to this it may be said how comes the politic Church of Rome to make so much of proselytes? I wish this were the only weakness in

[1] HN to Ld Perceval, 6 March 1724, *Society's Letters*.
[2] *Committee Minutes*, 19 Dec. 1723; *General Meeting Minutes*, 19 Feb. and 12 Aug. 1724.
[3] *Method of Proceeding into the Examination, etc.*, *Wake MSS.*, Arch. W. Epist. 27, f. 136.

which Protestants have endeavoured to copy after the Papists; for where have the Protestants convents endowed with ample revenues extorted from dying profligates to cloister new converts under probation; where have they an Inquisition to punish renegades as the Papists have; and till they have these barbarous advantages, they will in vain aspire to imitate the Papists in compassing sea and land to make proselytes, a character not mentioned with honour in the Gospel. And why a good proselyte must be relieved preferably to another good man of our own nation, known to be a worthy object of charity, is what I am at a loss to account for by the laws of Christianity.

But My Lord to put this matter in a proper light, suppose some man overgrown in wealth should out of compassion to reformed lewd women settle £500 or more p.a. for relieving such persons at the discretion of some particular friends. There is not a prostitute in Drury Lane but would put in a claim to this charity and bring certificates from the minister and church-wardens of the parish of their having attended the Sacrament and all other religious offices in publick, that they had taken the oaths to King George and, in short, passed all the qualification tests that could be invented, except being sincerely good. I dare say the managers of such a charity would in seven years experience make fewer mistakes in proportion than has been done in relieving proselytes.[1]

Percival's reply was that since "the gentlemen are intent upon new modelling the Proselyte Society", he wished them success, but they would not have his support any longer: "I fear they will be as much disappointed as we were, and therefore I am resolved to be no longer a Commissioner." So far had his disillusion gone since his enthusiastic acceptance of office less than seven years before. Newman felt the same. When the new scheme was completed he confessed: "I am sick of it before we begin to act upon it." He would have resigned also, but for his duty to the Archbishop of Canterbury and others. He felt "obliged to give my poor attendance, though it be only as a witness that what is doing is like hedging in the cuckoo, of which I believe a few months more will convince them".[2]

As Newman was Secretary, he could not be a nominal member while the Society continued, particularly since, more than ever, the work fell upon a few commissioners. No one was willing to succeed Chamberlayne as Treasurer, so the office was put into commission and shared among a Committee for Receipts and Payments, of which Newman was always a member.[3] The minutes show that the commissioners asked him to carry out many of their

[1] HN to Ld Perceval, 14 Dec. 1723, *Private Letters.*

[2] Ld Perceval to HN, 18 Dec. 1723; HN to Ld Perceval, 20 Dec. 1723, *Egmont MSS.*, Add. MSS. 47030, ff. 93, 97–8; HN to Rev Dr Bray, Sheldon, War, 14 July 1724, *Society's Letters.*

[3] *Committee Minutes, passim.*

routine tasks, whether signing receipts for subscriptions, investigating the circumstances of applicants, providing for the children of refugees, or arranging for the abjuration of converts. Since Lord Perceval, his most sympathetic correspondent in the past, was no longer a member, Newman's letters have fewer references to the work of the Society in this later stage, but to those whom he did write about it, his tone was as before. He was wearied still by frauds and fortune-seekers among the refugees, like "Mr Camillus Castiglione, a Proselyte from Milan, [who] finding no subsistence in England answerable to his expectations, is desirous to return to Holland and from thence to go seek his fortune in Prussia"; he thought it "a trust attended with so much trouble, and by which so little visible good has been done, and less is to be expected for the future, under a fund so scanty as it is like to be".[1]

It took a few years, rather than months as Newman hoped, before the commissioners were convinced of the hopelessness of their task, but at last, in 1728, "the Commissioners, considering of the difficulties of executing their Commission", reached agreement over "resigning the trust of the Commission".[2] Newman was ordered to write to Archbishop Wake to inform him "they are obliged to desire being excused accepting any more of the commission for that trust" and hoping "you will be of opinion that it will be a greater charity to drop than to continue it".[3] This must have been an agreeable order, and eighteen months later, after the inevitable delays of the time, he was able to report gladly to Lord Perceval that the Archbishop of Canterbury, the Bishop of London, and the Lord Chancellor had agreed to the discontinuance of the commission.[4]

Newman, however, never entirely abandoned the Protestant proselytes. The commissioners on their dissolution left him the task of granting certificates of genuineness to those who had been relieved by the Society to assist them in seeking further relief. Sometimes this was not enough; as, for instance, in the case of Joseph Avodio, "a native of Syria and a nephew of the Patriarch of Mount Libanus", who had "quitted his relations to the Church of Rome as a Maronite, wherein he was bred": Newman had not only to give him a certificate that he had been approved by the

[1] HN to Rev. Mr Declari, 8 Dec. 1727; to Mr Le Sueur, Canterbury, 27 Jan. 1728, *Society's Letters*.
[2] *General Meeting Minutes*, 18 Jan. 1728.
[3] HN to Abp of Canterbury, 10 Feb. 1728, *Society's Letters*.
[4] HN to Ld Perceval, 25 Sept. 1728, *Society's Letters*.

late commissioners as worthy of relief in 1727, but nearly ten years later assure an inquiring bishop that the certificate was genuine and commend him to a London incumbent for relief as a poor inhabitant of his parish.[1] There were also refugees, assisted by the French Committee, who wanted Newman's help in finding employment. There was Sarrante Desquerre, son of a gentleman to Louis XIV, who came to England "for the sake of embracing the Protestant religion". He could shave, dress a peruque, and write well, but lacked English. "When he came first to England, he appeared like a page to some nobleman, but since that he has been obliged to sell his fine clothes for subsistence." Now he was so poor that he would take any service, but in view of his father's position in France, "he would be glad to be excused wearing a livery".[2] Or there was Mrs Derville Bonneval, who received a pension of £5 from the French Committee; "she was formerly distracted, and the charity of her friends has put her into the way of peddling, purely to amuse her and keep her out of idleness, with a poor girl she keeps as an interpreter, on bread and water, which is all they can get by it"; and now she needed someone to "advance her the fees for taking out a regular license".[3]

It was also after the dissolution of the commission that Newman met the proselyte, who not only occupied more of his time than any other, but appears to have been among the most deserving. He was "the Revd Don Louis de las Torres" or rather "Mr Louis de las Torres", as Newman told correspondents he should be addressed—"for he does not love to be called *Don* that he might not be thought to be otherwise than an Englishman". De las Torres, nevertheless, was a Spanish priest, who, "having been entertained in Spain as one of Count Martajo's twelve Chaplains, when he was appointed Ambassador at our Court, he had the courage to execute a design he had long before proposed of leaving his service and renouncing the errors of the Church of Rome as soon as he should get to England. This he did publicly in St Martin's Vestry" in 1733 before Zachery Pearce, Vicar of St Martin-in-the-Fields and later Bishop of Rochester. Newman found him "a grave, good-tempered man, turned of 40 years of age". He agreed to solicit subscriptions for De las Torres' maintenance, and wrote with some success to the Bishop of London and

[1] *General Meeting Minutes*, 9 Nov. 1727; HN to Rev. Dr Pelling, St Anne's, Westminster, 1 Jan. 1737; to Bp of Bristol, 8 Jan. 1737, *Miscellaneous Letters*.
[2] HN to Mr Belcher, 22 Dec. 1729, *Private Letters*.
[3] HN to Capt. Degulhon, 20 Sept. 1733, *Private Letters*.

other prominent persons. The Spanish Ambassador sought "an order to arrest him as a deserter from his family and to send him to Spain"; but he had the protection of William Stanhope, first Earl of Harrington, who was Secretary of State for the Northern Department and had known him when British Ambassador at Madrid. This decided Newman, mindful perhaps of the enigmatical John Barrett, that De las Torres ought to "be out of the way of being poisoned or stabbed by his brethren till their resentments are cooled". He asked the Dean of Windsor whether he could "be dieted and lodged at Windsor in a plain, decent apartment near St George's Chapel, where he may have the benefit of daily attending divine service and enjoying good conversation with access to your public library" so that he could learn English. The Dean found him lodgings with "one of the poor knights", who, "being a French refugee, has soups, etc., that he likes better than our English dishes", so Newman placed him on the Windsor coach with "a guinea and a shilling towards defraying the expense of his journey", all that was left of the money collected for him.[1]

There, with the help of one of the canons, Daniel Waterland, the theologian, De las Torres translated the New Testament "into the Minorcan language". Newman hoped to have it printed "by obtaining an order from His Majesty to the Treasury to give directions for the proper for issuing so much as may be necessary for the service out of the episcopal revenues sequestered in Minorca", but this was not possible, and De las Torres had to admit the "printing of it will be of no service to religion because there are not six people in the island that converse only in that language that can read and that the polite people read and understand Spanish very well, but won't look into a Spanish New Testament that comes from Protestant hands for fear of displeasing their clergy". Newman then tried to have him appointed to a deputy-chaplainship in the navy, preferably in the Mediterranean, so that in addition "a grant of £60 per annum or more could be obtained upon the establishment of Minorca", but with no more success.[2]

Clearly some means of support had to be found for De las Torres. The Bishop of London, Edmund Gibson, was "pleased to approve

[1] HN to Hon. Mrs Charlotte Tichborne, 8 Sept. and 18 Oct. 1733, 25 Jan. and 10 Sept. 1734, *Private Letters*; to Rev. Dr Booth, Dean of Windsor, 17 March and 1 May 1733; to Bp of London, 22 March 1733, *Society's Letters*.

[2] HN to Rev. Dr Waterland, 3 May 1735; to Sir Richd Manningham, 27 Jan. 1736, *Private Letters*; to Hon. Mrs Tichborne, 24 Dec. 1733, *Society's Letters*.

of his orders as an ecclesiastic", and Newman got up a fresh subscription to provide him with a clergyman's habit, but he still needed money for "other necessaries as well as to discharge his lodgings at Windsor". Newman tried hard to have "a man of so eminent a character preferred to some living where he might be no longer a burthen to his friends". He urged these friends to use their influence with patrons of livings, suggesting suitable ways of approaching them. The Lord Chancellor, Charles Talbot, might be told, for instance, that though it might seem De las Torres would best be sent to Minorca, "he can hardly escape there being stabbed or poisoned by his malicious enemies, which will be a strong argument with my Lord Chancellor, whose compassionate temper is well-known". But none were persuaded. Bishop Gibson gave 5 guineas towards his clerical habit, but no hope of a living, despite Newman's plea that it would not be "ill-bestowed, considering his quality and zeal for the Protestant interest, besides such an encouragement might induce other persons of figure to follow his example when they see those that embrace the Protestant religion are to be supported".[1]

Moreover, De las Torres added to his own difficulties. A former colleague in the Spanish Embassy, John Gonzales, Equerry to Count Montajo, followed his example, "renounced the errors of the Church of Rome", and "took the opportunity of quitting his service in the Ambassador's absence". De las Torres gave him 6*d.* a day out of his own small income. Then it turned out that De las Torres had "married a poor widow". He had "too much honour to disown her and as God shall enable him will never abandon her"; but subscribers were "suspecting the sincerity of his profession" because of it, and some withdrew their support. Others suspected him "as a spy, as one that lives in good terms with the Spanish Ambassador and will ere long return to Spain to secure the reward of his services here to the Romish interest". De las Torres angrily spoke of taking legal action against his slanderers; but Newman urged patience and suggested he might better devote his energies "to acquire the English language", if he wanted at least "some curacy in the country till it shall please God to open a door for him for some better preferment".[2]

But it was not to be. Newman had to confess "his want of

[1] HN to Bp of Winchester, 15 Feb. 1734, *Society's Letters*; to Rev. Dr Booth, Windsor, 24 June 1735, *Private Letters*; to Rev. Dr Waterland, 21 June 1735, *Miscellaneous Letters*.

[2] HN to Rev. Dr Booth, Windsor, 24 April 1735, *Society's Letters*.

English has disqualified him from any of our Church preferments, except sinecures, which, you know, are jewels generally promised long before they are vacant to people of overbearing interest, which he could not expect". Then De las Torres' wife had a child. Newman redoubled his efforts to get "a provision for him and his family". He gave up the idea of posts in the Church; he forgot even the dangers of Minorca and commended him to General Kane, Governor of the island, as a man who "would make a good lay missionary in your government, either as a common soldier or a domestic in the meanest station in your Excellency's family, either of which, I believe, he would thankfully accept under his present circumstances". Even this was not possible.[1]

Eventually it was decided to provide for De las Torres in much the same way as had been attempted for Barrett. He was appointed Chaplain to the *Falmouth* man-of-war, proceeding with the squadron to Jamaica, in the hope he would obtain a living there. So he sailed early in 1738 with the good wishes of his friends, though the Dean of Windsor had to add that his late landlord had auctioned his books to pay his arrears of rent. The S.P.C.K. gave him tracts, which he reported he had distributed "among the ship's crew on board the *Falmouth* to so good effect that there is rarely any cursing or swearing on board". Gradually other news reached England about him. First, that he had "escaped the snare intended for him at Madeira to allure him under the merciful care of the Fathers of the Inquisition"; then that the Governor of Jamaica had presented him to the large parish of Queen's Castle St Mary's, but that "the climate does not agree with him and that he thinks of returning to England with the *Falmouth*"; and, finally the next year, that he had died "of a violent fever". His wife and child received help from his old patron, Lord Harrington, but upon Newman, as usual, fell the task of discovering what effects he had left in Jamaica, assisting with a petition to the Admiralty, and seeking relief in other ways.[2]

The case of De las Torres seems to stand apart from nearly all the others in Newman's correspondence. Newman never doubted the sincerity of De las Torres, unlike the Vaudois youth or the rest

[1] HN to Bp of St Asaph, 19 Oct. 1737; to Gov. Kane, Minorca, 17 Dec. 1735, *Miscellaneous Letters*.

[2] *S.P.C.K. Minutes*, 20 June 1738; HN to Capt. De Ribera, Plymouth Citadel, 17 April 1739, *Private Letters*; to Mr Commissary May, Kingston, Jamaica, 13 Jan. and 11 Nov. 1738; to Rev. Mr Louis de las Torres, 31 Jan. and 31 Aug. 1738; to Rev. Mr Galpine, Spanish Town, Jamaica, 2 Aug. 1739, *Miscellaneous Letters*.

of the Protestant proselytes. He continually complained of "impostors and vagabonds who came from abroad with no religious views".[1] And yet this was almost inevitable. England, and especially London, was then regarded on the Continent as a prosperous and hospitable refuge. "London", its social historian has said, "then to some extent took the place now taken by the United States as the obvious resort of those driven out of their countries by economic or political pressure."[2] The city was said to swarm with foreign refugees, criminals, bankrupts, and adventurers, "canaille chassé de leur pays". Many Protestant proselytes seem to have merited this description. The royal bounty naturally attracted mendicants of all sorts. To distinguish between false and genuine applicants was impossible for what Newman termed "incompetent judges" and "rules tried and amended over and over". London was a happy hunting-ground in the eighteenth century for foreign impostors, such as the Frenchman, going by the name of George Psalmanazar, who persuaded Henry Compton, Bishop of London, that he was a native of Formosa;[3] and the commissioners of the Proselyte Society were no wiser in sifting the tales of the Protestant proselytes.

Nor did those applicants whose conversion seemed genuine present a much easier problem. England was not as full of opportunities as foreigners hoped. In particular, the professions were, as Addison observed in 1711, "each of them overburdened with practitioners and filled with multitudes of ingenious gentlemen that starve one another".[4] The ranks of the clergy were not exempt from such overcrowding. Even a native-born convert like Barrett could not, at the height of his reputation, find any opening for his services beyond a temporary curacy, while the fate of De las Torres showed how impossible it was for the foreign ecclesiastic to find employment in the Church of England. Newman's humanitarian and Protestant zeal would not allow him to stand aside from helping the proselytes, but it was never work that he enjoyed, nor can it be ranked among the most useful that he did.

[1] HN to Ld Perceval, 26 Oct. 1723, *Egmont MSS.*, Add. MSS. 47030, f. 57.
[2] M. D. George, op. cit., 110, 133.
[3] R. Bayne-Powell, *Travellers in Eighteenth Century England*, 1951, 191–4.
[4] *The Spectator*, No. 21, 24 March 1711.

7

"A MAN OF INTEREST"

JOHN CHAMBERLAYNE'S death in 1723 left vacant both the post of Treasurer of the Proselyte Society and that of Secretary of Queen Anne's Bounty. Founded in 1704 from the annates appropriated to the Crown by the Reformation Parliament in 1534, the Bounty sought to augment small livings in the Church of England. Since it had some 200 Governors, including all the bishops, deans, lord-lieutenants, privy councillors, serjeants-at-law, and the mayors of every English city, "a numerous body selected from those already over-worked", its paid officials did much of its administration. Some of Newman's friends, with Archbishop Wake and Bishop Gibson's support, wished him to succeed Chamberlayne as Secretary of the Bounty, "an honour", Newman confessed, "I no more expected than I did to become one of the Lords of the Treasury".[1]

The Treasurer of the Bounty, however, requested the post on grounds of long service and ill health. The Governors, with the seeming indifference of the time to administrative efficiency, agreed, but unanimously recommended Newman for the Treasurership, an office held by patent from the Crown for which the holder had to find security for some £30,000. Newman asked Lord Perceval for his support, saying: "The Archbishop is much my friend on this occasion and in a manner over-ruled my declining the place of Treasurer, when I had in a manner absolutely refused it." Perceval replied: "I shall always be extremely pleased to hear your particular affairs succeed to your mind and heartily wish you may not fail in the point you do me the honour to mention. I am sure the publick will be the better for your service." Walpole had already put forward a name of his own, Mr Blackaby, for the post, but Newman told the Marquis Du Quesne: "The Archbishop and Bishop of London expostulated the matter with Mr Walpole, so that he seemed to them to give up his friend and in manner promised to comply with the recommendation of the Governors." The appointment was delayed by one of the King's

[1] HN to Marquis Du Quesne, 19 Nov. 1723, *Letters to Jamaica.*

frequent visits to Hanover, but Newman was confident: "I don't find there is any doubt to be made of success." The King's return still did not settle it, and Newman lost confidence: "The affair of the Governors of the Queen Anne's Bounty is still in suspense by Mr W's contrivance, so that H.N. has no dependence on it"; and when the appointment was finally made it went to someone else, presumably another of Walpole's nominees, Jeffrey Elwes, alderman of London, sheriff and man of property, who held the post until his death in 1776, being knighted in 1744.[1]

This seems to be the only time when Newman might have left the S.P.C.K. He was not the man to seek advancement, but the putting forward of his name on this occasion showed that he had the confidence of a number of important men in Church and State. Newman knew only too well the need for such support in eighteenth-century England. Little could be done without patronage, and though he never again sought it for himself, his work for the Society and other causes meant frequent searches for the support of some "man of interest", some figure with enough influence for the success of his schemes.

In telling the Marquis Du Quesne about the affair, Newman wrote: "I own I shall not be disappointed if I miss it, but the steps which I have been obliged to take in compliance with the advice of my friends has of late devoured all my time, and if I do obtain the patent I shall be the more pleased because I hope it may put it in my power to serve the Marquis Du Quesne better than I have ever done by the access it will give me to Privy Councillors, Bishops and other great men in that Commission." And, indeed, though Newman never applied the term to himself, he did act as "a man of interest" for the Marquis Du Quesne and many others throughout his life in England. It may seem strange that people should have asked him to act in this way. He had no power in politics and could command no patronage, and certainly those whose desires lay that way did not approach him; but, on the other hand, his activities brought him into friendly contact with people of some importance—bishops and courtiers, writers and scientists, traders and administrators. Above all, he had a kind heart and great patience; he seems never to have refused requests for help or interest, nor to have minded waiting upon individuals, writing letters of introduction, or attending courts or committees

[1] HN to Ld Perceval, 4 Nov., 2 and 14 Dec. 1723; Ld Perceval to HN, 6 Nov. 1723, *Egmont MSS.*, Add. MSS. 47030, ff. 63, 84, 90, 66.

to further such requests, though they must often have delayed his work.

Between the leaves of one of his letter books there still rests a scrap of paper on which he wrote (and presumably left on his desk before setting out on his errand), "Gone to the Court of Requests, Westminster.—H.N.". The Courts of Conscience or Requests were petty courts created by various Acts of Parliament for the recovery of small debts.[1] Doubtless Newman had gone to the court at Westminster on this occasion to act on behalf of some poor suitor with his usual readiness. It is no wonder, therefore, that he was approached by all manner of people, mostly in misfortune, and their requests afford a glimpse into the lives of the professional and poorer classes in England at this time.

As might be expected from his work and interest, the largest number of Newman's suppliants came from the clergy. They even included Archbishop Wake, who wanted him to ask Lord Perceval to vote for his nephew, Martin Folkes, the antiquary, for the Presidency of the Royal Society in 1727. "It is of so delicate a nature that only the commands of so great a patron could prevail with one to address your Lordship in it", Newman told Perceval in transmitting the Archbishop's request to him; but Perceval had already promised to support Sir Hans Sloane, and Newman agreed that his claims were so great "that I thought nobody would have courage enough to stand in competition with him".[2] Sloane was elected, though Folkes succeeded him in 1741.

A very different divine whom Newman assisted was William Whiston, who succeeded Newton as Lucasian Professor at Cambridge in 1703. Like Newton he unluckily combined scientific with theological inquiries and was deprived of his professorship for Arianism in 1710. He was an early member of the S.P.C.K., but, as he recounted in his *Memoirs*, "from the year 1708, I had gone into deeper enquiries and designs, no less than the discovery and restoration of truly Primitive Christianity, as our Saviour and his apostles left it, without all regard for modern ages; while this Society thought themselves only capable of supporting things as they then stood in the Church of England by law established", and, therefore, to avoid "contests and disputes", he sent his

[1] M. D. George, *London Life in the Eighteenth Century*, 309, 401; *Local Government in Westminster* (Report of the Vestry of the United Parish of St Margaret and St John the Evangelist, Westminster), 1889, 194.

[2] HN to Ld Perceval, 3 and 9 Nov. 1727; Ld Perceval to HN, 4 Nov. 1727, *Egmont MSS.*, Add. MSS. 47032, ff. 99–100.

resignation from the Society in 1710 "to Mr Secretary Newman, who had long been my great friend". Newman must have been glad the Society was relieved of such embarrassing support, but he remained Whiston's friend and with the help of Steele enabled him to find employment by lecturing on astronomy in Button's Coffee House. "I thank you for your kindness to Mr Whiston", Newman wrote to Steele, "as it is a charity, not only to him, but to the publick, in putting him upon an amusement which may divert him from those studies that have made him so obnoxious to the reproach of good men . . . I only beg leave to suggest one thing to you when he does, because it will come with more authority than perhaps any man in the kingdom beside, and it is that you will be pleased to conjure him silence upon all topics foreign to the mathematicks in his conversation or lectures at the coffee-house. He has an itch to be venting his notions about baptism and the Arian doctrine, but your authority can restrain him at least while he is under your guardianship." Whiston presumably was given and took the advice, for he confined his coffee-house lectures to scientific subjects and was perhaps the first person to lecture publicly with experiments in London; but he kept his other interests, and from 1715 to 1717 conducted a Society for Promoting Primitive Christianity at his house in Cross Street, Hatton Garden.[1]

Another divine with scientific interests whom Newman asked Steele to help was William Derham, "a worthy representative of that class of eighteenth-century country parsons who pursued both avocations with confident assurance of their essential harmony".[2] He had been presented by Mrs Bray to the living of Upminster in Essex, where he lived quietly studying natural history and mechanics and serving his parishioners as both pastor and physician. His researches made him known to his scientific contemporaries. He became a Fellow of the Royal Society in 1702 and in 1711 and 1712 followed such distinguished men as Bentley and Clarke in giving the Boyle Lectures, which he published in 1713 as *Physico-Theology, or a Demonstration of the Being and Attributes of God from his Works of Creation*, a statement of the argument from final causes which reached a twelfth edition within half a century and was translated into French, Swedish, and German, while Paley

[1] W. Whiston, *Memoirs*, 151–3, 257, 202; HN to Mr Steele, 10 Aug. 1713, *Society's Letters*.
[2] Basil Willey, *The Eighteenth Century Background*, 1940, 39.

used it considerably in writing his *Natural Theology*. At Derham's request, Newman asked Steele to recommend the book, which he promised to do and in the *Guardian* of 24 September 1713 wrote a general essay on the "Contemplation of the Heavenly Bodies, Seasons, etc.", but made no mention of the book or its author. Newman encouraged Derham by saying he considered the essay "to be a prelude to it [his promise], and fine as it is, he could not say less to introduce so honourable a mention of your work as he intends. I hope he will make it as often the burthen of the *Guardian* as Milton's Heroick Poem was of the *Spectator*, and that he will think himself obliged to thank you for furnishing him with matter for many of his papers." A week later Steele wrote another essay, which named both author and book, summarized its argument, and praised it highly. "I do not know what Upminster is worth," wrote Steele, "but I am sure, had I the best living in England to give, I should not think the addition of it sufficient acknowledgement of his merit; especially since I am informed that the simplicity of his life is agreeable to his useful knowledge and learning"; and he concluded the essay, "the author may hope to be rewarded with an immortality much more to be desired than that of remaining in eternal honour among all the sons of men". Perhaps this was a hint; at any rate Newman's hope of frequent notice for Derham was not fulfilled. The *Guardian* in which the essay appeared was the last. It stopped through Steele's immersion in politics, and when he resumed his essays in the *Englishman*, Derham and his book found no place.[1]

Other clergymen asked Newman's assistance to promote humbler publications. There was Mr Disney of Lincoln, who "had occasion the last fifth of November to make mention of the royal family", and at whose request Newman sent printed copies of the sermon to the chaplain at St James' for conveyance "to the royal grandchild", Prince Frederick;[2] and Deodat Lawson, who presumably had some connection with New England, for "being reduced to the most extream want", he asked both Newman and Jeremiah Dummer, as colonial agents, to raise £5 from the New England merchants in London to enable him to publish "some broken Meditations" prefaced comprehensively "with a Solemn Dedication, first to Almighty God, next to the High and Mighty

[1] HN to Rev. Mr Derham, Upminster, Essex, 24 Sept. 1713, *Society's Letters*; *The Guardian*, No. 169, 24 Sept. 1713; No. 175, 1 Oct. 1713.
[2] HN to Rev. Dr Wilcox, St James', 23 Jan. 1721, *Private Letters*.

Monarch King George, and finally to their Royal Highnesses the Prince and Princess of Wales, with all their Royal and Magnificent Progeny", and announced he would "frequent the New England Coffee House" until he heard from them.[1]

Such clergymen wanted to promote their sermons in print, not only to earn a few shillings from their sale, but still more, as their dedications showed, to gain preferment. Not only in the eighteenth century was there a considerable "disproportion between the number of persons entering into Holy Orders and the benefices available for their incumbency",[2] but the operation of the unreformed ecclesiastical administration of the time meant that clergy, apart from a privileged minority who enjoyed advantages of birth and influence, had a hard struggle for preferment. Several asked Newman outright to use his influence for them. He himself could do nothing, but he always tried to secure the support of someone who could. On behalf of Henry Shute, Lecturer of Whitechapel and Treasurer of the S.P.C.K., Newman wrote in 1721 to the applicant's distant kinsman, John Shute, Viscount Barrington, representing him as having been ordained for over forty years and never had a benefice—"one thinks he is rich and does not want preferment (which I know is a mistake), another thinks him what in the late reign was called a Low Church Man". He assured Barrington of Henry Shute's integrity and loyalty to the present government and that the Lord Chamberlain or Lord Townshend "will favour any recommendation your Lordship shall give". Why Shute had not told Newman he had been beneficed in Suffolk from 1685 to 1690 before coming to London, can only be conjectured, but, in any event, he died the next year still without preferment.[3]

So difficult was the clerical ladder to promotion that there was competition even for the inferior pastoral offices. The lectureships in the London churches were particularly desired as being prominent enough to give the occupiers a chance of further promotion, and Newman was asked to assist aspirants to these posts. Thus, he wrote to a parishioner of St James', Garlickhithe, "to recommend to your vote and interest" a young candidate for the lectureship there: "I have long known him for a good spiritual preacher and

[1] Rev. Mr Lawson to HN and Jeremiah Dummer, 24 Dec. 1714, *Rawlinson MSS.*, C.128, f. 12.

[2] N. Sykes, *Church and State*, 189.

[3] HN to Ld Barrington, 6 May 1721, *Private Letters*; *Alumni Oxoniensis, 1500–1714*, IV, 1354; *Alumni Cantabrigiensis*, Pt I, Vol. IV, 71.

can assure you he is of good principles as to politics."[1] Sometimes Newman could only advise the aspirant where he might look for influence to promote his wishes. To a parson who wanted two vicarages in the Lord Keeper's gift, he suggested "that he must procure either his Diocesan or some Member of Parliament that is in favour with the present ministry to recommend him to my Lord Keeper".[2] The constant reference to attachment to the government emphasizes the political use then made of Church patronage, and the necessity for the aspiring clergyman to make his loyalty clear.

If such seekers after preferment revealed the struggle for places in this overcrowded profession, other cases that came before Newman showed the poorness of many of these places. John Pauncefoot was Vicar of Oxenhall with Pauntley, Gloucestershire. He and his wife were about 60 years old. They had three daughters, two married and one acting as a handmaid to her parents, but the eldest and her family, through sickness and misfortune, were dependent upon the elderly couple, who had also to bring up a child of a dead son. The living was only worth £30 a year; Pauncefoot had no estate, pension, or allowance, but he had not yet fallen into debt. Newman got him a grant of £10 from a trust for the relief of poor clergymen.[3] Even worse was the plight of those clergymen's widows whose cases Newman forwarded for relief to similar charitable societies.[4]

After the clergy, the largest numbers of pleas for help came to Newman from the fighting services. Some were for entry into the service, as that of Christopher Jackson, on whose behalf Newman wrote to Brigadier Richards, whom he had known in Newfoundland, asking for a place for him in the "train of artillery" the Brigadier was raising in the Tower of London.[5] Some were from fathers asking the same for their sons. Particularly importunate was a retired army officer, Captain Morris of Carlisle, who at the time of the 1715 Rebellion asked Newman, as having "strong interest with many of the great ones", to help his son, Ensign Tom, and "please to get him a Lieutenancy either in Horsefoot or Dragoons . . . or may be . . . a Company or Troop". Perhaps New-

[1] HN to Capt. Wilson, 12 Feb. 1714, *Society's Letters*.

[2] HN to Rev. Mr Edwards, Embleton, Northumb, 6 Sept. 1712, *Society's Letters*.

[3] HN to Mr Warmsley, Snow Hill, 25 Nov. 1737; to Rev. Mr Pauncefoot, Oxenhall, 20 May 1738, *Miscellaneous Letters*.

[4] HN to Rev. Mr Goodwin, Tankersley, Yorks, 11 July 1723, *Society's Letters*; to Rev. Dr Pelling, Westminster, 16 April 1718, *Rawlinson MSS.*, C.933, f. 127.

[5] HN to Brigadier Richards, Tower of London, 25 March 1719, *Private Letters*.

man was successful, for three years later Captain Morris wished him to get a younger son into the navy. Newman spoke to a captain about to command a ship on a Mediterranean cruise, who agreed to take the boy provided he had the King's Letter for him, "for every boy on board is a diminution of the strength of the ship's crew and is a perquisite of the Captain under the notion of servants, unless warranted by the King's Letter". Newman could only suggest that Captain Morris should repeat his request, through the General under whom he had himself served, to the First Lord Commissioner of Admiralty, Lord Berkeley, "though it is a favour that several of the quality now stoop to solicit for their children, since many of our sea commanders have made their fortune in a short time".[1] Then there were those wishing to leave their service, like Private Elderton of the Guards, who told Newman "that after every Review it is usual to discharge some men out of the Guards and that the Colonel does it gratis at the desire of any M.P. or other friend of the Colonel", and at whose request Newman wrote to a Member of Parliament asking him to recommend the Colonel to discharge Elderton;[2] and Captain Burgess, who commanded "a customshouse smack cruising between St David's Head and Swansea", and on whose behalf Newman wrote to another Member of Parliament asking he might "quit her at Michaelmas owing to his ill state of health".[3] Finally, there were those with claims of pay due to them, such as Timothy Ireland, whose papers Newman forwarded to the Treasury to uphold his claim for "the two pences as Surgeon to the marines on board the *Worcester* from 1 July to 26 October 1711".[4]

At first sight it must seem strange that Newman was asked to assist these service requests. Clearly he had no influence here and could only refer petitioners to a Member of Parliament or appropriate official. These petitioners, however, were like Newman's clerical suppliants. The administration of War Office and Admiralty was as loose and inefficient as the Church of England, and in both patronage had to be sought from many hands. The army and the navy were like collections of self-contained units, the colonel being in effect proprietor of his regiment, the captain of

[1] Capt. Morris to HN, 30 Jan. 1716, *Rawlinson MSS.*, C.844, f. 112; HN to Capt. Morris, Carlisle, 18 Nov. 1718, *Society's Letters*.

[2] HN to Sir Francis Boynton, M.P., Burton Agnes, Yorks, 9 July 1737, *Miscellaneous Letters*.

[3] HN to Charles Stanhope, M.P., Hanover, 29 Aug. 1720, *Society's Letters*.

[4] HN to Mr Manley, Office for Examining the Debts of the Army, etc., 11 March 1720, *Private Letters*.

his ship. An individual with a grievance about pay or promotion or a desire to enter or leave the service needed the favour of the appropriate patron. The requests to Newman for help in doing this show how difficult it was for those who lacked friends or influence in the services.

In fact, so completely did the need for patronage pervade English life at this time that Newman fulfilled some strange requests. He wrote, for instance, to a Court official to commend "an honest mustard maker and heartily well affected to King George. If you can recommend him to serve His Majesty's kitchen with mustard, I dare say when his goods are tried he will need no further recommendation", and to Chamberlayne's coachman on behalf of a sailor who "having a family to provide for and no business to subsist them in the way he was bred at sea, would be glad to learn to drive a coach, and having no friend capable of instructing him therein, he has begged me to recommend him. I could not think of anyone so capable as you, and therefore I have taken the liberty to recommend him to your kindness herein." [1] It was natural that men about to emigrate to America should ask him for letters of recommendation to colonial governors and other important persons, and those whom Newman thus served included a barrister, a tallow chandler, and a barber and peruke-maker.[2]

If eighteenth-century England could be hard for a man seeking employment or promotion, it could be even harder for a woman in poverty, old age, or sickness; and Newman took as much trouble and care in such cases. In 1718 he wrote to the Lord Chancellor's Secretary:

I hear the daughter of the famous Milton is in great straits, several of her scholars having left her, and others not being able to pay her for their schooling. If my Lord Chancellor knew her case, I am persuaded His Lordship would find means to procure a small pension of £20 or £25 per annum from the Government which would make the remainder of her life easy, nor could it be thought a burthen on the Government, considering she is (as I think) turned of 70. Pray make her case known to Sir Richard Blackmore,[3] who wants neither inclination nor interest to procure some relief for her. It would be a great reproach to our time to let such a person suffer for want of the common necessaries of life, whose very rags would be sacred relics 100 years hence in the opinion

[1] HN to Mr Salter, James St, 4 Aug. 1718, *Private Letters*; to Mr Chamberlayne's Coachman, 8 March 1714, *Society's Letters*.

[2] HN to Gov. Belcher, Judge Dudley, and Judge Byfeld, Boston, 20 Aug. 1731; to Gov. Belcher, Boston, 9 Feb. 1727; to Lt-Gov. Drysdale, Williamsburg, Va., 1 Jan. 1723, *New Eng. Letters*.

[3] A royal physician and writer.

of a true admirer of her incomparable father. I shall with pleasure show you the way to her cell, whenever you think fit to command.[1]

The daughter was probably Mary Milton, born in 1648, who never married and would have been just under 70 then. There is no evidence that Newman's plea for her succeeded, but it was typical of him that he should have acted in this way when he heard of her distress.

He was as ready to help other women with no claims to distinction. Among those who sought his assistance were the wives of the "200 British captives now in slavery . . . in the dominions of the Emperor of Morocco". He wrote round to his acquaintances, depicting the men's plight, "several have turned Mohametans to have their hard usage mitigated, and others die under the miseries they daily suffer for the want of the common necessities of life", and asking them "to use their good offices for procuring private charities to be remitted to them". When some of the captives were released and returned home, he sought further relief for them and wrote to the Secretary of the Admiralty asking that "the common necessities allowed to them by the Government" might be supplemented; while on behalf of the widow of one of these men he used his influence to obtain for her "the next vacancy in Lady Michael's Almshouse, near Stepney Church, belonging to the Mercer's Company", and for another employment in Greenwich Hospital, since her husband, who had been thirty years in the navy, would have been a pensioner there, had he not died soon after his return from slavery in Barbary.[2]

There were others besides these unfortunate women. One, "a house-keeper seventy years in St Martin's Lane", was commended by him to the Vicar of St Martin-in-the-Fields and "the charity of your generous parishioners", because her husband, a jeweller, had deserted her, and she could barely support herself "by working plain work at a cabinet-maker's at the corner of Langley Street in Long Acre".[3] For sick women he tried to secure the benefits of the new hospitals in London, the foundation of which was a notable event in this period, requesting for one "as a pensioner in the Infirmary in James Street for some disorder she has", and for another advice from the physicians at St George's Hospital "to get rid of a cancerous humour that seems to be her malady"; and when

[1] HN to Mr Hughes, 29 Dec. 1718, *Private Letters.*

[2] HN to Lady D'Elwes, 1 Feb. 1720; to Mr Josiah Burchett, Whitehall, 3 Nov. 1721 and 10 Nov. 1729; to Lady Dollins, Hackney, 2 June 1735, *Private Letters.*

[3] HN to Rev. Dr Pearce, 28 Jan. 1740, *Miscellaneous Letters.*

approached by a woman with "a daughter-in-law lunatick that has put her family to greater expense than they are able longer to bear", in the hope of saving her from the horrors of Bedlam, he asked a doctor "for your recommendation to Guy's Hospital, if such a favour can be granted to one in her case".[1]

Newman's solicitude for women in need of help was equalled only by his sympathetic interest in children. Though a bachelor, he was fond of the young and asked his correspondents about their families and received elaborately composed letters from their sons at school.[2] In 1727 the Minister and Churchwardens at Fort St George, India, made him guardian of three orphans in England of servants of the Company, and in his will he asked his executors "to have a particular regard to such orphans".[3] He liked to help boys leaving school to make a start in life. Probably the most notable boy whom he helped was Vincent Perronet, son of a surgeon in St Giles-in-the-Fields, "a very honest man, but one in low circumstances with three other children to maintain. He never intended to bring up this son to learning, but after he was devoted to a trade, he proved so intolerantly bookish that it was thought better to give way to his genius." The boy wanted to be admitted upon the foundation at Queen's College, Oxford, but though educated at St Bees School, he was not a native of either Westmorland or Cumberland, the two north-western counties with which the College was traditionally connected. So Newman wrote in 1714 to James Lowther, Member of Parliament for Whitehaven, to ask him to use his influence with the Provost of the College on behalf of Vincent Perronet. Perronet matriculated a member of the College the same year and later became Vicar of Shoreham, Kent, and a friend of the Wesleys, by whom he was so often consulted on matters of organization that he was styled "the Archbishop of Methodism".[4]

Of all the children in Newman's life, however, and for whom he did most as a man of interest, were those of the spendthrift Marquis Du Quesne. Newman's connection with the whole family—father,

[1] HN to Mrs Mary Green, 19 Jan. 1741; to Capt. Hudson, St George's Hospital, 4 March 1743, *Miscellaneous Letters*; to Dr Mead, Ormond St, 18 Nov. 1730, *Private Letters*.

[2] Thos. Bannister to HN, 7 Aug. 1715; Noah Cholmondley to HN, 10 Nov. 1722, *Rawlinson MSS.*, C.933, ff. 10 and 144.

[3] HN to Mrs Chamberlayne, 10 Oct. 1730, *Private Letters*; P.C.C. Wills, 1743, Boycott, f. 205.

[4] HN to Hon. James Lowther, M.P., 4 Oct. 1714, *Society's Letters*; *Alumni Oxoniensis, 1500–1714*, II, 1148; *D.N.B.*

mother, and children—was more like that of a relation than a friend, so close was his affection for them and so constant his efforts to promote their welfare. Indeed, bachelor though he was, he came more and more to be placed in something like the position of the head of the family; and here he displayed perhaps the most tender and sympathetic side of his character.

Gabriel, third Marquis Du Quesne, was of French Huguenot origin. His grandfather, Abraham Du Quesne, the first Marquis Du Quesne, was Lieutenant-General of the Naval Forces of France under Louis XIV; his father went to Switzerland upon the Revocation of the Edict of Nantes in 1685, when he himself was not more than a year old. As a youth, having entered the service of the Protestant Cantons, he was sent to England in 1709 to petition Queen Anne on behalf of the French Huguenots. He never settled again in Switzerland, but became naturalized in 1711, married, and joined the Guards, in which he became a Lieutenant-Colonel in 1717.[1] He and Newman seem to have been brought together through their common acquaintance with the first Duke of Portland, son of William Bentinck, Earl of Portland, the Dutch favourite of William III. Probably, indeed, both men had known the Duke's father, Newman when in the service of the Duke of Somerset, Du Quesne when appearing for the French Huguenots.

At any rate, in 1721, when the Duke of Portland was appointed Governor of Jamaica, he made Du Quesne Commander of Port Royal. Du Quesne was apparently at this time, as so often, in financial straits, for shortly before he sailed for Jamaica, Newman had to convey his apologies to the Archbishop of Canterbury for failing to see him, because of "the circumstances of his affairs that have obliged him of late to keep within the verge of the Court".[2] In fact, the family seem to have had only two friends of any worth —Newman and Lady Torrington, widow of Baron Torrington, second son of the first Earl of Bradford. The bachelor and the childless widow between them tried to ease the lot of the Marquis's dependants. Lady Du Quesne was faced with the prospect of going overseas without a single English servant until Newman remembered Mary Jackson, whom he had first known when 3 years old, one of the eight children of John Jackson, the first chaplain sent by the S.P.G. to Newfoundland in 1701. When Jackson

[1] W. K. Lowther Clarke, *Eighteenth Century Piety*, 54–68; J. Beresford, *Mr Du Quesne and Other Essays*, 3–97.
[2] HN to Abp of Canterbury, 10 May 1722, *Society's Letters*.

returned penniless to England three years later, Newman asked Addison, then Under-Secretary of State, to have the girl bound, on behalf of the Sons of the Clergy Corporation, to a milliner in Soho, "where she acquired such a character of fidelity and skill in the use of her needle as occasioned my recommending her to Lady Du Quesne when Mrs Hawson refused to go abroad with her".[1]

Above all, Newman and Lady Torrington cared for the children of the Du Quesnes. There were five of them—Ann, William, Thomas, Elizabeth, and Henry. When their parents went to Jamaica, Ann was "left with the old Marquis at Geneva"; William and Thomas, aged 6 and 8, sent to a school in Church Lane, Chelsea, kept by Mr Lefevre, a Huguenot pastor; Elizabeth had teething fever and died some weeks later, though attended by Sir Richard Manningham, the chief male midwife of the day, who applied blisters to her neck and dosed her with astringent medicines; Henry, not yet a year old, was first left, under Newman's responsibility, with his nurse at Hackney, but soon sent to rejoin his parents, to Newman's sorrow: "I have never parted with a child with more regret than with him, for though he could not speak, every feature in his face made a thousand orations for him, and his incessant good humour obliged everybody that played with him to love him." [2]

The two boys, William and Thomas, were left to Newman's care, and he often visited them at Chelsea. "I heard Billy say his prayers and his lesson in French", he told Du Quesne; and again: "I examine the children almost every time I go to Chelsea and hope you will approve of the little rewards I give to encourage them, the weekly allowance of 6*d.* falling short of what is necessary to keep them in heart with the other children." He had them to stay with him and took them on visits to see the Duke of Portland's sons at Eton or to friends. Lady Du Quesne wanted them to learn dancing, but Lady Torrington thought them too young and the additional expense too much, so he had to be content to enjoin Mrs Lefevre to "make them sit and walk straight". When "the old Marquis" died at Geneva in October 1722, Newman informed Du Quesne: "Their cloaths being thin, I have put them in mourning for their grandpapa in a dark grey drugget trimmed with

[1] HN to Lady Torrington, 30 Dec. 1726, *Letters to Jamaica.*

[2] HN to Sir Thos. Lowther, Holker, 24 Sept. 1719, *Society's Letters*; to Mr Jacob Montross, 25 Sept. 1722; to Lady Torrington, 28 July 1722; to Marquis Du Quesne, 12 Nov. 1722, *Letters to Jamaica.*

In answer to this it may be said how comes the Church of Rome to make so much of Proselytes. I wish this were the only weakness in which Protestants have endeavour'd to copy after the Papists; for where have they Protestants Convents endow'd with ample Revenues or extorted from dying Profligates, to Chapter new Converts under Probation; where Have they an Inquisition to furnish Renegadoes as the Papists have, and till they have these barbarous advantages they will in vain aspire to imitate the Papists in compassing Sea & Land to make Proselytes a Character not mentioned with honour in the Gospel. And why a good Proselyte must be relieved preferably to another good Man of our own Nation known to be a worthy Object of Charity is what I am at a loss to account for, by the Laws of Christianity.

But my Lord to put this matter in a proper light, suppose some Man overgrown in Wealth should out of compassion to Reform lewd Women settle 500 l. or more for relieving such persons at the discretion of some particular friends. There is not a Prostitute in Drury Lane but would put in Claim to this Charity & bring Certificates from the Min.r &

One of Newman's Draft Letters

"To My Lord Percival at Charlton, 14 Dec.r 1723". (See pp. 146–7)

black." Another time he gave them twenty kisses from their mother, who missed them sorely, and told Du Quesne: "The less you suffer my Lady Du Quesne to live in sight of the ocean or ships, the easier she will be in her mind that she may not think of letters till they come." [1]

But the Marquis had his own troubles. At first Newman had good news from him: "I am glad to hear that you live very elegantly and get a vast deal of money, at which all your friends rejoice and those honest people that have called upon me sometimes with your bills have no doubt but that they will yield hard money one time or another, saying that the Marquis was always a man of honour." Before long, however, disenchantment set in, and Newman learnt that "the Marquis and his Lady begin to be weary of the climate they are in, the excessive heat proving unhealthy to them", and that he was asking Lady Torrington to use her "good offices to get them removed to England" with a pension from the administration. He also found it hard to live within his salary. He had £800 a year, while the Duke of Portland was voted £5000 a year, twice as much as the usual salary for a Governor, presumably because he was a Duke. The island's Assembly soon regretted having voted him as much, however, because it complained that the Duke's liberal entertainment made planters spend more than they could afford. The Marquis seems always to have been extravagant, and doubtless he also found it difficult to remain unaffected by the Duke's style of living.[2] Like other government officers, he took to supplementing his salary by illegal trade in indigo with Dutch and French ships, besides sending Newman money to buy lottery tickets or to be invested in the company for "planting mulberry trees and breeding silkworms in Chelsea Park", one of the short-lived schemes projected at the time of the South Sea Bubble, in which Du Quesne also lost money. He took no notice of Newman's suggestions that he should send money to pay his bills in England, now totalling £300. He would not even pay the school fees for the two boys, which came to £64 a year, clothes extra.[3]

Even Newman and Lady Torrington would not tolerate this

[1] HN to Marquis Du Quesne, 5 Jan., 18 Feb., 14 and 30 Aug. 1723, 25 April 1724, *Letters to Jamaica*.
[2] HN to Marquis Du Quesne, 25 Jan. 1724, *Letters to Jamaica*; Frank Cundall, *The Governors of Jamaica in the first half of the Eighteenth Century*, 1937, 106.
[3] *Calendar of State Papers, Colonial: America and W. Indies, 1724–5*, No. 810; HN to Marquis Du Quesne, 17 Nov. 1724, *Letters to Jamaica*.

indefinitely. Early in 1724 Lady Torrington decided to pay the £10 a quarter, which she had previously given to Newman for Du Quesne's account, direct to the school; and in 1725 Newman asked the Marquis either to send him a remittance or relieve him of his difficult trust. A year and a quarter's school bills were owing, and Newman had to be "very passive to Mr Lefevre's exactions". He wanted to move the boys to "a noble school at St Alban's", which would cost £20 a year less, but their mother would not agree.[1]

By now Newman was also responsible for the youngest boy, "my dear namesake Harry Du Quesne". He had often been in Newman's thoughts: "I have desired his lady to give him twenty kisses from me and I'll return them all when he comes back." He had feared that in Jamaica the boy would be corrupted by "the dissoluteness of the place", and was overjoyed when Du Quesne decided to send "his little boy over for want of health and for fear he should become a negro by the heat of the climate". Having taken him off the ship at Gravesend, he told Lady Torrington, "Last night little Harry lay at my chambers [in the Middle Temple] in good health". He was, however, suffering from skin trouble through the salt food on ship. The voyage had lasted three months, and "they were obliged to kill their cats and dogs to help out their provisions, not that they ate them themselves, but to save water and to feed the tiger and other wild creatures which my Lord Duke has sent over to the King". So he was taken to Sir Richard Manningham, and Lady Manningham agreed to take him into her nursery until he was cured.[2]

After that Newman would have to provide for him. Lady Du Quesne wanted him to join his brothers at Chelsea, but this would clearly be too expensive. The unpaid school bills there amounted to £72 1*s.* 4*d.*, which included fourteen pairs of shoes bought for them, but not clothes and linen. Newman wanted to send him to some nursery near London, which would cost about £13 a year and £16 when he began Latin; but he was a difficult child. "Harry grows as wild as a buck, and has spirit enough for six children", Newman told the Marquis's brother at Geneva. Eventually he was boarded with Mrs Hawson, his mother's former maid, for 6*s.* a week—"She makes his upper cloaths serve for under cloaths as

[1] HN to Marquis Du Quesne, 23 Jan. and 17 Nov. 1724, 8 May 1725; to Lady Torrington, 5 May 1725, *Letters to Jamaica.*

[2] HN to Rev. Mr Galpine, Jamaica, 20 April 1723, *Society's Letters*; to Ld Perceval, 14 Dec. 1723, *Egmont MSS.*, Add. MSS. 47030, f. 90; to Mrs Mary Jackson, 13 Aug. 1723; to Lady Torrington, 15 Aug. 1724, *Letters to Jamaica.*

long as they will hang to him", Newman told Lady Du Quesne—and sent to a dame school in Chelsea. Newman urged Mrs Hawson "to cure him of all ill habits he has contracted among the negroes and sailors . . . to make him kneel down before you morning and evening to say the first ten words of the Lord's Prayer, till by degrees he may be capable of saying all of it . . . to oblige him to speak and behave himself to you and all the gentlemen and ladies of your family with the same respect as he should to my Lady Torrington or to his father and mother". In a few weeks, however, he had to go to a boys' school, being "too ungovernable for a mistress . . . the master pins him to his gown". The boy grew rapidly beyond petticoat control, and a year later Newman told the Marquis: "I put him into breeches on the King's birthday, which he likes so well that, with his good will, he would go to bed with them and never put them off." [1]

Meanwhile, the Marquis' affairs went from bad to worse. The position of a government official in Jamaica seemed hardly easier than in New England. In 1725 a Committee of the House of Assembly reported that £150 a year voted for the repair of the fort at Port Royal had been diverted, and the garrison was ill-housed; it charged Du Quesne with ill practices, including unlawful trading. Du Quesne submitted in defence that he had done all that he could to speed the repair of the fort, even compelling local ships to bring in stone to Port Royal for the purpose; but this only added to his trouble, for the House of Assembly resolved that this action was arbitrary and illegal, "a high infringement of the liberties and properties of His Majesty's subjects of this island" in their oft-used phrase, that he had indulged in illegal trade and allowed a sloop to pass the fort not properly cleared and that a Memorial about his conduct should be sent to the King.[2]

The news was a shock to both Du Quesne's friends in England. Newman might have remembered how readily accusations were made against government officers in New England, but he particularly remonstrated with him—"I cannot help wishing you had never concerned yourself in trade, but lived frugally, trusting Providence on the produce of your command . . . with less envy from your neighbours than by a trade which some people call by very hard names, such as clandestine, smuggling, illegal, etc. At

[1] HN to Mrs Hawson, Chelsea, 22 Oct. 1724, *Private Letters*; to Mr Du Quesne, Geneva, 19 Oct. 1724 and 11 March 1725; to Marquis Du Quesne, 21 Nov. 1724 and 30 June 1726; to Lady Du Quesne, 25 June 1725, *Letters to Jamaica*.

[2] F. Cundall, op. cit., 112.

the same time you may be a great loser, you are represented here as a vast trader, and one that will soon be in a condition to compound all your South Sea contracts upon very honourable terms." Lady Torrington "paid three guineas" for a copy of his Defence before the House of Assembly at Jamaica, "which, when she had read, she was surprised to find so weak and insufficient for removing the scandalous imputations",[1] and Newman agreed: "I have the same opinion your Ladyship has concerning it, that his Defence will be thought in England to be of as little weight as it was in Jamaica." To add to the Marquis' plight, the Duke of Portland, who had defended him against the Assembly, died of a fever in the summer of 1726. Lady Torrington decided he had better leave Jamaica, and tried to get him a patent or pension up to £500 a year. Newman also agreed with her here: "It is true his indiscretions, to give them no worse name, have been very great, and he has been severely punished for them by the misfortunes that have attended all his schemes for getting wealth to support himself and family with honour in England; but when I consider that less merit, recommended by a less powerful interest than your Ladyship's, has sometimes obtained the compassion of a pension to relieve an invincible train of misfortunes, I cannot but hope that there may be room to admit him to the like favour." [2]

Nevertheless, Newman had more than one cause for displeasure with Du Quesne. There was his treatment of Mary Jackson, whom he had secured as his wife's maidservant. "I have often repented of this office," he told Lady Torrington, "though I meant it for Lady Du Quesne's service, as well as the good of the poor girl." She was the only English servant in the household, her wages were unpaid, and scandalous imputations had been made against her. Newman had at least the satisfaction of hearing from a gentlewoman of the Duchess of Portland "such an account of her virtue, patience and fidelity in spite of all abuses" as restored his opinion of her, but at the expense of her employer.[3] No wonder he wrote to Du Quesne about his conduct in Jamaica. He assured him of his devotion to the children and asked him "to accept with the most candid interpretation all the harsh expressions in this letter, which though they are wrote with great regret, the friendship I owe you and your Lady will not suffer me to conceal". He could

[1] HN to Marquis Du Quesne, 12 Oct. 1724 and 30 June 1726, *Letters to Jamaica.*
[2] HN to Lady Torrington, 27 Oct. 1726, *Letters to Jamaica.*
[3] HN to Lady Torrington, 30 Dec. 1726, *Letters to Jamaica.*

only hope he could "find yourself through the goodness of Providence happy by being once more undone and disappointed in all your romantick schemes of making an immense fortune". Lady Torrington was still doing her best for him. She aspired "to gain an interest in Mr Walpole, who is everything but the King and to speak in his favour for you"; but she had already approached Lord Townshend, who told her "that your conduct had so exposed you to the hatred of the people of Jamaica that it was impossible for him to recommend you to the King after so many flagrant proofs of dishonesty in the trust that had been reposed in you; that the Duke himself, if he had lived, must have been sent for home, to remedy some mistakes in his government, which there was reason to believe your advice has precipitated his Grace into." If Lady Torrington should still obtain a pension of £500 a year for him, Newman thought the Marquis should allocate £100 for the children and go to live in Boston on the rest. He sketched for him an idyllic picture of how he might live there, though in terms suited to his own taste rather than that of a man like Du Quesne: "You may live . . . in that town more happily than the Governor himself, if you can be content with a pretty box and garden such as you are well able to contrive, with a chariot and a pair of horses to take the air with and to pass your time in amusing yourself with a good book at home and such friendly society as that town affords, the most like to London for the way of living of any place that I know in America." [1]

But Du Quesne's career was not to have a leisurely close. The Duke of Portland's successor, Brigadier Robert Hunter, arrived in Jamaica early in 1727. Walpole had refused the Marquis a pension, but instructed Hunter to continue him in his post, but such was his unpopularity in the island that the new Governor declined to begin office under this handicap and dismissed Du Quesne.[2] Lady Du Quesne came home at once. She brought with her a black boy named Pompey, whom Lady Torrington would not allow her to keep. Once again this meant trouble for Newman, who accepted Pompey as a gift in order to find him a master. He offered the "little innocent black boy native of Jamaica, a beauty of his kind", first to Lord Perceval, "to wait on you, my Lady and your children", and then to the Bishop of

[1] HN to Marquis Du Quesne, 4 Nov. 1726, *Letters to Jamaica*.
[2] HN to Lady Torrington, 8 Feb. 1727; to Marquis Du Quesne, 21 April and 11 May 1727, *Letters to Jamaica*.

London, "in acknowledgement of your great tenderness to the souls of the whole race of negroes".[1] There is no hint whether either accepted the present, but presumably Newman had no great difficulty in disposing of him, for Hogarth's engravings suggest that a black page was common in fashionable households at this time.

To know what to do with the Marquis and his affairs was more difficult. Newman suggested that he should come home and live incognito until his debts were settled. If he had traded for two years and four-fifths of his creditors agreed, he was entitled to a Statute of Bankruptcy at a cost of between £70 and £100. Lady Torrington still helped the family. Newman told her: "If they that forgive seven times do an available act to Him to whose unbounded goodness we owe everything, how highly acceptable must they be who can forgive seventy times seven. I flatter myself that there will be no need of arguments to induce your Ladyship to choose rather on the side of immense forgiveness than of implacable resentment." [2] As soon as the Marquis arrived in London, Newman had to see him. "Go immediately", he wrote, "to your Lady at Mr Batchelor's, a mantua maker, at the end of Duke's Court in St Martin's Lane, where I will meet you." His situation was indeed desperate.[3] He had, Newman told the Archbishop of Canterbury, "not enough left to pay the expense of a Statute of Bankruptcy, nor can he with safety appear to solicit any favour without a statute from his creditors. This refuge several of his principal creditors are ready to consent to, but they will be at no expense for promoting the statute, and it is in the power of the least of his creditors to arrest and give him trouble till he has such an indemnity as the law allows to unfortunate men." [4] And he told Lord Perceval that the most he could do for the Marquis was "to seek an apartment to hide him in till matters can be accommodated with his creditors", though "the Archbishop of Canterbury has been so good as to promise me his assistance, in conjunction with other such friends as may be prevailed with, to raise the sum desired to extricate him".[5]

Until this was done, his wife and children had to be cared for.

[1] HN to Ld Perceval, 30 Sept. 1727; to Bp of London, 12 Oct. 1727, *Society's Letters.*

[2] HN to Lady Torrington, 9 Nov. 1727, *Letters to Jamaica.*

[3] HN to Marquis Du Quesne, 13 Sept. and 13 Nov. 1727, *Letters to Jamaica.*

[4] HN to Abp of Canterbury, 22 Nov. 1727, *Society's Letters.*

[5] HN to Ld Perceval, 1 Dec. 1727, *Society's Letters.*

Lady Du Quesne lodged "in Great Maddox Street, behind Hanover Square new Church", to be near Lady Torrington's town house in Bond Street.[1] She could no longer object to her two boys' removal from Chelsea. They were sent to St Alban's Abbey School in January 1727, and Henry, still "a rugged child", followed six months later.[2] Newman could not forbear to point out to the Marquis that if the boys had gone earlier, "I am sure you would have had £100 of what has been laid out where they are". Lady Torrington tried to get the oldest boy a post at Court, but Newman had to tell him: "Your mother desires me to tell you there is no likelihood at present of your being admitted to the honour of waiting on Her Majesty as one of her pages, from some hints that have lately been given to your Mamma, but don't let this discourage you, it may be you want to be humbled and have in conversation boasted too much of the honour your friends aimed at for you." Newman himself went to see two Customs-house officers about the possibility of getting him a patent place in London or on the coast, which would "be a comfortable support to him and all the family, and whenever he comes to be preferred to Her Majesty's service, it may be resigned to one of his brothers. These places are all capable of being officiated by a deputy, the salaries of them paid quarterly out of the customshouse." [3]

Gradually the affairs of the Marquis improved. A settlement was reached with his creditors. He took a house "at Teddington for the convenience of being near the Court, where the Marquis goes often, and to be near my Lady Torrington for the benefit of her coach". As well as using Lady Torrington's coach, he had an allowance from her, to which his wealthy connection, Mr Ducane, a Director of the Bank of England, added £20. Between attending the Court at Kew and Lady Torrington's country house at Twickenham, he took to writing. Early in 1728 there appeared in London a pamphlet entitled *The Marquis Du Quesne vindicated: in a Letter to a noble Lord from the Aspersions cast on his conduct, while Commander of Fort Charles, at Port Royal in Jamaica, under His Grace the Duke of Portland, which aspersions were published in a letter said to be wrote by a gentleman of that island and addressed to a member of Parliament.* No name was affixed to this lengthy title, but Newman said it was "drawn up and printed" by Du Quesne. In it he claimed

[1] HN to Marquis Du Quesne, 26 Nov. 1726, *Letters to Jamaica.*
[2] HN to Rev. Mr Fothergill, St Albans, 10 Jan. 1727, *Letters to Jamaica.*
[3] HN to Master Wm Du Quesne, 5 Dec. 1727, *Letters to Jamaica.*

that, in part at least, he was blamed by the Assembly for obeying the orders of the Governor and Council, and admitted that he had, as Newman warned him, given his enemies opportunities to attack him by engaging in trade.[1] He gained a new benefactor in 1729, Archdeacon Russell of Cork, whose remittance enabled him to set up in the wine trade.[2] In a year or two he seemed to be doing well. He went to Hampton Court weekly to sell "French wine, oil, olives, etc., and desires no other favour at Court but that they may buy his wines of his hands at the market prices". He and his family were reunited "in a commodious house they have taken in Old Bond Street".[3]

But his second venture into trade was to end as disastrously as his first. Early in 1734 he was "not a little incumbered by one cross accident or other, and he is once more obliged to shelter in the verge, but Lady Torrington still takes care of his lady and the children". Even Newman could not help him by buying more wine, as he had not drunk his previous purchases.[4] The next year Du Quesne's business came to an end; he was "still conflicting with adversities in the verge of Court, though he has obtained a certificate on the second Statute of Bankruptcy against him".[5] In 1736 Newman could only tell his brother: "He has some promises from a Great Person at Court, but as the performance has been delayed some years, I doubt there is little dependence on their being brought to execution." [6] By the end of that year Du Quesne had disappeared, Newman reporting he had "left his lodgings in Warwick Street, Charing Cross, and they cannot or will not give any account of him".[7] After that, there is only one more mention of him in Newman's correspondence, when Newman discovered him with difficulty early in 1738 living in a coffee-house in Spring Gardens: "I hear he is in health, but I don't find he applies himself to any business." [8] And the last known of the Marquis is that he presented an unsuccessful petition to the Lords of the Treasury in 1740, representing himself

[1] F. Cundall, op. cit., 113; HN to Mr Du Quesne, Geneva, 18 Feb. 1728, *Letters to Jamaica*.

[2] HN to Archdeacon Russell, 6 Nov. 1729, *Letters to Jamaica*.

[3] HN to Lt Wm Dodd, Jamaica, 28 Nov. 1732, *Private Letters*.

[4] HN to Rev. Mr Galpine, Jamaica, 22 Jan. 1734, *Society's Letters*; to Marquis Du Quesne, 11 April 1734, *Private Letters*.

[5] HN to Lt Wm Du Quesne, 24 Dec. 1735, *Private Letters*.

[6] HN to Mr Du Quesne, 13 Sept. 1736, *Private Letters*.

[7] HN to Sir Roger Bradshaigh, 20 Nov. 1736, *Private Letters*.

[8] HN to Lady Du Quesne, 31 Jan. 1738, *Private Letters*.

as starving and asking for a pension, which he claimed had been promised him in 1727, but never fulfilled because of the death of George I.[1]

The disappearance of the Marquis left his family once again dependent upon Newman and Lady Torrington, but they could not keep them forever. Lady Du Quesne went in 1735 with her daughter Ann to "the Isle of Wight, where they live on the benevolence of their relations". There she became "housekeeper to Carisbrooke Castle" until 1742, when the Duke of Bolton, who had been deprived of his post of Governor of the Isle of Wight on account of his persistent opposition to Walpole, was enabled by his opponent's downfall to resume the post, and Lady Du Quesne suffered "the inconsolable affliction" of dismissal "to make room for some distant relation that His Grace wanted a provision for". Her father, Sir Roger Bradshaigh, had not been able to prevent it, and Newman could only hope "the remainder of her life will be made as comfortable as can consist with her infirmities of gout and an advanced age".[2]

Of the children, William had already, before his father's disappearance, "by my Lady Torrington's interest with Sir Robert Walpole" become "a young clerk in the Lottery Office, which he attends every day from his father's house".[3] In 1734 he joined the army as a Lieutenant in one of the Independent Companies and was sent to Jamaica. Newman expressed the wish to his mother that the island would not "prove as unfortunate a place to him as it has been to his parents", and wrote to the young man himself to hope that "though heaven witholds from you some of the blessings which others lavishly enjoy, I hope you will live to see the clouds dispersed". He urged him to study nature and plantation management, which he might find profitable later on. He concluded: "When you are quartered in a desolate place, let the Holy Scripture or some other good book be your daily amusement, and if you can inspire the soldiers under your command with a love of virtue and religion when they are destitute of every advantage for acquiring it, such heroism will make you the darling of God and men and add a glorious lustre to your account hereafter. Adieu, my dear Billy."[4] Newman hoped that William could return for a

[1] W. K. Lowther Clarke, op. cit., 54, 62.
[2] HN to Sir Thos. Lowther, Holker, 17 Aug. 1742, *Society's Letters.*
[3] HN to Lt Wm Dodd, Jamaica, 28 Nov. 1732, *Private Letters.*
[4] HN to Lady Du Quesne, 5 July 1734; to Lt Wm Du Quesne, Jamaica, 24 Dec. 1735, *Private Letters.*

commission in the regular army in three years' time, but he died of fever before then.[1]

The second boy, Thomas, was more fortunate. Colonel Townshend, who had married Lady Torrington's niece, provided for his education. He became a scholar of Eton in 1729, of King's College, Cambridge, in 1737, and a Fellow of the latter in 1741. He never married and was a substantial pluralist. When he died in 1793, at the age of 75, he held three livings in Norfolk and was a Prebendary of Lichfield and of Ely and Chancellor Canon of St David's.[2]

The youngest boy, Newman's favourite, was the most difficult to settle in life. After leaving school, he was sent to sea, and in the summer of 1736 came home from the West Indies and settled himself on Newman: "To prevent his hindering my clerk and molesting the tranquillity of my little family, I have been obliged to put him to a writing school in my neighbourhood, but when I sent yesterday to know whether he was there, he was not, nor had been there all the forenoon." He had "gone to Tyburn to see the men hanged", and Newman showed how much he belonged to the age by commenting that it was "a curiosity I can't blame him for, provided he had asked leave and gone in a better appearance than a Black Guard or street robber". Newman sent him to a better school at Chelsea, from which he was expelled, and then to another, Mr Stotherd's Academy.[3] In the spring of 1737 the boy went back to sea; but before the end of the year he presented himself to Newman again: "Coming home last Saturday evening, I was surprized with the sight of Harry Du Quesne, who gave me no reasonable account of his leaving the *Gloucester* but that he had nothing to do." He had worked his passage back from Gibraltar to Amsterdam in a Dutch ship and then to Harwich, "from whence he footed it up to London".[4] Newman could still think of nothing for him but the navy, and got him aboard the *Hampton Court*, bound for the West Indies. He sent an encouraging letter to him at Spithead, gently rebuking him for the sleepless nights he had given his mother and sister. Althought only a ship's boy, Harry

[1] HN to Mr Du Quesne, 13 Sept. 1736, *Private Letters*.

[2] HN to Marquis Du Quesne, 12 Aug. 1736; to Sir Roger Bradshaigh, 20 Nov. 1736, *Private Letters*; *Alumni Cantabrigiensis*, Pt I, Vol. II, 77; W. K. Lowther Clarke, op. cit., 54–5, 65.

[3] HN to Marquis Du Quesne, 12 Aug. 1736, *Private Letters*.

[4] HN to Lady Du Quesne, 31 Jan. 1738; to Sir Roger Bradshaigh, 26 Dec. 1737 and 9 Feb. 1738, *Private Letters*.

was invited to dine with the officers, and promised the first vacancy as a midshipman.[1] By the end of 1738, however, Newman heard from De las Torres that he had deserted on reaching Jamaica and sailed in a merchantman for England. Newman despaired. "I am very much concerned for the account you give me of Mr Du Quesne," he wrote to De las Torres, "and if he goes in the same way, he will come to the gallows in spite of all the care his friends have taken to bestow a liberal education upon him"; and to Mr Galpine he complained: "I am sure he will be very unwelcome to his friends, who have at a great deal of expense fitted him out twice in two very good men-of-war, and he has run away from them both." [2] The rest of the story is silence. We do not even know whether the boy returned to England, for he disappeared from Newman's correspondence even more completely than his father.

There remained the only surviving daughter, Ann, who was with her grandmother at Geneva all the while her parents were in Jamaica. Though she was during those years only "Miss at Geneva" to Newman, he was thinking of a marriage for her as early as 1724, when Mr Ducane called on him with his two boys from St Paul's School, aged 12 and 13, and wondering whether one of them might "not in time be sent to fetch her home".[3] Ann was sent to school at Geneva until 1728 by her grandmother, who then said she could do no more, despite help from Lady Torrington. In a letter which Newman copied into his book, Mr Du Quesne complained: "My brother has ruined her to such a degree that she has no more than £50 a year left." [4] Despite the plight of her parents, there was nothing for Ann but to come to England, and Newman reported that she was "wonderfully improved for her age as to be in danger of being, through her beauty and accomplishments, the toast of the town". He wrote to Geneva: "She is now at board at Twickenham under my Lady Torrington's protection, where she learns English apace; I have not seen her since she went, but my Lady Torrington and the Marquis both tell me that she improves very much, so that Lady Du Quesne, her mother, can now freely

[1] HN to Lady Du Quesne, 31 Oct. 1738, *Private Letters.*

[2] HN to Rev. Mr De las Torres, Jamaica, 11 Nov. 1738; to Commodore Brown, Jamaica, 19 Dec. 1738, *Private Letters*; to Rev. Mr Galpine, Jamaica, 11 Nov. 1738, *Miscellaneous Letters.*

[3] HN to Mr Du Quesne, 13 Feb. 1724, *Letters to Jamaica.*

[4] HN to Lady Du Quesne, 9 July 1724; Mr Du Quesne to HN, 9 Jan. 1728, *Letters to Jamaica.*

converse with her, which she could not do for a long time but by signs which gave her some uneasiness." [1]

Though she first missed her grandmother so much that Newman "could never mention her with that respect as I ought, but Miss put her handkerchief to her eyes", while when he read her a letter from her grandmother, "she burst into a torrent of tears, and I could not help bearing her company, so that I had not power to go on reading the letter", Ann soon came to take the place in Newman's affections that had been held by her wayward youngest brother. He hoped more than ever that she would make a good marriage: "Let her read the Scripture as often as she did at Geneva, practise her writing and all kind of housewifery for her sex, and God will provide for her".[2] In 1738 Newman and her mother thought it time to assist Providence. Lady Du Quesne suggested that Newman should approach young Jonathan Belcher, son of the Governor of Massachusetts, but he had to report: "I took an opportunity to acquaint Mr B., but he told me frankly that though he has a great respect for the young lady you mentioned, he is under strict obligations to govern himself by his father's directions in an affair of that moment, that he dare not indulge himself in any inclinations to alter his condition without his consent, that being a younger brother and newly entering into the business of a laborious profession which has been very expensive hitherto." [3] Whatever the young man's real feelings, the ambitious Governor would certainly have wanted a bride bringing a larger dowry and influence than Ann, who also had her own ideas, for (Newman reported) she "dined with me last Sunday senight, when she assured me she had laid aside all thought of marriage to a Scotch jeweller who had made his addresses to her".[4] And in 1743, shortly before he died, he could tell Jonathan Belcher: "Miss Du Quesne, whom you had bespoke as a second, was happily married the 17th current to Mr John French, only son of a gentleman of the Isle of Wight, a discreet man in good circumstance, who was so pleased with Miss's charms that he told his parents he could think of no other person, and that he should think himself happy to have her, though without any fortune." [5]

Newman's intimate connection with the Du Quesnes, and his

[1] HN to Mr Du Quesne, 25 July 1728, *Letters to Jamaica.*
[2] HN to Lady Du Quesne, 6 March 1735, *Private Letters.*
[3] HN to Lady Du Quesne, 13 May 1738, *Private Letters.*
[4] HN to Mrs Chamberlayne, 14 Dec. 1738, *Private Letters.*
[5] HN to Jonathan Belcher, Jnr, Dublin, 31 March 1743, *Miscellaneous Letters.*

activities on behalf of others when appealed to as "a man of interest", reveal another side to Newman the Secretary of the S.P.C.K. or Newman the organizer of foreign missions and charitable causes. Often those in charge of such undertakings are men of great efficiency and industry, yet lacking the gift of personal friendship or compassion. Newman's forbearance and persistence in assisting these people showed that though an administrator, he was not blind to the needs of individuals, and though a bachelor, he was ready to take upon himself the domestic cares of another family.

8

AN AMERICAN IN LONDON

ON 23 May 1723, Esther Vanhomrigh, the unfortunate "Vanessa" with whom Swift tried to share his love for "Stella", died, it is said, of a broken heart. She left her fortune, originally bequeathed to the Dean of St Patrick's, between a Mr Marshall, an Irish judge, and another Dean—George Berkeley, Dean of Dromore since 1722. It was a strange bequest, for she and Berkeley never met, though he was a friend of Swift; but he accepted eagerly the £3000 to which it amounted, for it seemed to make possible his "fixed purpose of going to Bermuda" and founding there a college for training planters' sons as well as young American savages. He conceived this plan after a visit to England in 1720, when the gambling mania of the South Sea Bubble was at its height. He was appalled by the ample evidence of luxury, corruption, and spiritual decay, which seemed to him to indicate the fatal degeneracy of Britain, where "infidels have passed for fine gentlemen and venal traitors for men of sense". Above all, he felt that Britain was unworthy of her Empire to use it only for commercial gain, and agreed with Swift that it was a serious reproach that she had made no effort to protect and educate the natives of the lands where her people traded and settled. His Bermuda college was to remedy this by training native missionaries as "the fittest instruments for spreading religion, morals and civil life among their countrymen, who can entertain no suspicion or jealousy of men of their own blood".

A year after the Vanessa legacy, Berkeley's scheme seemed still more likely when he was appointed in May 1724, through the influence of his friend, Lady Perceval, to the richer deanery of Derry, said to be worth £1500 a year, and in the autumn he came to London to prepare his plans. He brought with him a letter, typically combining sympathy with irony, from Swift, who said that Berkeley's heart would break if his deanery were not taken from him and the exorbitant sum of £100 a year provided for him in Bermuda. In London Berkeley exerted his extraordinary persuasive powers upon all he met, and he received remarkable support. By the spring of 1726 he collected £5000, and in that year also obtained a charter for the college from George I and a vote by the House of Commons of £20,000 from the £80,000 given to Britain by the Treaty of Utrecht as the purchase money for the island of St Christopher in the West Indies.[1]

Newman was prominent among those who assisted Berkeley in London. Both as a native of the American continent and an official of a society for spreading Christianity, he sympathized with the project. Since missionary work in America and the West Indies was the concern of the S.P.G., the S.P.C.K. could not be directly interested in the scheme, but Newman still considered it his duty to give Berkeley what help he could. A college had already been planned in Barbados by General Codrington, who died there in 1710 and left his estates to the S.P.G. for its foundation. Newman believed Berkeley's project would similarly benefit the S.P.G., "to whom the College at Bermudas will also be of use to furnish missionaries when it please God to succeed the undertaking".[2]

Newman was able to be of considerable use to Berkeley, since the most likely supporters of his scheme were those members of the S.P.C.K. and similar societies who were prominent in all good works, like Lady Elizabeth Hastings, from whom Berkeley received his largest donation of £500. The speed with which Berkeley raised money for his college amazed Newman. He noted that Berkeley had obtained subscriptions or promises to the amount of £2000 within two months of his arrival in London, £4000 by February of the next year, and £5000 a month later. Newman recognized that, despite the support given to him, it was a personal triumph for Berkeley. "If the Dean himself", he told Lord Perceval, "had not had a great deal of patience and courage with a powerful interest, he could never have gone the length he has done." [3]

Newman's position and experience also made him realize Berkeley's difficulties. It was hardly practicable to establish the college in Bermuda. The distance of 600 miles from the American coast and the Indians for whom the college was mainly planned could outweigh the temperate climate and frugality and simplicity

[1] *D.N.B.*; B. Rand, *Berkeley's American Sojourn*, Cambridge, Mass., 1932, *passim.*
[2] HN to Rev. Mr Henry Robinson, Leeds, 4 Nov. 1725, *Society's Letters.*
[3] HN to Ld Perceval, 21 Oct. 1725 and 25 Sept. 1729; to Rev. Mr King, Topsham, Devon, 8 Feb. 1726; to Rev. Mr Cary, Bristol, 22 March 1726, *Society's Letters.*

of the colonists, which Berkeley imagined were the island's great advantages. To Newman it was a pity that the college was not planned "somewhere else nearer to the continent for whose benefit it is chiefly intended", and he later told Berkeley: "If you had made a short voyage to America before you had published your proposal, you would have very much have altered your scheme." To a correspondent he was very frank: "As to the Bermudas affair, you are pleased to desire my thoughts. I own to me the difficulties that attend the putting it in execution seem insuperable, but Providence may make the attempt a door to an establishment somewhere else for the purpose, when 'tis found to have miscarried there. Therefore I would not (nor would it become me) withhold any design of charity to it."[1] Dr Bray was of the same opinion, and one of the last writings he published before his death early in 1730 was a *Memorial*, in which he condemned, from his own experience in America, the idea of a college in Bermuda as impractical.[2]

The position of the college was not, in fact, the most serious difficulty. The whole idea was incompatible with the pervading commercial spirit. Esteem for Berkeley's character did not lead to payment of the parliamentary grant, and after nearly four years in London he resolved to sail to America and make such preparations as he could for the college. Here again Newman could help him. He gave Berkeley letters of introduction, asking colonial governors and other prominent New Englanders to help him; he also arranged for Governor Shute to give him a letter of credit for £6000 on Shute's agent at Boston.[3] From Newman's correspondence, it seems that the reason why Berkeley, when he sailed from England in September 1728, did not go directly to Bermuda, but went first to the American continent, was that he wished to make "a purchase of lands on or near Rhode Island with a view of furnishing the College designed at Bermudas with fresh provisions from it", and that he was also aided by Newman in selecting for his residence there such a suitable and agreeable place as Newport, Rhode Island.[4]

Here Berkeley bought a farm of ninety-six acres and built a

[1] HN to Col. Phenny, Gov. of the Bahamas, 18 Aug. 1725; to Rev. Mr King, Topsham, Devon, 8 Feb. 1726, *Society's Letters*; to Dean Berkeley, Rhode Island, 29 April, 1729, *New Eng. Letters*.

[2] H P. Thompson, *Thomas Bray*, 92.

[3] HN to Col. Jenkes, Gov. of Rhode Island, and others, 24 Aug. 1728, *New Eng. Letters*; to Gov. Shute, 25 July 1728, *Society's Letters*.

[4] HN to Rev. Mr Hales, 15 Feb. 1732, *Society's Letters*.

THE HOUSE OF COMMONS COMMITTEE ON THE FLEET PRISON, 1729

From the painting by William Hogarth

Chairman, General Oglethorpe. Other members of the Committee, Lords Morpeth, Inchiquin, and Perceval, Sir Gregory Page, Sir Archibald Grant, Sir James Thornhill, Sir Andrew Fountaine, General Wade, Captain Vernon, Francis Child, and William Hucks. Bambridge stands on the extreme left. (See p. 225)

small house. He entertained the most intelligent and educated of the colonists, and a letter from Newman shows how he sought to be accommodating to men of all persuasions and urged the duty of toleration: "I have just now received the enclosed from Lord Perceval and must let you know what the New England men here say of you, that you are so complaisant to the Quakers that you even go to their meetings and preach among them, and they in their turn go to church, where your dispensation of the use of the surplice and some other observances here, particularly the 30th January,[1] etc., would disgust weak people. I tell them I believe St Paul would have done the same if he had been in your place."[2]

Newman's letters also show that a few months in America were enough, as he foretold, to convince Berkeley that his college would be better on the mainland. Newman suggested that a good place would be New York, particularly "an island called Fisher's Island", owned by his kinsman John Winthrop, "who, I believe, would give you a good tract of land towards encouraging your settlement there". This would need a change in the royal charter granted the college, but Newman doubted whether Berkeley would obtain it:

> If the Government are in consent to erect the College where it may be most effectual to answer the purposes of it, I hope they will not refuse the leave you desire of a translation, especially when they see such good reasons for it as I doubt not but you have offered; but you know what it is to solicit at our Court, and though a thing may not be refused, yet by the delays given without a vigorous solicitation a man's life wastes and all projects built upon dilatory grants must suffer extremely in the execution, though never so well designed. If you could come over yourself for two or three months next spring, you would have a better chance to succeed upon your own solicitations than I doubt can be expected from your friends here, though they wish heartily well to the design, but there is a great difference between being a well-wisher and being the soul of an undertaking.[3]

Newman, in writing thus feelingly, doubtless had in mind his own recent five years' attendance upon the King's ministers for payment of the royal bounty promised the Society towards the Arabic Psalter and New Testament. It soon appeared that Berkeley's case was even less hopeful. In reporting this early the next year, Newman again urged him to come home, but for a

[1] Commemoration of the Martyrdom of King Charles I.
[2] HN to Dean Berkeley, R.I., 17 Sept. 1729, *New Eng. Letters*.
[3] HN to Dean Berkeley, R.I., 29 April and 17 Sept. 1729, *New Eng. Letters*.

different reason: "The Bishop of London and other persons of note here seem to think it impracticable to prevail with the Government to consent to a transfer of the settlement designed at Bermudas to Rhode Island. The objections made to Bermudas are with them so many good reasons for withdrawing the grant promised to the design in case it had gone on as first projected. Upon which considerations I believe you will think of returning to secure your Deanery before it can be liable to forfeiture. Dr Clayton is nominated for Bishop of Kildare, and when you return you will have a fair chance to be appointed to the first vacancy of that kind you may be inclined to accept." [1]

This decided Berkeley to resume his first plan of establishing the College in Bermuda in the hope of still obtaining the grant; but Newman had to tell him his chances of even that were not favourable. A month later he wrote to him: "I have acquainted several of your friends in our Society with your resolution to go to Bermudas as soon as the Government are determined to comply with their grant under the great seal, but they seem to think the Government will be less inclined to such a determination upon the advice of the mutinous disposition of the inhabitants since the withdrawing of the independent companies from thence to the Bahama Islands. And that thereupon many of the inhabitants at Bermudas are going and gone to the Bahama Islands and South Carolina." [2] Such excuses made it clear that the Government had really no intention of ever paying Berkeley the grant. In June 1729 his friend, Bishop Benson, told him there was little chance of it; and when, at last, in 1731 Bishop Gibson asked Walpole what was the true intention of the Government, he received the reply: "If you put this question to me as a Minister, I must and can assure you that the money shall undoubtedly be paid, as soon as it suits with public convenience; but if you ask me as a friend, whether Dean Berkeley should continue in America, expecting the payment of £20,000, I advise him by all means to return home to Europe and to give up his present expectations." [3]

Lord Perceval reported this to Berkeley, who bowed to the inevitable and returned home, a disappointed man, in the autumn of 1731. He scrupulously returned all the subscriptions he had received, and Newman obtained his permission "to intercede with

[1] HN to Dean Berkeley, R.I., 27 Jan. 1730, *Society's Letters.*
[2] HN to Dean Berkeley, R.I., 5 Feb. 1730, *New Eng. Letters.*
[3] A. C. Fraser, *Works of Berkeley*, Oxford, 1871, IV, 186.

such as may happen to be known to me or any of my friends for applying what they had devoted to a charitable use towards assisting some one or more of the religious branches of the designs of our Society, particularly the Protestant mission to East India, which only wants money to be prosperous under the blessing God Almighty has already vouchsafed to the beginnings made by our Society". Newman secured over £60 for the Indian mission in this way, while Berkeley made over £200 that remained unclaimed to the S.P.G., so his unwearying efforts to raise the money were not entirely wasted.[1]

Moreover, Berkeley continued to interest himself in America, though theological philosophy and Irish social problems were now to be his chief concern. The year after he returned from America he was "nominated by his Grace of Canterbury to preach at Bow Church" at the anniversary meeting of the S.P.G., and in "an excellent sermon", in Newman's opinion, "put the mission to America in the clearest light that has yet appeared". When the sermon was printed, the S.P.G. gave the S.P.C.K. 500 copies which Newman had "carefully distributed among their members and correspondents in town and country".[2] Also, while in Rhode Island, Berkeley had met one of the most outstanding S.P.G. missionaries, Samuel Johnson, a Tutor at Yale College, until, together with Timothy Cutler, Rector of the College, he had taken orders in the Church of England. As with Newman, Johnson's conversion did not destroy his affection for his College, and he brought it favourably to the attention of Berkeley, who saw in it a means of accomplishing something of what he had proposed in his own college. He made over to it the farm he had bought in Rhode Island to found scholarships "for the encouragement of classical learning", and when he returned to England he gave it nearly 1000 volumes of theological works, "the first collection of books that ever came at one time to America".[3]

Once more Newman could assist Berkeley by arranging for the shipping of this gift to America. His experience of sending articles to Harvard and friends in the colonies had acquainted him with agents able to do it. He conveyed the books to Yale through Andrew Belcher, a merchant of Boston and relation of Governor

[1] HN to Dean Berkeley, Greenwich, 20 Jan. 1732; to Bp of London, 18 Nov. 1732, *Society's Letters*.

[2] HN to Rev. Dr Humphrey, Sec. of S.P.G., Warwick Ct, 13 Sept. 1732, *Society's Letters*.

[3] HN to Mr Lewis Thomas, Dublin, 29 Feb. 1732, *Society's Letters*.

Belcher.[1] Berkeley also presented an organ to Trinity Church, Newport, Rhode Island, for which Newman not only arranged the transport, but found an organist from Cheapside for the church.[2] These were Berkeley's main gifts to America, but he also gave some books to Harvard, and it seems that this was through Newman's solicitations. When Berkeley was in America, Newman asked Benjamin Colman to introducc him to "Mr President Wadsworth, Mr Flint, etc. and show him how much we have improved a college in our wilderness in little more than four score years"; and he evidently continued to press his College's claims when Berkeley returned to England, for he told Edward Hutchinson, Treasurer of Harvard: "Mr Dean Berkeley's charity, though it did not go all to our College, I obtained as much as I could with decency ask and through his favour conferred on a sister or daughter of Harvard College was in a manner given to us." [3]

In fact, Newman was glad to assist Yale, not only as a deserving daughter of Harvard, but also because its theological teaching was the same. "It is a seminary in its infancy", he told a correspondent, "and therefore wants encouragement, and the principles of the Church of England are so much taught there that several of the most promising gentlemen educated in it have conformed to the Church of England, though they live in a country abounding with Dissenters." [4] He corresponded with Johnson, whose religious development was like his own and with whose outlook he agreed. "I congratulate you", he told him, "on the success of your and others' example in conforming to the Church of England, and while you and your brethren take care to maintain a Christian temper towards those that dissent from them, the Bishop of London and all that wish well to the Established Church will be better pleased than at a zeal which carries the appearance of persecution where Christian charity and good reason ought to be the governing principles." [5]

Yale valued Newman as a sympathetic and conscientious agent, and when, the year after it received Berkeley's books, it wished to

[1] HN to Messrs Andrew Belcher and Co., Boston, 1 June 1733, *New Eng. Letters*; "A Catalogue of Books for Yale College sent by Bishop Berkeley and shipped by Henry Newman, 1733", Yale University, Stirling Memorial Library, MS. Vault, Sec. 17:1.

[2] HN to Rev. Mr Honeyman, Newport, R.I., 19 Oct. 1733, *New Eng. Letters*, and 12 Aug. 1736, *Society's Letters*.

[3] HN to Rev. Mr Colman, Boston, 24 Aug. 1728; to Mr Hutchinson, Harvard Coll., 29 Sept. 1740, *Society's Letters*.

[4] HN to Rev. Mr Hales, 15 Feb. 1732, *Society's Letters*.

[5] HN to Rev. Mr Sam. Johnson, Stratford, Conn., 21 Aug. 1734, *New Eng. Letters*.

purchase a telescope in England, it commissioned Newman to do it. He was particularly able to do this through his own astronomical knowledge and acquaintance with members of the Royal Society. He told Elisha Williams, President of Yale: "I took the first opportunity of waiting on Dr Halley, Professor of Astronomy at the Royal Observatory, for his advice whether to send you a refracting or reflecting telescope. He told me by all means the latter because it would be attended with an apparatus that would facilitate all observations, and that a tube of the length I now send would show as much as a refracting telescope of twenty feet in length. I have tried it with all the planets, except Venus and Mercury, which were too near the sun to be seen while it was in my custody, and found it answered my expectations." [1] At least some service to the cause of American education resulted from Berkeley's visit, and Newman played an important part in making this possible.

On the whole, however, Newman's correspondence with Berkeley emphasizes the almost inevitable failure of the Berkeley project. Britain had not yet a consciousness of imperial obligations. Berkeley's success in raising subscriptions was a tribute to his gracious personality rather than public realization of a neglected duty. Walpole, though he subscribed £200 towards the scheme, had no intention that it should be carried out and knew that, once Berkeley's influence had gone from London, he could at first prevaricate and then openly oppose it. Newman's correspondence contains no expression of his own opinion. He was careful not to say more in writing than "his design for erecting a college at Bermudas [was] impracticable for reasons too long to mention";[2] but he must have realized that the country did not yet regard the care of backward races as one of the obligations of empire.

Berkeley's Bermuda project was only the most important scheme affecting America in which Newman was involved. Though he spent the second half of his life entirely in England without once returning to America, he did not lose his affection for his native land. As a contemporary American writer expressed it, Newman "went over and settled in England many years since and saw cause to conform to the Established Church. But he ever cherished

[1] HN to Rev. Mr Elisha Williams, Yale College, 31 Aug. 1734, *New Eng. Letters*; Henry Newman, "Account of the Telescope sent to Yale College, 1734", Yale University, Stirling Memorial Library, MS. Vault, Shelves—Yale.

[2] HN to Rev. Mr Cary, Bristol, 27 Jan. 1732, *Society's Letters*.

and expressed a warm and generous love and regard for his country, the churches and colleges here, and sought their prosperity and flourishing."[1] He corresponded continually with Americans—the colonial governors, the Presidents of Harvard and Yale, the clergy of New England, his relations, and old business friends. In a letter to President Leverett of Harvard, he said, "I earnestly beg your prayers that I may never disparage my native country",[2] and he always identified himself with it, considering himself an American rather than an Englishman, saying to his American correspondents "we" and "our". To his English correspondents he was ever ready to give a good opinion of America, as when sending Bishop Gibson a requested list of Harvard and Yale graduates, he observed, "I think one inference may justly be made from both lists that the country where those graduates live is very healthy", since of Harvard's 1193 graduates in 91 years, 749 were still alive, and of Yale's 291 in 31 years, 265 were still alive.[3]

In return for assistance to American institutions or individuals, Newman liked to be sent little presents, especially of foodstuffs, to remind him of his earlier days, such as "a barrel of salt pork, fed with the chestnuts of New Cambridge and afterwards with Indian corn" or "spruce bud from Newfoundland, of which I hope to brew next month some March Beer". He shared these gifts with New England friends in London. "If you love New England salt fish and oil", he wrote to John Winthrop in 1737, "let me know when you will honour me with your company to dine on it, and it shall be ready." Above all he liked to have a "cask of Indian flour" to make the already traditional New England baked Indian Pudding and "treat my countrymen with a dish that all England can't afford". In the last year of his life he was sent some squash seed, which he planted in the garden at Bartlett's Buildings, "but the London air did not agree with them and last summer was too cool to bring forward anything that required heat".[4]

As may be imagined, one of the strongest ties binding Newman to America was Harvard. His friend, John Leverett, became

[1] Ebenezer Turell, *Life and Character of Dr Benjamin Colman*, Boston, 1749, 146.

[2] HN to President Leverett, Harvard Coll., 22 Jan. 1713, *Harvard College Papers*, I, f. 98.

[3] HN to Bp of London, 1 March 1734, *Society's Letters*.

[4] HN to Messrs Andrew Belcher and Co., Merchants, Boston, 4 Aug. 1733; to Mr Geo. Rogers, Merchant, Boston, 4 Feb. 1737; to Mr John Winthrop, London, 26 Feb. 1737; to Messrs Edmund and Josiah Quincy, Merchants, Boston, 14 Sept. 1739; to Mr Thos. Hutchinson, Boston, 25 Oct. 1742, *New Eng. Letters*.

President of the College in 1707, and Newman corresponded frequently with him and also with Benjamin Wadsworth, who succeeded him in 1725, and Edward Holyoke in 1737. In writing to them, as to any Harvard tutor or graduate, he showed that he still considered himself a member of the College. It was "our College" and "my mother", and to the end of his life he retained an interest in its business and a willingness to assist it, while Harvard found it useful to have such a devoted and energetic graduate in England and relied upon his services in several important matters.

A difficulty facing the College at this time was its position under its charter, which had been granted by the Assembly of Massachusetts and led to constant disputes with that body, who disliked Leverett's liberal policy. As early as 1704 Henry Flint suggested to Newman that the College might be in a stronger position with a royal charter. Newman liked the idea, "especially if the advantages of education be not confined to one party of Christians only, but designed as well to instruct and encourage those that at present make up the main body of Protestants (I might say of Christians too) the Established Church of England". He thought also that it "would invite the generously disposed in England to such bequests to your revenue as would in time entitle you to the honour and respect of a younger sister to the famous universities of England".[1] Not until 1723 did President Leverett himself consider soliciting a royal charter from George I and write to ask Newman's advice. Newman still favoured the possibility, thinking an additional advantage would be that "it would be a means to attach the students there to the King's interest, who even now that they are dependent upon the orders of the Assembly, have dared to dedicate their theses to the Governor in his absence, as a mark of their respect to the King's Representative, and to pray for him publickly, while others are afraid of showing him so small a respect, for fear of incurring the displeasure of the mighty Lower House"; and he sent Leverett copies of the Statutes of Oxford and Cambridge to help him in drawing up a new charter. On inquiry, however, Newman found that the College could not "have such a favour now, nor indeed ever could, without being subjected to a Visitor appointed by the Crown or perhaps by the Archbishop of Canterbury, Lord Chancellor or Bishop of London, jointly or

[1] HN to Rev. Mr Henry Flint, Harvard, 30 June 1704, *Mass. Hist. Soc.*, Miscellaneous MSS., Vol. VII.

severally, besides several rules unavoidably imposed that would interfere with your present constitution in religious matters and cramp all that liberty you now happily enjoy". He thought, therefore, that the present charter "with all its faults, in my opinion, is to be preferred to a new charter under the Great Seal accompanied with several golden chains". His advice was taken and the scheme dropped. Newman and Leverett both realized that Anglican supervision at Harvard, even if possible, would send candidates for the Congregational ministry to Yale and make a royal charter ruinous for the College.[1]

Newman still thought there were ways in which the College might seek royal favour. After the failure of the Jacobite Plot of 1722, the Corporation of Harvard College directed Henry Newman and Thomas Hollis to present an address to George I "upon the discovery of the horrible and detestable conspiracy against His Majesty's life and Royal Family";[2] and in 1727 Newman sent President Wadsworth specimen addresses of loyalty to George II on his accession, saying: "In perusing those from our Universities, I could not help thinking it would become our Cantabrigian Mother in America to take this occasion of addressing the Throne. You have as good or perhaps a better title to it than many bodies here that daily do it, as you are a foundation of daring and undissembled loyalty to His Majesty, ever praying for perpetual blessings on the illustrious Protestant Succession." The College agreed, and an address was "sent over to Mr Thomas Hollis and Mr Henry Newman, to be presented by them and such as they should choose to go with them" as patrons or graduates of the College.[3]

A useful material service Newman performed for Harvard was the recovery of legacies left to it in England, as he did for the S.P.C.K. and other bodies. The first such task he undertook was when the Corporation of the College determined in June 1709 to try to secure the legacy of £500 of Governor Edward Hopkins. Over fifty years had passed since his death, and his heirs inter-

[1] HN to Rev. Mr Henry Flint, Harvard, 10 Sept. 1723; to Rev. Mr Colman, Boston, 20 Oct. 1722; to Rev. Mr Neale, London, 10 Nov. 1722, *New Eng. Letters*; to Mr Delafaye, 15 Nov. 1725, *Mass. Hist. Soc. Proceedings*, First Series, X, 350–1; S. E. Morison, *Three Centuries of Harvard*, 72.

[2] Harvard College Records, 5 Feb. 1723, *Colonial Soc. of Mass. Publications*, XVI, 482.

[3] HN to Rev. Mr Wadsworth, Harvard, 15 July 1727, *New Eng. Letters*; to Duke of Newcastle, *Col. State Papers—America and W. Indies*, 1726/7, 794: C.O. 5, 10, No. 11; T. Hutchinson, *History of the Colony and Province of Massachusetts Bay*, I, 383.

posed obstacles which made pursuit of the College's claim difficult, costly, and uncertain. In addition the vague terms of the will—"to give some encouragement in these foreign parts for the breeding up of hopeful youths in a way of learning, both at the grammar school and college"—did not make it clear whether Governor Hopkins meant the bequest to be shared between some school and Harvard and even also the College at New Haven, Connecticut, considered in his lifetime and since founded as Yale in 1701. Nevertheless, the Corporation appointed Newman as their attorney, sent him £40 for the prosecution of their rights, and promised him more if needed. He pursued his commission with such perseverance that a favourable decree in Chancery was obtained in March 1713, the legacy being divided: three-quarters to Harvard, one quarter to the Latin Grammar School, Cambridge, Massachusetts; and £800, the principal of the legacy with accumulated interest, was vested in a board of trustees, who bought with the money an estate which they named Hopkinton. The Corporation voted Newman £20 "as a gratuity for his care and service in managing the affair of Mr Hopkins' legacy". Newman, nearly thirty years later, looked back upon this as one of his most fortunate achievements, for he recovered the legacy "when it was on the brink of being irrecoverably lost, as it would have been if the old man, turned four score, who paid it, had been in his grave".[1]

Meanwhile, in 1710, the Corporation had asked Newman to inquire about another legacy left to the College by Sir Robert Thorner. Newman replied to President Leverett that he had received full satisfaction from the trustees of the estate and added: "Mr Thomas Hollis, one of the trustees, at the Cross Daggers in Little Minories, desires his will may be inquired for after his decease." This Thomas Hollis was the London merchant who founded in 1721 and 1725 the first two professorships at Harvard, in Divinity and Natural Philosophy; and Newman's news was very important, for it was the first hint of the beneficent intentions of the six Hollises whose names were to be so closely linked with the prosperity of the College.[2]

[1] Harvard College Records, 16 Nov. 1719, *Colonial Soc. of Mass. Publications*, XVI, 447; *Leverett MS. Diary*, 17, 20–1, 82, 164, Harvard College Library; *Harvard College Papers*, I, ff. 95, 98, 102; HN to Mr Edward Hutchinson, Harvard, 29 Sept. 1740, *New Eng. Letters*; S. E. Morison, op. cit., 56–7; T. Hutchinson, op. cit., I, 205.

[2] J. L. Sibley, *Harvard Graduates*, III, 391; T. Hutchinson, op. cit., I, 231; Josiah Quincy, *History of Harvard College*, 2nd ed., 2 vols., 1860, I, 232–41, 398, 399.

The College continued to employ Newman to recover legacies for it, but he could not repeat his early successes. In September 1729 the President and Fellows asked him to inquire about a legacy of £10 a year out of the tithes of the parish of Fremington, near Barnstaple in Devon, left to the College by Judge John Dodderidge by will dated 20 January 1658, but which had not been paid since 1687. Newman was again appointed attorney by the College and told not to spend more than £20 in recovering the legacy. At the end of 1732, however, he reported he had spent all this sum. He was granted another £20 with the assurance of still more if necessary, "provided there be any fair prospect of recovering the said legacy"; but it did not look as if there were. Newman's reports were discouraging, until at last in 1740 he had to confess failure. The sole surviving trustee refused to answer his letters, and he believed the estate was now so reduced in amount that it would not be worth the cost of Chancery proceedings to recover it.[1] He was similarly unable to recover £20 a year bequeathed to Harvard in 1679 by Owen Stockton, formerly incumbent of Chatisham, Devon, to support an "Indian convert or one that will study the Indian language that he may preach the Gospel among the Indians" and mentioned by Calamy in his *Life of Richard Baxter*.[2] Difficulties even greater than those of the charity schools faced Harvard College in attempting to recover lost or misappropriated legacies in England.

Perhaps the service to his old college in which Newman took most pleasure was procuring books for its library, of which he had once had charge. "I have been always sensible of the advantages accruing to my Mother by additions to the Public Library", he told Henry Flint in 1704, "and have therefore slipt no opportunity of addressing those that had ability or compassion to contribute to it." [3] He continued to do this for nearly forty years more. He collected a "box of Latin classical books, given him by friends",

[1] HN to Mr Wm Mervin, Heanton, Devon, 29 March 1729; to Rev. Mr Wadsworth, Harvard, 22 Feb. and 30 April 1729, 1 Aug. 1732, 24 Sept. 1736; to Mr Lewis Gregory, Barnstaple, Devon, 12 Nov. 1730; to Mr Lewis Stuckley, Biddiford, Devon, 1 April 1731; to Mr Wm Tallamy, Biddiford, Devon, 1 April 1732; to Mr Chas Challis, Plymouth, 25 July 1733; to Mr Edward Hutchinson, Harvard, 29 Sept. 1740, *New Eng. Letters*; Harvard College Records, 9 Sept. and 28 Oct. 1729, 1 Dec. 1732, 6 April 1737, *Colonial Soc. of Mass. Publications*, XVI, 567, 578–9, 605, 684; Ben. Wadsworth's Diary, 29 May 1730, *Colonial Soc. of Mass. Publications*, XII, 477–8.

[2] HN to Rev. Mr Chandler, 19 Oct. 1733; to Mr Edward Hutchinson, Harvard, 29 Sept. 1740, *New Eng. Letters*; Edmund Calamy, *Life of Richard Baxter*, 1702, 152.

[3] HN to Mr Henry Flint, 30 June 1704, *Mass. Hist. Soc.*, Miscellaneous MSS., Vol. VII.

and in sending White Kennett, Bishop of Peterborough, a sermon by Benjamin Colman, he asked him "sometimes to remember the Public Library of that Seminary where it was delivered", with the result that the Bishop gave him "a packet" of books for the library. Newman thought nothing too small, from Bishop Gibson's *Directions to his Clergy* to a letter from Prince William of Wales, which he sought from the Secretary to the Commission for Building Fifty Churches because "the students have a great esteem for His Royal Highness".[1] This was William Augustus (then aged 7), later Duke of Cumberland, known as "the Butcher" for his severity in Scotland during the '45.

Newman failed to obtain what would have been his most valuable accession to the library. Towards the end of 1740 he learned that Sir Richard Ellys, the theological writer and M.P. for Boston, Lincolnshire, "has taken a lease of two or three houses, where he now lives, for 99 years, to give himself and his executors time to think of disposing his library, which he is determined to leave to the publick in some manner or other". Sir Richard had married twice, but had no children by either marriage. The disposal of his estate, and particularly the fine library he had amassed, was therefore a matter of interest. Horace Walpole, who had written a Latin ode in Sir Richard's honour and given him his own portrait, was said to be seeking the inheritance; but Newman understood that Sir Richard "would be glad to give his library to any learned seminary among the Dissenters" and was most likely "to leave it to Dr Williams' Library for the Dissenting Clergy". Newman regretted this, since "nobody scarce knows of [it]", but could not agree with a clerical friend that it should go to Sion College if this meant the exclusion of "Dissenting clergy to study there as well as others . . . May God deliver us from such narrowness". Newman thought Harvard might urge upon Sir Richard "the usefulness of dedicating his noble collection to our College where it will really be of use to posterity for the service of religion and learning in many respects beyond any such dedication in England, where private advantages of books are so common that publick libraries are little resorted to except now and then by an author". He communicated his thoughts to Benjamin Colman, who wrote to Isaac Watts, as representing English Dissenters, to ask

[1] HN to Rev. Mr Wadsworth, Harvard, 31 May 1733; to Bp of Peterborough, 13 Sept. 1722; to Rev. Mr Colman, Boston, 20 July 1723 and 30 March 1728, *New Eng. Letters*; to Mr Philipps, Sec. to the Commission for Fifty Churches, 28 June 1728, *Society's Letters*.

his opinion about the destination of the library. Watts' reply was definite: "What you say from Mr Newman, I believe is true, that it will do more service in New England than in London"; and he added rather condescendingly: "I am glad to hear that Mr Newman, who appears zealous for the Church of England, has any remaining kind concern for the churches of New England as you intimate." Colman, however, wrote warmly to Sir Richard Ellys about Newman, whom he hoped would be able to tell the old man of Harvard, introducing him as "my dear countryman and once fellow-student in the said College . . . with whom I have had the pleasure of a free and lasting friendship these forty-five years past". In the summer of 1741 Newman went in a friend's coach to see Sir Richard "at his country house at Ealing, but he was so ill of the gout that neither my friend nor I could get access to him. After his coming to Town, he was inaccessible to everybody but his chaplain and physician." Nevertheless, Newman believed that he "does not exclude us from hopes of his favour in some shape or other to our College when he has considered of it"; but he died the next year. Newman understood that he left "his lady about £5000 a year, not including his library, which he referred to another and particular disposition, which he never lived to accomplish, so that now it is fallen to his lady and other relations as personal estate". In fact, Sir Richard's whole estate was entailed on his second wife and then to the Hobart and Trevor families. His library eventually was removed to Blickling Hall, Norfolk, a Hobart seat.[1]

The same concern for the welfare and prestige of his old College and friends led Newman to persuade the Royal Society to extend its membership to American scholars. John Chamberlayne and Sir Hans Sloane were Fellows of the Royal Society, whom he asked to propose such candidates. Cotton Mather was elected a Fellow in July 1713, and the next year Newman was able to secure the honour for his two greatest New England friends, when Chamberlayne asked him to "recommend it to Mr Thomas Brattle's executors in New England to bestow his manuscripts relating to astronomy, musick and other parts of the mathematicks on the Royal Society". Newman agreed to do this, but added: "I have been thinking that the request will go with the better grace

[1] HN to Dr Ben. Colman, Boston, 1 Oct. and 20 March 1740, 25 March 1741, 28 Sept. 1742, *New Eng. Letters*; Rev. Mr Isaac Watts, Newington, to Rev. Dr Colman, Boston, 18 May 1741, *Mass. Hist. Soc. Proceedings*, Second Series, IX, 383; Ebenezer Turrell, op. cit., 147–9; *D.N.B.*

if the Society be pleased to choose his learned brother, William Brattle, the Minister of Cambridge in New England, to be a Fellow of their illustrious body, he being, I believe, chief if not the only executor that Mr. Brattle has left." He also suggested they might at the same time elect "the learned President of Harvard College at Cambridge, John Leverett", since they were "the two great luminaries for learning in that country, and will, I am sure, in that capacity reflect honour upon the Society because to my knowledge they have many years since perused with delight their transactions and recommended them to their pupils as the best standards of natural philosophy now extant". Chamberlayne proposed them both, and they were elected Fellows in March 1714.[1] Later Newman acted as intermediary between them and the Royal Society in placing their communications. The Royal Society never received Thomas Brattle's papers.

Since the support of the Church of England in "the English plantations of America" concerned the S.P.G., Newman's appointment as Secretary of the S.P.C.K. did not enlarge his American correspondence by bringing him into contact with the Anglican clergy there. Though the S.P.C.K. sometimes made presents of books to individual clergymen in America, it could do no more, as Newman explained to Samuel Johnson, "without an immediate repulse from the appearance of invading the province of another Society, with whom they always desire to live in harmony, because they are engaged in the same work, though in different parts of the world." [2]

Instead of the Anglican clergy, Newman's American correspondence was largely with his contemporaries among the Congregational ministers in New England, whom many members of both the S.P.G. and the S.P.C.K. regarded as sectaries; and this was bound to place him in a delicate position. The occasion in 1714, when he had to defend himself for corresponding with them,[3] arose through a letter from Colonel Francis Nicholson, who as Governor of Virginia had upheld the Anglican clergy there. He accused Newman of "a constant correspondence with mongrel church people or Dissenters, but most of the latter". The matter was communicated to the S.P.C.K., who eventually held a long

[1] HN to Mr Chamberlayne, 23 Nov. 1713, *Society's Letters* and *Colonial Soc. of Mass. Publications*, XXVIII, 100; *Royal Society Council Minutes*, II, 270; *Journal Book of the Royal Society*, X, 525, 551.

[2] HN to Rev. Mr Sam. Johnson, Stratford, Conn., 7 Sept. 1737, *New Eng. Letters*.

[3] See above, p. 9.

debate on it in June 1714, in which Newman's conduct was censured, as well it might be, for the Anglican reaction had already produced its converts in the Northern colonies, and it must have seemed to many that Newman delayed the victory by corresponding with the enemy. Newman, however, did not even reply when censured, considering that enough of the Society's time had already been wasted, but he did defend vigorously to his friends both his own conduct and the reputation of his American correspondents, especially William Brattle and John Leverett. Not only had they been the means of making him an Anglican, but Brattle had "more than once declared to me that he was so much in love with the beauty and order of the Church of England and the learned men at the head of it, that if it were possible for him to take holy orders without the hazard of going ten thousand leagues for them, he would do it".[1]

Though Newman would not modify his letter-writing to America, he wanted to do what he could to help the Church of England in America. Gibson, who as Bishop of London was responsible for its oversight, seems to have consulted him several times as a man likely to know the religious position in America. Newman realized, for instance, that the real danger to the Church was not the Liberal Congregationalism of Harvard, but the rising tide of sectarianism in the colonies, the "Banditti of furious Dissenters", as an Episcopalian called it,[2] and in reply to an inquiry from Gibson about sending a clergyman to Providence, Rhode Island, he gave a sketch of conditions there which suggests that American Protestantism already displayed its fissiparous nature:

> I have been at the town of Providence several times and believe a prudent, circumspect minister would do a great deal of good there. As ignorant as the people are, they can generally read and many of them read the Scriptures in their families, by means of which there is a good appearance of common morality among the inhabitants, many of whom, when I knew them, were Quakers or Anabaptists or of a sect between both improved by themselves or their ancestors, which they would pretend zealously to maintain from some text or texts of Scripture, and for want of a discreet spiritual guide some of them, I fear, have disputed Christianity out of their families and reduced all religion to consist in one or two whimsical observations, as keeping the Sabbath

[1] HN to Mr Taylor, Sec. of S.P.G., 12 Feb., 29 March, and 5 April 1714; to Rev. Dr Smalridge, Dean of Ch. Ch., Oxford, 9 March 1714; to Mr Nelson, 5 April 1714; to Mr Dolins, 4 June 1714, *Society's Letters*; *S.P.C.K. Minutes*, 3 June 1714.

[2] J. C. Miller, *Origins of the American Revolution*, 1950, 138.

on Saturday or in keeping every day as the Lord's Day, wearing long hair, etc.[1]

Newman also realized that the Church suffered a great handicap by being an Episcopal Church without bishops in America, while dissenting sects enjoyed full privileges, and the necessity of going to England for ordination weakened it in the face of such rising sectarianism even in the Southern colonies where it was established. Soon after Gibson's translation to London in 1723, Newman told Governor Drysdale of Virginia that he had discussed this with the Bishop, who "seems fully convinced of the expediency of having suffragan bishops on your side of the water" and of encouraging such institutions as the College of William and Mary at Williamsburg as "more like to afford proper clergymen for your parts than either of our two Universities".[2] But the idea of an American episcopate was disliked by New England Puritans, as the beginnings of Popery; by English Dissenters, as increasing the power of the Church; by the British Government, as a threat to its policy of imperial centralization; and even by Anglican laymen in the Southern colonies, as inconsistent with the powers the vestries had gained over the clergy. The difficulties this placed in the way of creating a native clergy was shown by information Newman obtained from Gibson for a New England inquirer about the possibilities of ordination. The Bishop expected candidates to "understand to translate the Greek Testament into Latin or English . . . to render readily a plain Latin author into English and English into Latin . . . and have some knowledge of Divinity"; to possess "full testimonials of a sober life and conversation from credible persons", such as the Anglican clergy at Boston or a colonial governor; and to be accepted by "so many of the substantial inhabitants as may suffice to constitute a church and to maintain a minister with decency"; but the only assistance the Bishop could offer such candidates was to give them "a recommendation to the Lords of the Treasury for His Majesty's bounty of twenty pounds towards defraying the charge of their passage".[3]

Again, Newman knew that the character of the Anglican clergy in America left much to be desired, and was anxious that everything possible should be done to raise their reputation. He was grieved to learn that an S.P.G. missionary in New England was

[1] HN to Bp of London, 22 March 1723, *Society's Letters*.
[2] HN to Gov. Drysdale, Williamsburg, Va., 2 Aug. 1723, *New Eng. Letters*.
[3] HN to Rev. Mr John Emerson, Portsmouth, Mass., 3 Dec. 1725, *New Eng. Letters*.

engaged in a lawsuit over land: "I am sure the clergy will lose more of the affection of their flocks than they ever get by acquisitions in this manner. How can a minister of the Gospel be excused or expect to be followed, who preaches up self-denial and a contempt of this world, [but] at the same time he is grasping at every opportunity of litigating with his neighbours for a trifle?" [1] Another time, information about the character of a clergyman led him to write to the Anglican clergy of Boston, "desiring you would prevent his acting any part there to the dishonour of his profession or anywhere else in America".[2] Nor was this the only time he acted against an unsuitable man in the Church in America. In 1727 John Checkley came to England to be ordained to the charge of the episcopal church in Marblehead, Massachusetts. The two ministers of the town, John Barnard and Edward Holyoke (later President of Harvard), wrote to Gibson "to prevent so troublesome a man" coming there. Barnard later described how he "sent it unsealed, enclosed in another to Mr Newman, a very worthy gentleman, who I knew in England, desiring if he approved of it, to seal it and deliver it to his Lordship, but if not, to destroy it". Newman took it to Gibson, who read it and told him he could not probably "find leisure in the midst of so great a hurry as constantly attends him" to reply to the two ministers himself, but asked him to inform them "he was well satisfied that the gentleman you mention ought not to have orders, nor should have any from him while he remained under so vile a character". The result was according to Barnard, that "our town and the Churches of this Province, through the favour of God, got rid of a turbulent, vexatious and persecuting-spirited non-Juror. Blessed be God for his kind dealings with us!" [3]

Newman naturally welcomed not only peaceful relations between the Church of England and other Churches in America, but also ideas for reconciling them. He was glad to support Benjamin Colman, who became minister of the new Brattle Street Church, Boston, in 1699 and sought fellowship with all other Churches in Boston, despite the opposition of the Mathers and others. Newman commended him to Gibson as the "minister of that Church in Boston which is reckoned mid-way between the Church of England and Dissenters, some of the fundamental

[1] HN to Rev. Dr Colman, Boston, 30 Sept. 1740, *New Eng. Letters*.
[2] HN to Rev. Dr Cutler, Boston, 15 March 1731, *New Eng. Letters*.
[3] HN to Rev. Mr John Barnard, Marblehead, Mass., 25 Sept. 1727, *New Eng. Letters*; J. L. Sibley, *Harvard Graduates*, III, 393.

articles of it being that no man shall be denied communion with them for being a Church of England man, that the Scripture shall be read publickly every Lord's Day and the Lord's Prayer used at the end of their Morning and Evening Prayers without offence to the congregation. This establishment was occasioned by the narrowness of some other congregations, who denied the Sacrament to those who were of the Church of England, a weakness, I believe, they are now ashamed of, for Mr Colman's learning and moderation has drawn many of the gentlemen of sense and substance from the neighbouring congregations to his." [1] As they had been students together at Harvard under Brattle and Leverett, Newman could write freely to Colman about reconciling the Church of England in America with other Churches. One idea, rather too hopeful, was that Harvard might use in its worship some fixed liturgy, as that of Ostervald at Neuchâtel, which might encourage the New England Churches to adopt it and so "no longer be reckoned among Dissenters by the Church of England". Later he thought it would be more fruitful if each side considered what they had in common. While in places "where inveterate customs have established themselves, as Episcopacy is with the addition of temporalities blended with the constitution of England, and Presbyterianism in Scotland, it would be turning the world upside down to oblige people to alter an establishment that implies no idolatry nor deviation from the fundamentals of Christianity, and with which they may go to heaven, let them be on which side of the question they please", yet in other places, such as America, "If we consider every *Bishop* or *Superintendent* of the Christian Church as a great *Presbyter*, and every *Presbyter* with a cure of souls regularly ordained as a little *Bishop* . . . it might go a good way towards obviating the invidious distinctions that subsist among us".[2]

Such views perhaps justified the suspicions of some members of the S.P.C.K. of their Secretary, but he seems to have had the confidence of both Anglicans and Congregationalists in America, as was shown by his part in obtaining the royal gift to Christ Church, Boston, in 1733. Christ Church, the North Church, was the second Anglican church built in Boston—the King's Chapel being the other—and was completed in 1723, when Timothy

[1] HN to Bp of London, 26 Feb. 1726, *Fulham Palace MSS.*, American Papers, Mass. Second Box.

[2] HN to Rev. Dr Colman, Boston, 22 Oct. 1722 and 24 Sept. 1736, *New Eng. Letters.*

Cutler, the former Rector of Yale, was appointed to it. In 1730, when Jonathan Belcher arrived to take up the Governorship of Massachusetts, he brought a Bible, Prayer Books, Communion plate, and altar furnishings for the King's Chapel as a gift from George II. Immediately the vestry of Christ Church voted to ask Belcher and the Bishop of London to obtain a "like benevolence" from the King for their church. Both Belcher and Gibson turned to Newman to conduct negotiations for them. Newman persevered with this as untiringly as other solicitations he made in official circles, and his efforts were appreciated in Boston. Belcher wrote to him in 1731: "I am very thankful for your care to procure the King's Bounty for Christ Church"; and again: "The minister and vestry of Christ Church send you their humble service and most hearty thanks for your kind and diligent solicitations in the affair of the King's Bounty." The business took two years, because of opposition by the Lord Chamberlain of the Household, whom Newman eventually circumvented by petitioning directly to the King. The Treasury warrant for the gift was issued in May 1733, and it arrived in Boston early in September, Newman having also undertaken to ship it out, for which he had £26 16*s*. 10*d*. as expenses from Christ Church.[1]

Indeed, the causes assisted by Newman as an American in London were many. Whether Berkeley's Bermuda project, or the libraries of Harvard and Yale, or Christ Church, Boston, he was able and willing to act as an agent for them in the mother country. Moreover, the same services which he performed for American institutions were often requested by individuals. Thomas Prince, for instance, whose acquaintance with Newman was slight, limited perhaps to occasional contacts between 1711 and 1717 when Prince was in England, made use of him in 1729 to send some scientific literature and "a pair of the exactest globes", on the grounds that "none of my acquaintance is so well accomplished in the mathematick sciences to do it for me"; while ten years later Newman tried unsuccessfully to get him made a doctor of divinity at a Scottish university.[2]

[1] HN to Gov. Belcher, Boston, 18 Feb., 15 March, 7 May, 20 Aug., 18 Sept. 1731, 30 June 1732, 5 May 1733; to Messrs Andrew Belcher and Co., Boston, 1 June and 21 July 1733; to Rev. Dr Cutler, Boston, 28 July 1733, *New Eng. Letters*; to Duke of Grafton, 4 Nov. 1732, *Society's Letters*; P. Merrit, "The King's Gift to Christ Church, Boston, 1733", *Colonial Soc. of Mass. Publications*, XIX, 299–331.

[2] Thos. Prince to HN, 4 March 1729; HN to Thos. Prince, 16 July 1729, *Colonial Soc. of Mass. Publications*, XXVIII, 101–3; HN to Rev. Mr Robt Miller, Paisley, 2 Oct. 1739, *Miscellaneous Letters*.

Still more was Newman able to help fellow-countrymen in England. Once he obtained the release of two New Englanders who had been press-ganged into the navy; once he joined with others to pay for "all due attendance and other means for his recovery" for an American clergyman who had caught "smallpox in such manner that his life is in danger"; again, he commended a New Englander, who was sick and alone in London, to St Thomas's Hospital "to be admitted under the care of their physicians", offering to pay the usual charges to the House "in case it should please God he should do otherwise than well"; and another time he interceded on behalf of a Connecticut woman with her estranged husband who had left her and come to England. No wonder that when Thomas Coram thought of founding "a New England Bank" in London for the relief of visiting colonists in distress, he wished Newman to be one of its four managers. This scheme did not materialize, but if it had, Newman would almost certainly have accepted the duty and performed it with all the zeal and industry he was accustomed to display in helping anything that concerned his native country.[1]

[1] HN to Rev. Mr Drew, St Thomas' Hospital, Southwark, 4 Oct. 1727, *Private Letters*; to Mrs Winthrop, New London, Conn., 21 Sept. 1736, *New Eng. Letters*; Mr Thos. Coram to Rev. Dr Colman, Boston, 22 Sept. 1738, *Mass. Hist. Soc. Proceedings*, LVI, 51, 54.

9
THE COLONIAL AGENT

NEWMAN'S services to America were not confined to private causes and persons, many as they were. His willingness to help his native country soon brought him a post in which for a number of years he acted as an official link between the mother country and the colonies. This came to him through Colonel Joseph Dudley, Governor of Massachusetts and New Hampshire. Dudley may well have met Newman while he himself was in England from 1692 to 1702 and have recognized him as a man able and ready to assist American interests in England. At any rate, in 1709 he wrote to the Council of New Hampshire recommending that Newman should be agent for the colony in London as "a very good gentleman and very acceptable to those upon whom he depends", and the Council agreed.[1]

The office of colonial agent was well established, probably originating in the time of the Commonwealth and the conquest of Jamaica, and by now important as a recognized intermediary between colonies and mother country. A colony expected its agent to promote its interests in England, while the Government also regarded him as the spokesman of the colony. The office did not assume this importance without controversy over the appointment and authority of the agent. Disputes between governor and assembly over control of the agent and the claim of each to have its own agent occurred in many colonies.[2] Newman experienced such a conflict of authority from the outset, and his position was further complicated because New Hampshire and Massachusetts, though separate colonies, had the same governor from 1699 to 1741. The year after Newman's appointment as agent for New Hampshire, the agent for Massachusetts, Sir Henry Ashurst, died; his brother, Sir William Ashurst, was offered the post, but declined it. Dudley tried to have Newman given this post as well, but Sir William Ashurst and a number of London merchants trading with New England wished it to go to another New Englander settled in

[1] *New Hampshire Provincial Papers*, III, 417–18.
[2] *Cambridge History of the British Empire*, I, 434.

London, Jeremiah Dummer, a prominent lawyer and man of fashion. The General Court of Massachusetts, realizing that it was not likely to be in its interests to have the same agent as a neighbouring colony, also preferred Dummer and persisted in its preference. Dudley probably favoured Newman for several reasons, not the least being that both he and Newman were Puritans who had conformed to the Church of England, while Dummer was a sceptic in religion; but he thought it best not to add to his continual dispute with the General Court and accepted its wishes. Newman and Dummer continued as agents for their respective colonies for about the same period under several governors, though, as the General Court had foreseen, their work brought them into conflict more often than alliance.[1]

As a colonial agent, most of Newman's business was done with the chief body of advisers to the King in Council on all American matters. This had been set up by William III in 1696 by commission under the Great Seal as the Lords Commissioners for Trade and Plantations and was commonly known as the Board of Trade. It was a small group of eight men, supplemented by the occasional attendance of certain of the great officers of state named in the commission, including the Bishop of London from 1702. Its purpose was entirely advisory; "it was a board for the collection and presentation of information; action and execution remained in the hands of the King and Council." [2] Though its main attention was given to trade, it made inquiries into all aspects of colonial administration, so that it is not surprising that Newman should have been continually in contact with it while a colonial agent.

In 1729 Newman wrote: "I have been agent upwards of twenty years." [3] At first, however, he was not employed permanently by New Hampshire, but only as occasion arose. His most important commissions were warlike during these first years. The War of the Spanish Succession was nearing its end. Essentially a European struggle, British governments had been reluctant to extend the fighting to North America; but the New Englanders desired the conquest of Canada to put an end to border raids and attacks on

[1] T. Hutchinson, *History of the Colony and Province of Massachusetts Bay* (ed. L. S. Mayo), Cambridge, Mass., 1936, II, 140; "16 Nov. 1716. Mr Jer. Dummer is chosen Agent; had 63 votes. Barrington Shute esqr. 30. Mr Henry Newman 1." "Diary of Samuel Sewall", Sewall Papers, *Mass. Hist. Soc. Collections*, Fifth Series, VII, 111.

[2] A. H. Basye, *The Lords Commissioners of Trade and Plantations*, New Haven, Conn., 1925, 4.

[3] HN to Geo. Jaffrey, Henry Sherburn, etc., New Hampshire, 4 March 1729, *New Eng. Letters*.

their coastal shipping by the French. Since the Phips expedition of 1690, they had themselves made several abortive campaigns against Canada, the last being an attempt to take Port Royal, capital of the French colony of Acadie, in 1707. Recognizing that professional leadership, regular troops, and warships were vitally necessary, the colonists urged the British Government to support operations in North America. The Government finally agreed to an expedition in 1709, but events in Europe caused its postponement, to the great disappointment of the New Englanders; and in December 1709 Newman was instructed by the House of Representatives of New Hampshire to present an address to the Queen "that the expedition against Canada may be revived in the spring".[1] The next year saw the fall of the Whigs and the gradual restoration of a completely Tory ministry, which, while anxious to end the war, saw the political advantages of a victory in North America, both at home and at a peace conference. It agreed to support operations against Canada, and in October 1710, Port Royal, capital of Acadie, was captured. In January 1711 both Newman and Dummer presented the Queen with several addresses from their colonies "to congratulate her Majesty on the conquest of Port Royal, now Annapolis"; but in November of the same year, Newman was ordered by Dudley and his Council to present a memorial on the sufferings of the Province from French and Indian raids and ask for a further expedition. To the Board of Trade, which strongly supported the New Englanders' wishes, Dudley wrote to signify that Newman's commission was to urge the Government "to revive that just and honourable resolution last year taken by her Majesty for the reduction of Canada, thereby to make her Majesty the sole possessor of all North America".[2] The Government agreed to continue operations, but there followed the ignominious failure of the Walker expedition against Quebec in 1711. Before the end of the year, New Hampshire and Massachusetts both once again petitioned the Queen "to renew the expedition in the spring"; but peace came in 1713, and Canada was to remain French for fifty years more.[3]

The coming of peace both changed and increased New Hampshire's commissions for Newman; and in 1720 the General

[1] *P.R.O., Acts of the Privy Council* (*Colonial Series*), III, 412–13; 508–10.
[2] *Boston News Letter*, 4–11 June 1711; Gov. Dudley, Boston, to Board of Trade, 13 Nov. 1711, *Col. State Papers, America and W. Indies, 1711–12/167*, C.O. 5/865, 73 and 5/913, 363–8.
[3] G. S. Graham, *The Walker Expedition to Quebec, 1711*, 1953, *passim*.

Assembly, finding their affairs "frequently requiring the solicitations of some persons at Court", made him their permanent agent. This was reaffirmed in 1735, and he remained agent for another two years after that. For his services he charged the Assembly £10 a year: "I should not have taken it upon me to estimate my service, if the nature of the thing had not obliged me to it, and presume the allowance of £10 per annum will not be thought extravagant, considering how great a share my clerk has of it." But he did not keep an exact record of his expenses: "The particulars of my expenses of every occasion of attending either the Secretary of State, Council Office, Board of Trade, or Parliament House, when a Naval Stores Bill or other like matter have been depending, would have given you and me not a little trouble to enumerate." Instead, in 1729 he said he had "kept such an account three years", which amounted to £19 6*s.* 6*d.*, "for Petitions, Memorials, Orders of Reference to the Board of Trade, etc. by the King or Lords Justices, coach-hire and other incidental expenses", and so charged £6 8*s.* 10*d.* a year for expenses. Payment to him by the Assembly was erratic. It paid him only £18 in 1718 and voted him £100 on his permanent appointment in 1720, but he only received £36 the next year and £33 in 1723. Thereafter, he had £50 in 1727 and £60 in 1729. This did not, Newman calculated, entirely reimburse him, and he asked for more, since, "I hope I may be enabled to serve the Province without injuring myself"; but he had no further money until his appointment was reaffirmed in 1735, when the Assembly granted him £100.[1]

Upon his appointment in 1720, the Assembly instructed Newman that the matters they wished him to pursue particularly were the "dispute between this and the Massachusetts government about the dividing line"; the grant of stores for Fort William and Mary, "the stock being now very low"; "that the lumber from hence may be imported into Great Britain free of duty and the bounty continued on naval stores, that the forging of iron there may not be obstructed but encouraged and that some better encouragement may be granted for raising hemp and flax"; "that the Surveyor General of the Woods may be directed to preserve the mast trees after a better manner and not suffered to obstruct His

[1] Assembly of New Hampshire to HN, 22 July 1720, *New Hampshire, Miscellaneous Papers of Ebenezer Hazard,* Box 7, Library of Congress, Washington, D.C. (Manuscript Library); *New Hampshire Provincial Papers,* III, 779–80; Vote of Assembly of New Hampshire, 1735, *New Hampshire Hist. Soc. Province Papers,* Series of 1901, XI, 14; ? to HN, 1735, *New Hampshire Hist. Soc. Misc. MSS. 1703–39,* f. 19.

Majesty's subjects from getting such timber from hence as is not, nor never will be, fit for the service of the Crown." [1] In fact, they were to represent most of Newman's work as agent, and his efforts to solve them satisfactorily for New Hampshire give an insight into relations between the British Government and an American colony at this time.

The first, the boundary dispute between New Hampshire and Massachusetts, was long drawn-out and not settled until Newman had ceased to be agent. Such boundary disputes were prominent in American colonial history, and no colony avoided one with one or more of its neighbours. In this case, unfamiliarity with the geography of New England—a common cause of boundary disputes—led English officials in drawing up the Massachusetts charter of 1691 to define its northern boundary as a line three miles north of and parallel to the Merrimac River. It was not then known that this stream bends sharply north at an angle some thirty miles from its mouth, which meant that a literal interpretation of the charter would confine the royal province of New Hampshire to a narrow strip of land on the Atlantic. Against this, New Hampshire claimed that the Charter should be amended in a common-sense manner to extend the boundary line due west at the point where the Merrimac River turned sharply to the north.[2]

After the "affair of the lines" had been disputed between the two colonies for many years, the British Government was brought into it when the General Assembly of New Hampshire in 1720 instructed Newman to appeal against the literal interpretation by Massachusetts of its charter, and Jeremiah Dummer was told by a House committee to contest on behalf of Massachusetts any representations Newman made at Whitehall.[3] The result was that for nearly twenty years more the dispute was fought out in England, where the two agents were rivals for a favourable settlement. New Hampshire wanted especially to win because it wished to be independent of Massachusetts under a separate governor and would not be large or wealthy enough to claim this without the extended boundary. The Assembly marked its sense of the importance of the case by sending Newman in 1726 a special grant of £100 for its prosecution; but he warned them, "If this matter

[1] *New Hampshire Provincial Papers*, III, 779–80.

[2] J. J. Burns, *The Colonial Agents of New England*, Washington, D.C., 1935, 73–5; J. S. Barry, *History of Massachusetts*, II, 133; J. Belknap, *History of New Hampshire*, 2nd ed., 3 vols., Philadelphia, 1813, I, 234.

[3] *New Hampshire Provincial Papers*, XIX, 195; *Mass. House Journals*, II, 241, 262.

comes to a hearing by learned counsel at the Board of Trade or before the Council, I cannot retain less men than the Attorney or Solicitor-General with some other noted counsel with ten guineas each for a hearing and if, as commonly happens, they are put off the first time, they will expect four or five guineas each to refresh their memories, especially when they are told they are maintaining the quarrel of a province", and again, "I must not be stingy in fees to counsel, etc., which are grown exorbitant since the fatal year 1720, and what you have remitted will only make a beginning." [1]

Newman was handicapped by several difficulties. He had throughout to contend with an antagonistic Council in New Hampshire and a Governor who was also Governor of Massachusetts. Governor Belcher persistently tried to prevent his appointment as agent, so that he was in fact from 1729 the representative only of the popular Assembly of New Hampshire. And though Massachusetts was responsible for this situation, Dummer exploited it by doing his best to prove that Newman had no proper status as an agent.[2] Indeed, Dummer's awkwardness was another of Newman's difficulties, which were increased by the dilatoriness of the British Government and its officials. As early as 1722 Newman thought the most "summary way of ending this controversy" was to secure, through the Board of Trade, the appointment of a royal commission to decide upon it, and the Assembly of New Hampshire agreed. Though this device was finally adopted, it was not until after more than ten years—years in which Newman struggled against Dummer's manoeuvring and official procrastination. He began by submitting a memorial to the Duke of Newcastle, Secretary of State for the Southern Department, which had been given charge over the plantations in 1704, with the request that he would lay it before the Board of Trade. Despite several letters to the Duke, this never reached the Board, and Newman had to conclude it was "irretrievably lost in the Duke of Newcastle's office".[3] He sent another memorial in 1726, this time to the Privy Council, but with the same request that the matter should be considered by the Board of Trade. This succeeded, and

[1] J. Belknap, op. cit., II, 84; HN to Committee of Both Houses, New Hampshire, 20 Aug. 1726; to Lt-Gov. Wentworth, 12 Feb. 1728, *New Eng. Letters*.

[2] *New Hampshire Provincial Papers*, XIX, 249–51; *Acts of the Privy Council, Colonial*, III, 593.

[3] HN to Gov. Shute, 19 Feb. 1722; to Col. Wentworth, 4 June 1726, *New Eng. Letters*; *Col. State Papers, America and W. Indies*, C.O. 5, 931, No 14; *Journal of Commissioners for Trade and Plantations, 1726*, 281–2.

the Board asked Dummer and himself to present their cases before it. Newman was ready to do this and obtained evidence from New Hampshire, but Dummer was not, and for years put what obstacles he could in the way of the Board considering the matter. In 1731 Newman was still complaining of "Mr Dummer refusing to join with me" in reaching a settlement.[1] Finally, in 1737 a commission was agreed upon and appointed, which took the dispute away from the agents and the Board of Trade. Its decision favoured New Hampshire, but by then the old protagonists, Newman and Dummer, had both ceased to be agents. When Francis Wilks, agent for Massachusetts, made a final and unsuccessful appeal against the commission's decision in 1738, the agent for New Hampshire who opposed him was Newman's successor, John Tomlinson, Senior.[2]

The matter of the "stores for Fort William and Mary" concerned the supplying of this, the chief citadel in New Hampshire, with arms and ammunition. The Province passed a Powder Act in 1702, providing that an "impost or powder money" should be levied on British ships trading with New Hampshire ports to pay for these warlike stores, but in 1720 the Board of Trade ordered the suspension of the Act. A committee of the Council and Assembly of New Hampshire instructed Newman in that same year to ask for a gift of stores from the royal bounty for the fort. Having no encouragement from the Board of Ordnance, he petitioned the Board of Trade, urging the importance of the fort as "a frontier against the invasions of the Indians" and a safeguard for "His Majesty's naval stores", which had now only sixteen barrels of powder for its "forty-two pieces of ordnance". He asked, therefore, for 110 barrels of powder for the fort, "together with a suitable proportion of great and small shot".[3] That was in March 1721. After considering the petition intermittently, the Board in December 1723 recommended the Privy Council to accede to it. The Privy Council referred it to the Board of Ordnance, which coldly recalled it had supplied New Hampshire in 1708 by Order in Council with military stores worth £1077 6*s*. 7*d*., for which it had received no grant from Parliament, so that the "debt still remains

[1] HN to Lt-Gov. Wentworth, 29 July 1726, *New Eng. Letters*; to Sec. of the Council of New Hampshire, 2 May 1731, *New Hampshire Provincial Papers*, III, 832; *Col. State Papers, America and W. Indies*, C.O. 5, 869 ff., 340, 341–3 v, 346.

[2] *Col. State Papers, America and W. Indies*, C.O. 5, 198 f., 319 ff.; also B.M., *Add. MSS.* 15487, f. 2.

[3] HN to Bd of Trade, 31 March and 27 July 1721, *Col. State Papers, America and W. Indies*, C.O. 5, 868 ff., 43, 43 v, 44 v, 63, 64 v; also *Rawlinson MSS.*, C.379, f. 25.

unsatisfied to this Office". This latest requirement by New Hampshire would cost £1231 0*s*. 6*d*., and the Board's revenue was appropriated to the Royal Navy and garrisons in Great Britain and could not be diverted. Moreover, to meet New Hampshire's wishes would set a precedent for "other Provinces to bring extraordinary expenses on this Office", for which Parliament was unlikely to grant any money.[1]

There it rested for the remainder of Newman's time as agent. He was not allowed a copy of the Board of Ordnance's report until nearly a year later. Then he immediately wrote to Walpole to request him to "favour a further application to His Majesty for a special grant to the Board of Ordnance for issuing the stores desired or to recommend it in Parliament among the services unprovided for or otherwise as you in your great wisdom shall think fit". Neither this nor repeated appeals to the fountain-head availed. His letters were unanswered; attempts to see the minister were difficult, either because Walpole was "laid up with the gout and for that reason inaccessible to all people except his domestics or ministers of state" or was "very much at his seat at Chelsea or Kensington" or making "a long visit at his country seat in Norfolk". When Newman did manage to see him, he could only report "he told me he would consider my papers on that subject at his first leisure". But that time never came. In 1728 Newman reported that his continued efforts to obtain the supplies met with nothing "but favourable promises"; the next year Walpole told him he "must have patience to wait for his answer about stores until after Michaelmas"; and in 1731 he vainly presented yet another petition to the Board of Trade. Persistence met with no reward.[2]

These two matters, the boundary dispute and the stores for Fort William and Mary, simultaneously accounted for a large part of Newman's work as colonial agent. They show the effect of Walpole's policy of "salutary neglect" as applied to the colonies. His practice of letting sleeping dogs lie rendered the administration in

[1] *Journal of the Commissioners for Trade and Plantations, 1721*, 271, 308, 309; ibid., *1723*, 51, 56; Bd of Trade to the Lds Justices, 17 Dec. 1723, *Col. State Papers, America and W. Indies*, C.O. 5, 915 ff., 398–400; Report by Bd of Ordnance to Earl Cadogan, Master-General of H.M. Ordnance, 24 Dec. 1723, *Rawlinson MSS.*, C.379, f. 33.

[2] HN to Committee of both Houses, 29 Sept. 1724, *New Hampshire Provincial Papers*, IV, 146–7; to Sir Robt Walpole, 25 Nov. 1724, *Rawlinson MSS.*, C.379, ff. 58–9; to Lt-Gov. Wentworth, 3 Dec. 1725, 20 Oct. 1726, 3 Oct. 1728, 19 June, and 17 Oct. 1729; to Sir Robt Walpole, 22 Jan. 1726; to Committee of both Houses, New Hampshire, 6 April 1727, *New Eng. Letters*; to Sec. of Council, New Hampshire, 21 May 1731, *New Hampshire Provincial Papers*, III, 832.

Britain quite inadequate to deal with colonial affairs. Moreover, the subordination of all government agencies to the political exigencies of the great Whig magnates led to the more important powers vested in the Board of Trade, such as the right to nominate to colonial offices, being absorbed by the Secretary of State for the Southern Department.[1] This office was held from 1724 to 1748 by the Duke of Newcastle, of whom gossip said that he was so preoccupied with borough-mongering that his closet was jammed with colonial dispatches, all unopened.[2] The Board's influence was not revived until that able and vigorous administrator, George Dunk, second Earl of Halifax, became its President in 1748. Yet though the Board reached "its lowest level of ineptitude and indifference between 1730 and 1748, it carried out with a considerable measure of success the terms of its commissions"; [3] and Newman seems to have found it the most satisfactory body to deal with. In all, however, the slackness and inefficiency, then characteristic of British administration generally, was so great in everything concerning the colonies that even the most industrious and conscientious agent could not have hastened the slow and ineffective machinery of government, nor overcome the indifference and irresponsibility of officials and ministers. Newman never gave up, but at times he was near to despair, as when he wrote to Colonel Wentworth, Lieutenant-Governor of New Hampshire: "The delays attending my solicitations on behalf of the Province have given me so much uncertainty that I have no heart to write to you only to repeat what I have said before of promises." [4]

The fact was that eighteenth-century British imperialism was commercial. The ruling class thought about the colonies in terms of mercantilism and wished them to remain contributory to the power and prosperity of the mother country. This was bound to provoke opposition from the colonists when they felt it conflicted with their own interests, as was shown by the other matters undertaken by Newman for New Hampshire. The wars of the century showed the Admiralty the inconvenience and uncertainty of depending upon Sweden and the Baltic countries for naval supplies, which were, therefore, sought from the colonies. In 1705 an Act of Parliament fixed bounties on tar, hemp, timber, and other naval stores imported from the colonies and forbade in New England,

[1] A. H. Basye, op. cit., 24.
[2] J. C. Miller, *Origins of the American Revolution*, 1950, 33.
[3] *Cambridge History of the British Empire*, I, 413.
[4] HN to Lt-Gov. Wentworth, 4 June 1726, *New Eng. Letters*.

New York, and New Jersey the felling of pine-trees of certain dimensions.[1] The colonists welcomed the bounties, but not the restrictions on cutting timber. John Bridger, His Majesty's Surveyor-General of Woods, who was sent to New England in 1717 "to inquire into the state of the country", reported widespread destruction of trees suitable for shipbuilding.[2] The next year the Council of New Hampshire voted Newman and Dummer £15 "for their soliciting the liberty to cut timber, etc. within this Province".[3]

The Government's answer, however, was to introduce a Bill in 1722 forbidding in these colonies the felling of pine-trees of any size except those growing in townships.[4] This was more stringent than the previous Act which had excepted trees belonging to private persons, and, moreover, the Court of Admiralty was to be empowered to judge offences against these provisions. The Assembly of New Hampshire ordered Newman to protest against the clause, which he did by petition to the Board of Trade and letter to Lord Carteret, then Secretary of State for the Southern Department, but he reported to Governor Shute that "the Lords of the Admiralty insisted so much upon it, and the Commissioners of the Navy attending the House of Commons several times about this and other causes, Mr Bridger prevailed with them to believe, that if the clause did not pass, all the best pines in America would be destroyed".[5] This Act, however, did not have the desired result. Colonists construed its provisions to mean that trees growing in any established township were not the King's property and could be cut for private use; they took to forming townships where the best timber grew. In 1729 another Naval Stores Bill was introduced to forbid the cutting of certain timber "notwithstanding the said trees do grow within the limits of any townships laid out or to be laid out".[6] It was passed despite the protests of the colonial agents, though Newman reported they had prevented the ironmasters adding in the committee stage a clause prohibiting the making of bar iron in New England.[7] In the end, the whole

[1] 3 and 4 Anne, cap. 10.

[2] J. S. Barry, *History of Massachusetts*, 3 vols., Boston, 1855–7, II, 109–10.

[3] *New Hampshire Provincial Papers*, II, 719.

[4] 8 Geo. I, cap. 7.

[5] HN to Bd of Trade, 9 Jan. 1722, *Col. State Papers, America and W. Indies*, C.O. 5, 523, f. 8; also *Rawlinson MSS.*, C.379, ff. 26–8; to Ld Carteret, 9 Feb. 1722; to Gov. Shute, 19 Feb. 1722, *New Eng. Letters*.

[6] 2 Geo. II, cap. 35.

[7] HN to Gov. Burnet, Boston, 30 April 1729, *New Eng. Letters*.

business of the naval stores was more fruitful in disputes than benefits, and by its mismanagement exasperated all concerned.

If the disputes over naval stores illustrated the conflict of the interests of the colonists with the needs of imperial defence, another matter in which Newman was involved illustrated the conflict of those interests with British economic policy and was more successful in its outcome for the New Englanders. This was the Molasses Bill, designed by imposing a prohibitive tax to prevent the importation of foreign sugar, rum, and molasses into Great Britain and the American colonies. It was introduced into Parliament in 1730 at the instigation of the British West Indian interest, which was alarmed at the growing trade between the North American colonies and the French West Indies in these commodities. This was contrary to British mercantilist principles and a violation of the treaty of 1686 between England and France which prohibited trade between the subjects of the two countries; but it was profitable for the colonists to exchange their staple products for sugar, molasses, and rum, which were cheaper in the French than in the British West Indies. Representatives of the continental colonies immediately protested against the Bill. Newman with "as great appearance of merchants as I ever knew" attended in 1731 "a solemn hearing before a Committee of Council at the Cockpit" of a petition presented by Barbados against the trade, and later in the year he and other American colonial agents discussed opposition to the Bill with General Oglethorpe, M.P., at the Ship Tavern without Temple Bar one evening until midnight. The struggle between the island planters and northern colonists was long and bitter. The Molasses Act was passed in 1733,[1] but smuggling by New England merchants undermined its enforcement, and the tacit acceptance of defeat by the British Government was the first important set-back for that phase of mercantilist policy which had favoured the island colonies and their products to the disadvantage of the northern colonies.[2]

The whole-hearted manner in which Newman pursued his colonial commissions could not have been achieved unless he had sympathized with the aims and aspirations of the New Englanders. Despite his fondness for England and loyalty to the Crown, he

[1] 6 Geo. II, cap. 17.

[2] HN to Gov. Belcher, 8 Feb., 7 and 27 May 1731, 20 March and 30 June 1732, *New Eng. Letters*; C. M. Andrews, "Anglo-French Commercial Rivalry, 1700–1750", *Am. Hist. Review*, XX, 772.

realized that the colonies wanted to manage their own affairs and seek their own interests. He showed this when the Board of Trade tried to resume the colonial charters and establish stricter control over their trade and government and establish a uniform system of administration.[1] Before this policy was set aside by Walpole and Newcastle, seven Bills for the resumption of charters were introduced between 1700 and 1720 into the House of Commons, and though they were rejected, Massachusetts was sufficiently alarmed to present to the King an address for the continuance of its privileges, which was supported by its agent, Jeremiah Dummer, in his *Defence of the New England Charters*. Newman, in a letter, expressed views similar to those of his fellow agent:

> The truth is the charter governments are a check to that arbitrary power which the officers in the other governments want to introduce into all the plantations and that the reason that these officers have taken all opportunities to represent these governments at home as destructive to the King's (meaning their own) interest and violates the Acts of Trade—the contrary to which would appear manifest if the subjects in the governments that have not charters were admitted to speak. Perhaps they would so present the many grievances they groan under that the King in his abundant goodness and the Parliament in their great wisdom and justice, to gain the general good of true subjects instead of taking away, would confer charters on those governments that have them not, to screen the just liberties of true peoples.[2]

Newman would not, however, go further than this. He defended the rights possessed by the colonies in their charters, but would not join those in New England who sought to get round the charters and increase the power of the colonists at the expense of the Crown and its officials. He was only too aware of these attempts, since Massachusetts was long the chief centre of political disturbance in New England. This was partly because of its predominance in population. At the accession of George I the English-speaking population of New England was about 90,000, of which Massachusetts had about a half, Connecticut a fourth, and Rhode Island and New Hampshire the remainder in about equal proportions.[3] It was also partly because the Bay Colony had achieved unity and comparative freedom from internal discord such as the struggle between Scotch-Irish and

[1] *Cambridge History of the British Empire*, I, 385–6.
[2] HN to ?, 25 July 1715, MS. in New Eng. Historic Genealogical Society Collected Papers.
[3] *Cambridge Modern History*, 1934 ed., VII, 54.

Quakers that rent Pennsylvania.[1] Still more it was because of the political ambitions of the oligarchy which gained power in Massachusetts in the eighteenth century. The change in the franchise qualification in 1691 from church membership to property ownership led to the supplanting of the old aristocracy of learning and godliness by this new oligarchy of merchants and traders. And closely allied with this ruling class were the lawyers. It was a small oligarchy, composed mainly of wealthy and inter-related families, among whom were the Olivers, Hutchinsons, and Quincys, with whom Newman had ties of friendship or relationship. These merchants, administrators, and judges dominated the Assembly of Massachusetts and sought to extend its authority. This they did, not so much in the cause of democracy as in order to transfer power from the Crown to themselves and monopolize the most important political posts.[2] As agent for the less aggressive Assembly of New Hampshire, Newman's sense of loyalty to the Crown was not, however, strained, and he opposed the policy of the oligarchs of Massachusetts and supported the cause of each of the four Governors of Massachusetts and New Hampshire whose successive periods of office covered his most important years as agent.

"Every proprietary Governor", remarked a contemporary observer, "has two masters; one who gives him his Commission, and one who gives him his Pay."[3] The Governors of Massachusetts found this only too true. The Assembly used its power of the purse to induce the Governors to obey its wishes rather than the Royal Instructions. The salary dispute began under Sir William Phipps, the first Governor appointed under the new charter of 1691. He was instructed from England to demand a fixed and permanent salary of at least £1000 a year. The Assembly declined to comply, and when successive Governors were appointed with similar instructions, maintained its refusal. Governor Dudley, the first under whom Newman served, persisted in his claims until his enemies secured his dismissal in 1715. Newman wrote: "To above two months past, Mr Dummer and I have been earnestly engaged in using all the honest arts we could think of to keep Colonel Dudley in his government, but our pains have been to so little purpose that last week Colonel Burgess . . .

[1] J. C. Miller, *Origins of the American Revolution*, 51.
[2] Ibid., 44–8.
[3] E. B. Greene, *Provincial America, 1690–1740*, New York, 1905, 198.

obtained a commission to succeed him . . . His character, if it answers what we are told here, will by no means make him a suitable man for that country."[1] Eventually Dummer bribed Burgess not to take the post, and Samuel Shute was appointed in 1716.

Shute was conscientious and prudent, "one of the best Governors that ever was sent to the Plantations", in Newman's opinion,[2] but his administration was one of the stormiest suffered by a royal governor in the American colonies. Not only was he insulted by the Assembly over the perennial salary question, but it also made absurd and unwarranted claims to authority in connection with military operations against the Indians. Eventually, in 1723 Shute sailed for England to present a memorial to the Privy Council and lay his grievances before it. The Assembly sent to controvert the charges Elisha Cooke, a violent opponent of the Governor, who had negatived his appointment as Speaker.[3] Shute's case, however, was so strong that Dummer and other colonists in England wrote to the Assembly that they were harming themselves by their treatment of him, an opinion which Newman echoed to a friend in New England: "I reckon Mr C., instead of justifying the Province, will go nigh to lose the Charter, and nothing less could be expected from one that has so little a command of his temper, and who had by a long series of aggravated circumstances rendered himself so unacceptable to the Governor and by him to the Government here."[4]

Shute remained in England, trying to secure enforcement of the payment of the arrears of his salary; but the Privy Council would only repeat its order to the Assembly to pay him £1000 a year with the threat of settling a revenue by Act of Parliament over its head if it did not do so. Newman noted ominously that the Assembly "have made no advances towards satisfying the Government here of their resolution to pay arrears or to support His Majesty's Governor whenever he returns to New England".[5] In fact, the colonial desire for independence was already so developing as to mean disowning the sovereignty of the British Government, which was unable to assert the authority it claimed; but Newman was unaware of this. "I am sorry to observe that people here", he

[1] HN to Mr Dudley, Woodbridge, Barbados, 1 April 1715, *Society's Letters*.
[2] HN to Lt-Gov. Wm Dummer, Boston, 6 Sept. 1723, *New Eng. Letters*.
[3] *Acts of the Privy Council, Colonial Series*, III, 93 ff.
[4] HN to Mr Sam. Penhallow, 3 June 1725, *Mass. Hist. Soc., Belknap Papers*, f. 115.
[5] HN to Lt-Gov. Wentworth, 29 July 1726, *New Eng. Letters*.

wrote to Judge Paul Dudley, "seem convinced by our late conduct that we are for shaking off our dependence on Great Britain, though all that know our country are satisfied 'tis the furthest thing in the world from our interest or inclination; to whom shall we go for protection, etc.? And if one squadron of British men-of-war can make all America tremble, what could they not do with one single Province if they should do what they can do, and yet some of our infatuated politicians seem to dare to be visited by them, not considering how near all their valuable privileges are to being cancelled by one single touch of the paw of a British Parliament." [1]

In the event, Shute did not continue his turbulent governorship. In the spring of 1727, when about to return to Massachusetts, the death of George I vacated his commission. He was not re-appointed, but given the sinecure of Comptroller of the Woods in America with a no more certain salary of £400 a year, and he lived privately in England until his death.[2] In his place William Burnet, son of the Whig bishop, was transferred from the Governorship of New York and instructed to move the Assembly for a fixed salary of £1000 on pain of intervention by Parliament. Newman trusted no more would be heard of Cooke: "I hope he will not have it in his power to lead the country into any more infatuations, that he himself will be wiser for his voyage hither and less turbulent to his country, when he reflects on the first-fruits of his rashness";[3] but he was again chosen for the Council and on Burnet's arrival directed anew the opposition to a fixed salary. Burnet maintained a gallant and honourable, but hopeless, struggle until his death in 1729, refusing, at great personal sacrifice, liberal propositions, if he conceded the principle. Twice a year the representatives tried to bribe him by voting him larger sums which he never accepted.[4]

During the dispute with Burnet, the Assembly sent Jonathan Belcher, a Boston shopkeeper and virulent anti-Episcopalian, to urge its case in England. He was there when Burnet died and managed to succeed him as Governor, mainly through Lord Townshend's influence. Though a native of New England, Belcher had hardly more success than his predecessors in gaining a fixed salary. He did no more than persuade the Assembly to vote

[1] HN to Judge Paul Dudley, Boston, 13 Sept. 1723, *New Eng. Letters*.
[2] *D.A.B.*
[3] HN to Mr Edmund Quincy, 6 Dec. 1725, *Mass. Hist. Soc.*, *Trumbull Letters*, f. 26.
[4] *Townshend Papers*, 237 f.

his salary annually at the start of each session, instead of the half-yearly grant by which since Dudley's time it had sought to control the Governor. "They are daily endeavouring to incroach upon the little power reserved to the Crown in the Royal Charter", Belcher commented.[1] Newman counselled patience: "All your friends here are concerned at the difficulties you meet with respecting your salary, but you know the humour of our countrymen is so perfectly like the English their forefathers who had the character of being led to anything but drove to nothing, that I dare say you will choose rather persuasive expedients than coming to extremities with them." Mindful of Shute's fate, he advised him not to seek redress in England: "You suffer uneasiness now, but when all things are considered, perhaps you may well think that preferable to be endured rather than to come home and live an indolent pensioner in the prime of your days and to see a stranger sent over in your room." [2]

The Assembly in 1731 presented its claims in an address to the Privy Council, which declared that they showed "that their design is to assume to themselves the executive power of the government of the said province, and has a direct tendency to throw off their dependence upon Great Britain".[3] But Belcher was fond of office and not ready to uphold the royal prerogative more than necessary to satisfy the British Government. He preferred popularity at home by advancing colonial interests at the expense of the Crown. He asked to be allowed to accept an annual salary from the Assembly, and Newman, at his request, sought Bishop Gibson's support in the Privy Council. "The people", he told Gibson, "have been long since disposed to comply with the King's Instructions for giving £1,000 per annum to the Governor, but desire to be excused giving it in the manner proposed by the Instructions because they think it giving up one of the principal privileges of their Charter, as dear to them as *Magna Charta* is to the people of Great Britain." [4] Newman saw as clearly as the Privy Council that the Assembly's persistent attitude was not based upon personal animosity towards the successive governors, but upon a principle, the right to control their own affairs. But neither faced the final issue of the dispute. The British Government abandoned its

[1] *Col. State Papers, America and W. Indies*, C.O. 5, 898, nos. 84, 84 i, 87.
[2] HN to Gov. Belcher, 26 March 1731, *New Eng. Letters*.
[3] *Acts of the Privy Council, Colonial Series*, III, 329–34.
[4] HN to Bp of London, 6 July 1731, *Fulham Palace MSS.*, American Papers, Mass. Second Box.

previous stand and allowed Belcher to accept the Assembly's offer; Newman, despite his earlier condemnation of the New England politicians, hoped the decision would "make things easier in respect to the salary".[1]

Newman can hardly be blamed for not realizing what an ominous precedent this was likely to create. His desire for a solution to the dispute was perhaps made stronger by his personal friendship with Belcher, which was greater than with previous governors. They were at Harvard together, and their correspondence was more than official. A further bond between them was Jonathan, Belcher's third and favourite son, sent by his father to London to study law in the vain hope of obtaining a lucrative practice or marrying a rich wife. Newman befriended him as other young men. He put him up in his lodgings until the young man's own rooms in the Temple were ready, and sought useful introductions for him. Belcher was constantly tried by his son's extravagant and careless ways, but Newman represented him favourably. "Your son at the Temple is very well", he told him on one occasion. "I often call upon him and find him with a folio law book open before him"; and it is to be hoped that honest Newman was not the victim of the same sort of subterfuge as practised by Archdeacon Grantley in the rectory study at Plumstead Episcopi. Belcher expressed gratitude to Newman for his "great condescension, goodness and affection" to his son, whom he urged: "Converse much with Mr Newman. He is an upright, religious man"; and again: "Mr Newman is a gentleman of virtue and religion; his acquaintance is valuable and always to be sought after." [2]

Nevertheless, Belcher was not an easy friend. The politician was uppermost in him, and his political reputation his constant concern. Once, for instance, he wished some discourses by himself to reach Queen Caroline and wrote to his son: "I have no doubt but Mr Newman and you might find an opportunity of being privately introduced at the Queen's back stairs into her apartment by one of the Ladies of the Bedchamber or present one on your knees yourself." Another time he heard that the two had commissioned a copperplate portrait of himself. "How could you presume to do such a thing without my special leave and order?",

[1] HN to Bp of London, 13 Aug. 1731, *Society's Letters.*

[2] HN to Bp of London, 6 July 1731; to Gov. Belcher, Boston, 20 Aug. and 4 Oct. 1731, *New Eng. Letters*; Gov. Belcher to HN, 20 Nov. 1731; Gov. Belcher to Jonathan Belcher, Jnr, 25 Nov. 1731 and 28 April 1732, *Belcher Papers*, *Mass. Hist. Soc. Collections*, Sixth Series, VI, 60, 64, 127.

he angrily asked his son. "You should be wise and consider the consequences of things before you put them in execution. Such a foolish affair will pull down much envy and give occasion for your father's enemies to squirt and squirt and what not. It is therefore my order, if this comes to hand timely, that you destroy the plate and destroy all the impressions taken from it." But he was too late and could only write again: "I am sorry, I say I am sorry, for what is done about my picture, but there is no help for it, and all I can say is *cave in futurum*. Be very delicate in doing anything relating to your father that is showy and can be of no service. However, I rather charge this good step on my very good friend Mr Newman than you, and I forgive because I know he thought it might be an honour to the Governor, but you must all set it down as a wrong step." [1]

In a more serious difference between governor and colonial agent, Belcher showed how scurrilous and abusive he could be despite his constant and sometimes sanctimonious praise of Newman. Newman's friend, Judge Paul Dudley, opposed Belcher in New England. "I am sorry", Belcher told his son, "Mr Newman should retain any regard for Mr D----y, who has made himself such a prostitute to everything that's mean and vile." When Jeremiah Dummer died, Belcher heard that Newman had a letter written by Dudley to Dummer, which he wanted for his own purposes. He asked Newman for it: "It can be of no service to you, but may be considerably so to me, and as it shall always remain a secret how it came into my hands, I fully depend you will show me a new instance of your sincere respect by letting me be possessed of it." Upon Newman's refusal, he wrote again: "I still think it not in your power legally or honestly to withold any papers belonging to the late Mr Dummer from the demand of his Executors, nor could any friend justly find fault with you in delivering them up. The wretch that went into the measures of that letter for breaking up the constitution of his country, to compass his revenge, ought to be the abhorrence of all honest men and lovers of English liberties." But Newman persisted in his refusal, and Belcher never obtained "the vile letter wrote by P.D. to the late J.D.".[2]

In any event, he could not have used the letter, for while still seeking it from Newman, he was dismissed from his governorship.

[1] Gov. Belcher to Jonathan Belcher, Jnr, 7 Aug., 1 Oct., 4 Nov. 1734, ibid., 97, 121, 143.

[2] Gov. Belcher to Jonathan Belcher, Jnr, 2 June 1740; to HN, 20 Nov. 1739, 21 May and 1 Sept. 1741, ibid., 247, 299, 394, 411.

His enemies triumphed, despite his desire to have a foot in both camps and readiness to use every occasion to strengthen his position. The British Government rejected his nomination for the post of Lieutenant-Governor of New Hampshire in favour of a personal opponent, Colonel Dunbar, Surveyor-General of the Woods in North America, whom he thought had "endeavoured to represent him to the Lord President, the Duke of Newcastle, and other ministers as an oppressor of the people and no friend to His Majesty's interest". Above all, the people of New Hampshire felt that Belcher, in the boundary dispute with Massachusetts, had shown partiality to the larger province and abused his powers as Governor in seeking a decision favourable to Massachusetts. Finally, some enemies brought charges against him in England, some being signed with forged names, and secured his dismissal in May 1741. "Notwithstanding you and all my friends imagined my interest was so well established at Court", Belcher wrote to Newman, "yet you soon was acquainted that there's no faith in man . . . I believe mankind who are acquainted with how much honour and fidelity I discharged my duty to His Majesty must think my case cruel and severe, to be dismissed without fault or complaint. Such treatment must be a great discouragement to faithfulness in the King's service." [1]

Newman agreed. Belcher's dismissal, he told Benjamin Colman, had "been long effecting by all arts and contrivances, so that mistakes have been magnified to wilful crimes and real, honest services to the King have been represented as artifices to cover unpardonable faults".[2] Despite the difficulties in their friendship and Belcher's partisanship against his province, Newman still admired and supported him. Sympathizing with his son, he said: "I hear the late Governor resigned his command with the dignity of an old Roman." Belcher thought "the ministry obliged in justice and honour to make some provision for me", and told Newman: "If you can assist me in a solicitation of this kind by your friends at Court, I shall accept it with much gratitude"; but war with Spain and the fall of Walpole's administration made things "in so fluctuating a state" that Newman gave him no hope of success, and in the last months of his life urged Jonathan Belcher to advise

[1] HN to Gov. Belcher, 18 Feb. and 15 March 1731, 20 Oct. 1733, 29 May 1734, *New Eng. Letters*; to Bp of London, 10 March 1738, *Fulham Palace MSS.*, American Papers, Mass. Second Box; Gov. Belcher to HN, 1 Sept. 1741, ibid., 411–13.

[2] HN to Rev. Mr Colman, 16 Sept. 1741, *Mass. Hist. Soc.*, *Colman Papers*.

his father not to come over to England to seek a pension: "I see little prospect of [it] being any advantage to him as the interests at Court are so very much changed, that I doubt he will not be able so much as to obtain an imaginary allowance of what was promised, or never or but poorly performed, of a pension of £400 per annum to Governor Shute, which I suppose is what he aims at." [1]

The letters Newman wrote as colonial agent, with their references to Walpole's policy of *quieta non movere* and Newcastle's lethargy in Britain, together with bitter partisanship and conflicting interests in the colonies, show how many and deep-seated, even in the first half of the century, were the difficulties between Britain and America. Moreover, his relations with the Governors of Massachusetts show how determinedly the colonial ruling class was fighting for control of the government. These governors, at any rate, were not lacking in either ability or knowledge of American affairs. Dudley was the son of one of the Puritan founders of Massachusetts; Shute a conscientious man and an "independent" in religion; Burnet formerly a capable Governor of New York; Belcher a Bostonian, a violent anti-Episcopalian, who had acted for the Assembly in London. Whatever Governors had been sent to Massachusetts, the Assembly would have treated them in the same way. Its members attacked, not the persons of the Governors, but their office. They realized what they wanted and unhesitatingly pursued it. The British Government, ominously for the future, stood by principle and yielded in practice.

Yet few envisaged the breaking of ties between mother country and colonies. Newman's fellow agent, Jeremiah Dummer, typically declared: "It would be more absurd to place two of his Majesty's beef eaters to watch an infant in the cradle that it don't rise to cut its father's throat, than to guard these weak infant colonies to prevent their shaking off the British yoke." [2] Newman thought much the same, though he did see a little further, however uncertainly, into the possibilities of the future. He told a correspondent: "They can never become independent of Great Britain while they remain crumbled into little provinces and governments, who have all their governors and principal officers from hence and glory in the privilege of being subjects of England,

[1] HN to Gov. Belcher, 30 Aug. 1742, *New Eng. Letters*; to Jonathan Belcher, Jnr, 28 Nov. 1741 and 17 May 1743, *Miscellaneous Letters*.

[2] Jeremiah Dummer, *Defence of the New England Charters*, 1765, 72.

but what may be the consequences of old England's forfeiting the dignity of a wise mother country by yielding to a general deprivation of manners, oppression, arbitrary government and the encroachments of Popery, cannot be judged of any more than the wise men of Greece and Rome two thousand years ago could judge of their present miserable state." [1]

[1] HN to Mr Richard Cotton, Etwall, Derby, 21 Sept. 1732, *Society's Letters.*

10

GEORGIA AND THE SALZBURG REFUGEES

THOUGH convicted criminals in eighteenth-century England were usually hanged, transported, or whipped, and jails were for the detention of prisoners before trial, and still more for debtors, they were often terrible places. Though supposedly under the Crown's supervision, most were in the possession of local bodies or even private persons, who generally farmed them out to wardens empowered to appoint the jailers and make what they could out of the prisoners, while the buildings were often old, crowded, and insanitary.[1] The S.P.C.K. had the distinction of being the first organization in England to consider the state of the prisons. Soon after its foundation, it decided to investigate the London prisons, the most important being at this time Newgate, in the City, for all classes of offenders, the Fleet, at the foot of Ludgate Hill, for debtors, and the Marshalsea, in Southwark, also for debtors. In 1702 some members led by Dr Bray visited these and other London prisons and produced a report, *An Essay towards the Reformation of Newgate and the other Prisons in and about London*, which unfortunately was not published until 150 years later. It condemned much in the prisons, including the "personal lewdness of the keepers", "old criminals corrupting newcomers", "unlimited use of liquors", and "neglect of all religious worship".[2]

Dr Bray was also concerned about the reclaiming of prisoners into honest employment, especially the "thievish and lewd women" at Bridewell and Newgate, where to see them whipped or beating hemp under the overseer's cane ranked with the hangings at Tyburn as popular spectacles of the time; but when Bray visited these prisons he heard them "often complain with tears in their eyes that it is for want of employment, and to get bread, that they betake themselves to, or continue in, that abominable course of life". He would have liked to have seen "a Penitential Hospital for the Imploying and Reforming Lewd Women", supervised by

[1] Basil Williams, *The Whig Supremacy, 1714–1760*, Oxford, 1939, 130.
[2] R. S. E. Hinde, *The British Penal System*, 1951, 17, 21–6.

"some grave matron", where the incorrigible would be "corrected" and all prepared for domestic service at home or in the plantations.[1]

When Newman became Secretary, the S.P.C.K. was still concerned with the prisons. It naturally considered the religious welfare of prisoners, and in 1710 arranged for services to be taken in the Marshalsea, providing a pulpit, a Book of Common Prayer, and a Bible from its own funds, while Newman tried to interest "some of the clergy of greater name" to minister there.[2] Nor was this all. It supported "the Ordinary of Newgate" who urged "that it might be a Christian service to such criminals in Newgate as were reprieved if they were put into some workhouse instead of being turned over to the common side of prisoners, where they are exposed to the vile practices of such ill men as are for the most part there confined", only to find "it could not be done without a clause in some Act of Parliament for the removal of such persons out of Newgate before their pardons come down, which has sometimes happened to be several years". The Society pressed this upon Members of Parliament, as also the "procuring an Act of Parliament for making in every County Gaol separate apartments for condemned criminals".[3] Such suggestions had no effect, but a later one was more successful. In 1715 Newman wrote to Chamberlayne:

The Chaplain of the Marshalsea Prison assuring me by letter that 200 prisoners for debt by a moderate computation have been starved to death in that Prison in the space of two years past, it is the request of several worthy gentlemen who are well-wishers to humanity and the honour of the nation that you would be pleased to acquaint those worthy Members of Parliament who have the case of those miserable creatures under their consideration therewith, in hopes their wisdom may find some expedient to prevent the like barbarities for the future, at least that Commissioners may be appointed to enquire what provisions have been made for the support of that Prison and also what disorders and abuses have been committed therein and how the same and the loss accruing to the publick by the death of so many persons for time to come be prevented. And if this enquiry were extended to all the prisons in the Kingdom to be reported to the next session of Parliament, I believe it would disclose such a scene of cruelty as is not to be equalized in Turkey nor in Barbary itself.[4]

[1] H. P. Thompson, *Thomas Bray*, 24–5.
[2] *S.P.C.K. Minutes*, 8 June, 27 July, 3 and 10 Aug., 19 Oct., 23 Nov. 1710; HN to ?, 5 Oct. 1724, *Rawlinson MSS.*, C. 933, f. 171.
[3] Ibid., 18 Jan., 8 and 15 June 1710.
[4] HN to Mr Chamberlayne, 9 June 1715, *Society's Letters*.

Four years later, in 1719, a Parliamentary Committee investigated prison conditions, and its report showed that the facts given to Newman were not exaggerated. There were between 700 and 800 debtors in the Marshalsea, of whom 300 had died in less than three months.[1] But even this failed to effect any real prison reforms. In 1722 General Oglethorpe, who had served as a volunteer under Prince Eugene against the Turks, entered Parliament as a Tory member. Always zealous in good causes, he became known as a supporter of the interests of the American colonies, and a visit to a friend imprisoned for debt showed him the plight of such people. Another Parliamentary Committee was appointed in 1729 "to examine the state of the gaols within the Kingdom". Oglethorpe was chairman, and its large membership included Newman's friend, Lord Perceval. They brought to light the cruelties of Bambridge, Warden of the Fleet Prison, and in the Marshalsea found "upwards of 350" prisoners on the common side dying of starvation. They fed them, but before this, they reported, "a day seldom passed without a death, and upon the advancing of spring not less than eight or ten usually died every twenty-four hours".[2]

Oglethorpe also got through Parliament an Insolvent Act to release debtors owing only small sums, but there was a general fear that these freed prisoners would be useless unemployed paupers. This was much the same problem as had led Dr Bray to propose his plan for a reformatory for prostitutes, and towards the end of 1729, within six weeks of his death, he suggested to Oglethorpe the formation of an association to found a colony for released debtors and other necessitous poor without employment in England. This appealed to both Oglethorpe's imperial and humanitarian zeal. One of Dr Bray's last acts before his death was to extend Dr Bray's Associates into a charitable organization, which was confirmed by decree of Chancery in 1731. On Oglethorpe's proposal, Dr Bray's Associates were further enlarged to combine it with the philanthropic and reforming parliamentary group. This was done by July 1730, and two years later, on 9 June 1732, when the Trustees for Establishing the Colony of Georgia in America were founded by charter from George II, they included all the original members of the enlarged Dr Bray's Associates. Five of

[1] *Commons Journals*, 21 Jan. 1719.

[2] John Nichols, *Genuine Works*, 1817, III, *passim*; *Commons Journals*, 14 May 1729.

the twenty-one Trustees were Anglican clergymen, and most of the rest were Anglican laymen.[1]

Unoccupied land south of Carolina was chosen for Georgia, the colony for poor debtors, partly for the defence of South Carolina against Indian and Spanish raiders from Florida, partly for growing flax and vines and manufacturing silk. Indeed, the latter was Oglethorpe's main hope of raising the money needed for imperial defence, and the seal of the Trustees was engraved with figures of spinning-worms. The Georgia Office was in Old Palace Yard, Westminster, with Benjamin Martyn as Secretary and Harman Verelst as Accountant. The scheme owed much to the idealism of Oglethorpe and his friends. Each settler was to be granted forty acres of land, which he could not alienate. Although in Carolina, five thousand white settlers employed thirty or forty thousand negro slaves "to work six days in the week without pay", there was to be no slavery in Georgia. As Benjamin Martyn put it: "Civil liberty is to be established there in its full extent. No appearance of slavery, not even in negroes; by which means, the people being obliged to labour themselves for their support, will be, like the old Romans, more active and useful for defence of their government." [2]

Newman was closely involved in the scheme from the outset. As early as 1731 he told Berkeley in America of "a project vigorously espoused by Mr Oglethorpe and several other active Members of Parliament . . . for sending a Colony of our poor helpless people . . . to the southern parts of South Carolina", which he hoped would "succeed to the relief of many thousand of His Majesty's subjects that are now perishing in the streets of this city and its suburbs, or in the gaols of this Kingdom, leading a useless life".[3] Moreover, among the Trustees for Georgia were several of Newman's friends: Captain Coram, who had a similar plan for the colonization of Nova Scotia; Lord Perceval, the first President; and Sir Hans Sloane, who offered to pay for a person to go to the colony to investigate the vegetation and instruct the settlers in agriculture. Newman admired Oglethorpe. He thought it remarkable that he should leave England to "cross a perilous ocean for the sake of establishing a few distressed families undone by

[1] E. L. Pennington, "Anglican Influences in the Establishment of Georgia", *Georgia Historical Quarterly*, XV, 292–7; J. W. Lydekker, "Thomas Bray, Founder of Missionary Enterprise", *Historical Magazine of the Protestant Episcopal Church*, XII, 188–214; H. P. Thompson, op. cit., 97–100.

[2] Benjamin Martyn, *Reasons for Establishing the Colony of Georgia with Regard to the Trade of Great Britain*, 1733, 30.

[3] HN to Dean Berkeley, R.I., 5 Feb. 1731, *New Eng. Letters*.

idleness, intemperance, sickness or other ill habits, oppressed and all with poverty, to found a colony in a wilderness wholly uncultivated, abounding with pine barrens, crocodiles, bears, and wolves with other animals of no apparent use to the creation but to punish the posterity of fallen Adam", particularly as his colony "does not yield of any immediate visible reward but the distant expectation of an uncertain glory like what Julius Caesar enjoyed when he landed in Britain about 1700 years ago with a more promising people than are now the first planters of Georgia".[1] Yet Newman had himself high hopes for the colony and told Oglethorpe: "The examples which the Europeans under your discipline will set to the natives will give virtue an amiable lustre and let them see that the Christian religion is not only in name but in reality an improvement of the divine and social virtues which adorn the humane species." [2]

The Trustees collected subscriptions to pay the prison fees for debtors to be discharged and to provide for their transport to Georgia, and the S.P.C.K. for a number of years gave either the proceeds of its charity box or a collection at the anniversary meeting to this.[3] Oglethorpe sailed in November 1732 with the first party of 114 settlers, "40 able sensible men, the rest women and children". He established settlements on the Savannah River and at Frederica on the Spanish border as well as a fur-trading post at Augusta in the north. Newman praised Oglethorpe for going himself to the colony at the outset. He told Richard Reynolds, Bishop of Lincoln: "If other Members of Parliament should be induced by the same zeal to visit America, the interest of Great Britain with respect to the Plantations would be better known, and the British colonies in America would not want advocates in Parliament to defend them against the insinuations of those who industriously misrepresent them for private ends." [4] He wrote to the Secretary to the Lords of the Admiralty to suggest that Oglethorpe should be given "a letter to all the captains of the men-of-war" in American waters "to receive and convey him and his retinue from one province to another as he may occasionally desire it".[5] Newman was known as a helper of the scheme, and it was

[1] HN to Mr John Vat, Ebenezer, 10 Oct. 1735, *Miscellaneous Letters*.
[2] HN to Gen. Oglethorpe, Savannah, 4 June 1736, *Miscellaneous Letters*.
[3] *Egmont Diary*, II, 159; HN to Archdeacon Deane, 22 April 1738, *Miscellaneous Letters*.
[4] HN to Bp of Lincoln, 26 Oct. 1732, *Society's Letters*.
[5] HN to Mr Josias Burchet, 6 Nov. 1732, *Private Letters*.

to him that Coram appealed in 1733 to revise his unlettered account for the press of the sailing of the first emigrants.[1]

An event in Central Europe soon brought Newman into much closer contact with the settlement. Almost at the same time as the accession of George II in England, Count Firmian became Archbishop of Salzburg and determined to put down heresy in his diocese. The Lutherans in Salzburg were subjected to fines, confiscation, and imprisonment. When they invoked the toleration clauses of the Treaty of Westphalia, the Archbishop borrowed Austrian grenadiers to suppress the "revolt". Frederick William of Prussia supported their cause, and under the terms of the Treaty of Westphalia, the Archbishop finally agreed to allow them to emigrate to Prussia. Frederick William also secured a small dole for them, and nearly 30,000 eventually journeyed eastwards through Frankfort-on-Main to Prussia, Holland, England, and other Protestant countries.[2]

Early in 1732, Mr Ziegenhagen submitted an account of the plight of these people to the S.P.C.K., which considered it at several meetings and resolved to print 1000 copies of this "melancholy account of the barbarous treatment of about 20,000 Protestants in the Archbishoprick of Saltzburgh" to raise benefactions for them. It was decided, "in regard to the Bishop of London's rank in the Church and State", and because this was "an affair relating to religion and the Protestant interest abroad", to ask him "to lay this matter before His Majesty's Principal Secretary or Secretaries of State for their approbation for the design of this publication"; but when Newman waited on Gibson, he had to report: "His Lordship excused himself from doing what was desired by reason of his present indisposition which obliged him not to go abroad". The Society advertised the account in the newspapers; some members wished "to disperse [them] in the streets or coffee houses", but it was decided "only to put them into the hands of discreet persons to be dispersed occasionally in religious families".[3]

Despite this caution and episcopal lukewarmness, the publication achieved its purpose. By April £125 had been sent to Mr

[1] V. W. Crane, "The Origins of Georgia", *Georgia Historical Quarterly*, XIV, 104–5.

[2] W. B. Stevens, *History of Georgia*, 2 vols., New York, 1847–59, I, 107–8; R. L. Brantley, "The Salzburgers in Georgia", *Georgia Historical Quarterly*, XIV, 214–15.

[3] *S.P.C.K. Minutes*, 29 Feb., 11 and 28 March 1732; HN to Rev. Mr Fox, Reading, Berks, 11 March 1732; to Archdeacon Deane, 4 July 1732, *Society's Letters*; *Whitehall Evening Post*, 6 July 1732.

Urlsperger, an Evangelical minister at Augsburg, for the Salzburgers, and other sums were sent later. In June Newman told Governor Belcher that he had been very busy "in soliciting contributions" for the Salzburgers and that a total of £1000 had now been sent to them.[1] This was not Newman's only experience of German refugees, for a considerable number of Palatines had fled to England in 1709 and 1710. As late as 1717, Newman told Addison that Dr Bray had still 526 of them in his parish of St Botolph, Aldgate, who were unpopular among the people and described as "Hanoverians come to eat the bread out of the mouths of our poor". Eventually the government had transported most of them to New York, the Carolinas and Pennsylvania.[2] Newman pondered upon a similar plan for the Salzburgers and sent Urlsperger "a printed account published by the Trustees for settling the new colony of Georgia in the south borders of South Carolina", but cautiously added: "I have no authority to desire you to send any of the exiles . . . this way, yet there is reason to believe that if it were not for the greatness of the expense that would attend their transportation that they would be welcome to the worthy gentlemen concerned in the undertaking." [3]

Newman was right. Hopes placed upon the first settlers in Georgia had already evaporated. All were paupers, some from London slums, idle, worthless, and even criminal, who had, to quote an anonymous tract about the colony, "quitted their own Country to avoid Labour" and were not pleased when they "saw Labour stand before their Eyes in Georgia". The rest were "mostly Inhabitants of Towns" and "such seldom turn out good Husbandmen with their own Hands".[4] The Trustees recorded that "as many of the poor who had been useless in England were inclined to be useless likewise in Georgia", and the town of Savannah of forty wooden huts soon had court-house and prison, stocks, and whipping-post.[5]

Accordingly, when the S.P.C.K. agreed with Newman and informed the Trustees that the Society was "desirous that the

[1] *S.P.C.K. Minutes*, 25 April 1732; HN to Gov. Belcher, 30 June 1732, *New Eng. Letters*.

[2] G. N. Clark, *The Later Stuarts, 1660–1714*, Oxford, 1934, 330–1; HN to Mr Secretary Addison, 19 Aug. 1717, *Society's Letters*.

[3] HN to Rev. Mr Urlsperger, Augsburg, 8 Sept. 1732, *Letters to the Saltzburghers*.

[4] "A Brief Account of the Establishment of the Colony of Georgia under General James Oglethorpe, 1st February 1733", reprinted Peter Force, *Tracts Relating to North America*, Washington, 1836, 4 vols., I.

[5] "An Account shewing the Progress of the Colony of Georgia, 1741", ibid., I.

persecuted Saltzburghers should have an asylum provided for them in Georgia", the idea met with a ready response. The Salzburgers were not townsmen, but cattle-grazers, cheese-makers, and salt-miners. The Trustees hoped their industry and experience would make the colony profitable to Britain as had been planned.[1] "It is surely for the interest of England", said Benjamin Martyn, "to settle as many foreigners as possible in Georgia; when she knows that by every thousand, who will be transported thither, she will raise the means for employing four thousand more at home." [2] Public opinion agreed. For once finance was not, as Newman feared, the greatest problem. Even when the plan "to transport some of those glorious confessors to the new colony of Georgia" was still being discussed, he could report, "Benefactions are daily coming in from all parts of the Kingdom", including a promise from a gentleman, "who has contributed twenty guineas, that he will give £200 more if any number of them will become subjects of England in any part of the British Dominions".[3]

The Trustees for Georgia also applied to Parliament for a grant of public money towards the project. Their petition was presented in the House of Commons in May 1733 by Sir Joseph Jekyll, a barrister and steady supporter of Walpole. He urged "that it seems a particular design of Providence to erect a colony at this time for an asylum to the persecuted Protestants of Saltsburg", and explained that their products would "not interfere with England, nor even with our other Colonies, [being] such as silk, wine and potashes". Walpole "said he had the King's orders to tell the House that His Majesty had no objection to whatever they should resolve to give for the furtherance of the Colony"; but Thomas Winnington, a Lord of the Admiralty, said "he would have no foreigners sent thither, because we must be obliged to send English to mix with them", and later in private conversation with Lord Perceval "said we ought to have at least eight English to two Saltsburgers". Parliament granted the Trustees £10,000, the remainder of the purchase money for the island of St Christopher, which had been voted, but never paid, for Berkeley's college in Bermuda. The portion of the Princess Royal, on her marriage with the Prince of Orange, had come from the same source, leaving a

[1] L. F. Church, *Oglethorpe: A Study of Philanthropy in England and Georgia*, 1932, 142.

[2] Benjamin Martyn, op. cit., 35.

[3] HN to Rev. Dr Pardo, Oxford, 28 Sept. 1732; to Rev. Dr Payne, Saltwood, Kent, 31 Aug. 1732, *Society's Letters*.

residue, which Oglethorpe, with Berkeley's consent, induced the government to appropriate to the colonization of Georgia.[1]

Meanwhile, preparations were made to collect the first Salzburgers for Georgia. Newman acted as intermediary with Urlsperger, whom he asked to encourage refugees to accept the scheme. The Trustees would "pay their passage from Frankfort to Rotterdam and freight them to Georgia; grant them each fifty acres of land; give them tools, seed, and everything requisite"; "and maintain them for a year till they had settled themselves". Newman described the colony as "a large tract of fine land between two large rivers [2] in a temperate climate, capable of a vast variety of productions for the benefit of trade and comfort of life", and assured them they would "there enjoy all the rights and privileges, religious and civil, of English born subjects".[3] But they were difficult to persuade. The Trustees planned to send 300 over, but when Urlsperger could only "pick up the emigrants by dozens or less numbers", they agreed to 75 as a first shipload. When the party was at last ready at Augsburg in October 1733, it only numbered 42,[4] but the Trustees agreed still to send them, "being assured that their reception in Georgia will encourage others to follow them".[5] Newman arranged for them to be taken down the Rhine to Rotterdam by Henry Von Reck, nephew of a Hanoverian nobleman who represented George II at the Imperial Diet at Ratisbon.[6]

The S.P.C.K. had now decided what it would contribute towards the scheme, informing the Trustees "that they agreed to defray the expense of the Saltzburghers and other emigrants in their journey from Germany to Rotterdam and to support a Minister and Catechist".[7] As with the East India Mission, the Society decreed "that these persons receive their ordination at Augsburg or some other Protestant Church in Germany, before they depart thence". Newman turned once again to Halle and secured John Martin Bolzius, Deputy Superintendent of the Latin Orphan School at Halle, as Minister, and Israel Christian Gronau, a tutor

[1] *Egmont Diary*, I, 373–6; R. Wright, *Memoir of General James Oglethorpe*, 1867, 51.

[2] The Rivers Savannah and Altamaha.

[3] *S.P.C.K. Minutes*, 7 April 1733; HN to Rev. Mr Urlsperger, 13 Oct. and 29 Dec. 1732, 18 and 29 May 1733, *Letters to the Saltzburghers*; to Archdeacon Deane, 5 July 1733, *Society's Letters*.

[4] 78 including their wives and children.

[5] *Egmont Diary*, I, 288; "Journal of the Trustees for Establishing the Colony of Georgia in America", reprinted *Colonial Records of Georgia*, I, 77, 139–40.

[6] HN to Rev. Mr Lowther, Rotterdam, 26 Oct. 1733, *Letters to the Saltzburghers*.

[7] *Colonial Records of Georgia*, I, 137–8.

at the same school, as Catechist, who joined the Salzburgers at Rotterdam. In return, Professor G. A. Francke asked the S.P.C.K. to contribute "towards building an Hospital in Prussia for old, decrepit Saltzburghers", but Newman had to reply that the Society had no money to spare. Since March 1732 it had sent £1482 4*s.* 6*d.* to Urlsperger for the Salzburgers and still had the cost of their transport to pay. It had also put aside £2000 for the salaries of the two men in Georgia.[1] Newman, in fact, sought all the help he could for the emigrants, including a suggestion to Governor Belcher that the New Englanders might like to send a "shipload of boards and timber to make the first habitations", a matter which Oglethorpe had forgotten when he accompanied the first settlers to Georgia in October 1732.[2]

The Salzburgers embarked at Rotterdam, and the ship put in at Dover for a few days. They were received by Captain Coram and Mr Butjenter, one of the King's German chaplains, who tried to cheer some who "seemed very melancholy" at first "because there were some who told them they were carried to Georgia in order to be made slaves of". Coram hired a house for the ministers and a room in a public-house for the sick and children; the rest stayed on board ship, except when the magistrates of the town invited them to dine in the workhouse "where they were regaled with roasted sirloin of beef and plum pudding". They marched there in procession, singing hymns, and "abundance of the neighbouring gentry resorting to partake of the pleasure of this new sight". Afterwards they went to the public-house, where Butjenter preached to them from 2 Corinthians 6. 17, 18: "Wherefore come out from among them, and be ye separate, saith the Lord, and touch not the unclean thing; and I will receive you, and will be a Father unto you, and ye shall be my sons and daughters, saith the Lord Almighty." They then all took the oath of loyalty to the King.[3]

Finally, Butjenter consulted with Bolzius and Gronau "about settling the form of their publick worship", which "as near as may be, will be conformable to the Church of England". This was in accordance with the practice of the Lutheran congregations in

[1] HN to Rev. Mr Urlsperger, Augsburg, 3 July and 4 Dec. 1733; to Prof. Francke, Halle, 21 Dec. 1733, *Letters to the Saltzburghers*.

[2] HN to Gov. Belcher, 20 Oct. 1733, *New Eng. Letters*.

[3] HN to Capt. Coram, Dover, 11 Dec. 1733; to Rev. Mr Urlsperger, Augsburg, 18 Dec. 1733, *Letters to the Saltzburghers*; *Daily Post Boy*, 10 Aug. and 28 Sept. 1734; *Daily Advertiser*, 26 Dec. 1733 and 28 Sept. 1734.

England at this time which conformed on many points to Anglican rites and traditions. The Swedish congregation in London, for instance, observed—on 30 January and 29 May respectively—the commemoration of King Charles the Martyr and of the Restoration, while the clergy, in order not to offend the Protestant feelings of contemporary Anglicans, did not wear the chasuble at the Eucharist, though it was prescribed in the Swedish Church Law of 1686. Indeed, while many Anglicans had a special regard for Lutherans at this time, the Lutherans on their part seem to have been eager to approximate to the Church of England rather than to the English Dissenters.[1] The S.P.C.K. was very ready that the Lutherans in Georgia should do this and "delivered to them German books in which are the form of prayer, baptismal rites, the Lord's Supper, Matrimony and Burial, etc.". The Society also gave them a chalice and paten, while Newman's own gift to them was *Ludowig's Dictionary and Grammar* to help them learn English, for which he searched the London bookshops and sent it by the Dover coach just before their ship sailed at the end of December 1733.[2]

The emigrants were met at Savannah the next March by Oglethorpe, who had delayed returning to England to see them. Because of criticism in the House of Commons, the Trustees had resolved that the Salzburgers should "be so mingled with Englishmen as in time to become one people with us"; but they refused to be separated, so Oglethorpe and Von Reck chose the site of a new town for them, 19 miles from Savannah.[3] They called their settlement Ebenezer and planned, Bolzius told Newman, to erect there "a stone pillar in memory of God's having delivered them from persecution and led them to the utmost parts of the earth, where they may praise His name with freedom and be a light to the Gentiles". The two men also, Newman informed correspondents, "describe Georgia as a paradise capable of all manner of improvements which may hereafter redound very much to the advantage of Great Britain in the products it may yield of raw silk, wine, coffee, rice, etc.", while "Mr Oglethorpe recommends very much those already sent us as an honest, laborious, chearful set of people".[4] In order not to spoil this happy picture, when the S.P.C.K.

[1] Hans Cnattingius, *Bishops and Societies*, 42.
[2] HN to Rev. Messrs Bolzius and Gronau, Dover, 22 Dec. 1733, *Letters to the Saltzburghers*; to Mr Verelst, Georgia Office, 12 Feb. 1734, *Society's Letters*.
[3] *Egmont Diary*, I, 303; L. L. Knight, *Georgia Landmarks*, Atlanta, 1914, 183.
[4] HN to Rev. Dr Thomlinson, 18 June 1734; to Sir Thos Lowther, Lancaster, 27 July 1734, *Society's Letters*.

published Von Reck's *Journal* of the voyage, it removed "too frequent mention . . . of the changing of the wind and of its being sometimes quite contrary" as well as "all the complaints of the Captain's ill use of the Saltzburghers as what would be of no service to encourage others to follow them".[1]

In fact, the first reluctance of Salzburgers to go to Georgia was not repeated. As soon as July 1734, Urlsperger asked Newman whether another party might go, as the growing distress of the refugees made many want to leave.[2] Both the Trustees and the Society wished to bring the Salzburgers in Georgia up to the originally proposed number of 300, but found "that the expense of a transportation of persons from Germany to Georgia amounts to a much greater sum than was at first imagined", which made "both Societies apprehensive that they are hardly at present in a condition to transport and settle so large a number as 260". Before long the Trustees "signified that they are exhausted and must leave the expense of it wholly on the Society as to maintain them a year after their arrival in Georgia", but the S.P.C.K. still resolved "to send over an embarkation of fifty heads of Saltzburghers at their expense", and the Trustees gratefully "recommended to the Common Council to give the said Saltzburghers grants of land in Georgia".[3] The Salzburgers were so ready, this time, to depart that a party of 56, with a Swiss leader, John Vat, left Augsburg in August to embark at Rotterdam. This time the ship put in at Gravesend, and by special warrant of the Lord Mayor the Salzburgers were allowed to land on Sunday "and walk in procession to the German Church in Trinity Lane to return thanks for their happy arrival in England, the City Marshall and my Lord Mayor's officers being ordered to attend them to preserve order during their procession to and from the Church". Afterwards they were "entertained at dinner at the expense of the German congregation".[4] When they reached Ebenezer safely by the end of the year, Newman was pleased at the speed with which this transport had been accomplished and thought the Society might "expect another transport next spring".[5]

[1] HN to Gen. Oglethorpe, Old Palace Yard, 4 Sept. 1734, *Society's Letters*; *S.P.C.K. Minutes*, 10 Sept. 1734.

[2] Rev. Mr Urlsperger, Augsburg, to HN, 22 July, 20 and 23 Sept. 1734, *Letters from the Saltzburghers*.

[3] *Colonial Records of Georgia*, I, 181, 192–3; *S.P.C.K. Minutes*, *passim*.

[4] HN to Mr Verelst, Georgia Office, 25 Sept. 1734, *Letters to the Saltzburghers*; to Bp of Cloyne, 24 Oct. 1734, *Society's Letters*; *S.P.C.K. Minutes*, 29 Oct. 1734.

[5] HN to Ld Primate of Ireland, 28 Nov. 1734, *Private Letters*.

He had, however, to restrain a still more hopeful agent in the affair. When Von Reck returned to Germany he met Count Zinzendorf, who had invited the persecuted Moravian brethren to settle on his estate. Von Reck offered them a passage to Georgia, telling them "that God hath made choice of the English nation to deliver them, and that the day of their deliverance will ere long appear". News of this alarmed the Trustees and the Society; both instructed Newman to inform Von Reck: "They desire you will immediately put an absolute stop to your proceedings." "What the Society have collected", Newman told him, "for relieving the Protestant Saltzburghers is appropriated only to them", and while the Trustees might have land in Georgia for the Moravians, "you seem to forget the consideration of the great charge of carrying them thither and of maintaining them till such time as they may be in a condition of maintaining themselves." [1] When Von Reck urged the value of the Moravians as "manufacturers in glass and earthern ware", the Trustees answered that they did "not think it proper to encourage manufacturers in Georgia which may interfere with those of Great Britain".[2]

There were problems in Georgia also. The second settlement of Salzburgers did not produce as cheerful a report as the first. Vat wrote at length to Newman on the plight of the settlers in their "pine-barren lands", where the soil "is almost nothing else but sand". Beans and Indian corn, supplied by the Trustees, had been sown, but produced no crop. Of six houses ordered to be built at Ebenezer by Oglethorpe, three (for Bolzius, Gronau, and himself) were finished, but "are so wretchedly slight, that by making one single step, both houses shake so, as to be in danger of falling to the ground, and in any rain I am forced to shift my bed in one of the rooms therein, occupied by myself and three families besides". For fear of the Spaniards they had built "a block house 28 feet in length and 18 feet in breadth", now used as a church, school, and warehouse. They had also built a couple of bridges, because the river was too low for boats to come up, and they had to carry provisions on their backs or by small wagon. The swamps were unhealthy, unfitted for cultivation by white people. He had been very ill, and eight people had died since he arrived. He concluded: "In this the reputation of the Rev. Mr Senior Urlsperger

[1] *Egmont Diary*, II, 132; HN to Mr Von Reck, 5 Nov., 3 Dec. 1734, 15 March 1735, *Letters to the Saltzburghers*.
[2] Mr Verelst to Mr Von Reck, 6 Nov. 1734, *Letters to the Saltzburghers*.

and some of the chief magnates at Augsburg is highly concerned, for it was upon their publicly appearing in the affair, that these innocent people ventured their all, in leaving their services in good families, and the Roman Catholicks in that town will not be wanting in insults for sending people into such a desert, where in two years they cannot reap the corn or seed they sowed", and he urged the Trustees to "remove hence these illustrious and worthy people . . . in a new settlement".[1] He was supported by a temperate letter from Bolzius and Gronau, who said: "These good people acknowledge the great benefactions they have received, but they would also fain see themselves in such a condition that they might eat their own bread." [2]

The Trustees were not unaware of conditions in Ebenezer, for as early as February 1734 one of their number, who had been there, told them the settlers had not "applied themselves so much as we expected in clearing their lands", and the next month they had to agree that the Salzburgers "will be another year's charge upon us to maintain them, which was not in our scheme, for after the first year they were to maintain themselves out of the produce of their lands". The S.P.C.K. was placed in the same position by the second party of settlers, for whom it was financially responsible. The party's "freight and necessaries" cost it £786 4*s*., and it paid the Trustees £287 0*s*. 1*d*., "the charge of twelve months provisions supplied the Saltzburghers in Georgia under the care of Mr Vat over and above the three months provisions which they carried with them". The Society had also agreed to support a schoolmaster as well as a minister and catechist at Ebenezer. Bolzius had £50 a year, Gronau £30, and Ortmann, the schoolmaster, £10. Neither Trustees nor Society, therefore, wished to face the expense of moving the Salzburgers to a new settlement.[3] The only solace granted Bolzius and Gronau by the Society was "twelve dozen of Vidonia Madeira . . . to refresh you and your friends under the toils of your settlement".[4]

Oglethorpe was back in England, preparing to return to Georgia with more emigrants. Lord Perceval thought "the foreigners we are in treaty with to send should by prudent means be delayed";[5]

[1] Mr John Vat, Ebenezer, to HN, 30 May 1735, *Letters from the Saltzburghers.*
[2] Rev. Messrs Bolzius and Gronau, Ebenezer, to HN, 2 April 1735, *Letters from the Saltzburghers.*
[3] *Colonial Records of Georgia*, I, 192–3, 209, 243, 254–5, 269.
[4] HN to Rev. Messrs Bolzius and Gronau, 13 May 1735, *Letters to the Saltzburghers.*
[5] *Egmont MSS.*, Add. MSS. 47060, ff. 55–66.

but the S.P.C.K. still hoped to send as many as 100 more. Newman found, however, that not nearly as many Salzburgers could get permission to leave, so the Society, "with leave of several great benefactors to the fund, expanded their charity" to include a body of Protestants, expelled from Carinthia to Ratisbon, who wished to go to America. The Imperial authorities would not let enough of these people go to bring the number up to 100, and when Von Reck brought them to Rotherhithe in October 1736, just in time to join Oglethorpe, the party was only "58 persons, men, women and children, nearly half Saltzburghers and the rest Austrians".[1]

Two ships sailed for Georgia, the *London Merchant* and the *Simmonds*, escorted by the *Hawk* sloop-of-war. Von Reck's party was in the *London Merchant* with about 120 other emigrants. The *Simmonds* had 200 emigrants, together with Oglethorpe; a party of 25 of the Moravian brethren, finally accepted by the Trustees; and three "volunteer missionaries" for the colony, "Mr John Wesley, Fellow of Lincoln College, Oxford; Mr Charles Wesley, Student of Christ Church, Oxford; Mr Ingham of Queen's College, Oxford". These "well-disposed gentlemen", as Newman called them, had been recommended for religious work in Georgia by Dr John Burton, an Oxford don and Georgia Trustee, who took an unusual interest in the Oxford Methodists. The voyage lasted fifty-seven days, the emigrants undergoing the hardships common in Atlantic sailings during the autumn gales. In the *London Merchant*, the only incident recorded was that a boy was "whipt for stealing of turnips", but in the *Simmonds*, the women found relief in the ministrations of John Wesley, and he was impressed by the courage of the Moravians during storms. When the ships reached Savannah, Von Reck's party again refused to be divided. A few agreed to settle in the military post of Frederica, 100 miles away, but the rest joined the Salzburgers at Ebenezer. John Wesley began his ministry at Savannah.[2]

Newman knew John Wesley, who in 1732 was made a corresponding member of the Society and received books for his work among the poor and prisoners at Oxford, while his father was a member until his death. Wesley wanted to go to Georgia to preach

[1] HN to Rev. Mr Urlsperger, Augsburg, 20 June, 8 and 22 July 1735; to Mr Von Reck, Ratisbon, 12 Aug. 1735; to Gen. Oglethorpe, Georgia Office, 18 June 1735, *Miscellaneous Letters*; *Colonial Records of Georgia*, XXI, 446–8.

[2] P. A. Strobel, *Salzburgers and their Descendants*, Baltimore, 1855, 91; *Colonial Records of Georgia*, I, 240; *Daily Advertiser*, 15 Oct. 1735; HN to Lady Eliz. Hastings, Ferrybridge, 4 Oct. 1735; to Rev. Mr Urlsperger, Augsburg, 7 Oct. 1735; to Mr John Vat, Ebenezer, 10 Oct. 1735, *Miscellaneous Letters*.

the Gospel to the Indians. When Oglethorpe had returned to England in July 1733, he had brought with him an old Indian chief, Tomochichi, his wife, nephew, and some women and children. They had been presented to George II at Kensington Palace and stayed over a year in London, during which time Newman had helped in taking them on sight-seeing tours. Wesley went to Georgia as a direct result of the visit of these Indians. He was warmly supported by Newman, who had long hoped that colonization would mean the evangelization of the natives. He told Oglethorpe: "I hope you are the *white-man* that will, according to the tradition of the Indians, deliver them from the darkness that has for many ages overspread them", and asked Bolzius and Gronau, "What hopes have you of gaining the savage natives to the knowledge and love of the Saviour of mankind?", to which the harassed pair replied that "divers affairs have prevented our applying ourselves thereto".[1] He similarly hoped, therefore, that Wesley would "cultivate a sense of religion among the Europeans in your settlement and, if possible, among the natives, who for many ages have lived in the utmost darkness". Wesley sailed from England with a gift of books from the S.P.C.K., to be shared with Bolzius and Gronau, and a message from Newman: "I heartily wish you and your fellow-travellers with Mr Oglethorpe a prosperous voyage, and that it may please God to bless you with health and success in the high errand you have undertaken for His Glory, of which it will be a great pleasure to the Society to be as frequently informed as opportunities offer." [2]

Wesley sent the Society no information. Newman wrote to him twice in 1736—once to hope that the country in all respects answered his expectations and that he found the Indians "as tractable to religious instruction" as he had expected and was not meeting the difficulties of work among them which he himself remembered from his own New England days, such as that of "language" and love of "their old wild liberty"; and again to send him a gift of twenty Bibles and the Society's latest literature.[3] But by the time these would have reached him, Wesley was caught in the toils of his "unfortunate encounters with the daughters of Eve", as

[1] HN to Gen. Oglethorpe, Savannah, 4 June 1736, *Miscellaneous Letters*; to Rev. Messrs Bolzius and Gronau, Ebenezer, 13 May 1735, *Letters to the Saltzburghers*; Rev. Messrs Bolzius and Gronau, Ebenezer, to HN, 2 April 1735, *Letters from the Saltzburghers*.

[2] HN to Rev. Mr John Wesley, 13 Oct. 1735, *Miscellaneous Letters*.

[3] HN to Rev. Mr John Wesley, 9 June and 22 Sept. 1736, *Miscellaneous Letters*.

the *Dictionary of National Biography* expresses it, which was to lead to his return to England in 1738. The Trustees readily accepted his resignation. Lord Perceval thought him "a very odd mixture of a man, an enthusiast and at the same time a hypocrite, wholly distasteful to the greater part of the inhabitants, and an incendiary of the people against the magistracy".[1] He does not seem to have communicated with Newman.

Wesley was succeeded at Savannah by George Whitefield, also a member of the S.P.C.K. Whitefield was equally anxious to convert the Indians, but on missionary journeys, he found many European children in miserable circumstances without education, "hurt by bad examples and hard services". He resolved to acquire "a house and land for these children, where they might learn to labour, read and write, and at the same time, be brought up in the nurture and admonition of the Lord".[2] He returned to England the same year to collect funds for this orphanage. By the summer of 1739 he was ready to go back. He called on Newman before he went "to receive the final benediction in my hands for the Orphan House". He told Newman he had collected seven or eight hundred pounds and proposed to return to Georgia by way of Pennsylvania, Maryland, Virginia, and South Carolina, "in all of which places", Newman remarked, "he will have occasion to exercise his talents, though he can't expect such vast audiences as he has had here". For Whitefield had begun to exercise his great gifts for open-air preaching; but the only comment Newman had to make in his correspondence about "his frequent preachings in Moorfields and Kennington Common" was to note with approval that the Lord Mayor had warned him not to preach in the bounds of the City "for fear of ill consequences to himself and his followers".[3]

The orphanage was to be important in Whitefield's work for the rest of his life, compelling him to travel and inspiring him to preach. Within a few months of his return to America at the beginning of 1740, he brought his funds up to £2530. The Trustees granted him 500 acres at Savannah, and he began at once a building to be called Bethesda.[4] He told Newman: "I bless God all things are in great forwardness in respect to mine. In a few months I hope to have much land cleared and the house completely

[1] *Egmont Diary*, II, 481.
[2] L. Tyerman, *Life of the Rev. George Whitefield*, 1890, 2 vols., I, 83, 348.
[3] HN to Hon. James Vernon, Clare, Suffolk, 8 May 1739, *Miscellaneous Letters*.
[4] *D.N.B.*

furnished. I have taken in already many children and am daily taking in more." [1] Later, at his request, Newman sent him three dozen New Testaments and a dozen *Lessons for Children* for the orphanage.[2] In return, when Whitefield visited England again in the spring of 1741, he presented the Society with "several specimens of the work in cotton by the children of the orphanage in Bethesda", which Newman thought showed the undertaking "promises very well".[3]

Despite his admiration for the orphanage, Newman had already criticized Whitefield for his preaching in New England in 1740. At Boston he had addressed 15,000 people on the Common and preached to students and townspeople in the Meeting House at Cambridge, but his Calvinism did not agree with Harvard's liberal Congregationalism, and he found little to praise there. "The tutors", he said, "neglect to pray with, and examine the hearts of, their pupils." He also attacked the two great books of eighteenth-century religion, the *Whole Duty of Man* and the *Sermons* of Tillotson, stating, "It is my opinion that Dr Tillotson is in hell for his heresy", to which Henry Flint had replied, "It is my opinion that you will not meet him there." [4] Newman was indignant when he heard about this. "I wish I could say more than I can", he told a correspondent, "of Mr Whitefield's prudence for treating the memory of Archbishop Tillotson and the Author of the *Whole Duty of Man* as he has done after their labours have passed in the world, and done perhaps as much service in the cause of religion as any two authors in the last and, I may add, the present century. The Father of Lies is no doubt highly pleased with the scurrility thrown on two such advocates for truth that they may be less read and esteemed than they have been, but I hope the frenzy of the detractor will never prevail to extinguish lights that have been so long justly celebrated." [5]

The breach between the two men was made complete the next year. Whitefield's friends built him a preaching "tabernacle" in London, and his ties with the Church of England were already strained. His last connection with Newman was to complain that the S.P.C.K. had omitted references to himself in published letters

[1] *Colonial Records of Georgia*, XXII (2), 299–300.
[2] HN to Gen. Oglethorpe, Savannah, 25 Oct. 1740, *Miscellaneous Letters*.
[3] HN to Rev. Messrs Bolzius and Gronau, Ebenezer, 21 July 1741, *Miscellaneous Letters*.
[4] S. E. Morison, *Three Centuries of Harvard*, 85.
[5] HN to Rev. Mr Salway, Senr, Worcester, 9 Aug. 1740, *Miscellaneous Letters*.

from the Salzburgers in Georgia. Newman denied this, but added: "If any member has taken occasion to express a dislike of some things in Mr Whitefield's conduct in religious matters, 'tis no more than we could expect. The Society as a society ought not to be answerable for that any more than they are for Mr Whitefield's opinion concerning the *Works* of Archbishop Tillotson and the Author of the *Whole Duty of Man*."[1] Whitefield's success as a preacher did nothing in Newman's opinion to lessen the enormity of the attack on these two books, and thereafter his name disappeared from Newman's correspondence as completely as that of his predecessor in Georgia.

The S.P.C.K. had, of course, no immediate concern with English missionaries such as John Wesley and George Whitefield, but since it continued to pay the salaries of the German pastors at Ebenezer, it had a close connection with them. They wrote regularly about their work to Newman. In 1735 they reported proudly that the Salzburgers attended public worship for half an hour on week evenings when work was done and three times on Sundays.[2] When the usual salaries were paid that year, the Society rewarded a Mr Zwiffler, who acted voluntarily as a physician, surgeon, and apothecary at Ebenezer, with a gift of £20, and increased Gronau's salary from £30 to £40 a year.[3] The next year Zwiffler was sent some drugs he needed, but paid nothing, so early in 1737 he took a post in Pennsylvania. Newman regretted the Trustees had refused him a grant to remain, but undertook to find another physician for Ebenezer.[4] Again Professor G. A. Francke helped him by finding a Dr Thilo who was willing to go, paying his passage to England, and providing him with drugs from the pharmacy of the Halle orphanage. Newman promised that the Society would assist Thilo "from their own narrow fund", but in the end the Trustees agreed to allow him "a Dutch servant, several tools and 8*d*. a day". The doctor gave a glimpse of his living conditions at Ebenezer by hoping that they would be "not displeased to allow him some provisions instead of a servant".[5]

Life at Ebenezer, indeed, was not easy. The third transport

[1] HN to Rev. Mr Hall, Stanton Harcourt, Oxon, 10 June 1741, *Miscellaneous Letters*.

[2] Rev. Messrs Bolzius and Gronau to HN, 6 Feb. 1735, P.R.O., C.O. 5/636, No. 94.

[3] HN to Gen. Oglethorpe, Georgia, 25 Sept. 1735; to Mr Wm Tillard, London, 1 Oct. 1735, *Miscellaneous Letters*.

[4] HN to Mr Zwiffler, Ebenezer, 8 June 1736; to Rev. Messrs Bolzius and Gronau, Ebenezer, 2 March and 6 Oct. 1737, *Miscellaneous Letters*.

[5] *Colonial Records of Georgia*, XXI, 507–11; XXIII, 250–2.

gave it a population of nearly 200, but the situation described by Vat—a malarial climate, bad water, and poor soil—could not be remedied. The Trustees had to agree to the removal of the settlement, which was rebuilt on higher ground by 1738.[1] Whitefield gave Bolzius £52 19*s*. 9*d*. towards a new church, besides buying "a large bell" and "necessary ironwork" for it; but Bolzius was not so lucky in his own comfort. His house was too rotten to rebuild on the new site. He borrowed £40 from Oglethorpe to build a new one. The Trustees had already given him £10 towards his former house, and he wrote to Newman: "As the honourable Society are always strongly inclined to do everything to our and the Saltzburghers' welfare, I make bold to beg the favour of their intercession at the Board of the honourable Trustees to allow, besides the £10 which they have allowed for one house, something more, which intercession will, I doubt not, prevail very much to my advantage." Newman forwarded the letter to the Trustees, but without result, and over a year later Bolzius wrote again to ask him to recommend "the charges of the house" to his "dear benefactors, in the best manner you think proper".[2]

There were problems at home as well. By now over 150 Salzburgers had gone to Georgia in three transports, and the Society wanted to fulfil their original plan of 300. Even before news of the arrival of the third transport at Savannah reached London, Newman told Urlsperger that if not more than 60 nor less than 50 Salzburgers could come over before August, the Society would arrange their embarkation for America, but added: "The Society are not in a condition to allow them anything to maintain them in Germany till such time as they are all ready to set out together from thence in their way to Holland."[3] Indeed, conditions in Georgia made it increasingly difficult to find money to send more emigrants out; and by that summer both Trustees and Society had to abandon the idea of a fourth transport, so great was the continued cost of maintaining the entire community at Ebenezer, which seemed no nearer to being self-supporting.

Yet they were pressed to send more refugees. Towards the end of 1736, Dr Ayerst, a Prebendary of Canterbury, asked Newman to help three sisters and one child from Salzburg, who wanted to

[1] P. A. Strobel, *Salzburgers and their Descendants*, 11.

[2] Rev. Mr Bolzius to HN, 12 Dec. 1738 and 15 Jan. 1740, *Letters from the Saltzburghers*; HN to Rev. Messrs Bolzius and Gronau, Ebenezer, 23 Oct. 1740, *Miscellaneous Letters*; *Colonial Records of Georgia*, V, 77–8.

[3] HN to Rev. Mr Urlsperger, Augsburg, 12 Feb. 1736, *Miscellaneous Letters*.

emigrate. Since arriving in England, one had lost her husband and given birth to a dead child. Trying to get to Dover, they had collapsed at Canterbury and might well have starved to death if Ayerst had not cared for them in his house. They said they had "two sacks of clothes and goods, which they sent by the hoyman to Dover", but could not pay their way even there. He offered "to send them up by the Whitstable hoy"[1] to be interviewed in London. But Newman could do nothing, though he asked both the Society and the Trustees. The former "were concerned they could not give them any relief out of their Saltzburgh Fund, which is appropriated to those persecuted people"; the latter "don't care to send women without their husbands, except they are young and capable of working as servants when they come there to pay for the charge of their transportation".[2]

Early the next year Urlsperger had another tale of distress for Newman: "A fortnight ago eighteen persons arrived here from Saltzburgh, who were forced to fly on account of the strange religion, as it is called, and Lutheran Books." They included a woman with seven children, one born on the journey to Augsburg, who had travelled for eight days by wagon in the height of the winter. More refugees were expected. They would have to be supported, but he had only £10 left. He joined in asking with the refugees, "Whether there is not a new transport going to Georgia?"[3] Newman's reply again had to be unpromising. The Society regretted "that their Fund for relieving Saltzburghers is at present so low, that they are not in a position to engage for any new transports, but if you be under any agreement for assisting or supporting any persecuted Saltzburghers now at Augsburg, which you have made in expectation of assistance from the Society, either for old persons, invalids or apprentices", the Society would grant £50 "as a final discharge of the Society from any further expense for emigrants from Germany, and they would be very well pleased if some part of this money might be given to the poor woman mentioned in your letter who had made her escape from Saltzburgh with seven children".[4]

Despite their precarious existence upon external relief, the settlers at Ebenezer also pressed for another transport. In 1737 Urlsperger understood that they wanted "more single women to

[1] *Colonial Records of Georgia*, XXI, 231–2.
[2] HN to Rev. Dr Ayerst, Canterbury, 4 Nov. 1736, *Miscellaneous Letters.*
[3] Rev. Mr Urlsperger, Augsburg, to HN, 15 Jan. 1737, *Letters from the Saltzburghers.*
[4] HN to Rev. Mr Urlsperger, Augsburg, 1 Feb. 1737, *Miscellaneous Letters.*

marry", but as the Society's share of their provisions came to £14 15*s*. 6*d*. that year, it was not sympathetic.[1] In the spring of 1739 Bolzius reported that they expected a good harvest, "which will enable them not only to provide better than formerly for themselves and families, but [to] hope to be serviceable the better to another transport of Saltzburghers, which we hope will be sent over next fall by the generous care and goodness of the honourable Trustees and Society". The latter were ready to consider the possibilities, but were told "that the Trustees do not think this a proper season for carrying over a new transport of Saltzburghers. Another year they will be willing to contribute to it as far as shall be in their power."[2]

Before that came round, however, the Spanish War broke out, and the very existence of Georgia seemed threatened. Newman told Bolzius and Gronau that the Society considered "the fate of the colony at this juncture seems not quite as settled as it is to be wished before another transport be invited", while he himself thought, "While the war with Spain continues, there is no likelihood of any encouragement to favour another transport. And if you can enjoy tranquillity in your habitations without attack from the Spaniards or Indians during the war, you will be as happy as can be expected in the present ferment of affairs." [3] The Society did, however, print in 1740 a *Letter of Thanks* written by Bolzius and Gronau to express their "grateful thanks" for the "favours they have received from their benefactors in Europe". This the Society sent to all their "benefactors in Great Britain and Ireland" in the hope that they, "if it please God, may be excited to show some further favours" to the Salzburgers.[4]

Eventually the most valuable favour came from Parliament. Inspired by Oglethorpe's successful campaign against the Spanish in Florida and realizing the strategic value of the colony, in 1741 it granted the Trustees £10,000 "towards the support of Georgia". The Trustees decided to use part of this in taking the long-awaited fourth party of Salzburgers over to Georgia. They "ordered that

[1] Rev. Mr Urlsperger to HN, 6 May 1737, *Letters from the Saltzburghers*; *Colonial Records of Georgia*, I, 302.

[2] Rev. Mr Bolzius to HN, 15 May 1739, *Letters from the Saltzburghers*; HN to Hon. James Vernon, Clare, Suffolk, 8 May 1739; to Rev. Messrs Bolzius and Gronau, Ebenezer, 28 Dec. 1739, *Miscellaneous Letters; S.P.C.K. Minutes*, 24 July, 1739.

[3] HN to Rev. Messrs Bolzius and Gronau, Ebenezer, 23 Oct. 1740, *Miscellaneous Letters.*

[4] HN to Bp of Lincoln, etc., 24 May 1740, *Miscellaneous Letters.*

a letter be wrote to Mr Henry Newman, desiring him to acquaint the Society for Promoting Christian Knowledge, that the Trustees purpose to make an embarkation of 50 Saltzburghers upon the Society's paying the passage of them to Rotterdam, that he acquaint Mr Urlsperger of Augsburg thereof, and that they are to be in Rotterdam in July next".[1] The Society accepted the arrangement, and Newman proceeded with the plans. When the party reached London, he and Verelst had great difficulty, owing to the war, in finding a ship to take them to America, but by September that had been done, and they sailed for the colony, having been joined by "some able husbandmen from Scotland", whom the Trustees hoped would provide a further stiffening to the original debtors and paupers taken there.[2]

This was the last party of refugees to Georgia in which Newman assisted, but he continued to serve the settlers in the colony until his death. One of his last services for them was to forward to the Trustees a request for help "to build a small house for divine service . . . and also to support a School Master for instructing the children" in "the Plantations", an additional settlement started by them near the new Ebenezer.[3] The emigration of the Salzburgers played an important part in the settlement of the colony. By 1740 it had received 1521 settlers, of whom the Salzburgers and other German Protestants came to some 600, while between 1741 and 1754 only a quarter of the grants of land in the colony were held by men with English names.[4] Moreover, the Trustees hoped the Salzburgers would be better settlers than the first emigrants and treated them favourably. They each received 50 acres of land when English settlers were only getting 40 acres, though their grant was later raised to 50 acres as well. And in an *Account* of the colony published by the Trustees in 1741, the settlers at Ebenezer were praised as "industrious and sober", not one of whom had "abandoned his settlement".[5]

This good opinion of the Salzburgers continued during the discontent that Oglethorpe's paternal regulations were causing in the

[1] *Colonial Records of Georgia*, I, 302, 379; V, 454.
[2] HN to Rev. Mr Urlsperger, Augsburg, 13 Feb., 24 March, 5 May and 14 July 1741; to Rev. Messrs Bolzius and Gronau, Ebenezer, 15 Sept. 1741, *Miscellaneous Letters*.
[3] *Colonial Records of Georgia*, V, 647; HN to Rev. Dr Wilson, Tunbridge Wells, 10 July 1742, *Miscellaneous Letters*.
[4] Basil Williams, *The Whig Supremacy*, 292–3; George White, *Historical Collections of Georgia*, New York, 1854, 37.
[5] *S.P.C.K. Minutes*, 31 Dec. 1733; Peter Force, *Tracts Relating to North America*, I, *passim*.

colony. In 1738 over 100 freeholders at Savannah petitioned the Trustees against the restriction on the alienation of land and the prohibition of slavery. Their first grievance referred to the onerous provisions attached to grants of land, which were in tail male only, to prevent the accumulation by marriage of more than one lot of 50 acres to each settler. Perhaps the Trustees were influenced by the fact that the Salzburgers, even before setting out for America, had informed Newman of their dislike of this provision. At any rate, the next year they acceded to the petitioners' request and changed the grants of land so that they were held in fee simple and could descend to widows or daughters where there were no sons to succeed.[1]

The Trustees, however, rejected the second request of the petitioners, who had complained that they could not compete with their neighbours to the north who employed large numbers of negro slaves. The Trustees were "determined to prohibit negroes, the use of them seeming absolutely inconsistent with the design of this colony, and, besides this, in many respects inconvenient and dangerous". They feared that, if there were slaves in the colony, the Spaniards at St Augustine would entice them away or incite them to insurrection. Also an able-bodied negro cost £30, a sum which would transport an emigrant to the colony, provide his tools, and keep him for a year. Instead of negro slaves, the Trustees instituted, for both English and German settlers, a system of indentured servants, who were to work for their masters for from four to fourteen years before becoming free settlers. This had not satisfied the petitioners, who complained that such servants were too few and often escaped from service. The Salzburgers were no better served. In 1740 Bolzius, speaking of 61 German servants brought over in one vessel, said: "One-and-twenty grown persons are picked out at Savannah, partly by the magistrates, partly by the people, having paid £6; and the rest, being forty souls, mostly bakers, millers, shoemakers, some women and ten children, are sent to our place [Ebenezer], where I endeavoured to accommodate them in the best manner I was able. No more than nineteen husbandmen could be supplied with servants, each with one servant, and some of these with small families." He also complained that these servants were "refractory, filled with ideas of liberty, and clandestinely quitting their masters", who often "were compelled

[1] W. B. Stevens, *History of Georgia*, 2 vols., New York, 1847–59, I, 276–81; *London Gazette*, 8 Sept. 1739.

to resort to corporeal punishment or other summary methods to bring them to obedience".[1]

Nevertheless, the Salzburgers counter-petitioned against the introduction of negro slaves into the colony. In a letter to Oglethorpe in 1739 they asked him "not to allow that any negroes might be brought to our place or in our neighbourhood, knowing by experience that houses and gardens will be robbed always by them and white people in danger of life from them, besides other great inconveniences". This still further raised them in the opinion of the Trustees compared with the "negro-mongers" and "drunken idle sort" among the settlers; but it did not make them popular in the colony. The dissatisfied colonists said the Salzburgers would "never commix or associate with Strangers" and ascribed their greater prosperity to the fact that "they have been hitherto liberally supported both from England and Germany, and their Rights and Privileges have been much more extensive than any others in the Colony". Moreover, they believed that "the pretended Content and Satisfaction of the People of Ebenezer, without Negroes, will plainly appear to be the Dictates of Spiritual Tyranny, and only the wretched Acquiesence of People, who were in Truth unacquainted with the Privilege of choosing for themselves", since they were compelled to sign the counter-petition by Bolzius.[2]

Whatever the rights of this, the Trustees certainly treated the Salzburgers with favoured consideration in the hope they would grow the products most desired by the supporters of the scheme. Newman had shared these hopes and asked Vat: "Pray let me know by a line now and then . . . what prospect there is of its answering the expectations of those who wish well to it, in respect to the products of rice, raw silk, naval stores, and any other things for the benefit of Great Britain, where all our hopes and wishes must centre at last." [3] But experience was showing that such crops were not suited to the soil and climate of the country. Cuttings from Madeira, intended to produce wine for all the plantations,

[1] John Harris, *Collection of Voyages and Travels*, 2 vols., 1748, II, *passim*; W. B. Stevens, op. cit., 291–2.

[2] *An Impartial Enquiry into the State and Utility of the Province of Georgia*, 1741, *passim*; "A State of the Province of Georgia, Attested upon Oath, in the Court of Savannah, 10 November 1740", reprinted Peter Force, op. cit., I; *A Brief Account of the Causes that have retarded the Progress of the Colony of Georgia in America*, 1743, *passim*; P. Tailfer, H. Anderson, D. Douglas and other Georgia Landowners, "A True and Historical Narrative of the Colony of Georgia in America", Charleston, S.C., 1741, reprinted Peter Force, op. cit., I.

[3] HN to Mr Vat, Savannah, 3 June 1736, *Miscellaneous Letters*.

yielded only a few gallons before the vines were abandoned; hemp and flax never amounted to a single ship-load for England; silk was produced by a determined effort and at a cost of nearly £1500, but up to the surrender of their charter in 1752 the Trustees had not raised as much as 1000 lb. of raw silk. On the other hand, as early as 1738 the Salzburgers grew a small amount of cotton. The results were very encouraging, the crop being of abundant yield and excellent quality, but the Trustees' hopes were still fixed on silk and wine, and the experiment was not countenanced. The Salzburgers survived because of their native industry and favoured treatment, but many other settlers gave up the attempt to grow unsuitable crops on their small grants of land without black labour. During the period of the corporate existence of the Trustees, two-thirds of the settlers whom they sent over to Georgia left the colony.[1]

Such troubles naturally detracted from the reputation of the colony in England, and in the last year of his life Newman was forcibly shown this. He was asked by Oglethorpe to find two or three charity boys for service with him in Georgia. He thought this would be an excellent start in life for the fortunate boys who went, so he "went to all the great schools in and about London", where he "had a choice of seven or eight hundred boys", but in vain. He told Oglethorpe that he had "found several willing to accept of your service, but they were either of a dwarfish stature, hump-backed, squint-eyed, or bandy-legged, and mostly destitute of the main qualifications you desired". He found only two possible boys—one in St Dunstan's-in-the-West School and the other in St Margaret's School, Westminster—but the trustees of the first and the parents of the second would not let them be bound apprentices in Georgia. In the end, Newman could only suggest that the captain of Oglethorpe's ship should "carry over half a dozen of the most likely boys he could pick up" from the streets and let Oglethorpe have the choice of them. Such was the reputation of the colony that it was not considered suitable even for charity school boys.[2]

Newman ignored the troubles in the colony as long as he could, but in the last year of his life his letters mentioned them increasingly. He was glad when the petition presented to the House of

[1] W. B. Stevens, op. cit., I, 264–76; H. McCall, *History of Georgia*, 2 vols., Savannah, 1811–16, I, 199.
[2] HN to Gen. Oglethorpe, Georgia, 9 Feb. 1742, *Miscellaneous Letters*.

Commons by Thomas Stephens, who had been chosen by the settlers in Georgia to make known their grievances in this way, resulted in the upholding of the Trustees and reprimanding of Stephens.[1] He praised Oglethorpe for his intention to return to England and face his enemies. And, indeed, when Oglethorpe did return in 1743, it was for the last time, too wearied by his struggles and too disappointed ever to go back to America. The death of Newman and the retirement of Oglethorpe marked, therefore, the end of the first stage in the founding of Georgia. Many trials lay ahead of the colony, and it was to develop very differently from the plans of its first promoters, but eventually both English debtors and Salzburg refugees were to make good their frontier province.

[1] W. B. Stevens, op. cit., I, 300–5; *Journal of the House of Commons*, 1742, XXIV, 191.

11
CONCLUSION

As a young man Newman must have had good health and strength to have led such an adventurous life, and during his first years as Secretary of the S.P.C.K. he only once complained of illness. This was in the summer of 1712, when he and his clerk, Mr Banks, both had "a strange indisposition that has for a week past run through this City, so that scarce any family has escaped it". It seems to have been some form of influenza, for its symptoms were "a violent headache and with some a dizziness attended with a sore throat, want of appetite, a feebleness which lasts two or three days and then goes off, so that very few or scarce any have died of it. What it portends, God only knows, but so general a disposition 'tis thought is occasioned by some malignancy in the air. May it warn us to be wiser and better and then it will be good for us that we have been afflicted. Physicians compute that there could not be less than 40 or 50 thousand persons sick at one time in the City of this distemper." [1]

His first serious illness was in the spring of 1720 when, at the age of 49, he was confined to his chamber in the Temple "by a pleuratick fever which I am forced to nurse in time to prevent it growing to the head", and he believed he "narrowly escaped going to my grave". His employers treated him generously, resolving "that the charges of Mr Newman's sickness be defrayed by the Society", and twenty years later he recalled how "the then Treasurer, by order of the Society, sent after him a present of ten guineas with a message, which he received in bed after losing three score ounces of blood, to spare no cost for the recovery of his health, which the Society had resolved to bear and generously performed. The consequence was the humanity of the message at that juncture in the blessing of God soon set him on his legs beyond any cordials or advice from the physicians." In all the Society granted him £20 for "defraying the extraordinary charges of his sickness". He was attended by his friend Sir Hans Sloane, and on his advice he took

[1] HN to Rev. Mr Francis Fox, Devizes, Wilts., 2 Aug. 1712, *Society's Letters*.

"lodgings at Hampstead for recovering himself".[1] Eighteenth-century Hampstead was described by a writer as "a pleasant village in Middlesex, situated near the top of a hill about four miles from the north-west side of London. On the summit of this hill is a heath, which is adorned with many gentlemen's houses";[2] while Defoe thought it "so near heaven" that it was not "a proper situation for any but a race of mountaineers, whose lungs had been used to a rarefied air",[3] so that it must have been ideal for Newman's convalescence.

He sought recovery of his health not only in the air of Hampstead, but also through exercise and diet. "I was at death's door with a pleurisy about sixteen months ago," he told a friend, "and received so much benefit by Hampstead air and asses' milk that I can't help advising everybody to use them as being more or less good in every case." [4] To Lord Perceval he ascribed his regained health to "riding two or three times a week" on Hampstead Heath and "eating an orange chip now and then in the day", and would also "presume to recommend them in any case where a sharpness in the blood prevails over all other humours".[5] He retained his confidence in this regimen for the rest of his life. He made "excursions abroad now and then on horseback to get rid of the scurvy sedentary life has subjected me to", and when too old for this, he took to "a machine to ride on without going abroad for the sake of the motion it gives", as patronized by "Princess Amelia and several people of quality", and costing 3½ guineas. At first he got a joiner to make him such "a chamber horse"; then he was given one by a lady correspondent and found it admirable "to refresh my weak lungs that wanted such an exercise to promote respiration".[6] He took care "at the same time to refrain from all liquors, especially tea, white wine, very small or stale beer, tending to cherish such [a sharp] humour in the blood", but always to drink milk daily at breakfast. His faith in these means to bodily well-being enabled him three years after this illness to write optimistically of his "health which, I thank

[1] *S.P.C.K. Minutes*, 23 Aug. and 24 Nov. 1720; HN to Ld Perceval, 22 April 1722, *Egmont MSS.*, Add. MSS. 47029, f. 238; to Archdeacon Deane, Canterbury, 7 Aug. 1742, *Miscellaneous Letters*.

[2] R. and J. Dodsley, *London and its Environs Described*, 6 vols., 1761, *passim*.

[3] Daniel Defoe, *Tour of the Whole Island of Great Britain*, 1724, Everyman ed., II, 4–5.

[4] HN to Mr Robethon, 31 Oct. 1721, *Society's Letters*.

[5] HN to Ld Perceval, 19 Oct. 1723, *Egmont MSS.*, Add. MSS. 47030, f. 44.

[6] HN to Mrs Blunden, Hampstead, 3 March 1740 and 27 Aug. 1742, *Private Letters*.

God, I enjoy with less interruption than in the former part of my life".[1]

He certainly came through his next serious illness safely. Early in 1733 London was struck by an epidemic of fever such as in the eighteenth century often ravaged the overcrowded and insanitary city. According to Newman it "carried off 2754 persons in this City the two last weeks" and was so widespread that "scarce a family has escaped having the sickness where it has not proved mortal". Newman and his clerk, Mr Delagarde, caught it. They recovered, though Newman was "confined to his chambers three or four weeks"; but the Society's messenger, James Bell, died of it, leaving a widow and son, "a hopeful youth about eight years of age", and no sooner was Newman well than he typically helped the widow, who wanted her son to go to Charterhouse "for grammar learning", by asking Archbishop Wake for his "warrant to succeed in the next vacancy of that foundation for youths in your Grace's disposal".[2]

Apart from this fever, Newman seems to have had fairly good health for some years, though anxious about it always after his attack of pleurisy in 1720. He complained in 1723 that sometimes "a weakness in my eyes obliges me to make use of my clerk" in transcribing letters; in 1728 he suffered "constant indisposition from a violent headache for about six months past" and apologized for not writing to several New England friends because of this "late and present indisposition".[3] After the age of 60 he felt his years, and in 1733 apologized to Dr Cutler, Rector of Christ Church, Boston, for his travelling expenses on undertaking a mission for him: "I should have been ashamed of charging you with so much coaching if I had been younger, but now I make a poor solicitor without a coach, and there were several times that I attended when I have either saved that expense or divided it between myself and a friend or walked part of the way to be as frugal

[1] Newman's views on beverages were those of his time. In 1705, for instance, Lady Carnarvon considered Miss Coke was "extremely fallen away and her voice weak and inward" through "her having had stale beer all this summer" (*H.M.C. Coke*, 1889, p. 164), and though tea-drinking increased throughout the century, it met with criticism. Jonas Hanway in *An Essay on Tea*, 1756, blamed it for scurvy, indigestion, paralytic, and other nervous disorders, and John Wesley expressed similar views.

[2] HN to Mr Hastings, Birmingham, 3 Feb. 1733; to Mr Grant, 5 Feb. 1733; to Rev. Mr John Gibb, Bristol, 17 Feb. 1733; to Abp of Canterbury, 28 Feb. 1733, *Society's Letters*.

[3] HN to Lt-Gov. Wentworth, 15 March 1723; to Rev. Mr Colman, Boston, 30

as I could." [1] He was again ill in the winter of 1737 and wrote: "I am confined to my chamber by a pain in my side, for which I have been blooded and hope by other cautions to be able to attend my duty next Tuesday"; while just over a year later his clerk, Mr Norman, had to write to correspondents: "Mr Newman has for ten days past been confined by a violent fever and not able to despatch business." [2] He still felt fit, however, for a man of his age, and the next year, when busy with the approaching annual audit and anniversary meeting, wrote: "God be thanked, I enjoy my health and do my business with pleasure though in the seventieth year of, God knows, an unprofitable life." [3]

Newman was fortunate to attain old age without suffering more from disease or from doctors, for medicine, though on the eve of great advances, was still marked by crudities, and some popular prescriptions were at least useless. In 1740 Newman wrote to Griffith Jones: "I applied myself to obey your orders for egg-shell powder, but when I came to talk with the apothecary, I found there wanted an explanation. You desired egg-shell powder simply, but he believed you meant Mrs Stephens' egg-shell powder, which has snails calcined with the shells and is much more effectual to bring off the gravel." [4] This was the concoction, the secret of which Joanna Stevens, an ignorant and vulgar woman, induced Parliament to buy from her for £5000 as a remedy for the cure of stone, consisting of a powder of calcined egg-shells and snails, a decoction of soap and swines' cresses, and pills of snails, alicant soap, and honey. Sir Robert Walpole took a course of this treatment, and it was calculated he had consumed 180 lb. of soap and 1200 gallons of lime water before he died.[5]

Again, ague or malaria was still common in England, and remedies were legion. Two mentioned by Dean Swift in 1743 were "pounded ginger, made into a paste with brandy, spread on sheep's lether and a plaister of it laid over the stomach", and "a live spider put into a goose quill, well sealed and secured and hung low about the child's neck as low as the pit of the stomach".[6] Newman himself recorded two cures. One he jotted down in the

[1] HN to Rev. Dr Cutler, Boston, 28 July 1733, *New Eng. Letters*.
[2] HN to Rev. Mr Ziegenhagen, Kensington, 12 Nov. 1737; to Rev. Mr Morgan, Brightwell, Berks, 4 Jan. 1739, *Miscellaneous Letters*.
[3] HN to Rev. Mr Salwey, Senr, Worcester, 8 April 1740, *Miscellaneous Letters*.
[4] HN to Rev. Mr Griffith Jones, Landowver, 4 Oct. 1740, *Miscellaneous Letters*.
[5] *Johnson's England*, 2 vols., Oxford, 1933, II, 276–7.
[6] Quoted in J. H. Whiteley, *Wesley's England*, 185.

rough minute-book at a meeting of the Society. He described it as recommended by the late Bishop of Ely, presumably John Moore, whose famous library was bought by George I and presented to the University of Cambridge; and perhaps he received it from a member at the meeting: "Take half a dozen cobwebs, roll them into a pill with sugar and give it to the patient an hour before the fit." The other, more pleasant, he included in a letter to a correspondent: "Take three spoonfuls of juice of lemon in the cold fit, and as the cold fit goes off, take a pint of mulled strong white wine. The patient will thereupon sweat, and if it does not cure at once taking it, it must be repeated two or three times." [1]

Newman had shown his interest in medical science by the subject of his *quaestio* as a young graduate at Harvard, and he did not confine himself to such quack prescriptions. He occupied himself with a most important discovery—inoculation against smallpox. Though known earlier, it was little used in England until 1721, when Lady Mary Wortley Montagu, who had had her son inoculated in Constantinople, induced George II to order the inoculation of three male and three female convicts in Newgate; but two of Newman's New England friends were early pioneers in the movement. In that same year 1721 there was an outbreak of smallpox in Massachusetts. Cotton Mather, having read in the *Transactions of the Royal Society* about inoculation, urged against violent opposition its introduction into America. Later he wrote an article on inoculation in New England which, through Newman's intermediacy, was printed in the transactions of the London Philosophical Society.[2] He was supported by Benjamin Colman, who published in 1721 *Some Observations on the New Method of Receiving the Small Pox by Ingrafting or Inoculating*, and Dr Jewen, Secretary of the Royal Society, wrote to Newman of it: "One may, I think, in that little tract, see the philosopher and physician, as well as the modest and humble divine." Newman told Colman: "The Royal Society here seem perfectly to approve of your method of inoculation, and though it meets with opposition, so that I am told a reverend divine of the Church Established made a

[1] *S.P.C.K. Minutes*, 19 April 1720; HN to Sir Thos. Lowther, Guisborough, Yorks, 29 Sept. 1720, *Society's Letters*.

[2] J. S. Barry, *History of Massachusetts*, II, 114–16; "The Way of Proceeding in the Small Pox Inoculation in New England", communicated by Henry Newman, Esq., of the Middle Temple, *London Philosophical Transactions*, XXXII, 33; *Mass. Hist. Soc. Proceedings*, XLV, 460.

pulpit discourse the other day against it, yet many more of the sensible, as well as the more distinguished, part of mankind come daily to the practice of it"; and he several times sent him pamphlets from England about it, if "only to convince you that we are almost divided as you are in New England about the lawfulness of it".[1]

Newman himself believed in inoculation. He wanted young Henry Du Quesne to be inoculated, but Mrs Hawson refused to agree to it, lest any hint of smallpox should scare away her lodgers.[2] Some of his relations in New England also supported the new experiments, and one, Colonel Quincy, gave his life in the cause. He came to London and died after inoculation. His friends advised him against it, because of his age, but he had long been interested in the method and said he had a call to it, "for the service of his country and that if he died under the experiment, he should be more satisfied than with the torture of daily expecting the natural way, which he was pretty sure would be fatal to a man in his years". So Newman wrote his epitaph in a proud but melancholy letter to Governor Belcher.[3]

Though Newman gave thanks for his good health in his seventieth year in 1740, it did not continue so for more than another two years. From the spring of 1742 it declined seriously. The old weakness of his eyes worsened, and he was afflicted with the cripplingly dispiriting complaint of asthma.[4] Early in 1737 Sir John Philipps had died suddenly. Telling John Wesley in Georgia, Newman said: "To leave the world without the anxieties of a lingering sickness and the agonies that usually attend the separation of soul and body, is a privilege every good man is not to expect." [5] Newman was not to be granted this privilege himself.

He remained in his post to the end, working as hard as ever, but his interest and zest for life diminished. These last years were troubled. The long peace came to an end in 1739 with the War of Jenkins' Ear against Spain, and his last letters reflect the same anxiety about affairs as the first. Even the ceremonial declaration

[1] Ebenezer Turell, *Life and Character of Dr Benjamin Colman*, Boston, 1749, 78; HN to Rev. Mr Colman, Boston, 31 May, 14 July and 20 Oct. 1722, 20 July 1723, *New Eng. Letters*; and *Mass. Hist. Soc.*, Colman Papers.

[2] HN to Lady Torrington, 30 Dec. 1726, *Letters to Jamaica*.

[3] HN to Gov. Belcher, Boston, 1 May 1738, *New Eng. Letters*.

[4] HN to Mr Jonathan Belcher, Jnr, Dublin Castle, 17 April 1742, *Miscellaneous Letters*.

[5] HN to Rev. Mr John Wesley, Savannah, 10 Oct. 1737, *Letters to the Saltzburghers*.

of war did not arouse his earlier enthusiasm for State occasions, and he described it with a worried weariness:

This day . . . has been solemnized here with a pompous declaration of war with Spain at St James' Palace Gate, Charing Cross, Chancery Lane and in Fleet Street, Cheapside and at the Royal Exchange, attended by heralds and their officers in state, a troop of Life Guards and Horse Grenadiers, and my Lord Mayor elect and Sheriffs attending at the three places within Temple Bar, which drew a vast concourse of people, more than the streets could well contain. We have been long coming to this solemnity, but I hope we shall not be as many years coming to that of peace, if the war be prosecuted with that vigour our preparations for it threaten, and it please God to bless the King's council in the approaching sessions of Parliament.[1]

The first winter of the war was so exceptionally severe that nearly thirty years later Parson Woodforde noted in his diary that it was "excessive cold, as cold and severe weather on all accounts as in the year 1740".[2] The Thames was frozen over all January and a Frost Fair held on it. Newman thought it "one of the severest winters I ever knew in New England or Newfoundland".[3] "Many substantial shopkeepers" in London suffered "for want of employment and fire", since coal rose to 3 guineas a cauldron and was "hard to be come at in the river by reason of ice and the impracticableness of using boats or lighters". As for "the poor of this City", their plight was "very afflicting" and would have been worse but for "the relief they have had from many charitable persons".[4] But the war dragged on, and two years later Newman could give no more cheerful account of conditions at home: "The war has occasioned a scarcity of provisions here . . . which joined to the decay of trade, has very much distressed the poor, so that the present taxes for the poor in some places, with the 4*s*. in the pound paid to the King, reduces a man of £200 per annum to £100 per annum, and the poor notwithstanding in a starving condition in many places where trade has suffered most." [5]

News of victories, which seemed to bring the end of the war no nearer, did not cheer Newman, and he did not join in the celebrations as whole-heartedly as when younger: "The success of

[1] HN to Dean Copping, Dublin, 23 Oct. 1739, *Miscellaneous Letters*.
[2] James Woodforde, *The Diary of a Country Parson*, 6 Jan. 1768.
[3] HN to Mrs Chamberlayne, 4 March 1740, *Private Letters*.
[4] HN to Sir Erasmus Philipps, Rome, 29 Jan. 1740; to Rev. Mr Fenwick, Hallaton, Leics, 14 Feb. 1740, *Miscellaneous Letters*.
[5] HN to Rev. Mr Jones, Bonavista, Newfoundland, 3 April 1742, *Miscellaneous Letters*.

Admiral Vernon at Carthagena . . . has filled the town with more noise and illuminations than ever I knew upon any occasion, because it held two nights together to oblige the mob, it being holiday time; I shewed lights the first night, but I did not the second. My neighbours and I that omitted that respect to them had our windows broke." [1] He lived to see the resignation of Walpole, whom he had found so difficult to approach, but whose peace policy he supported. He lived also to see the new administration of the politicians whom he regarded as responsible for the war rather than the trading classes. He wrote sarcastically to his merchant cousins, the Quincys of Boston, that since it was claimed "that the nation makes a better figure than it did under the late administration, and that trade and navigation everywhere find a better protection than they did", then peace would only come when "the sturdy beggars called merchants . . . work their way out of the war which they were represented by the late ministry to have officiously brought the nation into".[2]

Walpole was not the only figure in Newman's world to have come to the end of his career. Some were already dead. Archbishop Wake had died in 1737, but had disappeared from Newman's correspondence some years before owing to "His Grace's great age and infirmities, which have in a manner deprived him of any more taking a pen into his hands, who was formerly so ready and great a master of it".[3] Jeremiah Dummer, his old opponent as colonial agent for Massachusetts, he had recorded as having died in 1739 "at Plaistow in Essex, not without the regret of many who knew him for his facetious conversation".[4] Others had retired from the activities which had brought them and Newman together. Von Reck, the Hanoverian nobleman who had escorted two parties of Salzburgers to Georgia, was now at Halle leading a life of religious devotion and theological study. The loss which Newman perhaps felt most was that of his clerk, Peter Norman, with him since 1734. In the summer of 1742 Norman was so ill "of a deep consumption" as not likely to "be able to return to the Society's Office". Newman paid him his salary of £20 a year and board up to Midsummer, but could not continue this and pay another clerk, nor could he "abandon him after ten years faithful

[1] HN to Dean Copping, Derby, 21 May 1741, *Miscellaneous Letters.*
[2] HN to Messrs Edmund and Josiah Quincy, Merchants, Boston, 8 Sept. 1742, *New Eng. Letters.*
[3] HN to the Missionaries at Tranquebar, 3 Feb. 1731, *Society's Letters.*
[4] HN to Sir Erasmus Philipps, 22 May 1739, *Miscellaneous Letters.*

service in the business of the Society without endeavouring at means for his support, though in a languishing condition". He offered to pay Norman £5 a year, "if the Society would be pleased to add so much as to make it up a subsistence to him"; but the Committee delayed, though Newman wrote again, saying that he was still paying Norman his salary and reminding them of the generous way they had treated him during his own illness in 1720. The Committee, however, was still considering the matter when Norman died at the end of August.[1]

Newman missed him particularly because of the "weakness in my eyes concomitant of old age", which, he confessed, "makes writing very disagreeable to me . . . so that I am constrained to use brevity in writing to my friends".[2] He obtained a new clerk, a Mr Thomson, a Scotsman, but in the spring of 1743 this man left "to accept of being an usher in a school". Newman wrote round to his friends asking them if they knew of a likely man. He wanted one "of a good character as to his morals, healthy constitution, single, and of a quiet disposition in a family" and "nearer forty than thirty" years old. As to qualifications, he should be one who "writes a good running hand and understands accounts, engrossing I seldom have occasion for, but if he understands Latin and French, he may sometimes be of use to me in those languages". In addition, he should be one "that will be content to lodge in the office . . . and can shave me and help me on with my shoes in a morning, never be absent above a quarter of an hour from the office without leave, be regular in his conduct every Sunday, attending divine service somewhere, and to be at home early in the evening".[3] He wrote, finally, to Thomson, telling him: "I am not yet provided with a clerk, though I have tried several, and as I have surmounted in good measure the distress you left me in, I intend to take time to provide myself"; but concluding, rather strangely: "You know the nature of my business and way of life, and if you can submit to these and promise never to desert me so abruptly as you did, I can bear with the defect of your writing in hopes you will take pains to improve it." [4]

[1] HN to Rev. Dr Thomlinson, Newcastle-on-Tyne, 18 May 1734; to Archdeacon Deane, Canterbury, 22 July and 7 Aug. 1742, *Society's Letters*; to Gov. Belcher, 30 Oct. 1742, *New Eng. Letters*.

[2] HN to Gov. Belcher, 30 Aug. 1742; to Messrs Edmund and Josiah Quincy, Boston, 8 Sept. 1742, *New Eng. Letters*.

[3] HN to Mr Grose, Cornhill, 17 Feb. 1743; to Mr Bernwitz, Bishopsgate, 22 Feb. 1743, *Miscellaneous Letters*.

[4] HN to Mr Thomson, Edmonton, 10 March 1743, *Miscellaneous Letters*.

But Newman's asthma grew worse. He could hardly do his work in the winter of 1742–3. He apologized to Bishop Gibson for being unable to call upon him in November, though he was able to call upon the chairman of the East India Committee about holding a General Meeting to debate the whole position of the Mission, but he was too ill to walk and had to make the whole journey to Westminster and back by coach.[1] He feared he was "afflicted with a violent asthma, which will go nigh to carry me out of life, in which God's will be done", and in April confessed to a correspondent: "I can scarce hold up my head to signify this." [2]

The atmosphere of London, since coal was burnt on every hearth, was notoriously oppressive. Even healthy people, according to Defoe, liked to go to the suburbs for a day "to draw their breath in a clean air" before returning to the "smoke and dirt, sin and seacoal (as it was coarsely expressed) in the busy city";[3] while King William III, who suffered from asthma, had lived at Hampton Court when he could, at Kensington when he must, but never at Whitehall. Newman remained in London, and as spring approached was more optimistic: "Though I am still confined to my chamber, my asthma is more tolerable and with the return of mild weather will, I hope in God, very much repair." [4] But it was not to be. He died on 15 June 1743 and was buried two days later in the churchyard of St Andrew's, Holborn.[5] He desired in his will to be buried "plainly and with little charge as may be", so it is not surprising that neither the place of his grave nor its inscription have survived. In one of his letter books, however, may be found the rough draft of an epitaph he composed for a physician friend who died at Greenwich in 1727—"His Friendship and Charity kept Pace"—and no better epitaph could be found for Newman himself.

He had appointed as executors of his will, drawn up in 1731, three members of the Society: Archdeacon Deane, William Tillard, and Benjamin Hoare. Except for some small bequests to his housekeeper and one or two friends, he left his estate to his executors "for the use and benefit of my own honoured masters, the Society

[1] HN to Bp of London, Whitehall, 8 Nov. 1742; to Mr John Philipps, Westminster, 14 Feb. 1743, *Miscellaneous Letters*.

[2] HN to Mr Vigerius Edwards, Bedford Row, 7 April 1743, *Miscellaneous Letters*.

[3] Defoe, *Tour*, I, 168.

[4] HN to Dean Copping, Dublin, 5 March 1743; to Rev. Mr Perronet, Shoreham, Kent, 9 April 1743, *Miscellaneous Letters*.

[5] *Burial Register*, St Andrew's Parish Church, Holborn, "Henry Newman, Bartlett's Buildings, buried 17th June 1743".

for Promoting Christian Knowledge". A codicil made in December 1742 changed his directions about the land he had inherited from his father at Rehoboth and Attleborough in Massachusetts. Originally he intended to divide this between his cousins, Samuel and David Newman, who were farming it; but he revoked this, "not out of any disgust with my said kinsmen, but so far as in me lies to do justice to my creditors". The land was to be sold, his cousins to have first refusal of purchase and to be paid for all improvements they had made; the proceeds of the sale, except for £10 to be given to each cousin, were to go to discharge his debts, and any residue "to be applied to the use of the Society for Promoting Christian Knowledge towards carrying on their excellent designs at home and abroad". Another codicil, made in April 1743, gave 2 guineas to Duncan Thomson, evidently his clerk once again.[1]

The minutes of the Society's first meeting after Newman's death record no expression of regret. His death was announced, his executors named, and his will produced. Then the meeting arranged for the appointment of a new Secretary and concluded by discussing the release of prisoners from the Marshalsea. The next meeting agreed to provide for Newman's housekeeper, Hannah Beavis, "now grown old and infirm, having been for many years servant to the Society", and "to give Duncan Thomson, late clerk to Mr Newman, a guinea as a gratuity from the Society". Formal expressions of regret were not the custom, and Newman left no relations in England. The members of the Society perhaps acted in the most fitting way. Newman never cared for his name to be mentioned more than necessary and would certainly have wished the Society's work to continue with no further interruption beyond charitable provision for his dependants.[2]

The Dictionary of American Biography speaks of Newman's "deep but unobtrusive piety, his broad tolerance and his joy in giving himself for the welfare of others". He was not a prominent figure in Church or State. He devised no important policy, nor led any great movement. He regarded himself always as the "servant" of the S.P.C.K., and the active members as his "masters". With them, however, he can take his place among the men of goodwill and capacity who encouraged the spread of religion, popular education, and humanitarianism. His letters reveal how earnestly

[1] *P.C.C. Wills*, Principal Probate Registry, 1743, Boycott, f. 205.
[2] *S.P.C.K. Minutes*, 21 and 28 June 1743.

these promoters of "the age of benevolence" pursued their aims. The constant correspondence, committee meetings, and diverse errands with which Newman's time was occupied do not suggest that they lacked either vigour or method. Nor could they be accused of narrowness of vision. For the Church of England they pursued education and charity at home, leadership of the Protestant Churches on the Continent, and participation in the mission field; and Newman's work ranged over religious publishing, charity schools, East Indian missions, Salzburg refugees, Protestant proselytes, and American libraries. They stand out as a body of men actuated by religious devotion, wide views, and far-reaching compassion.

Yet their movement had its blind spots. The S.P.C.K., despite the varied and extensive causes it supported, was remarkably a London organization. It is true that London then, with a population of over half a million—or more than a tenth of the population of England and Wales—was far more important commercially, industrially, and socially, in relation to the rest of the country than it has been ever since, and that eighteenth-century roads and communications were notoriously bad. Nevertheless it is strange to find that Newman never went out of London the whole time he was Secretary of the Society; that he never visited any of the local societies which he urged his correspondents to form; and that he never met country members, upon whom the Society relied so much, except the few who visited London and occasionally attended the Society's meetings to hear policies discussed and decided by the few active members in London who in effect controlled it.

Again, the emphasis placed by the Society upon the distribution of religious literature, books, and tracts of all kinds, is remarkable. Even considered in conjunction with the charity school movement, which it was hoped would teach the poor to read, this suggests a confidence in the power of the written word hardly based upon experience. Perhaps the Church of England has always been in danger of being too refined to be popular. "You can't expect a converted old boozer to get much out of choral Mattins", Wilson Carlile used to say, and it is difficult to see what success can have attended the dispersal of *A Kind Caution to Swearers* among soldiers and sailors or *An Admonition against Drunkenness* among Shropshire miners, to mention but two of the many publications which Newman dispatched in hundreds to the Society's correspondents.

Such failings go to explain the limited success of the Society during this period when Newman was Secretary. Despite its concern for education and literature, it left the large mass of the poorer population in the towns untouched; despite its zeal for the East Indian mission, it could not inspire a single English missionary to join the devoted Danish and German Lutherans. These failings stand out all the more against the Methodist revival which began so soon after Newman's death. The Society represented a practical and ethical rather than an evangelistic piety. Newman approved strongly of Whitefield's orphanage in Georgia, but not at all of his preaching in Moorfields. The fervent passion, tireless travelling, and organizing ability of John Wesley combined with the preaching of George Whitefield and the hymns of Charles Wesley present a very different way of winning souls compared to that of Newman and his friends, who were good, kindly, hard-working men, but not outstanding religious personalities like the Methodist leaders.

It was a time for shock tactics, but these are not always the best for upholders of the Gospel. When the original fervours of a revival die down, the work has to be continued in a calmer atmosphere. Archbishop Secker was thinking of this when he questioned whether the Methodist preachers always reserved "a due share of their discourses for the common duties of common life".[1] With all its weaknesses, the S.P.C.K. during the period when Newman was Secretary was very conscious of the need of a religion that fitted people for the common duties of common life, a need which still existed after the Methodist revival. And in the Church of England this was supplied, not only by devoted clergy working within the parochial system, but also by societies organized on the lines of the S.P.C.K. and served by faithful officials in the tradition of Henry Newman.

[1] Quoted in Charles Smyth, *The Art of Preaching, 747–1939*, 1940, 170.

BIBLIOGRAPHY

CONTEMPORARY MATERIAL

MANUSCRIPTS

The most important sources for Newman's life and work are his letter books in the possession of the Society for Promoting Christian Knowledge and arranged by him under the following headings:

Letters to Correspondents. Private Letters. Society's Letters. Miscellaneous Letters. New England Letters. Letters to Jamaica. Letters to the Saltzburghers.

Also in the possession of the S.P.C.K. are:

S.P.C.K. Minute Books. Abstract of Correspondence. Letters from India. Letters from the Saltzburghers. Minute Books of "a society of gentlemen to watch the advances of Popery". Minute Books of the Commissioners for Relieving Poor Proselytes.

Other letters from and to Newman are in:

Bodleian Library, Oxford: *Rawlinson MSS.*, C. 379, C. 743, C. 844, C. 933, D. 834.
Bristol Public Archives Repository: *Manuscript Letters.*
British Museum, London: *Sloane MSS.*, 4052, 4054.
Egmont MSS., Add. MSS. 47030, 47031, 47032.
Harleian MSS., 5853.
Add. MSS., 3780.
Stowe MSS., 748.
Christ Church, Oxford: *Wake MSS.*, Arch. W. Epist. 15.
Church Commissioners, London: *Fulham Palace MSS.*, American Papers, Massachusetts Second Box.
Commonwealth Relations Office, London: *East India Company Papers.*
Harvard University, Cambridge, Mass.: *Harvard College Papers*, Vol. I.
Hollis MSS., *1718–74.*
Library of Congress, Washington, D.C. (Manuscript Library): *New Hampshire, Miscellaneous Papers of Ebenzer Hazard*, Box 7.
Massachusetts Historical Society, Boston, Mass.: *Miscellaneous MSS.*, Vols. V & VII.
Belknap Papers.
Colman Papers.
New England Historic Genealogical Society, Boston, Mass.: *Manuscript Letters.*
New Hampshire Historical Society, Concord, N.H.: *Miscellaneous MSS.*, *1703–39.*
Public Record Office, London: *Colonial Office Papers*, C.O. 5.
Yale University, New Haven, Conn.: *Stirling Memorial Library, MS. Vaults.*

MANUSCRIPT DIARIES, JOURNALS, AND RECORDS:

British Museum, London: *Egmont Diary*, *Egmont MSS.*, Add. MSS. 47061.

Harvard University, Cambridge, Mass.: *Leverett MS. Diary.*

Royal Society, London: *Journal Book.*
Council Minutes.

Somerset House, London: *Will of Henry Newman*, P.C.C. Wills, Principal Probate Registry, 1743, Boycott.

PRINTED

Letters to and from Newman are printed in:

Allen, W. O. B., and McClure, E., *Two Hundred Years: The History of the S.P.C.K. 1698–1898*, 1898.

Clarke, W. K. Lowther, *Eighteenth Century Piety*, 1944.

Calendar of State Papers, Colonial Series, America and West Indies.

Historical Manuscripts Commission, 7th Report; 13th Report, App. VII.

Colonial Records of Georgia, 26 vols., Atlanta, 1904–16.

Colonial Society of Massachusetts Publications, Boston, 1895 *seqq.*

Massachusetts Historical Society Proceedings, Boston, 1791 *seqq.*

Massachusetts Historical Society Collections, Boston, 1792 *seqq.*

New Hampshire Historical Society Collections, Concord, 1824–1915.

New Hampshire Provincial Papers, Concord, 1867 *seqq.*

OTHER LETTERS, JOURNALS AND DIARIES NOW PRINTED:

Journals of the House of Commons. *Journals of the House of Lords.*

Acts of the Privy Council, Colonial Series, 1713–1783, ed. W. L. Grant and J. Munro, 6 vols., 1908–12.

Journal of the Commissioners for Trade and Plantations, 1704–28, 5 vols., 1920 *seqq.*

Journals of the House of Representatives of Massachusetts, 1715–27, ed. W. C. Ford, 7 vols., Boston, 1915–25, Massachusetts Historical Society.

Harvard College Records, 3 vols., Boston, 1925–35, Colonial Society of Massachusetts.

Belcher Papers, Massachusetts Historical Society Collections, Sixth Series, Vol. VI.

Commonplace Book of Joseph Green, Colonial Society of Massachusetts Publications, XXXIV.

Papers of Samuel Sewall, Massachusetts Historical Society Collections, Fifth Series, Vol. VI.

Thoresby, Ralph, *Diary*, 2 vols., 1830.

CONTEMPORARY PRINTED MATERIAL (AMERICAN):

A Brief Account of the Causes that have Retarded the Progress of the Colony of Georgia in America, 1743.

An Impartial Enquiry into the State and Utility of the Province of Georgia, 1741.

Bradford's History of Plymouth Plantation, ed. W. T. Davis, New York, 1908.
Dummer, Jeremiah, *Defence of the New England Charters*, 1765.
Harris, John, *Collection of Voyages and Travels*, 2 vols., 1748.
Historical Collections of Georgia, ed. George White, New York, 1854.
Martyn, Benjamin, *Reasons for Establishing the Colony of Georgia, with Regard to the Trade of Great Britain*, 1733.
Mather, Cotton, *Magnalia Christi Americana*, 1702.
Newman, Henry, *Harvard's Ephemeris*, Cambridge, Mass., 1690.
—— *News from the Stars*, Cambridge, Mass., 1691.
Tracts Relating to North America, ed. Peter Force, 4 vols., Washington, 1836.
Turell, Ebenezer, *Life and Character of Dr. Benjamin Colman*, Boston, 1749.

CONTEMPORARY PRINTED MATERIAL (ENGLISH):

Account of the Charity Schools, 1704–14.
Publick Spirit illustrated in the Life and Designs of the Reverend Thomas Bray, D.D., 1746.
Chamberlayne, John, *Magnae Britanniae Notitia*, 25th ed., 1718.
Defoe, Daniel, *Tour of the Whole Island of Great Britain*, 1724.
Dodsley, R., and J., *London and its Environs Described*, 6 vols., 1761.
The Journeys of Celia Fiennes, ed. C. Morris, 1947.
Hatton, E., *A New View of London*, 2 vols., 1708.
Mandeville, B., *Essay on Charity and Charity Schools*, 1723.
S.P.C.K., *Circular Letters to Correspondents*, 1699 etc.
Strype, J. (ed.), *Stow's Survey of London*, 1720.
Welsh Piety; or a Collection of the several Accounts of the Welsh Circulating Schools, from their first Rise in the year 1737 to Michaelmas 1752.
Whiston, W., *Memoirs Written by Himself*, 1735.
Woodward, J., *Rise and Progress of the Religious Societies*, 4th ed., 1712.

NEWSPAPERS:

The London Gazette. The British Journal. The London Journal. The Flying Post. The Daily Courant. The Daily Post Boy. The Daily Advertiser. Whitehall Evening Post. Boston (Mass.) News Letter.

SECONDARY MATERIAL

Dictionary of American Biography.
Dictionary of National Biography.
Cambridge History of the British Empire, Vol. I.

Johnson's England, 2 vols., Oxford, 1933.
Allen, W. O. B., and McClure, E., *Two Hundred Years: The History of the S.P.C.K., 1698–1898*, 1898.
Anderson, J. S. M., *History of the Colonial Church*, 3 vols., 1856.
Barry, J. S., *History of Massachusetts*, 3 vols., Boston, 1857.
Basye, A. H., *The Lords Commissioners of Trade and Plantations*, New Haven, Conn., 1925.

Belden, A. D., *George Whitefield the Awakener*, 2nd ed., 1953.
Belknap, J., *History of New Hampshire*, 2nd ed., 3 vols., Philadelphia, 1813.
Bliss, L., *History of Rehoboth*, Boston, 1836.
Brantley, R. L., "The Salzburgers in Georgia", *Georgia Historical Quarterly*, XIV.
Burns, J. J., *The Colonial Agents of New England*, Washington, D.C., 1935.
Carpenter, E. F., *Thomas Tenison*, 1948.
Chatterton, Eyre, *History of the Church of England in India*, 1924.
Church, L. F., *Oglethorpe: A Study of Philanthropy in England and Georgia*, 1932.
Clarke, W. K. Lowther, *Eighteenth Century Piety*, 1944.
Cnattingius, Hans, *Bishops and Societies, A Study of Anglican Colonial and Missionary Expansion, 1689–1950*, 1952.
Crane, V. W., "The Origins of Georgia", *Georgia Historical Quarterly*, XIV.
Cross, A. L., *The Anglican Episcopate and the American Colonies*, New York, 1902.
Cundall, Frank, *The Governors of Jamaica in the first half of the Eighteenth Century*, 1937.
Douglas, D. C., *English Scholars, 1660–1713*, 2nd ed., 1951.
George, M. D., *London Life in the Eighteenth Century*, 1925.
Holmes, Abiel, *History of Cambridge*, Mass. Hist. Soc. Collections, Vol. VII.
Hutchinson, T., *History of the Colony and Province of Massachusetts Bay* (ed. L. S. Mayo), 3 vols., Cambridge, Mass., 1936.
Jones, C. C., *History of Georgia*, 2 vols., Boston, 1883.
—— *Dead Towns of Georgia*, Savannah, 1878.
Jones, M. G., *The Charity School Movement in the Eighteenth Century*, 1938.
Knight, L. L., *Georgia Landmarks*, Atlanta, 1914.
Latourette, K. S., *A History of the Expansion of Christianity*, 5 vols., 1943.
Lydekker, J. W., "Thomas Bray, Founder of Missionary Enterprise", *Historical Magazine of the Protestant Episcopal Church*, XII.
Miller, J. C., *Origins of the American Revolution*, 1950.
Miller, Perry, *Orthodoxy in Massachusetts, 1630–50*, Cambridge, Mass., 1933.
Morison, S. E., *Three Centuries of Harvard, 1636–1936*, Cambridge, Mass., 1936.
—— *Harvard in the Seventeenth Century*, Cambridge, Mass., 1938.
—— "The Harvard School of Astronomy in the Seventeenth Century", *New England Quarterly*, VII.
McCall, H., *History of Georgia*, 2 vols., Savannah, 1811–16.
Murray, T. B., *Jubilee Tract; being an Account of the Chief Proceedings of the Five Original Members of the S.P.C.K. in March 1698–9*, 1849.
Overton, J. H., *Life in the English Church, 1660–1714*, 1885.
Pascoe, C. F., *Two Hundred Years of the S.P.G., 1701–1901*, 1901.
Pennington, E. L., "Anglican Influences in the Establishment of Georgia", *Georgia Historical Quarterly*, XV.

Penny, F., *The Church in Madras*, 3 vols., 1904.
Quincy, Josiah, *History of Harvard University*, Boston, 1840.
Rand, B., *Berkeley's American Sojourn*, Cambridge, Mass., 1932.
Secretan, C. F., *Life of Robert Nelson*, 1860.
Shipton, C. K., "Secondary Education in the Puritan Colonies", *New England Quarterly*, VII.
Sibley, J., *Harvard Graduates*, Boston, 1885.
Smith, V. A., *Oxford Student's History of India*, 2nd ed., Oxford, 1923.
Stevens, W. B., *History of Georgia*, 2 vols., New York, 1847–59.
Strobel, P. A., *Salzburgers and their Descendants*, Baltimore, 1855.
Sykes, N., *Edmund Gibson, Bishop of London, 1669–1748*, Oxford, 1926.
——, *Church and State in England in the Eighteenth Century*, Cambridge, 1934.
Thompson, H. P., *Into All Lands: The History of the S.P.G., 1701–1950*, 1951.
——, *Thomas Bray*, 1954.
Traill, H. D. (ed.), *Social England*, 1903.
Tucker, H. W., *The English Church in Other Lands*, 1886.
Tyerman, L., *Life of the Rev. George Whitefield*, 1890.
Walker, Williston, *A History of the Congregational Churches in the United States*, New York, 1894.
Weeden, W. B., *Economic and Social History of New England, 1620–1729*, 2 vols., Boston, 1890.
Weigle, Luther A., *American Idealism*, New Haven, Conn., 1928.
Whiteley, J. H., *Wesley's England*, 1938.
Wright, R., *Memoir of General James Oglethorpe*, 1867.

INDEX